An Invitation to Design

An Invitation to DESIGN

Helen Marie Evans

Late Professor, School of Applied Sciences and Arts,
California State University, San José

Carla Davis Dumesnil

ASID, Assistant Professor of Interior Design,
University of Utah, Salt Lake City

Macmillan Publishing Co., Inc.
New York
Collier Macmillan Publishers
London

Macmillan Publishing Co., Inc.
866 Third Avenue, New York, New York 10022

Collier Macmillan Canada, Inc.

Library of Congress Cataloging in Publication Data

Evans, Helen Marie.
   An Invitation to Design.
   Bibliography: p.
   Includes index.
   1. Design.   I. Dumesnil, Carla Davis.   II. Title.
NK1510.E9   1982   745.4   81-3784
ISBN 0-02-334540-3   AACR2

Printing: 12345678   Year: 23456789

Preface
to the Second Edition

The late Helen Marie Evans raised most eloquently many pertinent issues that face both designers and consumers of design. This book is her beautiful legacy for students and professional designers.

The change in title from *Man the Designer* to *An Invitation to Design* reflects current trends in our language and interpretations of the generic word "man." It is clear to me that the phrase *Man the Designer* was intended to mean "people as designers," that design is an activity and unique behavior of people. However, the pronoun *he* is used throughout because the English language has no unisexual pronoun in common use. The book with its new title retains the Evans' legacy: the topics covered are applicable to people, to individuals, male and female, designers, and consumers.

The table of contents is similar to the one in Evans' first edition. The changes made for the second edition will facilitate an understanding of the concepts in design. Part one, "Basic Concepts: Communication in Design" relates for the reader those concepts basic to design. Chapters 1, 2, and 3 are essentially what they were in the first edition, with some minor changes. Chapters 4 and 5 have been expanded to include additional elements and principles of design. For me, there are eight elements of design: line, form, space, *motion,* light, color, texture, and *transparency.* Motion and transparency have been added to the chapter. In Chapter 5, "Principles of Design," variety, harmony, and scale have been included.

Part Two, "Cultural Contributions to Today's Design," discusses significant historical and cultural contributions that have affected the contemporary design world. Chapter 7 begins this part with "Contributions of Western Cultural History." This chapter contains the essence of Chapter 7 in the first edition and is found in Part Two instead of Part One. Chapter 8, "Contributions of the Far East and Africa," recognizes that these parts of the world have often been sources of inspiration at certain periods of time and have been used for contributions to design detail throughout history. Chapter 9 is "Contributions of the United States." Chapter 10, "Contributions of the Last Century," looks at the important contributions of our most immediate history—the last hundred years.

Parts Three and Four discuss inorganic and organic materials. Knowledge of materials is often treated more lightly than it is in this text. The choice of a material is very important to the designer and consumer alike. Each material has unique characteristics and performs differently when shaped and used. The material is actually the medium for a design idea. For example, glass can be molded into a goblet and has yet to be successfully shaped into fibers for clothing. Wood is often used for furniture, but gold can't support significant weight. Therefore, when gold is used on furniture, it is generally used as a surface decoration rather than as the structural material. Navajo weaving has been introduced into Chapter 18, Textiles.

Part Five, "Man As Consumer of Design," develops a concept of man, design, and everyday living. As we provide for our daily needs we make design selection and purchases. Consumer decision-making needs to include aesthetic as well as economic issues. Today, a person's near environment consists of the traditional categories of food, clothing, and shelter. Part Five has been reorganized to reflect these topics of the near environment and includes art selection. "Designing with Food" is discussed in Chapter 21. "Designing Clothing and Adornment" is addressed in Chapter 22 and "Designing Shelter" is discussed in Chapter 23. Chapter 24 deals with "Art Selection." The topics covered in the previous six chapters in the first edition are integrated into these four chapters.

The role of the consumer is very significant today; the marketing of a product is a key step in our contemporary economy. The consumer of design can be involved di-rectly in design decisions which affect the history of art, as can the designer. The consumer is generally not faced with a "white canvas problem" in his decision-making process, as are most designers. The consumer makes choices from limited alternatives; he selects from what is available. The consumer's selection process can be improved through knowledge. The effective consumer's choice is a valid link in design history. African masks are important not only because they were made, but also because they have been used. So often the word *function* implies commonplace and art implies an elite; yet, the usefulness of a design is very significant in meeting the test of time. Social status remains just one of the possible functions of a design. The last part of this book expands the issues for the consumer of design.

Psychologists talk about human behavior, and for me, designing is one particular form of human behavior; it involves people producing many and varied hand-made objects. Within this text you will find examples of good design. You will find examples from many periods of history, from many countries. People are producers of art objects. A design becomes art after standing the test of time, and the test of time refers to enduring beyond the present. Critics and historians will argue about the length of time required to reach a verdict, but all will accept the role of the test of time. That is, a designed object must last beyond its immediate popularity or beyond its initial production. For it to be a fine work of art it must be significant a century later. The art that people produce reflects the social issues of the time and traditions of the past, and thus their art is a visual marker of a certain place or period in time. This art is used and some of it is left around for future generations. The consumer has input into the use of the art, and we have collectors and museums that store this art for future generations. This text deals primarily with production, decision making, and design language. In the last part the consumers are users. And thanks to many museums, we have many illustrations for this text.

My first postulate is that art and design are basic to people. Art is a product and a design is an action or behavior producing the art. My second postulate is that nature provides the given: the materials to be manipulated by people. Nature also provides the "natural" beauty to be left alone or protected for further generations. It is nature that provides inspiration and comparison for design in art. My third postulate is that mankind functions within society. Its components are economies, religions, varying family structures, political organizations, and technology, simple or complex. Cultures provide each generation with a heritage or tradition that is a historical reference point in time. Successful artists visually express their period of time as seen from a particular place on earth, their home and travels. Therefore, man designs art, uses art, and leaves some for future generations. And these art objects become the visual markers, the visual history of particular times and places on earth. Designing is a basic human behavior that takes place within the context of society. The history of art is a social history of this particular behavior of mankind where man uses visual language as the tool to record a visual history.

Thus, this book provides many lessons basic to reading, appreciating, and understanding the meaning of design and the beauty of art. The concepts basic to design, the contributions and traditions of the past and other cultures, the materials (media for design), and consumers designing for everyday life are all considered. These are all important issues in design education that are explained in this book visually through illustrations and verbally through the written text.

I am very grateful to John Beck and Ray Christiansen for helping me to begin this chapter of my life as an author. And to Jenny and Jeff Davis, who started my design education and encouraged my design career. Thanks also are given to George Hotte and Eleanor Boettke Hotte for my quality formal education and to Barbara Rindflesh and Alice Yeates for assisting me in the research. A final thanks to Tom Kovach, Vivian Terzaghi and Bretta Dumesnil for their support and sensitivity.

May design enrich your visual life.

CARLA DAVIS DUMESNIL
Salt Lake City, Utah

Preface
to the First Edition

When Marcel Breuer came to the United States to teach at Harvard University in the 1930s, he began one of his first public speeches: "Ladies and gentlemen, if I were asked what is the most important task of our time, I would say it is to select." Today his words are just as relevant. Selection can pertain to creeds, politics, literature, dance, music, and all forms of human activity. *Man the Designer* is limited to the selection of familiar objects in our everyday life, the intimate environment with which we surround ourselves or by which we are surrounded. It is my belief that we can make our lives richer spiritually and aesthetically, as well as practically, if we become educated to be discriminating. Whether we become more selective through a formally structured process or learn to be so through our self-directed activity is not important. To live a more intensely satisfying and creative life, we must live sensibly and sensitively with the materials around us. The attitude I have taken throughout this book is that we are a single complex of nature, man, and society.

The initial chapter, "An Invitation to Visual Design," is a brief, exploratory introduction to our visual world. In it the reader is encouraged to see man, society, and the materials of our natural world as interrelated. Nature's materials are integral to us: they provide our physical sustenance as well as our artistic pleasure. We are an ecology of man and nature, but man has greater responsibility because he has the ability to control nature and a mind with which he can relate to it intelligently.

In subsequent divisions of the book the elements and principles of design are defined and exemplified through photographic illustration, so that together we can speak a common language. Considerations in judging the design merit of the various objects are included as a basis for making intelligent choices. Because visual appreciation, like literary, mental, or musical appreciation, is a lifelong process, we should not be disturbed if we later become dissatisfied with a former choice. Instead, we should welcome evidence that we have progressed along a continuum of knowledge and appreciation to find new and more appropriate responses.

Included is a chapter on design that has continued to inspire man through the centuries. A chapter on the creative person offers the reader an opportunity to understand the temperament of creative people and the many forms creativity can assume. I hope it will also help him to realize that we are all creative, although our creative expressions may differ.

All the materials man uses and some of each one's special attributes are presented in turn so that we may be more aware of the composition of the world around us and learn to treat nature's resources with respect. There are examples of work by past and present designers who have lived with materials so intimately by thought, experiment, deed, and design that they have left us a rich heritage. Consideration is also given to the newer media that today involve all of us, such as light, plastics, kinetic structures, and technology—which Mies van der Rohe said "reaches its real fulfillment when it transcends itself as art."

As an instructor of design and art, I am well aware of the importance of communication through visual design. Hence, the art elements and principles are thoroughly presented in the initial chapters of *Man the Designer,* because understanding them is necessary if the artist and the observer are to understand the design merit of objects. The other primary divisions of this book offer a selection of designs from other nations, designs that utilize inorganic and organic materials, and designs that are related to us and our environment. After assigning the initial seven chapters, which lay the cornerstone for understanding what constitutes good design, the instructor may want to rearrange the remaining four parts to suit individual class needs. As with other texts, some sections may be omitted if their content has

been or will be included in other courses. I hope this topical organization will lend itself to flexibility. A glossary is also provided at the end of the book with definitions of some specialized words that pertain to the arts.

I have been mindful of many people as I wrote this manuscript. My Czechoslovakian heritage originally endowed me with the desire to create and to search for beauty in the commonplace. I was further motivated by a friend at the University of Minnesota who encouraged me to take a course in design along with one in biochemistry. At registration I sat across from an adviser whose placard read "Goldstein." Naively, I asked if she was related to the Goldsteins who wrote *Art in Everyday Life.* She laughingly responded: "Yes, I'm Vetta." Under her stimulation, my career plans changed. Even now I am grateful to her for her recent encouragement when, still acting as my adviser, she wrote: "We too had our bad moments but don't despair. Give it time. It will come." I hope that in this manuscript somewhere can be detected a glimmer of the gifts the Goldsteins imparted to all their students.

As I wrote I was also mindful of and indebted to many of my students, both undergraduate and graduate, at Michigan State University, Southern Illinois University, and California State University, San José, who perused with me some of the depths of design. In many ways, by a phrase, a sentence, a report, or a book given me to read, their contributions, though not obvious, are nevertheless incorporated in this manuscript. All my student typists I thank, particularly for their patience in trying to interpret my long-handed shorthand. I especially thank Marsha Barr, who not only typed but had an uncanny gift of knowing where some misplaced paper might be hiding. I am also grateful to departmental secretary Pat Klein, who so often could help me with an elusive word. My gratitude is extended to Dean Robert Moore of the School of Applied Sciences and Arts at California State University, San José, and to Dr. Elveda Smith, department chairman within the school, who arranged released time for my writing.

Commercial companies and architectural photographers have provided me with a wealth of beautiful photographs, as have craftsmen and museums. I extend my gratitude to them all. Photographer Vincent Bernucci never gave up until his photographs for the text had the degree of excellence he deemed necessary for reproduction. To Virginia Saale and Professor Anna L. Loze goes the credit for arranging the table settings and floral compositions in Part V.

I am much indebted to the many experts who read portions of my manuscript, thus providing me with authenticity. Among these are designers Anni Albers, Anna Ballarian, Charles Eames, Edith Heath, Alexander Girard, Freda Koblick, George Nakashima, Gertrud and Otto Natzler, Vera Neumann, James Prestini, T. H. Robsjohn-Gibbings, Paolo Soleri and Marguerite Wildenhain. Peter York of the Design Centre of London helped me with England's contribution to design. The companies of Ekco Housewares, Orrefors Glass, and Steuben Glass also provided information. I have appreciated Mrs. Vanderbilt Webb's information concerning the World Crafts Council and Janet Thorpe's about the development of the Cooper-Hewitt Museum of Decorative Arts and Design, Smithsonian Institution.

I am proud to be a contributor to The Macmillan Company, and grateful to all its members who made *Man the Designer* possible. My initial encounter was with Craig Anderson, who stopped me as I was hastening to class one day to ask: "Do you need any books?" I nonchalantly answered: "No. But I do have an outline for one." This was the genesis of my book. I have enjoyed working with Tim Adam, John Beck, and J. Edward Neve. They have all been very helpful and provided me with kindly advice, information, and encouragement along the way.

Someone who has assisted me in a unique manner is my colleague Professor Anna L. Loze, historian of decorative arts. She has not only read much of the manuscript and made valuable suggestions, but has weighed data for significance, helped select the best photographs to include, and provided me with some of her own personal and historical documents. Everyone who writes needs someone who functions both as a sounding board and a confidant—she has been these and more.

I am appreciative of David Winfield Willson's remark concerning *Matrix*, his huge sweep of undulating wall covering inspired by an agate millions of years old; his few excellently selected words convey the thoughts I wished to express in my text:

Those in the modern society who find sky, mountains, earth, water, grass, and clouds lost or distorted because of urban developments must look closer and deeper to find beauty. . . . The world is no less full of wonderment than it ever was.

To all the others who assisted in indefinable ways, I am grateful. Now I invite you to read the chapters that follow and hope that by so doing you will develop a greater awareness and appreciation of both natural and man-made design in your daily environment. Then, reinforced with a knowledge of the art elements and principles, you should become more critical of design and more confident in making wise choices.

H. M. E.

To those who care
not only about people
but also about the design
of their physical environment

Contents

Part One

**Basic Concepts:
Communication in Design**

Part Two

**Cultural Contributions to
Today's Design**

XV

An Invitation to Design

Part One

Basic Concepts: Communication in Design

An Invitation to Visual Design 1

We are constantly surrounded and bombarded by a kaleidoscope of demanding visual forms. As a result, selecting goods has become a highly complex activity. Knowledge of materials and design is essential if the consumer is to realize practical and aesthetic satisfaction in daily life. The consumer without visual training is less than what he potentially can be. With education he can be selective, critical, evaluative, and sensuously appreciative of forms, colors, and textures. He can express himself by selecting objects that reflect his particular responses to life: his emotions, intellectual propensities, aesthetic inclinations, and social values. His material possessions need not be extraneous to him, instead they can constitute an extension of himself. His possessions can be both personal expressions and personal space; he can accept today's "materialistic" environment in a positive way, by defining and expressing himself. Selection can lead to an appreciation of self and to an appreciation of man as he functions daily and integrates quality design into his activities.

Today we need to become discriminating consumers for deeper reasons than to promote our self-interest. Our age deplores the growing lack of communication with nature and sends up nostalgic wails for the passing of open fields and wooded hills. There is a need to reassess our relationships with the materials of our world. When nature is converted to steel and reorganized in the form of a chair, is the chair less than nature? Does a teakwood cabinet have less of the quality of nature after it has been transformed from a tree in the Malaysian jungle into a sculpture object for daily functional use? Is not clay greatly enhanced when converted into a glazed bowl?

Man may always want to maintain his liaison with the

1-1 *Roger Dupzyk. A natural bough with an added seat and foot-rest has been smoothed and fashioned into a hanging chair in which to contemplate nature and onself.* California Design X, Pasadena Art Museum. *Photograph by Richard Gross.*

open sky, the rough-barked tree, the hush of the pressed-leaf carpeting underfoot in some primeval forest, and with water and sand and a clear wind blowing. But in this age and in the ages to come, as man more fully utilizes and engineers the environment around him, these sanctuaries and private "Waldens" will increasingly become part of total design. National parks and forests must necessarily assume greater significance. Local communities will more fully realize the need to preserve and develop areas for all men to share and experience some of the beauty and restorative qualities commonly associated with nature. For in a jostling society, a retreat to nature can soothe, and one must grant with Mireille Johnston that

On the grass, on the lake, nature does not impose on me,
does not intrude, does not try to direct me.
I can be oblivious if I wish; I can be calm,
I can savor the fragile and delicious moment.
I can sit in the center of myself,
I slowly coincide with myself, at last.[1]

and with Robinson Jeffers that

> *There is wind in the tree, and the gray ocean's*
> *Music in the rocks.*[2]

As opportunities for experiencing nature in its pristine forms become more circumscribed and consequently more coveted, man must seek through purposeful reconstruction to bring nature into his daily living, and enhance it. The tree is felled, not in opposition to nature but in synthesis with it—in order to construct a shelter

[1] Mireille Johnston. *Central Park Country A Tune Within Us.* San Francisco Sierra Club, 1970, p. 85.
[2] Robinson Jeffers. *Not Man Apart.* San Francisco Sierra Club, 1969, p. 56.

or a chair. People have always found ways by which to interrelate with nature according to their needs. The social and survival interests of man are much like those of other creatures.

Swallows need mud for building shelters, so they remove it from the swamps. Birds transport twigs and leaves for their nests. Bees suck nectar from flowers. Squirrels deprive trees of their cones and nuts. Man is not alone in transporting, converting, and transposing the elements around him. Yet, man is often removed from nature by dozens of middlemen.

As man's environmental horizons close in, his vision is necessarily focused on his immediate environment. He can no longer see the sunsets on the plains because of the density of human habitation, but he can reveal the reflections of the sky in his man-made pool or in mirrored images of flowers in a bowl or a silver spoon on his table. He can live with an awareness of nature's materials: the wood of a chair, the stone of a wall. Nature can be brought into daily life: rocks and pebbles from the ocean into the garden; graceful plant forms from the fields and forests into a weed pot. Clay from the earth can be transformed into brick for walls, hearth, and terrace. Man can delight in the presence of these materials—in their color, form, and uniqueness. He need not be separate from nature, because he can compose an organic unit with nature. Moreover, as the transformation of nature for human use increases all over the world, man must be more conscious and purposeful in utilizing nature's elements. As he consumes wood for domestic furnishings, he can respect its intrinsic character by treating it congruently with its fiber. Each material, whether wood, clay, steel, silver, or plastic, has its own potential for development. Each has a chemical and physical composition that influences its aesthetic potential. Each has a range of manufacture and of application to daily use that is limited only by man's inventiveness and appreciation of its particular attributes. There is evidence that in initial designs with a new material man often imitates materials already familiar to him; it is only after further experimentation that the new materials

suggest their own forms and unique uses. The artistic development of any material at its height is always characterized by individuality and exclusiveness.

Hence, we will not think of ourselves as adrift in a world of material goods, but as part of a culture that values and respects materials. We can renew ourselves in nature by revering it and through aesthetic joy in well-designed products. To this end we must not only understand the nature of the materials but also their modifiable elements and the organizing principles that aid us in forming valid aesthetic judgments.

In this text we will consider the plastic elements—lines, form, space, transparency, motion, light, color, and texture—as necessary for communication. Principles of design—proportion, harmony, balance, emphasis, rhythm, variety, scale, and unity—will be regarded not as a set of rigid criteria, but as guides to help us to form qualified conclusions about the design merit of familiar objects in our daily environment. The authors will present some of our heritage of past achievements that continue to delight and satisfy us. Recognition will be given to societies and the forces within them that are influencing the design of today's products.

1-2 *Cow dung bowls, Kadero, Nuba Hills, Kordofan. These pots are freely painted in white and red earth on a dark brown surface. The proportions, rhythm, unity, textural quality, and contrast through light and dark exemplify the craftsman's sensitivity to design elements and principles. By permission of the Trustees of The British Museum, London.*

1-3 *Glass presentation Goblet, American, about 1788. This glass, transparent and refracting light, is a product of man's technical manipulation of material.* John Frederick Amelung, New Bremen Glass Factory Collection, *The Metropolitan Museum of Art, New York.*

We will explore our use of both organic and inorganic substances. Man has always utilized materials with a purpose and with some degree of artistry. He has converted reeds and clay into vessels, stones into weapons, and mud into shelters. Shells, horns, teeth, leaves, and wood have been pressed into functions and decorative service. In some African societies even cow dung has been used to construct domestic containers and shelters. Other more highly developed industrial societies have refined or created glass, formed concrete, and through the chemical manipulation of air, water, petroleum, and gas, produced sophisticated plastic substances for furnishings and housing.

Man's inventiveness in using materials is extensive in its range. Significant aesthetic utilization of materials will be included here, as well as periods in the development of materials that are considered to be outstanding or that relate to the principles of good design. Not all the high points in man's use of materials are included; this does not reflect lack of achievement in other times, only the necessity for limitation here.

In the chapters that follow, the authors' intent is

1. To explore the elements and principles of art as a basis for communication and design merit of objects.
2. To develop good examples of good design and some familiar objects in everyday use.
3. To present some of the contributions to contemporary design from various nations.
4. To describe some of the qualities integral to both natural and man-made materials that influence their design potential.
5. To review some of the significant function and aesthetic uses man has made of materials.
6. To communicate the philosophies of some outstanding designers in various media and their considerations during the creative process.
7. To provide a brief resumé of the development of modern art.
8. To include a section on design in our near environment, which contributes to the enhancement of daily living.

This book will next look at man both as a designer and consumer of designs.

Designers and Consumers of Design 2

Man As Designer

Design is everywhere. It can be seen in the marching rhythms of a redwood forest, a leopard's spotted pelt, the hexagonal pattern of a honeycomb, the dimpled surface of a pool pelted by raindrops, and in the flickering patterns of light and dark as sunlight is reflected on moving leaves.

People can effortlessly enjoy design in nature, where it appears so abundantly. In a grocery store, however, marketing purposes come into play. Fruits and vegetables are arranged for sale in orderly displays. Produce is collected and organized to fill an allotted space. For further enhancement it may be polished or sprayed with a mist, packaged in cellophane, or displayed in colorful cartons. Appeal is made not only to taste, but also to

vision. The grocer makes a deliberate attempt to stimulate our vision—to increase or heighten our desire for an object. This selecting and organizing of materials to achieve a desired effect is *designing*. It is the process of structuring by using the basic elements of the visual arts—line, form, space, light, color, transparency, motion, and texture—to compose a unified whole in order to satisfy a particular purpose. It is giving visual form to the essence of something. As such, design is part of every person's daily activities. Everyone is a designer, whether he consciously wills to be one or not. The expectant mother awaits her baby with a plan, a layette; in design terms, a layout. Garments are selected and arranged with a consistent relationship to the needs of an infant. A mother does not necessarily think of design, but the singleness and definition of her purpose results in an organization of related materials.

From the time that we first rise and select our clothing to project a particular visual image to ourselves, our families, or the public, to the time that we dispose of these articles of dress in the evening, we are designing. Tidying the glove compartment of a car, arranging (or disarranging) the papers on the top of one's desk, combing one's hair, tying one's shoelaces, altering the tilt of one's hat—all these are design activities. They involve selecting, arranging, and ordering. They move from a state of randomness or indifference to a higher state of organization in order to create a desired impression.

Man himself is constantly moving in rhythms of walking, sitting, or dancing, which he can structure at will for the occasion. He designs with his body and with the dress and adornment he selects. All dance—from rock and roll to ballet—is design through selected physical manipulation. Man constantly designs and redesigns his personal and immediate environment, whether it be his house, his furnishings, or his garden. As an interior designer or architect he may design the environment of others or of the public as well. Only death takes away his design faculty—but mortuary services assure him that he will go to his final rest in a neat and tidy state of design.

This design activity of every man is not a casual and simple process. On the highest level, designing is a conscious and knowledgeable manipulation of the art elements to produce an expressive statement. It is purposeful creation in which emotion, knowledge, imagination, and intellect are all operative. It involves the cerebral and psychological processes necessary for decision-making. If man can define his problem and have some awareness of the effect he wishes to achieve, the act of design is facilitated. But designing is not a comfortable process. The ancients believed that the world began when a divine being created order out of chaos. Design begins when perceptive man views his world and does not like what he sees; hence he must affect or modify it. Design begins with dissatisfaction, not lethargy.

As an example, Art Nouveau, a period of design toward the latter part of the nineteenth century in which nature's forms were taken as a unifying theme, had its origin in some designers' dissatisfaction with what seemed to them the excessive ornateness of the Victorian period. The eclectic composite of forms and patterns common to design in the late nineteenth century seemed to them too undisciplined and too dependent upon historical antecedents to be able to affirm man's living in the present. Visually disturbed, promoters of the Art Nouveau movement attempted to make design contemporary by insisting that objects have relatedness with the botanical and biological patterns of nature. The best of design during that period showed man in control of the use of nature's motifs, ordering them in such a way as to reinforce or become one with the structure of an object. Eventually excesses developed that paralleled the lack of restraint in design common to the Victorian era, which the movement's originators had so abhorred. Elements from nature were allowed to flourish in profusion over the surface of objects. Dissatisfaction with this excessive decorativeness led, once again, to the development of new expressions and forms of organization. The right angle of the Bauhaus, a German school of design, displaced the sensuous botanical curve of Art Nouveau and ushered in the simplified style of the twentieth century.

This dissatisfaction, man's apparent need to constantly alter the appearance of his environment and impress his mark upon it, is indicative of the creative urge. One person's need to change the arrangement of his living-room furniture periodically and another's decision to design an arch symbolic of a nation's westward expansion (Eero Saarinen's sculptural arch at St. Louis, Missouri, is shown in Figure 2-1) are merely different expressions of man's desire to impress himself upon his environment—to organize and shape it in ways meaningful to him.

Creativity is reflecting oneself in relationship to the environment and the objects that compose it in an individual and personal way. This human need ensures that design will always be changing, because man does not remain content with static images. As the world changes and will continue to change, he will devise new symbolic systems to reflect changes in his perception and experience of life. Recent art forms—optical art, pop art, hard-edge art, constructions, happenings, poster art, and process art and sculpture—are some of the means by which man integrates and binds himself visually and physically to his daily environment. The only certainty about the future of design is that as events, responses, and attitudes change, new expressions will be developed.

Man As Observer of Natural Design

Man not only daily engages in designing, but he also observes the manifold designs of nature. Infinite generations of men have observed the orderly process of the sun's rising and setting, the rotation of the seasons, and a seed's germination to its flowering and production of multiple seeds, which in turn are eventually scattered to the winds. The budding of leaves in springtime, the darkness of approaching thunder clouds against a serene blue sky, the design of plump, ripe blackberries, and the spilling patterns made by rivulets of rainwater bulging from the opposing tensions of liquid against solid have been observed by men through time in many places. We still respond to these unless in our frustrations from meeting the demands of contemporary living we are, as T. S. Eliot phrased it, "distracted from distraction by distraction," so that we no longer see the sunrise, and the sunset is only the cue for beginning an evening's scheduled activities. Living the repetitive rhythm of a routine, a man may lose his sensuous wonder and his enjoyment of the colors, forms, and textures of nature. He may come to respond like an automaton, without animation.

2-1 *Eero Saarinen. The Gateway Arch to the West, of stainless steel, was constructed in commemoration of man's westward progress. The shape of the arch is equilateral, the distance from the outside northerly leg to the southerly being 630 feet and its maximum height also 630 feet, making it the nation's tallest monument. Transportation to the top and an observation room are contained within the structure. Photograph by Art Witman—Black Star.*

One who has maintained his sensitivity to design will get a constant recharging of his human battery from the patterns and designs of nature. He will enjoy not only those that seem to suggest order—the balance of veins on a leaf, the uniformity of the hexagons on a turtle's shell, the rhythmic lines of sand dunes, the radial pattern of blossoms—but also nature's disorders: driftwood and flotsam randomly swept upon the shore, old cars piled high in junk heaps with grass struggling for growth among upturned wheels, tumbleweed trapped by sagebrush. Nature does not always present a perfectly fin-

Man As Consumer of Man-made Design

Man also consumes his own man-made objects visually. In this respect we can speak of degrees of visual literacy. How do we "read" an object? There are those who pay little heed to the artifacts of their daily life. Spoons, cups, cars, chairs, vacuum cleaners—these are functional objects that fulfill needs for eating, transporting, sitting, and cleaning. Some people ask only that an object be a least common denominator, that it work in some way to fulfill a human need. They see it merely as function. They may make a few qualitative differentiations—some cars are less noisy; some cups are heavier and don't break as easily; some vacuum cleaners pick up dirt better than others. Generally speaking, such people constitute the part of the population that is not disturbed by the stereotypes and dulling duplication of housing designs in tract developments, by the ride through depressing streets when making the transition from air terminal to city hotel, or by billboards and telephone wires that make it difficult to take photographs of scenes in resort centers renowned for their natural beauty.

Those who see and demand more—who are more literate visually—are disturbed when their environment displeases them. They ask that objects be more than merely functional; they want them to provide the senses with a feeling of satisfaction or elevation and stimulation. It is not enough for an object just to work; it must express some quality valued by the viewer beyond merely serving a function, for function is the lowest ceiling that must exist if an object is to have any worth. It is not in the nature of a sentient and critical man who is engaging all his faculties to accept levels of value that he associates with the "vegetative" minimum. An object that will be seen and used daily must become an extension of the self. As such, it must reflect, express, and project the individual.

2-2 *Earth's cycle. Photogram by Helen M. Evans.*

ished design. There are random as well as ordered patterns to be found. For the man who seeks surcease from a highly structured world and requires variety in his experiences, there are times when he will appreciate "nonform for the sake of unrest" as well as "form for the sake of rest." It has been observed that men who keep alive, or better still, develop their appreciation of nature seem more responsive to life as a whole, find it more exciting, and enjoy and invite its daily surprises more than those who do not see because they are not aware.

Selective man thus requires that his material world contribute to or reinforce his identity. When one is continually living and working in groups, objects of daily use are instrumental in asserting oneself. An object is not only required to be efficient in operation—it must also communicate to some extent one's personality. It must say "me," and when seen in the intimate environment of the owner, the members of the group must think: "This is just like him"; "How well it expresses him"; or "I didn't know him like this before." Possessions reveal values, tastes, and even the deeper internal self, which one may not dare express otherwise. As such, they become personal emissaries and help establish communication and understanding between men.

This is beyond function. It is establishing a difference by what one owns. Objects can reflect a person's values, personality, education, social status, economic viability, provincialism or cosmopolitanism, philosophy, sensuousness, ethnology—and they may tell how confused or literate he is visually. Man's life is in constant relationship to objects.

Man may also manipulate natural materials to produce new media and expressions. Taking the natural elements, he can combine them into novel, workable relationships such as pewter, composed of tin and copper, and plastics in which various amounts of water, air, coal, petroleum, salt, and natural gasses are combined. Thus he extends his world both functionally and aesthetically. Because he cannot be disassociated from his materials, it is valuable for him to understand and appreciate them as affecting and enlarging the human experience. Only when he becomes avid to accumulate objects for their own sake or lives in an economic era when survival depends upon sustaining life minimally are materials per se, in all their expressiveness, not fully appreciated.

Objects perform other functions beyond serviceability, defining man, and helping establish his identity. They can also provide him with human associations by evoking memories. Robert Browning wrote a verse commemorating a friend:

> Beautiful Evelyn Hope is dead.
> Sit and watch by her side an hour.
> This is her book-shelf, this her bed;
> She plucked that piece of geranium flower.

Conrad Aiken in his poem *Music I Heard* also remembered a loved one through objects:

> Music I heard with you was more than
> music,
> And bread I broke with you was
> more than bread
> Now that I am without you, all is
> desolate,
> All that was once so beautiful is dead.
> . . . .
>
> Your hands once touched this table and
> this silver,
> And I have seen your fingers hold
> this glass.
> These things do not remember you, beloved,
> And yet your touch upon them will
> not pass.

Objects can create enjoyable sensations in man and as they become familiar and old, provide feelings of security, longevity, and continuity. They can become friends, create feelings of familiarity, and provide emotional support, just as people do. Antique objects may arouse feelings of kinship with ancestors who faced the same kinds of human problems we do and found resolutions to them. Newly designed objects suggest oneness with our own day and adventure into the future. Possessing some of the old and the new may provide some of the sensations of the role of two-faced Janus, the Roman god who could look simultaneously eastward to the rising sun and westward to its setting. Thus our cherished possessions can elevate our spirits by creating feelings of continuity between us and the past or of greater relatedness to our present. Through them is preserved the life of the human spirit.

They also preserve the traces of man's social history.

2-3 *Queen Anne armchair of walnut and tapestry c. 1710. This chair is a statement of the 18th-century in England. Collection, Metropolitan Museum of Art, New York.*

Gertrude Thomas has expressed this view exceptionally well about a single object—the chair:

A chair, in any period, has combined within its contours volumes of history—social, economic, and political. It stands as a symbol of its time. By its very existence it bespeaks authority, since for centuries the chair was only for the master or his guest, while women, children, and retainers sat upon stools or benches. By its very size and shape, a chair subtly indicates the degree of authority it confers. As for the rest, every turn or carving of its members suggests an anecdote, real or fanciful, of people or events important in its time.[1]

As a consumer of design, man also has an opportunity to develop his visual literacy, a lifelong process in itself. Visual literacy is seeing perceptively, emotionally, and with insight and intelligence. Visually literate people see the world intimately and intensely; they are aware of omnipresent design, both in nature and manmade objects. A falling leaf is an event; so likewise may be the rusting of a nail or the gleaming of the sun on a silver spoon. Those who are aesthetically sensitive attach values to an object that go beyond mere appreciation of its service. They can evaluate its design for the expressive qualities it gains from the designer's use of line, form, space, color, and texture, all of which serve to heighten a person's encounter with it. Appreciating the designer as both practical man and artist, both craftsman and poet, such people may try to enter into his motivation and purposes in order not only to understand his approach to the design problem, but to establish empathy with him as a man. They are, of course, rationally aware of qualitative differences between objects, based upon design principles; however, they also value the emotional responses, ranging from joy and delight to distaste and revulsion, that objects can evoke. They are liberal in their responses, enjoying art that exists for its own sake as well as the art that serves a utilitarian function.

Visual literacy means substituting visual involvement, for visual indifference. It means working the eye to make it a selective receptor. It is seeing with awareness, appreciation, insight, and knowledge. People who are visually literate create more aesthetic daily environments. Such milieux increase our enjoyment of, and capacity for, living. We are all enriched by feeling more intensely and deeply in all aspects of our lives. As design contributes to these feelings, it extends our humanity.

[1] Gertrude Z. Thomas, *Richer Than Spices* (New York: Knopf, 1965), p. 59.

Approaches to Design 3

The fields of art and design encompass such diverse activities as land and city planning; shelter design; product, advertising, and industrial design; interior and landscape design; design in apparel and personal appearance; design in food services; painting, sculpture, ceramics, weaving, and photography. This book will concentrate on those design activities and products that are most immediate to daily living.

Past approaches have differentiated between art, crafts, and design; no sharp delineation will be made in this text, however, because these authors consider any activity that engages the greatest portion of man's creative energies to be his art. The distinction drawn in the past between craft and art, between the creation of objects through skill and industrial craft to fulfill practical human needs as against the production of works whose chief service is to elevate the spirit by providing aesthetic satisfaction, has reflected man's higher esteem for what he considered to be more elevated functions. To state it briefly, fine art was considered the art of expression and applied art, the art of utility. Not so to George Santayana, who professed that liberal arts are brought to "spiritual fruition" by turning apt materials into "expressive forms." The fact that applied design and art have elements in common that make division between them arbitrary was well expressed by him:

It remains merely to note that all industry contains an element of fine art and all fine art an element of industry; since every proximate end, in being attained, satisfies the mind and manifests the intent that pursued it; while every operation upon a material, even one so volatile as sound, finds that material somewhat refractory. Before the product can attain its ideal function many obstacles to its transparency and fitness have to be removed. A certain amount of technical and instrumental labor is thus involved in every work of genius, and a certain genius in every technical success.[1]

More recently, in 1971, Lee Nordness, an art dealer commissioned by Johnson's Wax to acquire craft articles for the traveling exhibit *Objects: USA*, wrote in the brochure *Objects: USA; The Johnson Collection of Contemporary Crafts:*

Placing paintings and sculpture into a convenient "fine arts" category, and objects—whether functional or non-functional—into a craft category no longer sustains any aesthetic validity. The "presence" of many an object made in clay or wrought in gold is as satisfying as a sculpture in bronze or a painting in oil. . . . During the past twenty years the interaction between the once separate worlds of painting-sculpture and crafts has become so intimate that separating the expressions into "major" or "fine" and "minor" or "decorative" can now only be done on a quality level, not on a media one. That is, when one puts a contemporary painting beside a contemporary object in glass, the painting may well be deemed the "decorative" object and the work in glass the "fine" one. . . . In a world in which most objects are fabricated with a built-in obsolescence, are made to be thrown away, these artists have created objects which, because of their aesthetic presences, may be protected by their owners, and hopefully last through the years to one day tell a future century of the culture of our time.

The museums of the world are filled with articles dating from the Neolithic period when artist and artisan were one. They are valued today not only as historic records of how man fulfilled his functional needs but also because they provide visual pleasure. The sharp cleavage between what is categorized as "fine" versus "applied" art is thought to have begun with the Industrial Revolution of the nineteenth century. At that time considerations of art became separated from the manufacture of articles and buildings. Machines produced a proliferation of objects that lacked design quality and man became conditioned to accepting ugliness as the norm. What was gained in convenience for the masses was lost in aesthetic appreciation. Today the demands of modern man increasingly include satisfaction of his aesthetic interests as well as serviceability in the objects he uses. Hence there are now "artist-designers," variously called industrial or product designers, who create objects that are useful while simultaneously fulfilling man's need for visual delight. The education of these artist-designers includes not only engineering and production methods but the study of art and design.

The distinction between fine and applied art is becoming further blurred as artists and designers take advantage of the advances in science and technology. Paintings may be three-dimensional and include incandescent bulbs and fluorescent tubes. Textiles are being produced that are no longer repeat designs but single-image paintings. Where designers used to ask what art could do for technology, today artists are asking what technology can do for art. In this connection it is interesting to note that our word *technology* is derived from the Greek word for art: *techne*.

The coordinated role that art and industry must assume in the future was recognized in the exhibit *Art and Technology*, held in the Los Angeles County Museum in June, 1971. There was an echo of the Bauhaus philosophy—that a synthesis needs to be achieved between technology and art. The aim of the exhibit was to place some of the technical and financial resources of American firms at the disposal of a group of artists, to give them an opportunity to construct more ambitious works than their limited studio facilities might allow. The founding principle of modern art, that of *experiment*, was recognized as "a metaphor drawn from science and industry." Increasingly, sculptors, artists, and industry are realizing the need for supportive roles. If art is to be valid and enrich man's environment in our scientific age, sculptor James Prestini believes it must fuse the humane with the technological, as the superior art of past centuries used to do. Prestini's quo-

[1]George Santayana, *Reason in Art,* Volume IV of *The Life of Reason* (New York: Collier Books, 1952), p. 28.

tation in the caption under his *Construction 231* (Figure 3-1) clarifies the approach to his own sculpture and a future-oriented vision.

One can also note that whether labelled as artist, craftsman, architect, or designer, those who produce our objects have certain characteristics in common. They are knowledgeable, sentient, and emotionally responsive in relation to the impact of the cultural forces in their society. Working independently, they frequently arrive at similar visual interpretations and expressions of their environment. At any given time painting, sculpture, architecture, interiors, and the design of furniture and costume may have recognizable similarities in line and form.

Also, despite their professional designation, all designers value certain attitudes and engage in some common activities. They share a concern with aesthetics as well as function. As they interpret the changing world around them, they give visual and tactile form to their ideas and deeply felt emotions. The objects they create are symbolic of their subjective perceptions, thoughts, and feelings.

In ordering materials toward higher levels of organization, they transform them into coherent structures of greater significance. In a sense, they edit the gross disorderly details of an environment, omitting those that are superfluous and combining the pertinent elements into harmonious forms and images that give greater pleasure to man.

By solving some of life's problems through structuring materials for use, comfort, and beauty, they contribute to the efficiency and enhancement of our life style.

Today the attitude of those who are design-conscious has reached a degree of maturity that offers encouraging prospects of elevating the aesthetic level of man. The values inherent in the classical and romantic approaches to art have coalesced into acceptance of certain guiding principles in the production and selection of design objects. Both the sustaining values of the past and those of today's space age are held in respect.

The canons of good taste in Western design had their

3-1 *James Prestini.* Construction 231, *29⅞″ x 29⅞″ x 15½″. Prestini says of his work: "The basic concept of my sculpture is to communicate the influence of science and technology on our culture through art. I have used standard structural steel elements: I-beams, H-beams, channels, angles, pipes, and tubes. The elements have been machined and finished by industrial methods. The spaces generated by the sculpture are the result of elements used and compounded by the reflections of polished surfaces which create a virtual transparency and a mirror of the environment— all interacting. The precision, crispness, and discipline of the forms result from the use of industrial products and the control of technology." He adds: "Photographing the content of my work has been an art form in its own right." Courtesy of James Prestini.*

origins in the criteria for acceptable art formulated by the French Academy, which was founded in 1648 in the reign of Louis XIV. The tradition was reinforced by London's Royal Academy of Arts, established in 1768 as a "society for promoting the Arts of Design, providing a well regulated school and an Annual Exhibition." Both emphasized the classical values of the Greco-Roman world. In England, Sir Joshua Reynolds' *Discourses,* a text presented to students of the Royal Academy at its annual prize-winning event, further propagated the idealism of the day. Reynolds stated: "I would chiefly recommend that an implicit obedience to the Rules of Art, as established by the practice of the great Masters, should be exacted from the young students." Such was the temper of the day that led to the romantic revolt, which began during the latter part of the eighteenth century and was to lead into the scientific revolution of the nineteenth.

The standard of good taste had held that the highest beauty was marked by an absence of individuality. This restriction of the human imagination proved antithetical not only to the pioneers of the romantic movement, but to the very nature of man, who, if he is totally self-accepting, must express himself in all the ways he can. Hence art eventually became infused with more of man's capacities—turbulence, movement, power, emotion, imagination, freedom, and thrust.

The classical emphasis on uniformity was alien to the romantic spirit of later centuries. Experiencing the freedom to express himself, the artist would not confine himself to a classical world. Moreover, as he was no longer responsible to a patron who directed and sup-

ported him, the artist's direction came from his own personal experiences and aesthetic impulses; he was free to choose. If he wished to utilize the past, he saw it through his own eyes, not through group focus. He could interpret it aesthetically and give it form in terms of his own internal dynamism. He would be conditioned to some extent by what he saw, for man cannot completely escape the visual contagion of his day, but at least there would be a variety of visual expressions from which to take his cues.

That this freedom in expression should miscarry in the field of design during some of the ensuing eras is not surprising. After periods of suppression, freedom of expression is often characterized by lack of clarity of purpose, for abandon and freedom do not necessarily lead to design that has merit. Some of the Victorian pastiches in architecture, home furnishings, and decorative objects, which were designed in an era that succumbed to romantic flamboyancy, are examples both of miscarriage in the arts and of factory methods of reproduction. Industry frequently hired artists to produce patterns for dies, molds, and blocks that would emulate Renaissance, Gothic, and Greek stylistic features.

On the other hand, there is sustaining merit in the genuine orderliness of Georgian architecture, in the beautiful symmetry of the gardens of the Palace of Versailles, or the exquisite detail of interiors and décor under Louis XVI. Though one may reject the autocratic approach to art in periods of academic control, certain values from those periods still have relevance for today's design. Among these are a desire to appeal to the universality of man, to elevate or ennoble his spirit, to apply a restraint to design, to value order and simplicity, and to make a clear and forceful statement. The work of architect and designer Ludwig Mies van der Rohe and of today's Scandinavian designers continues to appeal because of their incorporation of many of these values.

In contrast, the romantic inclination to experiment with new ideas and forms and to project visual objects

3-2 *Gardens of the Palace of Versailles. The formality of the gardens, the fountains, and the palace add to the radial symmetry of the city's boulevards. Variations in the size of floral beds and the wings of the central palace create varied spatial relations. French Government Tourist Office.*

with sensuous appeal is more respectful of man's comprehensive self and vitality. Today we are living in a highly experimental age. No longer bound by tradition, we can be selective in utilizing the forms and designs of other periods as they meet our purposes. We have a wholeness of approach that need not constrain us either to depend upon or to demean the past. Moreover, not only is the world of the past available for our re-creation, but the mass media offer us the visual images of neighboring cultures, so that our vision can be expanded to phenomenal proportions. We have the potential to reach new heights of design.

In succeeding chapters the elements of art and certain guiding principles related to the design of objects will be presented. These should be viewed not as rigid criteria like the Royal Academy's "Rules of Art," but as guides to appreciation and creativity. They can help impart more significance to objects than they formerly held. They also provide us with a vocabulary so that we can communicate more effectively with others about design.

Before further presentation of the elements and principles of design, these are some important remarks to make about values. This book deals primarily with aesthetics, but the aesthetic value is only one among many. Men sometimes cherish objects they recognize as ineffective in design but that have pleasurable human or sentimental associations. Designs that offend are also sometimes retained in households for economic or practical reasons; for instance, unattractive chairs can be comfortable. In addition, although they are lacking in design quality, some objects may be valued for historic reasons, because of their links with the past, or because owning them provides a degree of status or prestige. In other eras, kings, queens, and persons of wealth have used artifacts to reflect the sumptuous splendor and luxury of their domains. In this case, interest would often be focused on the intricate workmanship involved in producing objects rather than on the aesthetic use of materials. But one can recognize limitations of design while still respecting the priority of others' values. Having developed critical taste in evaluating the design of objects, one has to learn to combine it at times with a parallel development in visual tolerance when living in an environment shared with other people.

4 The Elements of Design

Certain basic concepts constitute the language of design. They are *art elements* and *principles*. Through familiarity with them, we can communicate with others about design. The elements are the visual components used in creating an object or composition. To create, the designer uses some or all of these devices: line, form, space, transparency, motion, light, color, texture. Because they can be manipulated and modified to produce unlimited visual effects, these elements are often referred to as plastic. *Principles* are the basic guides to organization, the ways in which the elements are combined. Success in the application of the principles depends on the complementary functioning of each of the elements. To bring them into a working relationship and to unify the whole is the function of the designer.

Although the art elements are considered individually, they are all interdependent, as are the principles. *Forms* exist in space. Motion indicates a flow through space. *Color* and visual texture are qualities visible through *light*. *Line* is a graphic shorthand device for symbolizing forms by drawing boundaries of objects or representing cultural symbols such as letters.

Humans are a composition of the art elements. The human body is a symmetrically balanced structure, a form that moves through time and space. Its periphery is an outline. Because of the underlying skeletal, glandular, and muscular structure, a feminine form is associated with curved lines and a masculine form with angular lines. Humans come in different colors: white, olive, pink, black, or brown. Were it not for light, forms could not be differentiated. We are textured: hairy, smooth, glassy-eyed, freckled, wrinkled.

4-1 *Pablo Picasso.* The Deer. *(1936) One of 31 aquatints for Buffon's* Histoire Naturelle. *Published: Paris, Fabiani, 1942. Aquatint, 10⅝ x 8⅛". Collection, The Museum of Modern Art, New York. Gift of Abby Aldrich Rockefeller.*

4-2 *Alexander Calder.* The Hostess, *1928, wire construction, height 11½". Line can be partially supplied, and the eye and mind complete the form. Collection, The Museum of Modern Art, New York.*

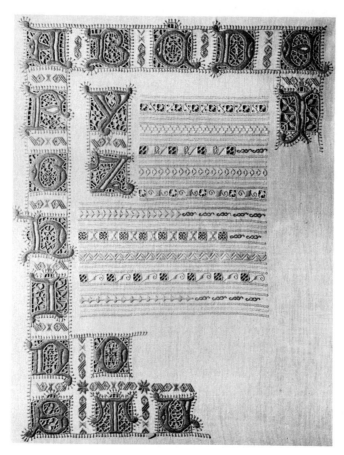

Our daily lives are directed by line. From the numerals on the alarm clock that summons us to action to the alphabetical symbols on medical prescriptions that help in maintaining our life, line is ever-present. As it informs us of the lives of others, it provides us with vicarious living. Through line, events are interpreted and emotions transmitted; richness and depth of experience are developed through the printed word of newspapers, periodicals, and books. Thus line extends and supplements our lives, taking us far beyond our personal and geographic limits. Because it enables us to live many roles, our understanding of others and of the peoples of the world is increased. Thus line both educates and humanizes us.

Writing, which is known as calligraphy, is considered an art in itself in some cultures. In China and Japan the art is developed from childhood. In Persia script is extensively used in the design of architectural detail, rugs, and ceramic ware. The illustrated manuscripts of the Middle Ages are masterpieces of fanciful line.

Psychophysical Communication

Line communicates in other ways than as a narrative symbol. Each of the art elements has psychophysical powers of communication and provides man with a symbolic language. The designer selects certain of these for their ability to project the desired image and as devices to create illusion. The direction of line and its breadth and forcefulness suggest particular attributes. As evidence of this, communication through line has made handwriting a means of determining an individual's personality, a fact often useful to criminologists.

The potential of lines to communicate through their direction results from man's observation of nature. Tall, stately trees create strong verticals, suggesting majesty and dignity; low shrubs suggest earthiness. High mountains seem austere and inaccessible; low hills appear close and intimate. Hence vertical lines become associated with uprightness, elevation, and formality whereas horizontal ones suggest the approachable and informal.

Line

Line is the lifeline of civilization. It is man's most useful symbol and is particularly significant among the elements because it has been instrumental in making us what we are today. The thread of recorded history is a line. Major advances in civilization have depended upon line as both symbol and means of communication. Man has used line in the shape of pictographs, cuneiforms, hieroglyphics, and letters to make himself a social being and to give continuity to his culture.

seem more active. The continuous progression of the spiral line, seen in the tendrils of vines and the boundaries of seashells, suggests infinity. Zigzag lines, like lightning, give an electrical and exciting effect. Very actively curved lines may be visually enervating or produce feelings of restlessness and agitation. Moder-

4-6 *Kitagawa Utamoro. Yam Uba combing her hair with the infant Kintoki on her back. The diagonal line illustrates the motion. Collection, The Metropolitan Museum of Art, New York.*

4-5 *Kitagawa Utamaro. The mother bathing her baby in the tub is expressed in line in this Japanese print. Collection, The Metropolitan Museum of Art, New York.*

Diagonal lines, as seen in the bending of boughs during a storm, appear more dynamic than horizontal and vertical ones because, being neither upright nor perpendicular, they produce psychic tension. Can they maintain themselves and defy the pull of gravity? Also by creating the illusion of their moving into depth, they

4-7 *Henri de Toulouse-Lautrec, French.* Troupe de Mlle. Eglantine. *Colored lithograph poster, 1896. The diagonal lines lead the eye into space. Victoria and Albert Museum. Crown Copyright.*

nal movements or ceilings of diagonal line structure seem not only more spacious, but more vital and energetic than rectangular ones.

Other Line Classifications

Line is also referred to as *contrasting, transitional,* and *repetitive.* Contrasting lines are horizontal opposed to vertical. These make a strong statement and establish a center of interest where they meet or intersect. A transitional line is a curved line that joins the horizontal with the vertical in a graduated manner. It establishes rhythm by creating a flow of movement between the contrasting elements. For instance, a contour davenport or chair placed between two abutting walls would be an example of fluid line movement using objects.

4-8 *Chinese bronze ceremonial covered vessel of the Kuang type (enlarged detail). Chou dynasty, late 11th century or early 10th century B.C. Spiral form; soft green patina with scattered incrustation outside and inside provides textural interest. Courtesy of the Smithsonian Institution, Freer Gallery of Art, Washington, D.C.*

ately curved lines, on the other hand, are more restful, suggesting gracefulness and lyricism.

Spatial Illusion

Space can be manipulated through the use of line. Increasing either the vertical or the horizontal aspect of lines produces differing spatial sensations. Because the eye follows the lines of the horizon more readily than it moves up and down, a room seems more spacious with horizontal wall structures or furnishings. Strong vertical lines increase the apparent height but do not appreciably increase space, because vertical eye movements require more physical effort. Interiors with diago-

Repetitive lines create pronounced rhythms, as seen in grid patterns.

Various lines have come to be associated with the social and political climates of particular eras and seem expressive of the values prevalent in a culture at a given time. For example, the *classical* line, which is basically horizontal and vertical and balanced bisymmetrically, as seen in Greco-Roman temples imparts an aura of the dignity and order characteristic of the classical world.

On the other hand, the *baroque* line, which began to be favored in architecture, art, and decoration in Italy during the late sixteenth century, is characterized by large scale, bold detail, and sweeping curves. It is the exuberant line of Michelangelo; the bulging muscles in his giant figures in the frescoes of the Sistine Chapel move in an equilibrium of thrust and counterthrust. The baroque line spread throughout Europe and was particularly popular in France during the reign of Louis XIV. Bold and impressive ornamentation in fabric and furniture commanded attention and effectively communicated the robust prowess and masculine energy of the French king and the general temper of his era.

The softening of the line into what would eventually become the *rococo* began in the reign of Louis XIV's great-grandson, Louis XV, perhaps reflecting the influence of feminine court favorites. By the mid-eighteenth century, the time of Madame de Pompadour, the rococo line had emerged as the most characteristic feature of the decorative arts. As befitted its name, derived from *rocaille*, "rock," and *coquille*, "shell," the rococo line was light, curvaceous, asymmetric, and often whimsical. Rococo art frequently combined the fantastic with the real. Fanciful trees, clouds, and waterfalls might be connected by series of garlands or ribbons tied in bowknots. Cavorting cupids frolicked in puffy cloud banks. Men and maidens, flirting with joyous abandon, played in roseate gardens canopied by dense sheltering boughs. Design motifs too captured this atmosphere of fantasy and their organization was expressive of an era when it seemed men still had unlimited space for play and freedom and for stretching their imagination.

For other eras, other lines. The sinuous asymmetric line is characteristic of the Art Nouveau period when botanical forms inspired the designer. Right angular and planular lines are associated with the greater severity and restraint of German Bauhaus design, which emphasized functionalism as opposed to ornateness and exuberance. Thus it seems that line can reflect what is in the mind and emotions not only of man but also of organized society.

4-9 *Wallpaper, probably by Reveillon, noted for his beautiful wallpapers in France about 1780. The imagery is characteristic of that time: two griffons uphold a flower basket, and female figures sheathed in foliage rest upon a circular medallion enclosing a butterfly. Courtesy of the Cooper-Hewitt Museum of Decorative Arts and Design, Smithsonian Institution.*

4-10 *Jean Honoré Fragonard. Love Letters, 8" x 10". An idyllic period is captured by Fragonard. Note the soft rococo lines and the impression of unlimited space. Copyright The Frick Collection, New York.*

and stars. Less rigid and organic are the ellipses and the parabola. Recognizing the abstraction present in nature, the French artist Paul Cézanne proposed reducing all forms to three: "Everything in nature is modeled on the sphere, the cone, and the cylinder; we must teach ourselves how to paint these simple figures, and then we can do whatever we wish." Cubism, an experiencing of the world geometrically rather than naturalistically, as in the Renaissance, reflected this position.

Forms have power to evoke feelings similar to those of line. Cubes seem static and rigid to us, whereas spheres seem mobile and rhythmically soothing. Those forms that are round, kidney-shaped, and womblike suggest warmth, comfort, and protection. Variations in

4-12 *David Smith, American. Cube IX, 1961. Stainless steel, 106¼" × 56" × 46". Varied rectangular forms are in taut balance with incidental light and shadow clarifying form. Collection, Walker Art Center, Minneapolis, Minnesota.*

4-11 *Architectural model of Karnak, Egyptian, 19th dynasty, 1350–1205 B.C. One can discern a multiplicity of forms: the cylinder, rectangle, sphere, ellipse, cone, and truncated cone. Note the spatial relationships and the textural decorative design relieved by plain surfaces. Collection, The Metropolitan Museum of Art, New York.*

Form

Form, a basic element of design, is sometimes referred to as *area, mass,* or *shape.* Three-dimensional forms with length, height, and depth measurements are *solids.* Two-dimensional flat forms, having only length and width, are often differentiated as *shapes.* All forms and shapes may vary in size or in the area they occupy.

Forms can be enduring. England's monolithic Stonehenge, the pyramids and rock-cut temples of Egypt, and the castles of Europe are all testimony to man's concern with form. It is the dominant element in both sculpture and architecture.

Forms are based upon the geometries and fluid contours of nature. Geometric forms include the cone, cylinder, square, rectangle, triangle, and circle. Composites of these are trapezoids, pentagons, hexagons, octagons,

4-13 *Pablo Picasso.* Guernica, *1937. Mural in black, white, and gray, oil on canvas, 11'5½" x 25'5¾". The mural was executed to memorialize the frightful bombing of civilians in the Basque town of Guernica, Spain. Almost all the forms and imagery are symbolic of some aspect of terror, pain, fear, and death. Much use is made of conical forms, which suggest despair, severity, agitation, and the destructiveness of war upon the human form, mind, and emotion. Collection, The Museum of Modern Art. On extended loan to The Museum of Modern Art, New York, from the estate of the artist. (Guernica has since been returned to Spain.)*

4-15 *Antoine Pevsner.* Torso, *1924–26, translucent brown plastic and copper, height 29½". The abstract sculpture resembles cubism in painting and stresses negative concave volumes in contradiction to nature's contours. Collection, The Museum of Modern Art, New York.*

4-14 *Jean (Hans) Arp.* Human Concretion, *1935, stone, height 19½". The soft, comforting forms resemble man's curving bone structure or stones bathed by the ocean. Shadow and light are adroitly used by the photographer to provide contrast of dark and light. Collection, The Museum of Modern Art, New York.*

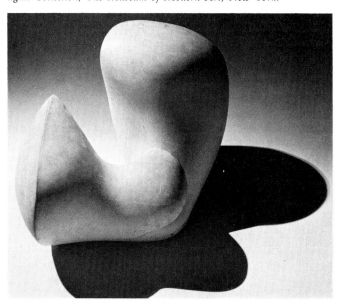

tall forms may suggest elegance, austerity, idealism, and spirituality, or they may induce feelings of elevation, such as joy and ecstasy. The slender Gothic cathedrals as well as the tall headdresses of the medieval era seem expressive of man's aspirations toward the heavenly. A prevalent form in church design today is the elongated vertical arch, which suggests man's communication with heaven and raises his eyes upward creating a feeling of spirituality. Low horizontal forms, on the other hand, are used to suggest man's approachability, as they were in the Renaissance, when developing excellence was considered the ideal.

In furniture design elegance, dignity, and stateliness are achieved through emphasis on the vertical. The low forms of Oriental furnishings, on the other hand, seem expressive of our close relationship with nature and earthly life. Because the sharp points of cones are associated with spears, daggers, and the jagged lines of lightning, the conical shape is most frequently assimilated into the décor of homes in a truncated form, as in lamp shades and the tapered, blunt legs of chairs. That pointed forms create a staccatolike effect is very evident in some of Picasso's paintings in which conical

tance of space is expressed by the Chinese philosopher Lao-Tse:

> *The wheel's hub holds thirty spokes*
> *Utility depends on the hole through the hub.*
> *The potter's clay forms a vessel*
> *It is the space within that serves.*
> *A house is built with solid walls*
> *The nothingness of window and door*
> *Alone renders it usable.*
> *That which exists may be transformed*
> *What is non-existent has boundless uses.*

We experience space as existing within certain limited and measurable boundaries, as in cylinders and cubes. These not only occupy space but have dimensions of volume: *length, width,* and *height.* Space is also experienced as a limitless nonmeasurable dimension, a dynamic field of force, which appears atmospheric in quality and is described in Webster's *New International Dictionary* as "extension in all directions, boundlessness, and indefinite divisibility."

forms are generously used. Contrast with these the soothing sensations you may experience when smoothing rocks that have been ground down by the waves or looking at the biomorphic fluid sculptures of Hans Arp (Figure 4–14).

Space

The element of form implies space. Time and movement in turn are dependent upon space. The impor-

Space has many characteristics that can be exploited by the designer. It can be private or public, formal or informal, personal or impersonal, social or solitary, warm or cold, enclosing or expanding, confining or liberating. It can attract or repel.

László Moholy-Nagy, the Bauhaus artist who founded the Chicago Institute of Design in 1937, was particularly intrigued with the elements of space and light. In analyzing man's response to space, he differentiated these four perceptual levels.

Man perceives space:

1. *through the sense of sight* in such things as sticks, rods, wiring, columns, bodies; surfaces meeting and cutting one another; interpenetrating objects; wide perspectives; relationships of mass, light, shadow; transparency; reflection; mirroring.
2. *through the sense of hearing* by acoustical phenomena; reflected sound; echo.
3. *through the sense of equilibrium* by circles, curves, windings (spiral stairways).
4. *through the means of movement* by different directions in space (horizontal, vertical, diagonal); intersections; jumps, etc."[1]

Many other optical devices have been employed, from the ancient Egyptian period to the present day architecture and landscapes. Prints of Roman architecture by eighteenth-century engraver Giambattista Piranesi can be photographically enlarged to cover an entire wall and create the illusion of extended vistas that overcome the confinement of walls.

Other devices may be used. Objects whose definitions are lost in mist or atmospheric haze will appear more distant. So will those that are smaller or placed higher on the picture plane. Combinations of diagonals, with occasional horizontal lines, gradually lead one into depth. Progression of sizes also creates movement and increases an object's spaciousness.

[1] László Moholy-Nagy, *The New Vision and Abstract of an Artist* (New York: Wittenborn, 1947), p. 58.

4-18 *Emilio Castellar, Brazilian.* Spherical Cosmic Orbs.
Castellar's heroes are our astronauts and his subjects the sights and sounds they explore for us. As a painter of space, meteors, and planets, he attempts to show man's heroism. He uses polyester paint to create a smooth glowing surface and combines the medium with plastic forms, pieces of machinery, and objects, such as the metal rope that combines the lower orbs. He invites you to touch, "Go ahead. You should feel them, see how they are made. Examine their surfaces. They are alive." Pan American Coffee Bureau, New York City.

Motion

Related to Moholy-Nagy's fourth perception is movement through time. Man's life on earth is a space, bounded by life and death. Our lives are kinetic pathways through space—time-and-motion studies of greater or lesser significance, efficiency, and aesthetic distinction. We recognize this whenever we refer to "the dance of life." The joy we take in observing ballet, theater, movies, and sports involves personal and psychological satisfactions gained from experiencing the articulations of forms in space. These also involve movements through time.

Although we are most familiar with the visual aspect

4-20 *Henry Moore. Family Group, 1945, bronze, height 9⅜". Henry Moore was among the first to relieve the heaviness of traditional sculpture by creating deep perforations. The family's home is the garden of The Museum of Modern Art, which makes it one of the most familiar families in the United States. Collection, The Museum of Modern Art, New York.*

4-21 *David Smith. Royal Bird, 1948, stainless steel, 21¾" x 59" x 9". The skeletal membranes of the sculpture enclose open space and emphasize line. Collection, Walker Art Center, Minneapolis, Minnesota.*

4-19 *Constantin Brancusi. The Kiss, 1908, stone. This is an example of closed sculptural space in which the sculptor extracts from stone the essence of embrace. The funerary sculpture was placed over a tomb in Montparnasse Cemetery where Brancusi himself is buried. Valuing the attributes of materials, the sculptor preserved the texture of the rough quarried block and retained its rectilinear character. The Kiss is symbolic of life and death, and the duality of life—man and woman. Life and love triumph over death—the woman within the embrace is pregnant. Philadelphia Museum of Art: The Louise and Walter Arensberg Collection.*

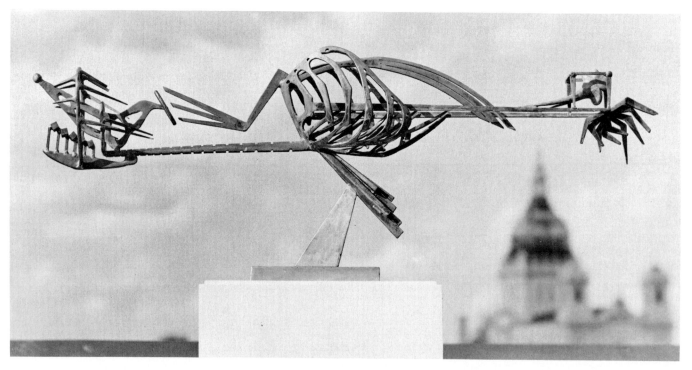
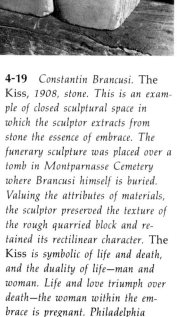

of space, the kinetic is coming into greater recognition through the media of sculpture, architecture, painting, and the cinema. In this age where jet planes circle the globe, rockets are orbited into the stratosphere, and man has set foot on the moon, the world seems diminished and penetrable. Space, time, and motion now become the elements that challenge the designer.

In other centuries sculpture was static. Forms, poised in balance, had specific horizontal, vertical, and oblique definition and were arrested on a supportive base. The visual impression was that of heaviness, produced by an impenetrable volume of unrelieved positive space. Gradually, as the sculptor began to perceive differently, mass came to be lightened by various means. These included an increase in plastic treatment of the material to create deeper recessions; development of negative space in the design, achieved either through perforation or by membranous structures surrounding empty space; poising of volumes suspended in relation to each other; and interpenetration of forms and spaces. The last element to be added was movement. In the first sculptures that made use of rotated volumes, we experienced motion as a new visual volume.

Forms in motion remained to be experienced visually. In the 1930s, Alexander Calder developed mobile forms in sculpture. More recently, architects have developed structures that pivot on a central base. Homes can now be constructed to rotate with the rays of the sun and utilize solar energy to provide light and warmth throughout the day. In 1968, architect Richard T. Foster designed a house in Connecticut that takes forty-eight minutes to four hours for a 360-degree rotation. Glass-walled, it permits a continuously changing panorama, including its own reflection in an adjacent lake. In Atlanta a revolving restaurant in the turret of the Regency Hyatt Hotel has a dome of transparent blue plastic through which one can enjoy a kaleidoscopic view of Atlanta's skyline and the Blue Ridge Mountains ninety miles away. Thus the experience of dining is enhanced by a constant change of scenery.

In painting, the artist was long confined by the two dimensions of a canvas—length and width. His challenge throughout the centuries has been to overcome this limitation by providing psychophysical experiences of depth and movement. Toward this end, he has employed numerous illusory devices, among them the building up of the third dimension by thickness of oil or painting substances (impasto), as can be observed in the paintings of Vincent van Gogh. Using a palette knife instead of a brush also creates depth through adding levels of paint. Including a filler applied in relief to the canvas or in the paint itself so as to create variations in height is a common procedure. Employing the collage technique of adhering semiflat or three-dimensional objects to a surface and painting over them also increases depth. Today the use of acrylics, which bind as well as color, has greatly facilitated the art of collage.

Transparency

Concern with motion has also influenced the use of materials. The American sculptor James Davis has stated why transparent plastics and artificial illumination are so useful to the artist today.

For me, the important problem in contemporary art is motion. In the fourteenth century, the art of painting made the revolutionary transition from the flat, two-dimensional effect to the illusion of three-dimensional space and solid sculpturesque form. Now we are entering a stage of further development where the element of motion must be considered. For this purpose, the traditional media—the tools and materials of painting and sculpture of the past—are obsolete because they are static, not dynamic, tools. The visual artist must adopt new tools and materials which modern science and industry provide. As the modern architect uses modern materials, so the artist who wishes to decorate this modern architecture must also adopt new materials. Transparent plastics and artificial illumination are two tools which have great potentialities for this new sculpture of movement.[2]

[2] Eleanor Bittermann, *Art in Modern Architecture* (New York: Reinhold, 1952), p. 168.

architect Frank Lloyd Wright through horizontal slab construction and the adroit use of glass, which allowed the space of landscape to flow backward and forward with the interior of the building. Boundaries and interior walls were fluid, creating inner penetration of space. Movement thus extended from the outer landscapes to the periphery of the building, through the interior of the center, and outward again. The slabs of geometric construction were suspended in equipoise through an equilibrium of top forces held in balance. Other architects, such as Walter Gropius or Le Corbusier or Mies van der Rohe, used the same elements but in vertical thrusts. These constructions were developed when energy was cheap and heat loss through windows was not as significant as it is today.

4-24 *Architect Richard T. Foster's home, Connecticut, 1968. This solar eight-room rotating home, with glass walls and cedar shingle construction, makes use of light as a plastic medium. The New York Times Studio.*

4-23 *Alexander Calder.* Lobster Trap and Fish Tail, *1939, mobile, steel wire, and sheet aluminum, about 8½" high and 9½" in diameter. Variations in the currents of air create ever-changing linear relationships and configurations emphasizing time, space, and movement as significant design elements. Collection, The Museum of Modern Art, New York.*

Architecture has reflected a development similar to that of sculpture. Static space containment is exemplified in the Egyptian pyramids and temples, the Greek Parthenon, and the mansions of the Georgian period. Transparency in space was achieved by the American

4-25 *Giambattista Piranesi.* The Prisons, *Plate III, etching. Much contemporary use is made of Piranesi etchings to promote the illusion of unbounded space. Courtesy, Museum of Fine Arts, Boston, Massachusetts.*

4-29 *Edward Hopper. Office in a Small City, 1953. Oil on canvas. This painting shows the role of light and shadow for interior and exterior structures. Collection, The Metropolitan Museum of Art, New York. George A. Hearn Fund.*

Light

Importance of Light

Although light, color, and visual texture are as inseparable as are space and form, for the purpose of emphasis each is considered individually here.

Of the elements, light has recently generated much excitement and influenced the design of fabric, clothing, art, sculpture, interiors, and architecture. Today it is regarded not only as a supportive medium but as a raw material, like paint or clay. Luminosity has become a plastic element that can be shaped and directed. The contemporary fascination with light has many possible explanations. One of them is that now we have increased leisure, we are becoming more aware of all our senses and have more time for cultivating our sensory reactors. Light, being a form of energy, makes a strong impact upon our senses. The designer of light may be challenging us to see. Also, because we live in a state of constant bombardment from visual data, organized design in all its forms must take on new intensities in order to compete. The urban neon nightscape has contributed to accommodating the eye to boldness and to the flashing and blinking of lights. Transparent plastics and reflective metals encourage designers to experiment.

Light appeals because of its mystery and magic. We can neither touch, hold, nor feel it. As the symbol for gods, saints, angels, or rulers regarded as divine, it has always been valued by the architect in his temple structures. The stained-glass rose windows of the Gothic cathedrals, the pulsating glass mosaics of Byzantine Ravenna, and the crenellated windows of Le Corbusier's chapel at Ronchamp, France, illustrate the power of light to transmit the essence of divinity.

Among the many painters who have been fascinated with the mystique of light are Caravaggio, Turner, Constable, Rembrandt, and El Greco. Monet and Seurat gave scientific representation of light through color by leaving unpainted areas of white canvas between colors to compound light through reflectance. Van Gogh's canvases are flooded with intense light by his use of heavy dabs of color which reflect glowingly like mirrors. Picasso's paintings frequently contain mirrors that reflect light, and his many-faceted cubistic paintings emphasize refracted prismatic light.

Definition of Light

The visual is the most highly valued of all the senses for cueing us to our environment. Eighty per cent of all our sensations have been estimated as visual ones.

Light is radiant energy coming to us in various wave lengths which act upon the organs of vision, enabling

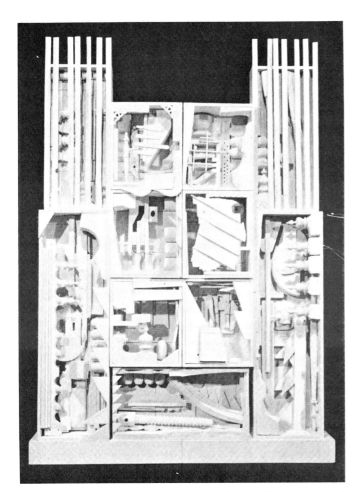

4-30 *Louise Nevelson.* Dawn's Wedding Chapel II, *1959, painted wood. Light and shadow highlight this relief sculpture. Courtesy, Whitney Museum of American Art, New York.*

4-31 *Nicholas Vergette. Ceramic garden sculpture (enlarged detail from Figure 12–16). The interplay between surfaces and their depressions relative to incident light creates shadows that help to differentiate form. The boldness of the forms suggest power and thrust. Courtesy Nicolas Vergette.*

them to perform their function of sight. Our retinas, however, are limited in their ability to receive all the light there is in the atmosphere. X rays and infrared, ultraviolet, gamma, and cosmic rays are beyond visual perception; only the rays that fall within the prismatic range are visible.

Light makes the world around us intelligible in many ways. The interplay between the surfaces and their depressions or contours relative to incident light creates shadows, which help to differentiate form. Moreover, all materials are modulators of light. Each has a certain light reflectance depending upon its molecular structure. Wood reflects differently from glass; velvet absorbs more light rays than does satin. This quality we call *texture*. Finally, the difference in various pigments' ability to absorb some light rays and reflect others—that is, *color*—also increases our awareness of form.

4-32 *László Moholy-Nagy.* Light Space Modulator, *1923-30, height 59½", 27½" x 27½". Courtesy of the Busch-Reisinger Museum, Harvard University.*

Functions of Light

Light is both functional and aesthetic. A few illustrations will point up its role with respect to the human body. Life is dependent upon light; for instance, children with rickets are helped by treatment with ultraviolet rays. On the other hand, too much ultraviolet may cause skin cancer. Atomic radiation is most effectively reflected by light colors. Burns were patterned on the bodies of the victims at Hiroshima according to light and dark areas in the fabrics they had worn. Blue-dye solutions applied to wounds accelerate healing because of their greater absorption of red and infrared light.

To illustrate the significance of light and color upon organic development, a simple test was conducted. Three green tomatoes of identical characteristics were placed in cloth wrappings—one in white, another in red, the third in black. These were placed without benefit of a glass cover to ripen in the sun. When the tomatoes on the vine had ripened, the cloths of the experimental tomatoes were removed. The one enclosed in white had ripened like any other vine-ripened tomato. The one in red was ripe, but had traces of black filament around the seeds. The tomato in the black cloth, completely depressed, had withered and decayed. It would seem that white light promotes healthy development, red rays are stimulating and fermentative, and blackness is deadly.

Artistic Use of Light

A recent designer who found light of significance to design was László Moholy-Nagy. Early in the 1920s he envisaged that light would become a new visual art. His experimentation with it was extensive. He studied the relation of light to sculpture, display, photography, cinema art, and architecture. Through his use of plastic and glass in sculpture he promoted interest in their potential. His revolving metal and glass sculpture, *Lichtrequisit,* of 1922–30 is considered not only one of the first light sculptures but also among the first kinetic works. One hundred colored bulbs, attached to a revolving motor in its base, threw a kaleidoscope of changing patterns of light on nearby surfaces.

Frank Lloyd Wright believed light to be one of the most significant elements in imparting the magical touch of beauty. In his interiors, continuous movement and shifting of aesthetic patterns were brought about from morning to dusk through the interplay of light and shadow. Windows and skylights were so placed that sunlight would shine in each room at some time during the day to cast provocative shadows. Sunlight was supplemented by artificial light, which was incorporated into the structure. Fixtures were recessed with no wires showing so that light seemed to emanate naturally from out of doors. In today's housing, the use of spot, cove, cornice, terrace, recessed ceiling, and sky lights reflects a greater awareness of light as an integral element of design.

Gyorgy Kepes, researcher into light as an art medium, believes in the creative application of light to clarify architecture and illuminate the night cityscape. He would use light on a huge scale, professing

The isolated, sheltered, small space of a room in the home or in a museum is suffocatingly narrow for the fluid power of light in action. The new, rich intensities of artificial light sources, if used creatively, must be woven into the bigger fabric of the night cityscape. The mirroring of the shop windows, the interpenetration of mobile vistas, with their continuous transformations of space and form, must be accepted as background to creative figures shaped by the moving contours of actual lights.[3]

[3]Gyorgy Kepes, "Light and Design," *Design Quarterly* **28.**

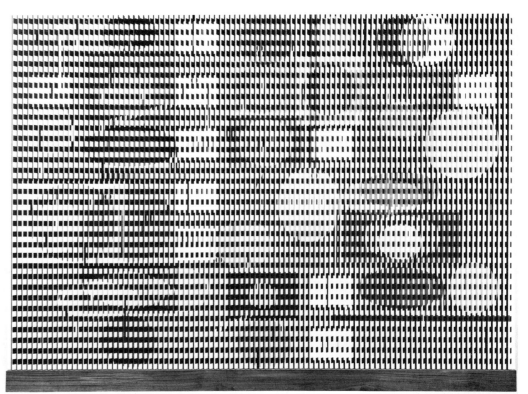

4-33   *Agam (Yaacov Gipstein).* Double Metamorphosis II, *1964, oil on aluminum in 11 sections, 8'10" x 13'2¼". As the viewer moves, the design configurations change. These views represent only two of multiple possibilities. Collection, The Museum of Modern Art, New York. Gift of Mr. and Mrs. George M. Jaffin.*

Commissioned to design a light mural for the New York office of KLM (Royal Dutch Airlines), he devised a complex program of fluorescent, incandescent, and spot lights to flicker through random color-filtered perforations. The ever-changing fluid configurations suggest night flights over cities. He intended that the mural become "part of the larger space of the street outside,

4-34   *Agam (Yaacov Gipstein).* Double Metamorphosis II, *1964, (view from the left), oil on aluminum, 8'10"x 13'2¼". Collection, The Museum of Modern Art, New York.*

4-35 *John Healy, English.* Box 3, *1967, 24″ x 38″. Sculpture in light. "When I first saw Healy's grandly classic* Box 3, *I knew of course that an intricately boxed-in mechanism of light and lenses, pattern discs, and color wheels was projecting a series of forms—in dead silence—onto a translucent screen, yet my involvement with the image was total, and as I became more and more absorbed in the changing geometry of the form, moving so slowly that my perception was virtually a subliminal one, I knew I was looking at a piece of sculpture, of sculpture made entirely of light." R. H. W.*

"It is difficult to adapt our thoughts to the conception that there might be, that indeed there are, different kinds of art, of space, of time. Yet only through enlarging our categories of thought can we adjust ourselves to those new forms of experience that scientific discovery is bringing to our door." Pierre Elliott, optical physicist and friend of John Healy. Photo Courtesy Woddell Gallery, New York.

sometimes blending and sometimes competing with the rivers of light generated by moving automobiles, giving and taking light from the surroundings, both invading the outside space and being invaded by it."[4]

[4] Ibid.

Contemporary artists' interest in movement has led to the development of vibratory effects through optical illusion. Their interest has been further satisfied with the creation of constructions that appear to move along with the viewer. Light has been added to multiply the visual images through reflection and shadow. By the latter 1960s several artists were producing "plugged-in" paintings. These generally consisted of fairly shallow boxes, opaque on all sides but the front. Abstractions created by such devices as reflectors, filters, motorized sculptures, phototransparencies, or programmed lighting were projected from behind against a screen of glass or fabric. Still other painters were using light bulbs in combination with canvas.

Many sculptors utilized the principles of Moholy-Nagy's *Lichtrequisit* in their constructions. They used light not only for its own effect but for its modulation of other materials or for the reflections it casts. A band of young Russian artists, the Dvizdjenje group, used electric light in conjunction with sound and odor in metal and plastic sculptures. Other sculptors used light and the electric equipment necessary to transmit it as their only medium.

Light was being used for environments and performances. Jack Lenor Larsen professed we are still in the dark ages with respect to the use of light. He advocated "painting a room with light," and through skillful devices he could bathe his own living room with lights ranging from blues and lavenders to magentas and golds, to create many moods. Also interested in mood was the Italian designer Lucio Fontana, who used extensive expanses of neon tubing to suggest the bold and mysterious. Choreographers and other artists have experimented with slide designs projected from different machines upon people in an environment, to produce novel and arresting images. Use of these techniques has unlimited possibilities for the expansion of moods in home environments too. Strobe-lighted floors have been predicted for living or family rooms. The use of mirrors, prisms, neon light sculptures, multiple projection of light and pattern, and time-lag sounds can create the illusion of unlimited space and provide us with multiple sensory experiences. By getting art off the wall, we become the performers in environments designed to stimulate us psychologically. Increasingly today man can live his own science fiction.

Color

Light is reflected from surfaces, and color is dependent upon the composition of the materials that are accessible to the light rays. When light comes into contact with a surface that reflects all the wavelengths equally we call our visual experience *white*. When the surface reflects none of the wavelengths but absorbs them all, we say it is *black*. A surface that does not absorb the green rays of white light but absorbs all the others is *green*. Color, then, is the name given to the reflections of wavelengths from surfaces. Because the composition of a surface material determines whether it will absorb or reflect the light rays, the manufacturer who is making a red object must put into its composition materials that will absorb all hues except red.

Mixtures of colored light produce effects that are different from mixtures of pigments, which are insoluble substances. Mixing colors in light produces more light; mixing pigments subtracts light. The stage designer manipulating both color and light will have different experiences from an artist who is mixing paints. The ceramist needs a knowledge of chemistry if he is to control the color of an object in the firing process, as does the artist who utilizes dyes in his fabric design that depend upon oxidation for the development of their hues.

Theories of color have been developed according to use. The physicist deals with colors in light; the psychologist with the sensations, moods, and emotions that color of an object in the firing process, as does the artist body systems; and the designer with many of these effects but also with the chemistry of pigments, glazes, and dyes.

The Prang System

The physicist found that mixtures of red, green, and violet light could form yellow, blue, and purple—so he considered the first three as *primaries*. The artist working with pigment instead of light found he could produce the colors orange, green, and violet by combinations of red, yellow, and blue paint. So the latter became *his* primaries, with orange, violet, and green constituting the *binary* or secondary hues. *Tertiary* or intermediary hues result from mixing a primary with a secondary, such as yellow with green to produce yellow-green.

The Three Dimensions of Color

The three dimensions of color—hue, value, and intensity—are useful in communicating about color.

Hue is the name given to primary, binary, or tertiary colors, such as red, violet, or red-violet. It indicates a color's position in the spectrum and on the color wheel, a circular device to show colors in relation to each other.

Value describes the lightness or darkness of a color. Values range from *tints*—which are very light or high in value—to *shades*—which are medium-dark or extremely dark and medium to low in value. For instance, pink, a light red, is high in value. Red is medium in value; maroon, a dark red, is low. A color can have its value lightened by adding water to a transparent water pigment or by adding white pigment to opaque paints. A deeper color or lower value is obtained by adding a darker pigment.

Intensity, or *chroma*, describes the brightness or dullness of a color. It indicates the degree to which it has been neutralized or grayed. Intensities range from maximum clarity of color, as in those colors on the outer periphery of the color wheel, to colors approaching gray, those near the center. Red is full or high in intensity; maroon is diminished or low. Pink is high both in value and in intensity for its level of value, because it is light and has not been grayed; what is commonly known as a dusty pink is lower in intensity.

Maroon is low both in intensity and in value, because it is both grayed and dark.

An efficient way to lower the intensity of a color is to add some of its complement (the color opposite to it on the color wheel). Hence, adding blue to orange produces rust, a neutralized orange. One can also gray colors by adding gray or black, but some color distortion may result with the use of black—for instance, yellow becomes muted green instead of being merely grayed. Carefully mixed proportions of any two complements on the wheel will produce a neutral gray. With opaque colors a small quantity of white may need to be added to produce the desired value.

Color Schemes

For appreciation and understanding of color a knowledge of the wheel and of the conventional color schemes is helpful. However, all colors can be combined harmoniously and effectively with proper manipulation of value and intensity. Persons who use color frequently often develop a sensitivity to its use and produce harmonious relationships quite unconsciously. Moreover, in most paintings and room designs no one color scheme is strictly adhered to. Complementary color arrangements may be used but analogous movements on either side of the complement are more frequently employed.

The related or close color schemes are monochromatic and analogous.

A *monochromatic* harmony consists of using one color in varying values and intensities, such as light blue, royal blue, and navy blue. Even though it employs only one color, such a scheme need not be monotonous if a range in value and intensity is provided. In addition, one can always add the neutrals—white, gray, or black—to create nuances of dramatic impact. Sparkling color schemes can be achieved through strong contrasts in values.

An *analogous* color scheme consists of colors immediately adjacent to each other on the color wheel, such as yellow, yellow-orange, and orange.

Because both these color schemes fall within a narrow spectrum on the wheel, they are unified in effect. The beginning designer usually encounters fewer problems in handling them than he does with the contrasting ones.

The contrasting color schemes are the complementary, double complementary, the split complementary, the triad, and the tetrad.

Complementary colors are those directly opposite each other on the color wheel, such as orange and blue.

Double-complementary color schemes contain two sets of complements, such as orange and red-orange, blue and blue-green.

A *split complementary* is a combination of one basic hue and the colors on either side of its complement, such as orange, blue-green, and blue-violet.

A *triad* consists of three colors equidistant from each other on the wheel, hence any colors that form an equilateral triangle. Both the primary and the binary colors qualify as triadic schemes.

A *tetrad* is formed by any four hues equidistant on the wheel, such as yellow-orange, yellow-green, red-violet, and blue-violet.

Because the colors in the contrasting schemes are more distant from each other, the task of combining them effectively is more complex but it can provide a visual excitement unlike that produced by the related colors.

In addition to the conventional harmonies, one may wish to design with an *accented neutral* scheme. Although white, gray, and black are the true neutrals, beige (made up of orange, low in intensity, which actually is a brown, raised in value by the addition of white) sometimes functions in this capacity. Many interior designers prefer the neutrality of off-white interiors so they can be free to use accents of intense color. Neutrals combined with a splash of vibrant color can make a strong dramatic statement.

The Munsell System

Further appreciation and refinement in the use of color can come through study of the Munsell system. To many it seems more sophisticated than the Prang, not only because it is more scientific but because combinations of its primary and intermediary colors seem more distinctive.

In 1912, in order to devise a systematic numerical color system, Albert Munsell established five principal hues: red, yellow, green, blue, and purple. Combinations of these yielded these intermediate hues: yellow-red, green-yellow, blue-green, purple-blue, and red-purple. Numerals were used to indicate hues and gradations between hues. In order to function within a decimal system of tenths, each principal and intermediate hue was assigned the numeral 5. Thus blue became 5B; blue-green, 5BG. Ten steps were assigned between blue-green and blue to indicate the comparative amount of blueness or greenness. Values in the Munsell plan were also assigned numbers. A gradual change from dark to light can be seen on the central pole of the Munsell Hue Value Chroma Chart.

Given this structure, Munsell could define a color with precision, starting first hue, then value and intensity. For instance, the symbols 5R/5/10 indicate a red with 5R, symbol of the hue. The red is of middle value (5: in scale value on the vertical pole). It is intense (very bright): 10 is a far extension on the chroma horizontal. Further refinement may be made by indicating steps in tenths not only between gradations of hues but between their values and intensities.

These data illustrate the fact that color can be defined with some precision. Although reliance upon analyses of color may depress a person's urge toward creativity, reference to a color system can suggest new and exciting color combinations and so extend one's color repertoire.

The successful use of color will depend upon an individual's development of sensitivity to subtle variations in hue, value, and intensity or chroma. This sensitivity is achieved not only through study but through extensive visual experiences and through repeated experimentation with color.

Designing with Color

All the design principles (which will be dealt with at length in Chapter 5) may be applied to composing with color. As far as proportions of color used are concerned, it is usually more visually satisfying to have one color predominant rather than proportions of color that are equal in their power to attract. This is closely related to the principle of emphasis.

If one wants to balance colors, a smaller amount of a light color will balance a quantity of dark color. Light rooms seem larger than dark rooms. Clothing that is light makes the person wearing it seem larger than clothing that is dark. A small amount of an intense color will balance a larger area of neutralized color.

A balance of hues may be established between warm and cool colors. The eyes function naturally to maintain balance of color. Prolonged looking at one color tends to induce its complement as an after-image. To provide this balance, the artist often includes a thrust of red in a painting that is predominantly blue and green. The designer may add a bowl of orange bittersweet, a splash of orange in a painting, or a terra-cotta ceramic to a blue room. Color is also balanced in a design either by placing it toward the center of the design or by repeating it in various areas.

Rhythm in color is achieved through gradation and repetition of hue, value, and intensity. In gradation of hue, the progression is gradually from one hue to another, as in an analogous color scheme. Gradation of value involves progression from a selected value to one that gradually becomes lighter or darker than the original. In gradation of intensity there is progression from a given intensity level to either higher or lower levels.

Emphasis of color is gained in all the ways of making one element dominant over the other. These include repeating the color; providing a foil by contrasting the color with its complement; providing sufficient background space around it; combining a color high in intensity with other colors that are low; placing it toward the center of a design; and using the color in an object of unusual and conspicuous design in order to arrest attention.

Many contemporary artists and designers prefer the visual excitement produced by abutting complements against each other. For those who would control this sensation, the following means are suggested:

In working with pigments one can bring blue into closer unity with its complement, orange, by neutralizing. To neutralize one may

1. combine some orange with the blue.
2. combine some blue with the orange.
3. combine some orange with the blue and some blue with the orange (equivalent to adding gray to each color).
4. combine a small quantity of any other hue with both the blue and the orange.

Surface treatments can also provide closer unity. One may

1. glaze, that is, paint a wash over the surface.
2. spatter, sponge, or streak colors over the complements.
3. place a transparent colored sheet of paper over them. The parallel in fabric treatment is using a sheer material over fabrics of strong contrasts.

Other means include placing a neutral color between the orange and blue. The use of coarser as opposed to smooth textures tends to subdue colors, because shadows are formed by the grain, as in velveteens and tweeds.

Effects of Color

Knowledge of the effect of colors upon each other is useful to artists and designers. They can use color to expand space, to increase or decrease the illusion of light, and to influence human reactions. Here are some of these effects.

Complements placed next to each other in appreciable quantities intensify each other. In narrow bands these neutralize to gray.

Prolonged looking at a color tends to induce its complement as an afterimage. Employing neutrals or increasing the spatial interval between intense colors lessens their intensity. An intense color combined with the same color of lower intensity seems more intense and the latter seems more grayed. This is particularly evident with blues. A light-grayed blue fabric becomes drab and almost indistinguishable from gray when placed next to an intense blue.

Colors higher in value than the background upon which they are placed seem lighter in value. Conversely, colors lower in value than the background upon which they are placed seem darker.

Light colors tend to increase apparent size because they reflect light. Conversely, dark colors reduce size because of light absorption.

Warm colors seem to advance, cool colors to recede.

Intense colors seem to advance, neutralized hues to recede.

Colors placed in close proximity to each other and mixed by the viewer's retina are more luminous than those mixed on a palette. Yellow and blue splotches of color applied to a canvas create a more vibrant green than a green taken directly from the tube. This effect was exploited by the French impressionists and pointillists to achieve the effect of brilliant sunlight on canvas.

A light, a bright (intense), and a dark color used in combination can make a sparkling, effective color scheme.

Not only are illusions created when colors are used

together in certain combinations, but during the last half century extensive research has been conducted to determine the effect of color upon the human mind and body. Faber Birren has made extensive contributions in this area and his research findings have been put to practical use by color consultants, psychologists, and the medical profession. Industrial psychologists have studied the relation of color to machinery and to factory interiors in order to increase safety and to promote production. Light and color are used in schools to facilitate learning, and in hospitals to reduce tensions and to hasten recovery. Recognition of colors' ability to soothe or arouse is also useful to the designer. Some of these effects follow.

Warm intense colors, such as reds and red-oranges, tend to stimulate the human organism. Bodily states—blood pressure, pulse rate, and respiration—are accelerated. Feelings of restlessness and excitation may follow. Time seems to pass very slowly. Conversely, grayed, cool colors—dull blues and greens—are relaxing and retard bodily processes. If no contrasting relief in color is provided, they can be pacifying but depressive. Yellow and yellow-green tend to be neutral in effect.

Colors commonly associated with nature and growth, such as green, are restful because they produce no marked elevation or depression of spirit unless the individual has suffered negative experiences with them.

Light colors seem to be more cheerful and ethereal than dark colors which, though restful, can seem somber and heavy.

Colors close in value are restful whereas those that are at opposite ends of the value scale are dynamic and stimulating. Hence checkerboard designs in black and white, hound's-tooth checks, and light-on-dark polka dots are visually fatiguing.

Colors that are equally intense combined together as in psychedelia are visually exhausting.

Unrelieved large expanses of white strain our vision, because they constrict the pupils of the eye, and glare lowers visual acuity. For efficient seeing, bright light

should be localized to areas where tasks are being accomplished, with surrounding areas in hues of lowered value. This principle is adhered to in hospitals, where white is used for the operating table and the localized task center, but walls and floor are in subdued tones of gray, green, or blue-green, as are the gowns and skullcaps of the persons participating in an operation. The complement of a cool hue to that of human blood and tissue also aids the surgeon's vision. Glare and eyestrain would be present in an all-white environment.

A combination of colors, provided there are not too many, may be more space producing than the use of

4-36 *Gene McDonald.* Tapet, *a contemporary woven fabric, which is comparatively quiet in effect compared to the David Hicks's design because of the designer's rhythmic gradation of values. Gene McDonald Inc., New York.*

4-37 *David Hicks.* Navajo. *Strong contrasts in color from white to black with no intermediaries can produce a staccatolike effect and appear dynamic.* Connaissance Fabrics, Inc.

a single color. One sometimes feels hemmed in by a single hue when no contrasting relief is provided.

Combinations of colors of the same values and intensities tend to be visually trying. Also exhausting is the use of equal proportions of colors that have the same power to attract. Visual satisfaction comes from sensitive handling of a balance between the intense and neutral and between the light and dark.

Color Symbolism

All societies have developed color associations and symbolism, which may acquire a certain sanctification through tradition. These differ depending upon political, religious, or racial origins. In addition each person has color biases as a result of his personal experiences. Some symbolism is held in common. For instance, in our society emotional moods are commonly associated with various colors, often more as colloquial expressions than as scientific fact. Anger is seeing red, depression is feeling blue, envy is green, rage is purple, hope is white, cowardice is yellow, feeling good is being in the pink, being deep in thought is being in a brown study, and despair is black.

Color symbolism may also be dual or ambivalent. Yellow, though associated with Judas's robes and with aging in Christian cultures, is indicative in Oriental and Central American cultures of the sun God, and power. The Russians' esteem for red as a color is reflected in their using the same word *krasnyi* both for "beautiful" and for "red." In the Orient, red is a happy color, symbolic of life and joy, and formerly the color worn by brides. On the other hand, to many Americans red is disturbing and ostentatious, and associated with the illicit. Blue in the orient is a color that can be associated with pestilence and disease: on the other hand, it is also the color worn by students, for, like the constantly changing hues of the heavens, students have the potential for limitless change. In the United States, blue is also associated with honesty and dependability, as when we say a person is "true blue." Whereas black is our color of mourning, white is for the Chinese.

Color symbolism can also apply to sound and movement. Recognition of movement as having color associations is evident in nursery schools, where children are told to dance yellow or red, thus calling into play their powers of interpretation and association. Musicians, too, have responded to sound as color. Beethoven is reported to have considered B minor the black key, while Schubert compared the key of E minor "unto a maiden robed in white with a rose-red bow on her heart." Sunlight to him was like C major, whereas all cold colors were minor keys. For Debussy, music was an attempt "to catch these violet rays of emotion." That artists use color as symbolic is particularly evident with the abstract expressionists, who use color as the visual language for expression of the emotions.

Color associations are particularly pronounced with respect to food. Part of the art of food preparation lies in preserving and enhancing the colors of food acceptable to man. Gray meat or strawberries, green cottage cheese, and bleached vegetables may perhaps be tasteful and nutritious, but they are unappetizing. When the color of food is not what is expected, not only is the appetite affected but intense feelings of sickness have been scientifically recorded.

Texture

We like the old and the new, the slick and the worn, though our two boys see to it that the slick soon becomes the worn.
Industrial designer Don Wallance

Texture is both a tactile and a visual quality. It is experienced when a person brushes his fingers over the surface of an object, which may seem rough or smooth, soft or hard. Texture as a visual quality results from light

4-38 Hair and Egg. *Contrasts in textures act as foils to each other, dramatizing the unique qualities of each. Photograph by Vincent Bernucci.*

4-39 *A Ballatore design, Baobab, a Moroccan crazy-quilt pattern as broken up as a map of Africa itself, from the Africa 2 Collection. Velvet: 54% rayon, 32% cotton, 14% mohair; 48" wide, repeat 36". The design was inspired by the Moorish tradition of Morocco where Larsen found pattern everywhere: "Pattern on pattern. Tiled floors scatter it; polychromed ceilings reflect it; Moroccan rugs blaze with it. No important surface is untreated, and yet this overall pattern gives unity to the whole." Jack Lenor Larsen Inc.*

being reflected or absorbed by the surface of objects. Velvet and tweeds absorb much light; satins and wet plastics reflect it. Thus texture may be sensed both manually and optically.

The organic and inorganic substances that compose our earth have particular textural qualities, which result from their structural composition. The units of composition of these elements and their organization produce varying surface tensions to which we respond. The small child spends many hours during infancy learning the feel of his environment and binding it to himself visually. Few can recall when the associative bond was formed between touch and sight, which no longer makes it necessary to touch an object in order to know

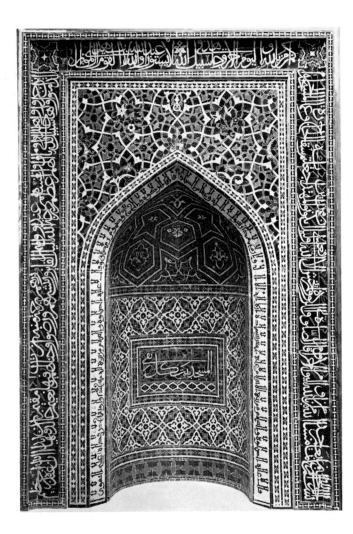

4-40 *Iranian Mihrab (prayer niche), faïence mosaic of glazed earthenware set in plaster, 1334. Here is a rich diversity of tracery, including Iranian script as a decorative element. Collection, The Metropolitan Museum of Art, New York.*

4-41 *Rock with lichen. Contrasts of light and dark in the formations of lichen create fascinating diversity on the rock's surface. Photograph by Helen M. Evans.*

MUNSELL HUE VALUE/CHROMA CHART

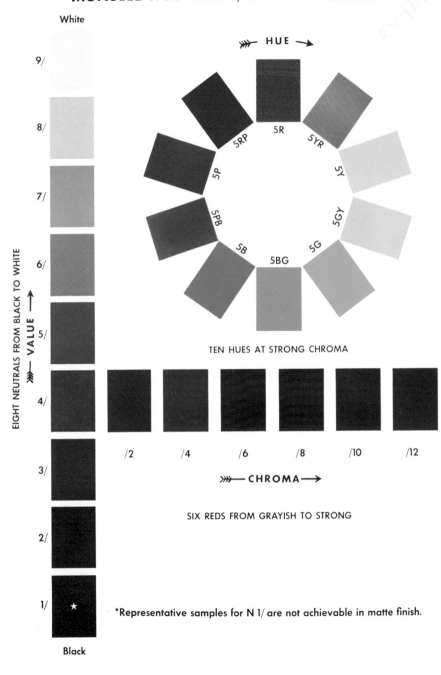

White

9/

8/

7/

6/

5/

4/

3/

2/

1/ ★

Black

EIGHT NEUTRALS FROM BLACK TO WHITE → VALUE →

HUE →

5RP 5R 5YR

5P 5Y

5PB 5GY

5B 5G

5BG

TEN HUES AT STRONG CHROMA

/2 /4 /6 /8 /10 /12

≫—CHROMA→

SIX REDS FROM GRAYISH TO STRONG

*Representative samples for N 1/ are not achievable in matte finish.

Munsell Hue Value/Chroma Chart. Ten Hues at Strong Chroma. Eight neutrals from black to white on the vertical pole. Red is shown at value 4 and extends from 2, low in chroma or intensity, to 12, very bright and high in intensity. Courtesy, Munsell Color Company, Inc.

Prang Color Chart. Painted by student Janet Gervin Martin. A conventional color wheel based on the three primaries, red, yellow, and blue. Mixing red and yellow makes orange; blue and yellow, green; and red and blue, violet—these latter are the *binary* colors. Combining the hues adjacent to each other yields *intermediary* hues. Adding white (or water to transparent paints) lightens the *values*. Combining colors opposite each other on the wheel (complementaries) *neutralizes* or grays them as can be seen toward the center of the wheel. Photograph by Vincent Bernucci.

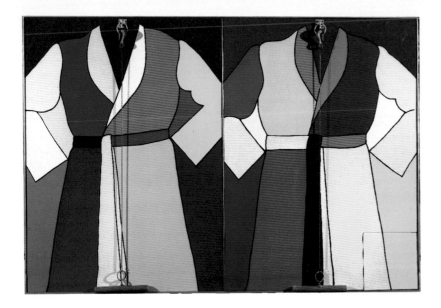

Jim Dine, *Double Isometric Self Portrait* (*Serape*). 1964. Oil with objects on canvas. Outlines help define the robes illustrated. Changes in color, whether subtle or strong, provide contrast of form. Collection, Whitney Museum of American Art, New York. Gift of Helen W. Benjamin in memory of her husband, Robert M. Benjamin.

Ellsworth Kelly. *Green, Blue, Red,* 1964. Oil on canvas. The complementary colors, green and red intensify each other and the green shape begins to vibrate around the edges. Collection, Whitney Museum of American Art, New York. Gift of the Friends of the Whitney Museum of American Art.

Roland Dorcely. *When to Relax?* Tempera on panel. Strong black outlines and expressive color are used to show a static chair and a female human figure in motion. Collection, Museum of Modern Art, New York.

4-42 *Jackson Pollock.* Number One, *1948. Oil on canvas. 68" x 8'8". Although seen here in black and white, this shows the action and movement of Jackson Pollock's painting. The subtle lines crisscross throughout the painting, not only projecting varying values of color from white to black, but also showing how an abstract series of lines and blocks can be well designed. Collection, The Museum of Modern Art, New York.*

how it feels. Our vision now cues us to such an extent that we seldom take time for the pleasure of feeling through touch.

Surfaces are constantly being modified by interaction with the atmosphere and through elements in contact with each other. Air carries gases, and water carries minerals, both of which modify the surface aspect of objects. When iron becomes pitted and rusty, its tactile as well as its visual textures are modified. Antique Oriental bronzes have become greatly enhanced through oxidation processes and mineral deposits, which have made the surfaces so varied in color as to create differing illusions of textural depth. The forces of nature are unrelenting and can soon reduce the gleaming textures of man-made objects to harmonize with their own more natural textures and colors. We must be constantly vigilant in polishing and protecting our man-made materials or they may corrode, develop a patina, or revert to a more natural state. One culture that values this attrition by nature's elements is that of

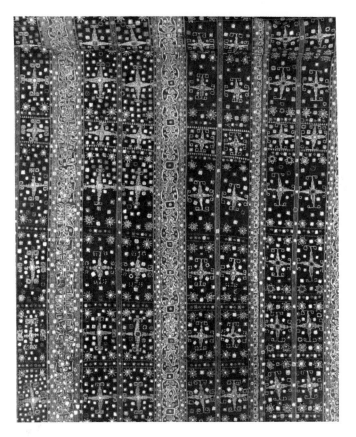

4-43 Indonesian sarong of cotton, silk, and glass, embroidered with mirrors, 19th century. Courtesy of the Cooper-Hewitt Museum of Decorative Arts and Design, Smithsonian Institution.

4-44 Philippine blouse of piña cloth woven from pineapple fiber during the first half of the 19th century. The transparency of the cloth and the delicate lacy lines contribute to the lightness of texture. The Metropolitan Museum of Art, New York.

Japan. The Japanese appreciate objects more as their surfaces become altered with the passing of time. Rocks are considered more beautiful as they collect lichen, and copper more fascinating as it develops a bluish patina. Newly manufactured articles are looked down on as brash and unaesthetic. Only after what is termed the *wabi* and *sabi* of time, do surfaces develop a muted subtlety of texture and so achieve a beauty that is considered worthy of contemplation and reverence.

Textural effects can also be simulated or contrived. The textural quality of fabrics is modified by printing various patterns such as floral or geometric designs on them, or dyeing them by such processes as batik and tie and dye. An artist may deliberately affect the surface tension of an object by crosshatching, jabbing, puncturing, twisting, or pasting things on it (the process called collage). Jackson Pollock threw sand and paint on plywood to produce textural compositions. All these devices the artist uses in an attempt to modify the surface that confronts him, to evoke a more highly charged sensation than the surface formerly provided. Man seems to have a need for sensual stimulation whether it be kinesthetic, auditory, visual, tactile, or olfactory. The artists' environments and "happenings" so typical of the 1960s appealed to many people precisely because they stimulated several senses simultaneously.

Textures have many nuances for the designer. The weaver and embroiderer are particularly engaged with texture, varying it to be gauzy, smooth, lacy, nubby, or open and closed. Illusion is also created through texture. Transparent objects seem lighter to us than opaque ones. Objects of varying densities produce differing textural sensations. A crystal glass has a different textural quality from that of a heavy glass mug, though both may be equally smooth to the touch. Dark, warm colors seem heavier than light cool colors. Glossy textures create different impressions of weight than matte ones. Large objects seem heavier in texture than small, delicate ones. These variations are of great importance to the designer who wishes to combine textures that are compatible, yet varied and stimulating.

Twentieth-Century Art

It is in the kinetic sense that the painter has moved farthest from these traditional ways of rendering space. Cubism, a movement begun in 1908 to convey artistic ideas through abstract geometric forms, is credited with the first rendition of objects as if they were being rotated, allowing one to see their many-sidedness simultaneously in an attempt to show "true reality." With the advent of Futurism, which started in Italy in 1909, artists began to suggest dynamic and simultaneous movement by superimposing an identical object in a sequence of linear poses, as in Marcel Duchamp's *Nude Descending a Staircase* (Figure 4-26). In photography, shifting of the image and multiple exposures can create a similar kinetic sensation, motion.

Since the time of Wassily Kandinsky, artists of abstract expressionism have been using the elements of line, form, color, texture, and light to create a backward and forward animation in the picture plane. Through them they suggest the spatial depths of the universe in its varying tensions. Depth is created by the inherent properties of the elements themselves, which have the potential to be fused with action. Colors, reflected light rays of varying lengths, produce depth as red, the longest, advances and blue, which is shorter, recedes. Lateral movement is also produced by differences in the colors' projective power. Equal cubic amounts of white, yellow, green, blue, and black, placed in horizontal alignment create a sideways visual motion because they are recorded visually in a descending quantity with white appearing largest and black smallest. White, seemingly largest, will move in front of the black, creating an experience in depth. Thus colors can pull, relax, or recede in order to portray tensions. This phenomenon illustrates the forces that are operative in color alone. If the dynamics of other elements are added, such as differences in line direction, forms suspended in interlocutory positions, textural variations, and light modifications, a canvas can pulsate with overwhelming vibrancy.

As a result of these recognized forces many paintings today reflect an attitude of reciprocity instead of concentration upon a single focus. Although a composition may have a gravitational point of interest toward which the rhythms flow, usually there is no bull's-eye target of concentration. Philosophically, man can take the entire world for his canvas, no one part commanding his attention more than another. As in architecture, where the commanding central doorway has yielded to a flow of line and form that merges with the landscape, so too the movement on the canvas is both toward and from—a reciprocity in vision.

It was only a short step from creating the illusion of depth on a canvas to actually incorporating it. In the 1960s with the development of constructions and wall sculptures, the third dimension was added to painting by building up plastic forms. With the incorporation of mechanized moving elements, the fourth dimension of time and space was provided. Depth and motion no longer necessitated illusory means but became realities for us.

5 The Principles of Design

The principles of design govern relationships among the elements of design. Elements are visual components, and principles are underlying assumptions applied to visual interpretation. For designers and consumers alike, excellence in design depends on an understanding of these principles. The principles of design are developed and discussed in this chapter.

The principles of design involve organization of the elements for visual effectiveness. Through them the elements are brought into meaningful relationships. The successful designer makes decisions in terms of these principles. He may have to decide whether to use a light or a dark color, a bright or a dull one, and a large or small quantity of it; he will also have to decide where the color should be placed. He may have conscious thoughts and be guided by considerations of proportion, rhythm, and balance, or he may unconsciously work in terms of these. Whatever his mental processes, all effective designs show evidence of an ordering process which can be broken down into definable principles. This organizing process is designing. It applies as much to the conception of an article for daily use as it does to a painting.

The principles of design that will be used through the succeeding chapters are *proportion and scale, balance, rhythm, emphasis,* and *unity and variety*. These relate to our near environment. We are already familiar with them on a human scale and use them in our daily speech. We speak of a man's having a sense of proportion. He has perspective and sees things in their true relationships. He may be well balanced; he neither "goes off the deep end" nor is he "lopsided" in his views. In his conduct and bodily movements, he may be uncoordinated and jerky, or smooth and rhythmic. The stagger of a drunken person disturbs our psychological need for a sense of balance and for rhythm in movement. In addition, a person may create a dominant impression or emphasis, thus establishing a personal theme, which may be one of masculinity, feminity, sophistication, exoticism, or unpretentiousness. He may live in unity with society—that is he may "fit in"—or be at odds with it. He may be consistent, or inconsistent and unpredictable. At his best, he does not "rub people the wrong way" but lives in harmony with them. Yet, as a man of many facets, he selects his associates not only because of common interests and qualities but also for the interest and stimulation their differing attributes provide. Replicas of ourself are boring, just as complete visual harmony seems unchallenging and dull. Harmony exists within the bounds of stimulating tensions among men as well as in the design of objects. Man has need for unity with variety in both his human and his material worlds.

Proportion and Scale

Proportion is basically a mathematical concept, and much training in vision is required before the eye eventually becomes the "sovereign judge." In design, proportion is the principle that involves ratios, the quantitative comparisons of parts of a design to each other and to the whole. Instances in which these ratios apply are to sizes (length to width to height); to amounts of color used (the amount of red, for instance, in a design in relation to the amount of white); to spaces (the quantity of open spaces in relation to closed ones, and the intervals between these); to forms (the size of small forms in relation to larger, or the number of round forms as compared to square); and to texture (the amount of smooth surface as compared to rough).

5-1 *Photogram of a butterfly. Note the subtle proportions and diversities, each spatial interval differing in size but unified with the whole through repetition of similar forms. Photograph by Helen M. Evans.*

With man, the eye is small in relation to the head. Man's head is usually about one seventh the height of his total body. Note the design relationship of the distance from the tip of your forefinger to the first joint, from the first joint to the second, and the spacing from there to the third. These subtle relationships in proportion exist throughout the world of nature.

In an object such as a chair there is the proportion of the leg to the back of the chair, to the seat, and to

5-2 *Stefan Siwinski. Plastic pedestal chair. This chair is a statement in simplicity and has proportions in pleasing relationship to each other and to the whole. Stefan Siwinski.*

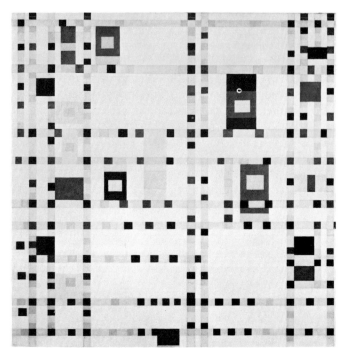

the arm. There is the proportion of the height of the leg to the height of the chair. In adding the human factor, consideration is given to the proportion of the distance from the floor to the chair's seat, as related to the distance between the ball of our foot and the knee. The most satisfactory designs for chairs and other furnishings are those in which our anatomy and spatial needs have been taken into consideration when determining the proportions of the object's structural elements. Scandinavian designers are well-known for their extensive anatomical studies to serve as bases for the design of furnishings. The dimensions of their storage

5-3 *Peter Schlumbohm.* Coffee maker, *1941, pyrex glass, wood, height 9". The functional ware captures the essential fluidity of glass, which contrasts with the textural qualities of wood and leather. The spout looks adequate to prevent dripping. The proportion of the upper half to the lower has pleasing diversity. Collection, The Museum of Modern Art, New York.*

5-4 *Piet Mondrian.* Broadway Boogie-Woogie, *1942–43, oil on canvas, 50" x 50". A Mondrian is more visually challenging than a checkerboard design. Collection, The Museum of Modern Art, New York.*

units are also determined by the sizes of the objects to be contained.

Certain proportions have traditionally been considered more pleasing and psychologically challenging than others. Although it is difficult to differentiate learned responses from those that may stem from a greater faculty for appreciation, certain preferences have been held by those with marked artistic ability. We will note some of these in a moment, but in each case it should be kept in mind that successful designs have been made that violate them. Perhaps this is because, in a total environment, objects are not viewed in isolation but as elements that contribute to the over-all design.

These are some of the proportions preferred in the past that still have validity for some designers:

Uneven numbers seem more interesting than even ones. Three or five buttons on a blouse or coat are preferred to two or four. A two-to-three linear proportion is preferred to a one-to-one. A rectangle, longer than it is wide, contains more differences and therefore more interest than a square. Rooms that have differences in length and width measurements seem more satisfying than those with identical measurements.

In three-dimensional design, the five, seven, eleven proportion—as is approximated by the height, width, and length of the Parthenon—is preferred to the proportions of a cube. (In recent years, very extensive use has been made of the cube, but it is often seen in combinations that extend its linear dimension, or we can see through the cube because of its transparency.)

Diversity in spatial relations is selected over uniform regularity. Spatial variations in the intervals of stripes on fabrics are more interesting than equal spacing. A painting by Piet Mondrian remains visually rewarding for a longer period of time than a checkerboard design.

A checkerboard design contains regular spaces; a scale drawing is based on regular spaces and proportion to a larger design. Scale can also mean a graduated series of shapes. In Figure 4-17 one finds graduated squares, each one smaller than the next. Albers was a master of graduated squares.

Balance

Closely allied to proportion is the principle of balance. In fact, the two principles are so interrelated that it is sometimes difficult to evaluate a work without referring to both of them.

Balance may be defined as the quality that creates a sensation of equilibrium. It provides a reconciliation of opposing forces, which results in a feeling of stability

and the capacity to maintain a secure, upright posture despite gravitational pull.

Two forms of balance, *bisymmetrical* and *asymmetrical,* are easily recognized and may be taken directly from the physics of vision.

Equal weights on either side of a central fulcrum will balance each other. Our common childhood experience provides us with the example of the ubiquitous seesaw. Fifty pounds of girl will balance fifty pounds of boy on

5-5 *David Smith.* Head, *1938, cast iron and steel, height 19¾". Through careful consideration of proportion, the negative enclosed space also results in an appealing form. Collection, The Museum of Modern Art, New York.*

5-6 *Greek embroidery, 17th century, island of Cos, border fragment, with formal balance. Courtesy of the Cooper-Hewitt Museum of Decorative Arts and Design, Smithsonian Institution.*

its equilibrium. Such balance is bisymmetrical, bilateral, or formal.

Weights cannot always be matched so easily nor does one necessarily wish to match them. Twenty pounds of girl may want to seesaw with fifty pounds of boy. Through experience, children quickly learn the physical principle involved—one can balance weights by increasing the distance from the central fulcrum. The lighter girl moves farther from the middle to balance the greater weight of the boy. Thus she overcomes the limitation of smallness in a rather elegant fashion, and creates asymmetrical or informal balance.

Translated to a visual format, we find that the same principle holds true. Increase of spatial distance from a hypothetical center will make it possible to balance a smaller object with a larger, or one can shift the fulcrum toward the heavier object as in Figure 5-8. However, visual impacts are not necessarily the equivalents of avoirdupois weight. Our vision produces illusions of varying weights. Opaque objects seem heavier to us than transparent ones of identical volume. Intense dark values outweigh light ones, and warm colors make objects seem heavier than those that are dull and cool in hue. A unique object seems heavier than its size warrants. A clock designed as a ladybug can balance a conventional clock of greater volume. Objects placed above the horizon line of a design seem lighter than those of equal volume placed below, because those below seem to have succumbed to the pull of gravity.

We speak of the bisymmetrical balance of identical objects as being *formal*. This balance stems from the classical need for dignity, order, restraint, and uniformity. It is the balance that has been valued since Greco-Roman days, through the Italian Renaissance, the neoclassic period in eighteenth-century Europe, and in Federalist America at the turn of the nineteenth century. It is still cherished by those who enjoy classic qualities, who value our heritage and like to maintain continuity with the past. Some find security in employing formal balance; it has withstood the so-called test of time. Others may not find it so satisfying because in clearly

the opposite end, provided both are equidistant from the central fulcrum. In design and décor, the image holds. A picture may function symbolically as the fulcrum in the middle of a fireplace mantel. Candlesticks may be added equidistant from it on either side. One feels secure the mantel will not tip but will maintain

defining space, it tells all at a glance. One's imagination has less opportunity to wonder where the limits of space are or to enjoy the play of variations in the spatial intervals. It may seem static, confining, nonexperimental, and lacking in adventurousness.

Asymmetrical or *informal* balance consists of unequal weights and spaces on either side of a hypothetical center. In its variety it has more of the charm and intrigue of the occult than does formal balance. Being characteristic of nature, it is highly valued by the Japanese, who see man and nature as a composite unit, and so establish no rigid boundary between the two. Frank Lloyd Wright, who also had great respect for nature, integrated the linear quality of his shelters with the irregular contours of the surrounding landscape to increase the apparent flow of movement; the designs of his houses were asymmetrically balanced. Space, not obviously defined, seemed to flow in an extended manner. Thus, not knowing exact limits can create an illusion of extensive space.

Sometimes two or more objects that produce the same aggregate visual weight are used instead of identical objects to create balance. We can balance a large sofa on one side of a fireplace with two chairs and hassocks on the opposite side. Though not identical in contour, these may have the same visual weight. The resulting balance is termed *equivalent,* or *obvious.* It is closely allied to symmetrical balance, because it evokes a similar feeling in us.

Balance can also be conceived of as *static* or *kinetic.* Static balance is related to symmetrical, in that the tensions between forms seem consistent. A rectitude of structure is equally present in the solidity of Egyptian pyramids and temples, the exactitude of Grecian temples, the staid quality of Asian Buddhas, and the frontality of African sculpture and of Indian totems. Static balance is of the earth—solid, unchanging, and unyielding. It comforts through its support.

Kinetic balance is evident in the forms that spring from the earth—plants, trees, rivers, canyons, mountains, and volcanoes. They are directed by an internal force into directions of no predictable compass. Responsive to their environment, they are shaped and hollowed and directed by air, wind, water, and heat. They change as the earth changes or as the geographical conditions of their locales are modified. Photographs made of sprouting beans show the eruptive, kinetic quality of forms in motion, of internal necessity dictating outward expression. This kinetic quality can be experienced in the rhythms established by forms that are arranged to produce varied tensional relationships, or by objects in actual motion, such as mobiles and moving sculptures and architecture.

5-9 *Jean Arp.* Growth, *1938, bronze. This biomorphic structure, informally balanced, parallels much of nature's growth and form with thrust balanced by counterthrust. Collection of the Philadelphia Museum of Art.*

5-10 Walter Crane. *An English nursery wallpaper: "Oranges and lemons say the bells of St. Clement." Machine-printed about 1939 after a design of 1890 for Jeffrey and Co. of London. Obvious or equivalent balance is illustrated by the children who circle the tree being of equal visual weight but not identical in appearance. Courtesy of the Cooper-Hewitt Museum of Decorative Arts and Design, Smithsonian Institution.*

5-11 *Franz Marc.* Blue Horses, *1911, oil on canvas, 41″ x 71½″. The undulating curvilinear movements of the horses' manes and torsos move backward and forward in the picture plane. Collection, Walker Art Center, Minneapolis, Minnesota.*

Both bisymmetrical and asymmetrical balance are of value to the designer. The petals of a flower are symmetrical and radially balanced, the foliage and the stems may be symmetrically or asymmetrically balanced. The veins of the leaf are obviously balanced but often with infinite variety and unity. *Radial balance* is also seen in round objects. It is the repetition of the pattern from the center. This balance is also called radial rhythm and is discussed in the following section. Figures 5-16 and 6-20 are excellent examples of balance from the center: radial balance.

In designing, we can impart unity and dominance of an idea by expressing one central theme more emphatically than others. But the areas of variation in a statement serve as foils or reliefs and can be used to point out the central theme more dramatically. Nature is the master of projecting and illustrating differences under controlled central themes. Thus we have seen that balance may be bisymmetrical (formal) or asymmetrical (informal); equivalent (obvious); or static versus kinetic or radial.

Rhythm

To most people rhythm is probably the most sensuously appealing of the principles. It is particularly familiar to us in music and dance, but we also recognize rhythm in the restless lapping of the tide over time-washed rocks, the maddening drip of a leaky faucet, the flub of a flat tire on the road, and the regular passing

5-12 *Jack Lenor Larsen.* Ebb Tide, Baedeker Collection. *A luminous cloth of shimmering velvet by Larsen's new batik printing method, which illustrates rhythm through continuous line movement. Jack Lenor Larsen Inc.*

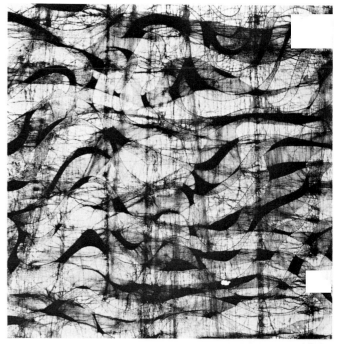

of the seasons. We may wish to hold back the spring and be reluctant for summer to come, but we know that nature is repetitive and that recurrence is inevitable.

Rhythm is regularity and recurrence, which lead to expectancy. As such, it implies an expected sequential movement of perception. In music, rhythm is indicated by a consistent number of beats to a measure. In design, it is the pattern established by lines, forms, textures, colors, light and dark patterns, and spatial intervals. Rhythm facilitates the movement of the eye from one part of the design to others and helps in maintaining a reciprocal flow of visual attention between areas. Because it provides progression or movement, it involves our kinesthetic sense as well as our visual; hence the strong effect that rhythm may have upon us.

A *continuous line movement* is rhythmical. The wash of a wave against the shore establishes a moving, continuous pattern of lyrical quality. The so-called streamlining characteristic of automobiles, planes, and household appliances has this quality. William Hogarth the great English painter and engraver, established what he called the "Line of Beauty"—the line produced by the

flow of movement from a woman's shoulders, down to the waist, and descending toward the buttocks. The Greeks also valued the elliptical line. The greater beauty of their work as compared to that of the Romans can be attributed in part to the rhythms they employed in designing moldings for their capitals. The curves of Greek moldings were freely drawn and elliptical, whereas the Romans used the compass to produce geometric curves of mechanical precision and correctness.

Another means of achieving rhythm is through *repetition*. Repetition may be of a motif or of any of the art elements. Fabrics in which a motif is repeated regularly have an expected pattern. Furniture that is consistently of greater horizontal length than vertical height establishes a rhythmic line movement. If one values the rhythm of color in interiors, a color can be selected from one room, utilized in an adjacent hallway, and subsequently used again in a connecting room.

Rhythm may also be secured by *radiation*. The petals of a flower emerging from a central corolla establish a radial rhythm. Cathedral or umbrella-type ceilings do

5-13 *This carved wooden vase, from the Kusai District of the Congo, Africa, has evident rhythm through repetition and flowing line. Courtesy of the American Museum of Natural History, New York.*

5-14 *Marcel Breuer. Reclining chair with frame of laminated wood and upholstery of foam rubber over plywood provides rhythm of line movement and contrast in light and dark patterns. Knoll International.*

5-15 *Electrical transmission tower, photographed from ground level looking skyward, presents radial rhythm or balance and an interesting interplay of spatial divisions. Photograph by Vincent Bernucci.*

5-16 *Robert H. Seyle.* Nail Relief #12, diameter 42". *Radial rhythm—nails of varying metals and elevations create subtleties in light reflection and shadow as well as textural nuance.* California Design X, Pasadena Art Museum, *from The Ankrum Gallery. Photograph by Richard Gross.*

5-17 *Leon C. Meyer, architect. The house is located in the San Francisco Bay area and contains 1,300 square feet of living space. Materials were cut and assembled at the site. Rooms are arranged like wedges of pie around a central core containing two bathrooms. Circulation is around the central core. "In an average three-bedroom house there's some 75 square feet of hall space. Our plan saves that wasted space." Windows are of tinted acrylic to reduce glare and heat loss. The walls are of tongue-in-groove redwood. Photograph by Morley Baer.*

likewise. In each case the rhythmic aspect is further intensified by the repetition of similar lines and forms. Because radial patterns are centrally balanced, reference is sometimes made to *radial balance*.

Lastly, rhythm is achieved through *gradation*. We may apply gradation to any element. Forms that slowly evolve from small to large are rhythmic. They establish in the viewer an expectation of moving toward a culmination. Colors that move in slow succession from light to dark, from intense to dull, or from hue to neighboring hue produce states of rhythmic tension.

Thus, we may create rhythm by a continuously fluid line movement and by repetition, radiation, and gradation.

Emphasis

Emphasis is dominance and accentuation, as opposed to subordination. The feature that is emphasized emerges from the mass. Emphasis implies a sequential time element. Certain visual images enlist the viewer's attention before releasing him to move on to others. If all parts of a design command equal and competing attention simultaneously, the viewer tends to become visually perplexed. In confusion he may ask, "What is this design about?"

When we wish to emphasize the rectangular form in the furnishings of a room, we do not include an equal number of round forms. If we want to emphasize blue, we will not make it compete with an amount of red that is equal to blue in its power to attract. Confusion of idea can be prevented by avoiding the combination of textures of rustic quality with those suggesting elegant refinement.

Ways of securing emphasis are

1. by repeating a design element or idea.
2. by juxtaposing a design element or idea with a contrasting element or idea.

5-18 *Edward Hopper.* House by the Railroad, *1925, oil on canvas, 24" x 29". Emphasis results by freeing the background area from any competitive forms—not even a bird disturbs the lonely desolation. This painting illustrates expressiveness; the Victorian mansion no longer functions, but even in its faded glory it stands proud and haunting and fills us with nostalgia for America's bygone days. Collection, The Museum of Modern Art, New York. Given anonymously.*

These are not as antithetical as they may at first appear. To emphasize the color blue in a room, one can repeat it. Draperies are blue; walls are blue; chairs are blue. Blueness is communicated, even to the point of

5-19 *René Magritte, French.* The False Mirror, *1928, oil on canvas, 21¼″ x 31⅞″. The "pupil" supplies a bull's-eye target of emphasis through its central location, strong contrast in value, and precision of form, as opposed to the softness and irregularity of the cloudlike forms. Collection, The Museum of Modern Art, New York.*

5-20 *Pavel Tchelitchew.* Hide-and-Seek (Cache-Cache), *1940–42, oil on canvas, 78½ x 84¾″. Tchelitchew was a neo-romanticist who reacted against abstract cubism and sought a return to fantasy and emotion. The colors in the painting have a psychedelic intensity. Through line direction, all faces are directed inward, so emphasis is drawn to the child in the center. Collection, The Museum of Modern Art, New York.*

maddening monotony. On the other hand, we can emphasize blue by contrasting it with its opposite on the color wheel, orange. A contrasting hue intensifies the other's visual impact.

The concepts of *dominant, subordinate,* and *accent* refer to the relationships of the parts in the total concept of emphasis. Of these three levels of emphasis, dominant means most obvious. Subordinate and accent are also important considerations in the whole design. Subordinate means the second most obvious; accent means the least obvious. The concept of dominant—subordinate—accent thus can be called more—less—least. Figure 5-21 shows an accent with the one black pigeon and dominant with the white pigeons. Figure 5-23 has the largest of the figures (dominant), somewhat smaller figures (subordinate), and three even smaller figures (accent). Dominant can be exposed by the largest object, largest volume or convergence of radial movement. Lines in a composition lead the eye to a culminating center, much as arrows point to what one should see, or as the spokes of a wheel direct the eye toward the hub. See Figure 5-16.

5-21 *Dora Jung.* The Pigeons, *long damask linen panel in gray, white, and beige, 1958. Emphasis is achieved by conspicuous difference—the one black pigeon stands out among the lighter ones. Notice the groupings for their pleasing variations in number and size and how the spatial tension between them is visually calculated for rhythmic progression. Courtesy of the Cooper-Hewitt Museum of Decorative Arts and Design, Smithsonian Institution.*

Unity

Every part is disposed to unity with the whole, that it may thereby escape its own incompleteness.

Leonardo da Vinci

When all the elements in a design are satisfying in their relationships, the design is said to have *unity.* This idea was well expressed by Hogarth in his first chapter of *Analysis of Beauty:*

Fitness of the parts to the design for which each individual thing is form'd . . . is of greatest consequence to the beauty

5-22 The Beatles' Rolls Royce. *1965 Phantom V touring limousine. This automobile is most asymmetrical in balance. The symmetrical balance and form have been accented with curvilinear patterns and symmetrical balance, as well, and the wheels have a radially balanced design. Courtesy, The Cooper-Hewitt Museum, The Smithsonian Institution.*

that they all, whether the art is painting, sculpture, or architecture, have the interdependence of nervous ganglia. They function together to achieve organic harmony and coherence. In achieving unity one finds that harmonious forms, lines, and textures have characteristics in common. Similarities of any kind—whether of form, color, texture, or line direction—help to establish oneness. A room has a marked unity when the forms of the furniture repeat the dominant forms and lines of the structural design of the interior, and seem related

5-23 *Alexander Calder.* The Brass Family, *1929. The sculpture here, made of brass wire, shows symmetrical balance and the use of dominant subordinant accent. The large figure at the base is dominant, the three figures in the center are subordinate, and the three smallest figures are accent. Collection, The Whitney Museum of American Art, New York.*

of the whole. . . . In ship-building the dimensions of every part are confin'd and regulated by fitness for sailing. When a vessel sails well, the sailors call her a beauty; the two ideas have such a connection.

Unity, then, is compatibility of the design elements with each other and in relation to the whole, which includes function. As such, unity is the master design principle. Each part should be so related to the other

5-24 Euphronios and Euxitheos. *Two warriors arming. Detail from reverse of a calyx krater. Attic, circa 515 B.C., terra cotta. The proportions of the arms and garments are here drawn in relationship to the human size. Courtesy, The Metropolitan Museum of Art, New York.*

to it in spirit. Textures are in harmony when they reinforce an idea or theme. Satiny textures look strange to us in a rustic interior, whereas heavy linens or raw silks do not. The element of light needs consideration, too. In cafés, where intimacy and conversation are usually encouraged, subdued, low, warm lighting may be used; in classrooms, however, bright, high ceiling lights are considered appropriate.

Yet complete unity can become dull and lifeless. The concepts *unity in variety* and *variety in unity* have been called the twins of historic beauty. They imply unity, with sufficient tension through contrasts to keep us visually alert. As architect Moshe Safdie aptly phrased it, the designer's problem is "to create freedom without chaos and order without sterility." For example, a framed rectangle the same color as the wall on which it is hung would harmonize completely with the shape and color of the rectangular wall, but the monotony that

results might provoke us. We prefer to look at paintings that suggest resolutions of visual tensions. The dominant form used in a painting may be rectangular, in keeping with the length and width of a canvas, but the artist will introduce enough opposition to satisfy our need for greater complexity. He will also counter areas of concentrated interest with areas of rest.

In interior design rooms that are rectangular and whose furnishings are all of the same dimension can depress one by their rigidity; they require secondary curves for relief and interest. Just as silence is magnified by a thunderclap, roughly textured fabrics are enhanced when supplemented by smooth ones. The ideal is to have a single idea or theme that is predominant, but to allow enough contrast to prevent ennui. The skillful designer is sensitive both to visual lags, produced by excessive conformity, and to visual anarchy, which results from unrestrained diversity. Designing is the art of balancing similarities with differences to produce visual enjoyment.

5-25 *Mary Wiggin.* Sampler. *1797. Silk on canvas. This sampler shows symmetrical balance and a rhythmic border on three sides. Collection, Philadelphia Museum of Art, Philadelphia, Pennsylvania.*

Principles of Design in Other Cultures

In many ancient, primitive, and folk cultures, art has not been approached as consciously as it has in the West. Yet the same principles seem to have been intuitively observed; merely different elements have been emphasized. The native tribes of Africa, the South Seas, New Zealand, and North America are among those who have utilized what seem to Western man to be distorted and exaggerated forms. Yet these impart to the total configuration of their objects an arresting and compelling quality. Respect for the principles of art is extremely obvious in their work. Idioms differ: the principles remain.

The Chinese Hsieh Ho developed six principles of painting in the late fifth century to serve as guidelines for Asian painters. These included:

(1) Spirit Resonance, for vitality of life movement; (2) Insight of Brushwork, to indicate bones of structure; (3) Careful Drafting of Object, to give likeness; (4) Adaptation of Color, to fit character of object; (5) Planning and Design, for thoughtful composition; and (6) Accurate Drawing, to bring model to beholder.[2]

Spirit Resonance is related to the concept that a great work of art must have an expressive quality, an aura or charisma. Great painting has *ch'i yun,* the spirit and breath of life. The significance of this first principle is pointed up in Huang Yüeh's *Twenty-four Qualities of Chinese Painting:*

Of the Six Principles, Spirit Resonance is of first importance.
Idea leads Brush. Wonder beyond the painting!
Like melody lingering on strings; like fog fading into mist.
Heaven's fresh wind, vibrating waves. . . .
The apparent, large or small, becomes intangible, fluid.[3]

Though not stated as a principle in Western art, expressiveness is a critical concern of the artist-designer. A work must convey his strong feelings or conviction about some aspect of life. By the removal of extraneous detail to bare the vital essence of the artist's talent, a work becomes expressive.

The second principle emphasizes line as a significant element. Line is used to show the vitality of life. The third refers to likeness, but in Oriental painting this is merely suggested and the viewer is required to provide the detail. The fourth principle, giving emphasis to the element of color, suggests adapting color to the object, not slavishly reproducing it. The fifth, organizing the elements into a composition, most closely parallels the concern of the Western artist. The last principle reflects the Oriental's veneration for the past. Reproducing the inspired movements of the masters helps the young apprentice to gain control of his brush strokes. Moreover, according to Chinese critics, copying is not mechanical imitation of the art form and conventions of a painter but the transferral of his thought and spirit to canvas. To some extent this discipline parallels that employed in some Western schools where reproducing past masterpieces was thought to develop greater visual awareness and understanding in the student, along with a facility in handling the elements. Copying can certainly develop mastery of admired techniques. Picasso freely admitted copying elements from paintings he appreciated; van Gogh copied Japanese paintings; and Paul Klee ultimately found self-expression by copying Chinese calligraphy. Eastern artists also have admitted attempting to reproduce selected art from the West that they admired, in order to gain a desired aesthetic effect.

[2] Tseng Yu-ho, *Some Contemporary Elements in Classical Art,* Honolulu: University of Hawaii Press, 1963, p. 16.
[3] Ibid., p. 8.

Evaluation of Design 6

I have considered an esthetic judgment to be one which expresses itself in the phrase, "It is a good work of art" or, "It is a good specimen of its type." Such a judgment is different from an expression of personal preference or taste which usually takes the form of "I like it." . . .

Taste, or purely personal preference is often confused with esthetic judgment. For instance, we often speak of an 'acquired taste' for Scotch, olives, Watteau, Haut Médoc, Dr. Samuel Johnson, or acid rock. But part of what is *acquired*—and sometimes it is the crucial part—is the information or experience upon which judgment depends. Only with information can one relate, cross-refer, collate, weigh, compare—in other words, *judge*.

Such information or experience can be acquired unconsciously, osmotically or informally, but usually isn't. The teenager who listens for hours to certain genres of popular music on the radio or hi-fi, is doing essentially the same thing as the scholar who reads around and through Dr. Johnson, and then starts all over again.

After a man has achieved a certain knowledgeability about a class of objects, he is perfectly capable of saying about a particular painting or vintage of song: "It is a good example of its kind," *and adding*, "but I really don't care for it myself." The former judgment (an esthetic one) can only occur after a certain learning process has taken place; the latter judgment (an expression of taste) can be made by a three-year-old child, and to that extent is less authoritative.[1]

Though art and design movements come and go, we still enjoy articles from past centuries. Through his artifacts, man has achieved immortality. His products are an index to his interest, skills, way of life, thoughts, feelings, and perceptions. They serve as evidence of his existence and reflect his human concerns. Fortunately

[1]Irvin L. Child, "The Experts and the Bridge of Judgment That Crosses Every Cultural Gap," *Psychology Today,* **2**:7 (Dec. 1968).

for us, many have been preserved and are dateless in the visual pleasure they provide.

Throughout the world, museums and homes are filled with treasured and valuable primitive and historic art objects—from spoons and textiles to architectural fragments. The artists of former days seem to have desired elegance in the design of products for daily use, just as they do today. There must be some criteria that can be applied to help us determine why some of these objects not only possess historic value but have the potential to continuously inspire and delight the viewer.

Furthermore, because man cannot escape being both a daily designer and a consumer of design, there must be some way he can learn to fulfill these roles more effectively. How can he become literate visually as well as verbally? That the aesthetic education of an individual is critical to his total functioning is emphasized by Herbert Read in his statement that aesthetic education is

the education of those senses upon which consciousness and ultimately the intelligence and judgment of the human individual are based. It is only in so far as these senses are brought into harmonious and habitual relationship with the external world that an integrated personality is built up.[2]

There are certain standard guidelines that can make one a more skillful and aesthetic designer, and that can make the consumption of everyday goods from both the past and present more rewarding. Though these may be violated for the sake of novelty and stimulation or from man's need to explore new artistic expressions, over extended periods of time one finds there are certain elements of consistency in objects that have survived and become classic in character. These artifacts not only indicate how man felt about materials and design at a particular time, but they have an integral aesthetic value.

[2] Quoted in "The Meaning of Aesthetic Growth for Art Education," *Everyday Art* (The American Crayon Company, vol. 39, 1960) p. 5.

Structural Design

To illustrate these basic recurring elements, let us begin with an analysis of the design components of various objects. These components may be classified or differentiated for the purpose of communicating about design. All objects have a structure or framework, which

6-1 *Ernest Moore.* Chambered Nautilus. *The chambered nautilus is presented here as a sculptural object. It has inspired many forms of man-made design, such as architect Frank Lloyd Wright's configuration of the Guggenheim Museum in New York City. Nature provides all the elements of rhythm: continuity of line, gradation of sizes, radiation, and repetition. Kamco, Paterson, New Jersey.*

we term *structural design*. Our bones form our skeletal structure. Buildings have studs, joists, and beams. A coffee pot has a body, spout, handle, and lid. Structure is integral and essential; it defines objects in space. Appreciation of nature's structure is found in artists' collections of such objects as animal skulls, driftwood, rocks, fish skeletons, sea shells, antelope horns, and sharks' teeth. We can also find pleasure in man-made forms, such as the old shoe, Figure 6-3, whose history tantalyzes us.

Structural Or Integral Decorative Design

In addition to structural design, there is often a decorative quality that is inherent in the texture of particular

6-2 Fossil in Formation, *1965 (photomontage). Photograph by Barbara Morgan. 1972. Man delights in "found" objects, both natural and man-made. From the ICP Exhibition, R; Ten Women of Photography. Collection, International Center of Photography, New York.*

6-3 *An old shoe, hallowed by time, can have a sculptural quality— and produce wonderment. What fields or walks has it trodden? What were the thoughts and deeds of its wearer? It is cherished by photographer Vincent Bernucci.*

6-4 *Staved teak: oval salad bowl, diameter 14", and salad servers. Dansk Designs Ltd.*

materials or may result from structuring during the production process. The beauty of a salad bowl or a cabinet may result from the designer's selection of distinctively grained wood. A textile with open and closed intervals of space, which create a lacy effect, has a decorativeness that results from the weaving process, and that is integral with its structure. A ceramic object may have a beautiful surface texture, which was formed during the firing process. Stones bound with mortar to form a wall make a decorative pattern. Exposed joints of furniture, such as the dovetailing and interlocking junctures of structural members, can function as decorative elements. In architecture, the ribs of Gothic vaults, the framework of open timber roofs in medieval halls, and the grids created by our contemporary steel-and-glass walls are structurally decorative. These forms of decoration may be called *structural or integral decorative design.*

Applied Decorative Design

Decoration may also be applied to the surface of structures. Tattooing, for instance, modifies the outward appearance of the human body. Buildings may be adorned with friezes, carvings, or with pictorially painted designs. Some household furnishings are carved, tooled, appliquéd, embroidered, or painted. Such surface embellishment may be called *applied decorative design.*

Evaluating Structural Design

In analyzing the structural design of an object, certain questions may be asked to determine its merit. Included are the following considerations:

1. Is the Form Conducive to Fulfilling the Function for Which the Object Is Intended; That Is, Does It Work Efficiently?

A chair should be so designed as to support the human body when in a sitting position and it should also provide comfort. This means that the seat, back, arms, and legs must be related proportionally to each other and to a seated body. The most successful design is that in which the designer takes into consideration man's anatomy and functioning. The resulting design may be ornate and exuberant or it may be trim and severe—in either case it has to be functional.

2. Is the Material Composing the Form Appropriate to the Function to Be Performed?

Among the materials chosen for a living room chair may be wood, metal, plastic, paper, or cane, with leather and fabric as accessories. Stone and ivory have also been used. Today chairs are made of wood, plastic, and paperboard because these materials are available, durable, portable, and supportive. A ceramic chair might break in being shoved and its weight would make it less portable. A glass chair could fracture or break. Stone is heavy; lacquer and ivory are scarce.

3. Has the Nature of the Material Been Respected and Allowed Its True Expressiveness in the Manufacture of a Form; in Producing the Object, Do the Tools Used and the Processes Employed Develop the Potential of the Material?

To illustrate, wood can be quartered or plain-sawed to capitalize upon variations in grain in order to produce veneers of intricate design. In the manufacturing process, standard parts of whole furniture pieces can be made uniformly at one machine setting. However, the finishing processes such as joining, veneering, sanding, and oiling might well be done by hand in order to develop the grain and pattern of the wood, thus fully realizing its aesthetic potential.

As another example, Edith Heath, the California ceramist, fully exploits the potential of clay. As an artist she values creative design and as a product manufacturer she values the machine for its efficiency in producing stoneware dishes that do not require a hand-crafted look. Thus she weds art with industry.

To illustrate her respect for materials, she uses clay in a way consistent with its many possibilities. Clay is plastic and can be shaped to any form, either elaborate or simple. No other common material is so responsive to the human touch. In producing hand-crafted ware on the potter's wheel, slight variations in touch and pressure produce subtleties in surface design that add aesthetic interest and provide man with pleasure in recording his oneness with clay. Ceramic wares always inform us of the degree of human pressure applied in their production. A hand-crafted ceramic piece that reflects honesty between the materials, tools, and processes used in its construction will not attempt to erase evidence of this human touch by making the surface machine-smooth, but will acknowledge the tools of the hand and fingers and value their traces.

Hand-crafted ceramic pieces reveal more of the hand of their creator, whereas machine-made ware reflects more of the creative mind of the producer. In recognition of this, Edith Heath employs the machine in the manufacturing process where it makes a valid contribution, and she employs hand-crafting where it contributes in ways the machine cannot, such as in glazing.

To begin with function, it is advantageous to be able to stack and store tableware. For this purpose dishes need to be uniform in size and shape. It is not possible by a hand process to secure the degree of uniformity that may be desired for ease of handling; nor is it efficient use of an individual's time and effort to try to duplicate identical pieces to form a set of dishes for mass production.

In using the machine to emulate—not to imitate—hand-crafted design, it is necessary to start with a basic design suitable to the application of machine methods, such as jiggering or slip-casting. The Heath plates are jiggered to produce uniformity. Teapots are intricate in

6-7 *Edith Heath. Bowl made on potter's wheel. Note the subtle application of hand pressure, which creates integral design, and the melting through of some of the minerals to provide a lively texture. Courtesy, Edith Heath. Photograph by Lisa Stephens.*

design, so slip-casting molds are used. The resulting machine forms are reminiscent of the plastic qualities of wheel-formed products but do not duplicate them.

With respect to decorativeness of design, glazes contribute to the distinction of Heath ware. Mrs. Heath uses glaze in a subordinate fashion to preserve as much of the nature of clay as possible. A proportion of approximately 22 per cent clay is combined with the glaze to produce a rich, matte surface. During the firing process the melting through of some of the minerals in the clay body, such as manganese dioxide, produces the lively brown speckles that are characteristic of Heath ware. This is an excellent example of integral decorative design, the design that results from the nature of the material and the process of manufacture.

Heath ware is equally suited to both indoor and outdoor living because the textures and colors repeat those of land and sea scapes and of pebbles and rocks. Glazes are applied by hand to facilitate greater versatility and individuality in techniques. The variations in human handling and in the temperature and duration of firing create subtle differences in dinnerware. Thus on each is recorded echoing traces of both man and machine.

Mrs. Heath describes her respect for both the material and the machine:

I still use the potter's wheel as a sketch pad for working out size relationships in the round. I then refine the shape and form in a more rigid material (plaster) to obtain the tailored contour that is characteristic of a machine-turned design. This transition from a sketch which succeeds because of its freedom to a hard line requires a fine degree of sensitivity and discipline, so that the final result will be a positive statement of the qualities of the clay and the limitations of the machine.[3]

4. If the Material Has Been Used in an Imitative Manner, Does It Make a Positive Aesthetic Contribution?

The fact that men have used materials to serve an imitative function since prehistoric times, is a tribute to

[3] Personal communication.

nature's potential for inspiration. Man's first containers for food and drink came from the sea, land, and forest—sea shells, ostrich-egg shells, coconut shells, animal bladders, and plant gourds. Their material forms had a structural and integral decorative quality that man emulated in designing new materials. This use of materials to serve imitative functions is not necessarily negative: imitation can lead to experimentation. Through this process, man can accidentally gain a greater knowledge of the potential expressiveness of a particular material. As he does so, he may become dissatisfied with reliance on imitation. Though it may be clever to duplicate, discovering a material's unfamiliar possibilities is more rewarding.

That these imitative forms do have an aesthetic appeal and can lead to the development of more advanced design is evident in many of the art forms of ancient man. Early American Indian pottery vessels were deco-

6-8 *Pre-Columbian corrugated bowl with additional incised ornamentation, suggestive of a woven basket pattern, southwestern United States. Man draws inspiration for design from nature's forms. Courtesy of the American Museum of Natural History.*

rated with designs to simulate basketry, a familiar imagery. In the pottery of neolithic southeast Asia, too, surfaces were often incised to emulate the weaves common to basketry. It has been theorized that ceramics may have developed as a result of clay-lined baskets being placed in such proximity to the fire that they burned, leaving the baked clay residue with a woven incised design.

In Oriental cultures we find that the beautiful celadon wares known as "celestial" porcelain began in an attempt to reproduce the exquisite colors of jade. Ceramics were also made in emulation of prized bronzes, with beautiful glazes being developed to duplicate the patina that bronze acquires through prolonged exposure to weathering.

The ancient Greeks referred to glass as *lithos chyte,* "cast stone," and attempted to make glass that would have the jewel-like qualities of stones. The Egyptians and the Romans successfully made glass in the striated patterns of agates. Today we find that designers with a comparatively short history of experimentation in plastics are making plastics imitative of such familiar materials as fabrics and wood. Through their experimenting, however, they are gradually developing plastics' own intrinsic beauty.

With many new materials on the market and with the possibility of creating art by technological means, there has been a relaxing of the condemning attitude toward imitation. Wallpapers and rugs, for instance, are made in patterns looking like ocelot fur and snakeskin. Jack Lenor Larsen has produced an exotically textured velveteen reminiscent of the batik process. Boris Kroll, a contemporary textile designer, has designed an attractive cotton stretch fabric that is hand-printed in imitation of a tied-and-died material. Wood grain is being printed on the underside of vinyl film which can then be bonded to any substrate—wood, plastic, or metal.

6-9 *Boris Kroll.* Bokashi. *Inspired by the hand-crafted tie-and-dye printing technique, the factory-produced textile can have a parallel abstract textural beauty. Boris Kroll Fabrics, New York.*

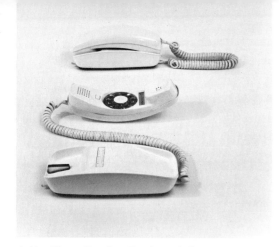

6-10 *Henry Dreyfus. Trimline telephone, 1965. In design often "simple is beautiful." Plastics have pre-empted the use of other materials for telephones because of their lightness of weight and ease in handling. Collection, The Museum of Modern Art, New York.*

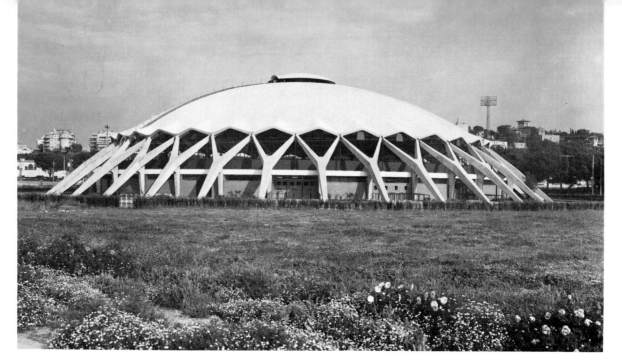

6-11 *Pier Luigi Nervi, Small Sports Palace, Rome, built for the 1960 Olympics. The interior has a webbed, flowerlike ceiling composed of prefabricated concrete, diamond-shaped sections. The triangular sections transfer the load outward and downward to the exterior Y-shaped buttresses and vertical supports. The cupola in the center provides a central source of natural light. Capacity: 5,000 seats. Alinari-Art Reference Bureau.*

6-12 *Oscar Niemeyer's house in Rio de Janeiro, Brazil, 1953–54. Ferroconcrete, a new material, has led to innovative 20th-century design, which in its fluidity and freedom deviates from traditional rectilinear forms. Collection, The Museum of Modern Art, New York.*

Plastic sheets are being made for use as furniture veneers; they simulate wood, but can be wrapped around small areas which is not possible with wood veneers.

In evaluating these designs one might ask if the resulting patterns and textures contribute aesthetically, and if individuality is gained. The reproduction of large forms, such as designing wallpaper to look like fieldstone or brick, seems obviously artificial. However, wallpaper that looks like grasscloth or silk shantung merely assumes an interesting texture. At the same time we must recognize that at the height of the artistic development of a material, it ceases to be imitative and takes on its own unique forms and exclusiveness. For instance, oiled teak has a quality aesthetically superior to that of a wood-textured synthetic. On the other hand, plastics reached a height of development when used for the simply designed bakelite telephone.

5. Do the Form and Materials Used Reflect the Particular Culture or Historic Era?

Materials and forms should preferably be relevant to the culture from which they stem. They should be both expressive of and consistent with their time. Frank Lloyd Wright confirmed this value: "Only when art is indigenous, the work of a particular time, according to the nature and character of the people at that time, is it for all time."

This means that it was fine for ancient man to shape bones and stone for his daily use; for the Greeks to erect temples of local marble, utilizing the post and lintel system of construction known to architects of their day; and for the Pueblo Indians of the Southwest to rely on sandstone cliffs for shelter and on clay for household objects. In turn, twentieth-century man will use the technology and materials available to him: steel and reinforced concrete, metal, plastic, glass, paper, and laminated wood. A culture's development of tools necessary for man's manipulation of the materials is also critical. Man's particular use of materials reflects a particular time and place in history.

6-13 *Charles Eames. Plastic side chair, 1951. A new technological material, plastic reinforced with fiberglass, leads to a logical original design for this century. Courtesy, Charles Eames.*

Architects Mies van der Rohe and Eero Saarinen used steel and glass to proclaim their time. Pier Nervi and Oscar Niemeyer have created hyperbolic-paraboloid forms of architecture from ferroconcrete. Designing for the twentieth century, Charles Eames used plastic reinforced with fiberglass, innovatively joining a plastic shell to a metal base by means of a neoprene mount. The *International Movement* developed the materials (paper, plastics, and metals) and used them for furnishings of all kinds. Designers of many countries experiment with new substances, forms, and processes to create a new vision and to extend the definition of *function* beyond the mere accommodation of human physical needs. One must also stress the emotional requirements of individuals as they relate to materials and space. Those who are artistic have asked for more than practical service from the objects they create and have recognized the need to provide psychological and aesthetic satisfaction.

6. Is the Design a New Expression Or Is It Merely a Superficial Change in Structure?

By way of example, fins on automobiles were a styling feature in the 1950s. Their addition to automotive design was a departure from the look of previous years. These fins soon became outmoded and today they seem dated and meaningless. They were a form of styling that became quickly obsolete, the kind of design that is new and attracts initially but that lacks continuous appeal and does not improve the functioning of an object. The superficial quality of styling in the long run may cloy our senses. In contrast to this the Ford Model T of the 1920s continues to charm because of the directness and honesty of its design conception. It antedated the concept of styling—the aim of which is not necessarily to advance design but to create consumer dissatisfaction with a present model in favor of the "new look." Through a yearly change of design the public is influenced to discard models whose function may be quite unimpaired. Those objects that survive through time achieve a perennial look, because they express a relevance to men of any era.

In contrast, the development of stretch fabrics for sportswear in the later 1950s led to the acceptance of a new silhouette for the human body in the 1960s. Pleats, gathers, and ease in the construction of garments were no longer required to facilitate movement. In taut clothing, the silhouette changed to one of slenderness and verticality. Likewise, Eames's plastic side chair of

6-14 *The Group 14 (Gianfranco Facchetti, Umberto Orsoni, Gianni Pareschi, Pino Pensotti, Roberto Ubaldi) "Fiocco" (Bow) armchair, 1970. Manufacturer, Busnelli, Italy. This armchair is made of iron tubes covered with stretch fabric. There is unity in the undulation of both the form of the chair and the curve outline. New technological materials can lead to new creative design. Courtesy of Busnelli, Italy.*

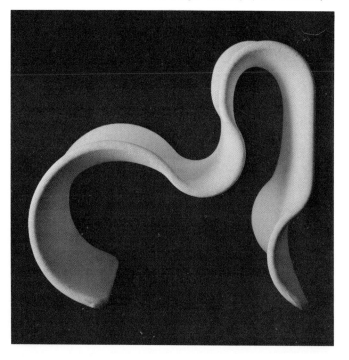

1960 used a form so natural to plastic that it subsequently served as a prototype. Also stretch fabrics manufactured for the upholstery business in the 1960s could accommodate the design of new forms, such as Pierre Paulin's ribbon chair with its complex curvature of plastic and metal composition. A criterion for the validity of new expressions was forcefully summarized by designer Henry Dreyfuss:

A change in technology, improved efficiency, added safety or comfort, a new utility development, an improved method of fabrication, the introduction of a new material—all these warrant a new physical expression. But to put a new look on an existing piece of merchandise—this to us constitutes the duping of an unsuspecting public.[4]

7. Have the Aesthetics of Form Been Observed?

In 1949, the Danish designer Hans Wegner, renowned for his ability to extract the potentials of wood, created a chair that had such marked aesthetic distinction that it became known as The Chair. Its proportions are varied and pleasing. The legs, slightly splayed, promote a sense of balance and security. Much of The Chair's beauty comes from the sculptural treatment of the back, which flows down to meet the leg. The back is oiled teak, the legs of waxed oak—both waxing and oiling are matte treatments that reveal the beauty of wood grain. It can be contemplated both as a seat and as a sculpture.

The Chair not only suggests comfort; it expresses how Hans Wegner felt about people and beauty. After seeing his chair, many people looked at chairs differently, expecting them to communicate as well as to function. This quality of expressiveness was described by the Victorian designer poet William Morris:

The presence of any beauty in a piece of handicraft implies that the mind of man who made it was more or less excited at the time, was lifted somewhat above the commonplace; that he had something to communicate to his fellows which

[4]Henry Dreyfuss, *Design 231* (March 1968) p. 19.

6-15 *Hans J. Wegner's classic chair, 1949. Wegner's furniture is renowned for its sculptureesque beauty and retention of the appearance of hand-crafted aesthetic qualities in machine-produced objects. Notice how the joinings contribute to the design and how all parts relate well to each other and to the whole. Though more refined in its simplicity, it is reminiscent of a Windsor chair. Georg Jensen Inc.*

they did not know or feel before, and which they would never have known or felt if he had not been there to force them to it.[5]

[5] Quoted by Ray Watkinson, *William Morris as Designer* (New York: Reinhold, 1967), p. 49.

Others who voiced the need for expression were the architects Louis Sullivan and Le Corbusier. An architect needs said Sullivan, "first of all a poetic imagination; second, a broad sympathy with human character and a thoroughly disciplined mind; third, a perfected technique and fourth, . . . an abundant and gracious gift of expression." Le Corbusier believed that "passion can create drama [expression] out of inert stone."

Evaluating Applied Decorative Design

In evaluating applied decorative design it is important to be aware of the purposes of the artist, for decorativeness fulfills many social and psychological functions. Among them are the following:

To Educate Or to Record
Typical highly decorated forms are the walls of the royal tombs and mortuary temples of the Egyptian Pharaohs. Their murals and carvings depict the Egyptian zest for life—the pleasures of the harvest, of the hunt, and of feasts and games. The decoration of Grecian vases also reflects the life of the ancient Greeks and their cherished events.

In the Romanesque, early Christian, and medieval periods, mosaics and decorative columns and statuary on architecture were used to inform an illiterate public about Biblical events. The Mayans and Aztecs also used decorative devices on architecture to educate the people about their gods. The excellent artistry in these edifices would seem to indicate that in preindustrial societies, the most outstanding artisans were recognized and employed to create decorative art.

To Honor
Historically, one finds expert craftsmen employed by the affluent to create decoratively. Glass goblets were

6-16 *Victoria and Albert vase made by Charles Mugh and Sons, Hanley. Portrait of Queen Victoria and an exterior view of the 1851 exhibition building on the reverse side. This vase, displayed at the Great Exhibition of 1851, is an example of historic decorative design intended to commemorate and honor. Victoria and Albert Museum. Crown Copyright.*

6-17 *Johan Rohde's silver pitcher of 1920 is timeless, needing no superfluous decoration. Notice how the line of the lip of the pitcher flows in one continuous line toward the base of the vessel. Georg Jensen Inc.*

elaborately etched; plaques and vessels of gold and silver were designed to commemorate events such as victories and coronations. The habit has persisted up to the present. The Eisenhower *toile* of 1959 depicted historic incidents in the life of the President. In 1968, Richard Nixon received a needlepoint design of the United States seal from his daughter Julie to commemorate his election to the Presidency. These kinds of articles may communicate honor, loyalty, love, or historic significance. Hence decorative consideration from the standpoint of the most effective use of a material may sometimes be of secondary importance.

To Identify or Symbolize

The use of applied decoration to identify or symbolize is a useful device to promote instant recognition of rank and status. Color has been used to differentiate those of higher status from those of lesser rank, as, for instance, in the use of purple for royal costume, or the bejeweled decorative splendor of court robes. Differentiation of status by means of decorative devices is evident in the use of banners, heraldic symbols, family crests, and monograms. Napoleon used the honeybee as his personal decorative device. Today the designer Vera uses a ladybug to establish her identity.

To Stimulate

Decorativeness may seem more stimulating to the senses than plain surfaces. Man fulfills some of his need for change of pace by decorating surfaces, whether it be his objects or his own body. The current revival of the decorative Art Nouveau and the perpetual appeal of fanciful paisley designs are illustrative of this. So is the decoration of the body either with cosmetics, or tattoos, or scarification.

6-18 *This owl is on the reverse side of an Athenian tetradrachm of the late 5th century B.C. The earliest Athenian coinage depicting Athena and her owl was first struck about 520 B.C. was widely used throughout the ancient world. For instance, the reverse side of the owl was still being copied in Arabia at the end of the 1st century B.C. Courtesy of the Smithsonian Institution, Washington, D.C.*

To Increase the Aesthetic Appearance of an Object

Many of the purposes we have listed may result in objects that provide a heightened experience when they are viewed. However, when these objectives are not based on artistic considerations, the design may be lacking in merit. Successful decorative design implies enhancement of the object through its application. In evaluating this, these questions might be asked:

1. Is the Applied Design Necessary? Does It Enhance the Object?

If the form is sufficient in itself and if it makes a clear and positive statement, there is no need for additional adornment. Also, if in the selection of the material or through production processes, the object has an integral decorative quality, further embellishment may detract from it. One cannot improve upon beautiful wood grain by painting or carving. The application of embroidery may be superfluous to a fabric composed of textural yarns with exciting variations in the spaces formed by the warp and woof. Or consider the design of a pewter pitcher. Would decorative design enhance or detract from the softly reflecting sheen of the metal? In the classroom, does a wastebasket need applied decoration if it would be consistent with the restraint in design of other functional objects in the room? Yet would not housewares and fabrics be dull if they were never decorated? And although coins and stamps only really need numerals to identify them, their decorativeness certainly provides man with added pleasure.

2. Is the Applied Design Harmonious in Color, Line, Form, and Idea with the Structure?

Colors that focus attention upon themselves and disregard background color do not contribute to unity of design. Lines and forms that are in opposition to the basic form may provide variety, but they create feelings of disturbing tension if they are too contradictory and demanding of attention. Dainty designs applied to an object of robust proportions seem inappropriate in character. When design is applied that is consistent with the structure, decorative and structural design function as one.

3. Is It Ordered to Relate to the Space upon Which It Is Placed?

All decorative design, if it is to relate to a form, needs to be structured to some extent. One example of this ordering is in the pediment of the Parthenon, now in the British museum, where Attic goddesses are so positioned as to form two abutted right triangles, thus creating a gable. You can also note the obviously triangular structuring in *Two Women Talking,* Figure 6-19. In Gothic cathedrals, stone sculpture was utilized to illustrate Biblical history; for the sake of design, the anatomy of the characters was elongated, foreshortened, or distorted to repeat the structure of archways, portals, and columns.

6-19 Two Women Talking, *painted terra cotta, Hellenistic art from Myrina, in Asia Minor. The forms are purposefully ordered to form a pleasing triangle. The Trustees of the British Museum, London.*

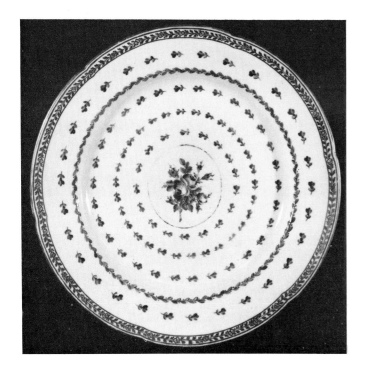

6-20 *Porcelain with overglaze decoration, Paris, France, circa 1775. Forms on this plate are ordered to be in harmony with the roundness of the plate. Compare the decorative design with that of Figure 6-21 and 6-22. The center medallion of roses serves as a point of emphasis. Courtesy of the Cooper-Hewitt Museum of Decorative Arts and Design, Smithsonian Institution, New York.*

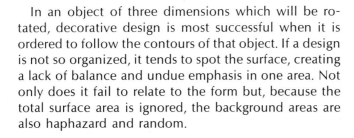

6-21 *Porcelain with overglaze decoration, Sèvres, France, 1770. Compared to Figure 6-20, the decorative design is spotty and lacks basic unity with the form of the plate. Courtesy of the Cooper-Hewitt Museum of Decorative Arts and Design, Smithsonian Institution, New York.*

6-22 *English fruit plate. Porcelain with overglaze painting, 1753–1758. Little attempt has been made to relate the decorative design to the structural design of the plate. Courtesy of the Cooper-Hewitt Museum of Decorative Arts and Design, Smithsonian Institution, New York.*

6-23 *Amphora, white-painted Cypriote ware, 750–500 B.C., height 31⅝". The lotus blossoms are stylized and reinforce the structural form. The spatial relations are noteworthy. Collection, The Metropolitan Museum of Art, New York.*

In an object of three dimensions which will be rotated, decorative design is most successful when it is ordered to follow the contours of that object. If a design is not so organized, it tends to spot the surface, creating a lack of balance and undue emphasis in one area. Not only does it fail to relate to the form but, because the total surface area is ignored, the background areas are also haphazard and random.

4. Is the Background Space Pleasing in Design?

The design motif itself is often called *positive design space* to differentiate it from the background, which is termed *negative design space*. The motif is considered foreground or *field;* it is seen against *background.* Negative design space does not mean space that can be ignored, because the act of placing a motif on a surface simultaneously creates another form—the background, which has its own rhythmic lines and patterns. The relative proportion of background to foreground space also contributes to the total design. Generally, when the impact of background space is equivalent with foreground space in its power to attract, visual fatigue results from the competition between the two to command attention. Our fascination with motifs that are familiar to us tends to focus our attention upon them with little regard to the abstracted background design they are creating. The successful designer will structure foreground and background simultaneously, realizing that the *relationship between the two is the design,* not the motif itself.

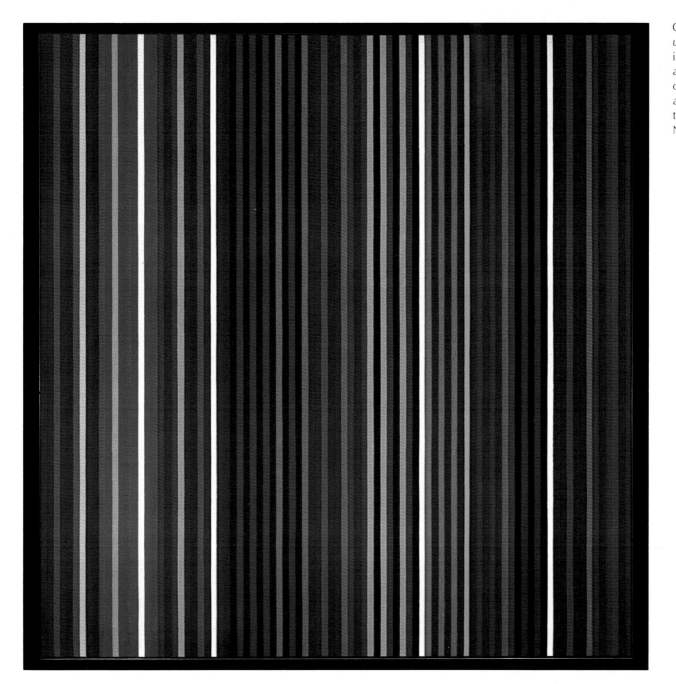

Gene Davis. *Anthracite Minuet,* polymer, 1966. This painting illustrates various means of attaining rhythm, a linear flow of color, gradations of color, and repetition of line. Collection, Museum of Modern Art, New York.

Man vs. Nature

Upper left: Photograph by Carla Davis Dumesnil. The underside of an automobile. The automobile is a symbol of the power of man and his effect over nature. *Upper right:* Photograph by Carla Davis Dumesnil. Flamingo tongue on coral. This is a photograph of a natural sea animal on the natural habitat of coral.

Man and Nature

Lower left: Photograph by Carla Davis Dumesnil. *Sea Creature and Hand.* This photograph shows one of the many relationships people may have and illustrates the importance of an ethic of compatibility of man and nature. *Lower right:* Photograph by Carla Davis Dumesnil. *Stairs and Snow.* Cement stairs and the fallen snow give a rhythmic pattern of light and dark as the snow melts. Structures built by humans also interact with nature.

6-24 *Detail of quilted and embroidered petticoat, linen and wool. France, first half of the 18th century. The background and foreground areas are equally beautiful, to the extent that the positive space and negative space each create equal attention in different ways. Courtesy of the Cooper-Hewitt Museum of Design, Smithsonian Institution, New York.*

6-25 Floral Fantasy. *Reversal of foreground and background space in fabric design can create differing moods. Thaibok Fabrics Ltd.*

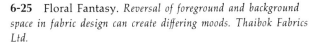

6-26 Floral Fantasy. *Light positive space on dark negative space. Thaibok Fabrics Ltd.*

6-27 Vase with gilding, Bohemia, perhaps mid-19th century. The decorative design becomes textural and enhances the basic verticality of the vase. The decorated surface contrasts pleasingly with the undecorated. Courtesy of the Copper-Hewitt Museum of Decorative Arts and Design, Smithsonian Institution, New York.

5. Does the Decorative Design Reinforce the Structure of the Object?

Applied design can reinforce structure by repeating the dominant line movement or by emphasizing the main structural points. To illustrate, decoration applied to a tall vertical pitcher would be predominantly vertical in character, with only sufficient secondary horizontals to satisfy our need for variety through contrast. To emphasize its structural points, a band of decoration might be placed near the rim of the vase, at the swell of its body, or near the base, as in the amphora shown in Figure 6-23.

Design is sometimes used to consistently cover the entire surface of an object, in a fashion similar to the gilded vase, shown in Figure 6-27 which appears textural in quality and creates a single impression that does not direct attention to any one part of the design. This all-over surface pattern is often used by the Japanese, who combine many designs over the entire surface of an object to create a uniform visual impression. Chinese blue willowware is, likewise, basically allover scenic and textural. As in Oriental design, many of the still lifes painted by the French artist Henri Matisse are flat and decorative with an all-over design of varying textural impressions.

6. Has the Design Been Applied for Valid Aesthetic Reasons?

Formerly, articles of great structural simplicity and restrained decoration were thoughtfully conceived and valued by the members of a culture. In these days of

6-28 Joseph Angell. Silver-gilt ewer, London, 1854. Contrast this bristling textural treatment with that of the vase with gilding for reinforcement of structure. Courtesy of the Cooper-Hewitt Museum of Decorative Arts and Design, Smithsonian Institution, New York.

6-29 Charles Kandler. Tea kettle and stand, 1727–37. In this design is the material valued for its own unique aesthetic and are unity or harmony recognized as major design principles? Victoria and Albert Museum. Crown Copyright.

extended travel, it is generally assumed that the tourist will not buy unless his attention is arrested by ostentatious surface design. Simple wooden bowls may be garishly painted and wood sculptures in vulgar forms are often highly varnished. Ceramic glazes are fre-

6-30 *Carved figures illustrating Maori legends. Art can function as literature. For instance, the center man, Lorabario, paid frequent visits to his neighbor's wife. The husband became suspicious of the footprints, so Lorabario conceived the idea of using stilts. Thinking the marks were made by an unknown animal, the husband slept contentedly. The design on the face and body represent the peculiar method of body decoration among the Maori known as* moko, *tattooing by cutting off the skin in narrow strips. The totemlike figures, decorated frontally, retain the basic form of a tree trunk. Courtesy of The American Museum of Natural History.*

quently glossy and harsh and sea shells are lacquered. In these cases, decoration and surface treatment are applied not to enhance structure but simply to catch the eye of the tourist, who is generally considered visually illiterate; by buying the wares designed to trap him, he maintains this image.

In another category, some designs are more conducive to telling a story than to performing an aesthetic function. If a story is told visually, with consideration of aesthetic values, the message may be enhanced because mental and emotional satisfactions are also realized. That this is true can be seen in the delightful Maori wood sculptures in Figure 6-30. It has also been projected that the drawings in the caves at Lascaux, in France, had symbolic and narrative significance and were instrumental to prehistoric man in securing him benefits during the hunt. They are valued today, of course, as art, quite independently of these functions. On the other hand, many designs have been made on glass and metal to commemorate events or to indicate the wealth and status of privileged individuals. Though these designs may be vital and expressive, they often reflect greater concern with the designer's ability to embellish in order to communicate respect, reverence, or obeisance toward an authority figure than genuine aesthetic concern.

7. Has the Decorative Design an Appeal That Can Be Sustained During the Length of Time That the Object Will be in Use?

Much decorative design is aimed at attracting attention and creating excitement. It would be a dull visual world without ornamentation. There are times when we may wish to be immersed in sound, color, pattern, light, and movement. Carnivals and fairs provide us with that opportunity. Psychedelic design with its titillation of color and light serves a similar function.

But just as we may want stimulation, so we need surcease from it. Things that will be viewed for extended periods of time produce fatigue less readily if their decoration is restrained. Expendable articles such as paper plates and cups, occasional apparel, and posters can be highly decorative because we usually do not live with them for long, or they may be valued because they

6-31 *Malcolm Leland. Cast bronze door pulls, length 12". Manufacturer, Forms and Surfaces, Santa Barbara, California. Forms may express boldness and strength—and the mind of the designer who extracts the essence of an object in its most concentrated form.* California Design XI, *Pasadena Art Museum.*

6-32 *Jun Kaneko. These glazed ceramic forms, which are about three feet high, have such expressive vitality that they approximate live forms that might be indigenous to the natural environment.* California Design X, *Pasadena Art Museum.*

contribute color and pattern to a quiet environment. Cosmetic body art is fun and temporary; tattooing is usually regretted. Wallpaper in a game room could well be active in design; in a living room, more restraint is appropriate. Cars were merely sensational and fun when painted psychedelically.

8. Does the Design Have Merit and Individuality?

Design merit, like aesthetic distinction, is an abstraction that defies easy description. One can approach it obliquely by stating that some designs are obviously not very satisfying when viewed over long periods of time. Hsieh Ho was speaking of design merit when he declared the first principle of art to be Spirit Resonance, the vitality of life movement. A work of art must not only appeal to the senses; it must have an expressive quality that intensifies one's awareness of life and creates a magnetic field of interaction between man and object. Expressiveness relates not only to the designer's incorporating some of his own life and vitality into a work but also to his capturing some of the dynamic force within objects instead of merely duplicating their outer static form. The object then has a "presence."

Classifications of Decorative Design

Various classifications can be given to applied design. *Naturalistic designs* are those that exactly duplicate the familiar aspects of nature. When applied to objects other than nature, design is spoken of as being *realistic;* both naturalistic and realistic designs represent the familiar aspects of objects. Although naturalistic design can be attractive, for the forms of nature have an inherent beauty, it may appear superficial when only surface aspects are captured. Moreover, design that leaves nothing to the imagination and employs forms that have been seen many times before does not enlist one's interest for long.

However, even treating objects realistically, the artist is free to use his imagination to vary the structure for greater meaning and involvement. He need not make

6-33 *Henri Rousseau.* The Dream, *1910, oil on canvas, 6'8" x 9'9½". Here is jungle beauty of a dreamlike quality in a naturalistic design that has been stylized to some extent. Collection, The Museum of Modern Art, New York.*

a literal translation of natural phenomena but can allow his emotional responses to become incorporated into an image to give it vitality. This vitalized expression is admirably demonstrated by Andrew Wyeth, whose paintings are recognizable scenes or portraits and yet are so highly charged with mood and emotion as to approach mysticism. They remain communicating and provocative.

Stylized, or *conventionalized, design* consists of simplifying the visual aspect of an object by eliminating all unnecessary details and exaggerating lines to produce dramatic forms and pronounced rhythms. This reduction of detail and purposeful distortion places

6-34 *Andrew Wyeth.* Christina's World, *1948, tempera on gesso panel, 32¼ x 47¾". The painting is realistic, but with emotional overtones.*
The inspiration was an older crippled woman, but here she is shown as youthful. She seems trapped by the vastness of space and her incapacity to
move. Collection, The Museum of Modern Art, New York.

emphasis upon the essence of form. Hsieh Ho, in his principles of art, recognized the value of economy. This was expressed in *Twenty-four Qualities* by Huang Yüeh under Verse XX, Terse Purity:

Let others squander effort; get all in one stroke.
Suggest in minimum the mighty; find freedom in mediums.[6]

Stylized designs tend to reduce three-dimensional forms to flat shapes of two dimensions. Because walls, floors, bodies, and other objects upon which design is placed are flat, stylized design provides greater unity with structure than naturalistic design, which suggests depth. The lasting beauty and versatility of Chinese, Japanese, and Persian prints in costume and décor are attributable in part to their flatness. Moreover, the omission of superfluous detail leaves the viewer free to complete the design in his imagination. Because he enters into the design process by providing part of the visual data, he creates along with the creator. Thus appreciation becomes a two-way process, with the viewer enlisted in the act, and his interest is prolonged through human involvement.

In *abstract design* forms are so organized that the identity of an object may be lost, or ambivalent images may appear through the lack of a sufficient number of identifying cues. Moreover, abstract design does not rely solely upon objects for its content but includes ideas, emotions, and qualities. It calls upon us, the viewers, to appreciate variations in light and dark, in color, in lines and forms, in spatial intervals, and in textures. We must also appreciate the way all these elements interact dynamically to produce varying fields of tension and force. The viewer is required to allow these elements to suggest the artist's intent without benefit of familiar cues and associations. To appreciate such art, one must value an artist's need to represent visually the ideational,

6-35 *Joan Miró.* Person Throwing a Stone at a Bird. *Oil on canvas, 29" x 36¼". The amorphous forms of Miró contrast with the precision of Léger. Collection, The Museum of Modern Art, New York.*

emotional, mystical, mysterious, ambiguous, and undefinable.

Abstract design may be structured either with geometric regularity and precision or with organic variance and fluidity. Machine design has come to be associated with the former, handcraftsmanship with the latter. Neither is mutually exclusive, but it is characteristic of design from a machine to be precise and duplicable, whereas man's production is variant and unpredictable,

[6]Tseng Yu-ho, *Some Contemporary Elements in Classical Chinese Art* (Honolulu: University of Hawaii Press, 1963), p. 14.

6-36 *Fernand Léger*, Three Women (Le Grand déjeuner), *1921, oil on canvas, 72¼ x 99''. The painting suggests mechanized precision. Collection, The Museum of Modern Art, New York.*

reflecting his many moods and changing physical states.

As examples in the design of textiles, some of Alexander Girard's geometric designs are less humanely warm than Jack Lenor Larsen's exotic and sensuous floral patterns. Joan Miró's paintings of biomorphic forms contrast with Fernand Léger's mechanical symbols. Frank Lloyd Wright's eulogizing of organic architecture contrasts with Mies van der Rohe's paean of song to steel and glass. The sculptures of Henry Moore, Hans Arp, and Alexander Calder contain fluctuating rhythms produced by irregular curves; cubic precision characterizes those of Jacques Lipchitz, Alexander Archipenko, and Antoine Pevsner. See Figure 4-15.

Increasingly, in design, one finds that machine and hand are not resisting each other—that there is a fusion of hand and machine processes, a liaison between the geometric and the organic. Industrially precision-cut wood is used in the production of hand-crafted furniture. Factory-spun and dyed yarns are woven into organic forms on a hand loom. This relationship between men, materials, and methods is a promising one.

Part Two
Cultural Contributions to Today's Design

Foreword

Many societies have contributed to our world's design heritage. In design, adaptation reflects the continuity of culture. Ancient Greco-Roman design is one of the most familiar and historically famous because of its profound influence on world art and architecture. Fluted columns, caryatids, acanthus leaves, rosettes, and frets continue to adorn buildings and furnishings. This period of history remains significant in the cultural development of the Western world.

A great redirection of visual imagery was effected when the East Indian companies of the seventeenth century introduced the culture of the Orient to the West. The rage for all things Oriental—porcelain, fabrics, embroideries, lacquered screens, ivories, wallpapers, and jade—was felt throughout mercantile Europe and gave rise to factories that attempted to produce similar wares. Japanese woodblock prints influenced impressionist and postimpressionist painters as well as designers of the Art Nouveau period. Negro and island arts were catalysts for the imagery of the later nineteenth century.

Of the many societies that have contributed to today's design, some have provided us with an understanding of the philosophy and a rationale behind their creation to a greater extent than others. Because the intention is to encourage an understanding of the dynamics involved in the creative process, only selected societies will be presented here, not because their contribution is more significant, but because they have provided a literature that informs us. Through intensive study of these societies one can develop insights into the creative process, designer's philosophies, and the societal conditions that contribute to the production of good design.

Contributions of Western Cultural History 7

Continuity in Nature and Design

In these words the California poet James Broughton has indicated the value of allying the present with the past:

A poem is, was, and will be. It is of the present only if it is connected to the past and to the future. A contemporary poem needs some fragrance of the ancient, an echo of the primordial, a taste of the everlasting: otherwise it has no parents nor progeny.

Design, too, can benefit from integrating some of the past with the present. Art that provides pleasure to man in one culture and to one generation has the potential to provide satisfactions to others far removed in time and place; the continuity of the universe provides a corresponding continuity in man's expressions. The artist is only familiar with what surrounds him and which he experiences. As man experiences nature visually, he converts its forms, colors, and textures into paintings, sculpture, architecture, and stitchery.

Thus one finds that artists' canvases reflect land, prairie, and mountain scapes. Sculptures bear a similarity to such forms as stones and birds. Architecture may have a likeness to the chambered nautilus, to rock strata, or to honeycombs. Portrait artists take man himself and his personality as the object of their intensified study. From the beginning, nature has been the great progenitor of art. The forms that man of any civilization or century develops necessarily derive from his visual images and from the emotions and internal sensations he experiences. Moreover, just as nature provides

have their own vitality. As symbols of civilization they bind the past to the present and the living with the dead. By bringing the far distant near in both time and place, they bring nations into proximity and serve to unite mankind. Thus a spiritual economy is provided for the family of man.

Over the years man has developed a sensitivity for the design forms that remain pleasing. Upon analysis, those that survive show a structural organization in which the principles of design are respected and which possess a quality of expressiveness. Cultural anthropologists suggest that in various societies the most capable artisans have been recognized and given creative assignments. Examples of designs of lasting quality are

7-1 Hermit—Fisherman in the Autumn Forest. *Fan mounted as an album leaf by Sheng Mou, Chinese artist active about 1810–1860. This ink and color on silk is dated 1394. It reflects the near and far of a Chinese landscape. Collection, The Metropolitan Museum of Art, New York.*

continuity in its many aspects, so man's interpretation of it finds relatedness of expression and a degree of meaningfulness in designs of other eras.

Works of art can be created at any technical and social level. They can be created consciously or unconsciously, either by primitive or highly sophisticated cultures. Those that are not as dependent upon stylistic criteria have more potential for survival. Their merit does not diminish with time and technological advance, for they

7-2 *Egyptian wall decoration from Traditions II Collection of wallpapers. This classic design, which has lasted through history, can be equally at home in a contemporary setting. Wall Trends International.*

7-3 *June Schwarcz. The interior of this enameled bowl was inspired by the shell of a turtle. Courtesy of June Schwarcz.*

7-4 *William Morris,* The Trellis, *1925. Wallpaper in the style of an 1862 design. Printed from woodblocks. A flower and bird pattern interwoven through a trellis repeated for wallpaper. Courtesy of the Cooper-Hewitt Museum of Design, Smithsonian Institution, New York.*

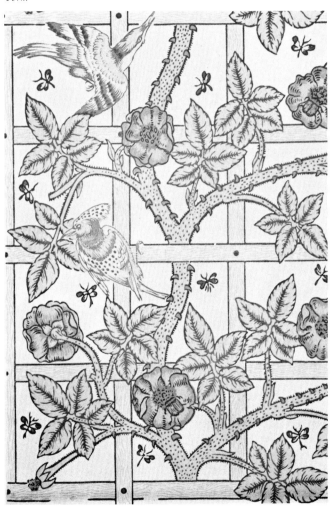

7-5 *Grant Wood.* American Gothic, *1930, oil on beaverboard, 29⅞ x 24⅞". Man interprets nature— man himself. The painting certainly qualifies as expressive. Unity and rhythm result from the repetition of spirelike vertical lines. Courtesy of The Art Institute of Chicago.*

7-6 *The "Whirlpool." Spiral nebula in Canes Venatici, whose form is often repeated in both nature and man-made design, as in Samuel Ayres's* Whirlpool Vase, *Vincent van Gogh's* Starry Night, *Chinese bronze ceremonial vessels, and Maori wood sculptures. Photograph from the Hale Observatories.*

so numerous that only a selected few can be cited to show that continuity exists and that the values in design for one age can persist in others.

Continuity in Art, Sculpture, and Architecture

Architecture has been called the great mother art. Sheltering abodes have continuously expressed man. As

7-7 *Samuel Ayres.* Whirlpool Vase, *height 14½ ". Steuben Glass.*

lean-to in order to provide for family expansion, to the building of related structural wings, and later the addition of the breezeway with connecting garage.

Le Corbusier built a multiple dwelling house in Marseilles, France, between 1947 and 1952, which had a pillar foundation (*pilotis*) with free circulation space

7-9 *Victor Horta. Staircase of the Tassel House, 1893, Brussels, Belgium. Collection, The Museum of Modern Art, New York.*

7-8 *"Favrile" glass vases, Louis Comfort Tiffany, New York, 1848–1933. Man interprets nature and then expresses himself in available materials. Unity and rhythm in this glass result from repetition of line and shape. Collection, The Metropolitan Museum of Art, New York.*

Frank Lloyd Wright observed: "Architecture is man's sense of himself embodied in a world of his own. As the man is, so will his buildings be." Looking back historically, one finds both the post-and-lintel and the simple truss construction, which are engineering methods for space containment, employed by the Greeks, Romans, English, and the early settlers in America. These constructive devices have continuously provided Americans with their most prevalent type of shelter. The well-proportioned and flexible colonial design has allowed for modifications, from adding a simple

7-10 *Piet Mondrian,* Composition, *1925, oil on canvas, 15⅞ x 12⅝". Notice* de Stijl *design of lines bypassing lines and the spatial relations. Collection, The Museum of Modern Art, New York.*

on the ground floor. He was using the same principle of construction as the neolithic man who built his house on stilts along a riverbank in about 12,000 B.C. Another kind of continuity in architectural design can be illustrated by Victor Horta's balustrade, developed circa 1895–1900, for a residence in Brussels. It reflects the Art Nouveau linear quality drawn from Japanese woodcuts of the seventeenth and eighteenth centuries. In the 1960s Art Nouveau had a renewed appeal for use in fabric design, glassware, wallpaper, and poster art.

There has been continuing use of *de Stijl* devices. *De*

7-11 *Charles Eames. Façade of Eames's home, in Venice, California. Machine-fabricated parts can create beauty, as in this textural composition. Courtesy of Charles Eames.*

Stijl was a group formed in the Netherlands in 1917 that took its name from the Dutch periodical *de Stijl,* meaning "The Style." Its design was characterized by simple angular treatments inspired by the simplicity and linear composition of Japanese architecture. Its influence is evident in the paintings of Piet Mondrian and the architecture of Frank Lloyd Wright and Mies van der Rohe. The facade of Charles Eames's California home is reminiscent of *de Stijl.* In the 1960s Yves St. Laurent used a similar configuration of line and form for dress design. In recent years, home furnishings have also been designed with emphasis upon the angularity of the cube and the rectangle, much as in *de Stijl* and Bauhaus design.

7-12 *Mies van der Rohe. Farnsworth House, Illinois. The design parallels the simplicity of Mondrian. The utility core is in the center of the plan, with space flowing freely around it. Hedrich-Blessing photograph.*

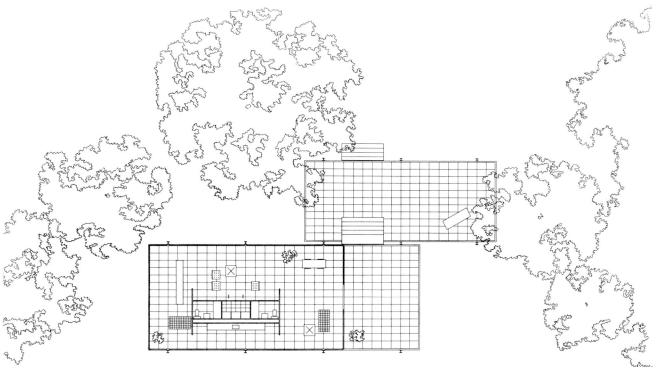

7-13 *Mies van der Rohe. Floor plan of Farnsworth House. Note the simplicity of the furniture arangement which follows the basic structural form of the architecture. Hedrich-Blessing photograph.*

95

Design of Ancient Cultures

Ancient cultures whose furnishings seem dateless include the Chinese and Japanese. Their designs have proved extremely viable, scarcely needing any adaption to blend with the décor of various periods. The mandarin chair of the Chinese has retained its exotic beauty through the centuries. The Oriental splat-back chair, with its yoke top rail, later simplified to a horseshoe curve, appealed to designers of the Queen Anne and Georgian periods as well as to Hans Wegner, two centuries later. The low table of the Chinese, looking as

7-14 *Hans Wegner. A contemporary chair (1944) inspired by an ancient Chinese design. Fritz Hansen, Inc., New York.*

7-15 *A hand-crafted re-creation of a Greek klismos chair in walnut with leather thongs, taken from a design on a lekythos of mid-5th-century B.C. "I tried to recapture the spirit that made them timeless." T. H. Robsjohn-Gibbings for Saridis of Athens.*

though it were sculptured from a single wooden member, can readily be combined with both the ancient and new. The Japanese have created beautiful chests in which fine woods, lacquered finishes, and distinctive metalwork continue to provide textures that satisfy.

Another constant in design is the Oriental rug. Brought from India, Persia, China, Japan, Turkey, and Afghanistan, antique rugs remain treasured heirlooms. They complement contemporary furnishings as readily as they do traditional interiors, for their use requires only sufficient background space and restraint of pattern in other areas. Other timeless *objets d'art* include Oriental paintings; Persian miniatures; and ceramics, glass, and metal wares from the Near and Far East.

Greek Design

The design of chairs can serve as an index to civilizations. Chairs are man's tool for sitting, relaxing, traveling, dining, working, studying, and sleeping. Their designs are acknowledged as expressive of social values.

One of the oldest classic chairs is the Greek *klismos*. Its splayed legs and graceful back-arm curvature were incorporated in furniture design of various periods, including the French Empire, English Regency, and American Federal. T. H. Robsjohn-Gibbings, who traveled widely in Greece in order to study the furnishings depicted in ceramics, statuary, and architecture, developed furniture that was based upon Greek forms. He demonstrated that one can take the simplicity and refined proportions from the design of an ancient era, translate that design into contemporary materials, combine these elements with excellent workmanship, and achieve a product that is equally satisfying today.

Spanish Design

Spanish design, influenced by the Moorish invasion of Spain in the eighth century with its subsequent imposition of Arabic design elements, coordinates well with today's interiors because its abstract contours harmonize with the geometry of the contemporary. The perennial appeal of Spanish design lies in the interplay of textures—deeply carved wood, stucco walls, glazed tiles, iron grillwork, and leather upholstery. Mexican design, which is of Spanish derivation, has a similar appeal. The popularity of Mediterranean furnishings,

7-16 *Greek kylix of black-glazed terra cotta, 5th century B.C., width 5¼". Compare the structural simplicity of its design with that of contemporary hotel saucepans. The Metropolitan Museum of Art, New York.*

7-17 *Hotel saucepans of stainless steel. Collection, The Museum of Modern Art, New York.*

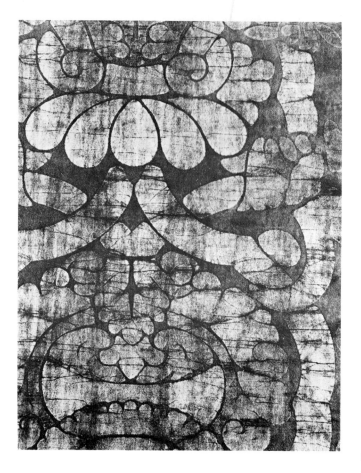

7-18 Conquistador, *a design in velvet adapted from a Spanish colonial motif. Jack Lenor Larsen Inc.*

which incorporate many of these elements, is a response to forms and textures that remain pleasing to man.

In the area of housing, some architects are re-examining the traditional central placement of a house as though it were a handkerchief on a lawn, and are proposing that the atrium plans of Spain, the Mediterranean, and Mexico provide a better solution to land usage. In past times, row housing with dwellings that shared common walls used to be associated with Old World and early American tenement living. Today the aesthetic of row housing is being re-evaluated, and the solid wall front, which opens unexpectedly upon inner vistas of garden and perimeter walls facing a central courtyard, has won fresh consideration for its unifying potential upon exterior design and for the pleasures and privacy provided by a central patio.

French Design

Louis XV furnishings with their soft curves and pleasing proportions are used in interiors to this day, and are referred to as French Provincial. Those of Louis XVI, with a straighter classical line, have a continuity with the Roman furnishings excavated in Pompeii, evidence of man's continuous delight in a return to things classical. These are used in interiors where an air of graciousness is desired. Adaptions of Empire furnishings are similarly employed because their wooden frames provide a pleasing sculptural quality.

English Design

The vitality of European Gothic design was recognized by William Morris and other nineteenth-century craftsmen and architects. Today the vertical lines so typical of Gothic style are being used not only in furnishings but in architecture, particularly that of the Japanese architect Minoru Yamasaki.

Other lasting English designs are the Queen Anne and the Georgian, which are renowned for their pleasing proportions and traditional refinement. The total design concept of Robert Adam, in which he integrated the architecture, interior design, and furnishings of the late Georgian period, found a new expression in the 1960s with designers such as American Milo Baughman, who created "total atmospheres" in which all the elements —materials, color, fabrics, and furniture—were coordinated to produce a controlled total concept. Even English Victorian design, long out of favor because of the surfeit of differing styles that were employed, has been reassessed and found to have elements of survival value.

American Design

During the first quarter of the eighteenth century, a provincial type of chair was produced in England, which was known as the Windsor, or captain's, chair. Made by English wheelwrights adept at bending rims and turning spokes, the Windsor became known as "the chair that went to sea." This spoked chair, whether in the wheelhouse, on the captain's quarterdeck, or in the parlor, suggested simplicity, dignity, and comfort. Transported to America, it became a perennial favorite in homes with a domestic air and served as a prototype for designers.

Other chairs of similar genre were the Brewster, Carver, and ladder-back chairs. The ladder-back chair was designed to a high level of artistry by the Shakers, a religious sect in eighteenth-century New England, who were dedicated to simplicity and worked in the folk art tradition. Their religious philosophy supported restraint, which was reflected in furniture design without turnings, applied decoration, veneers, or carvings. Today, though the Shakers are almost extinct as a religious group, they have left us a design legacy of integrity of

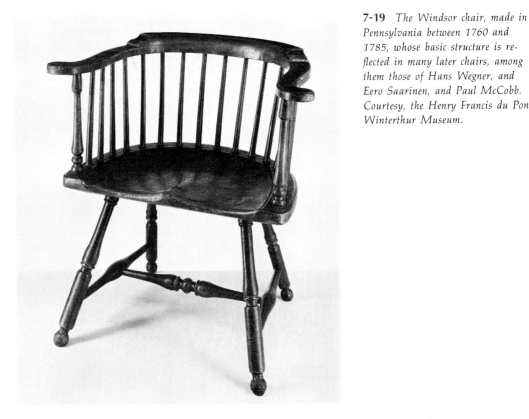

7-19 *The Windsor chair, made in Pennsylvania between 1760 and 1785, whose basic structure is reflected in many later chairs, among them those of Hans Wegner, and Eero Saarinen, and Paul McCobb. Courtesy, the Henry Francis du Pont Winterthur Museum.*

purpose and respect for materials. Beauty resulting from order, modesty, and economy is evident in their solidly built dwellings and meetinghouses, in their drawers, cupboards, and cooking arches built integrally into interiors, and in their great stone barns and mills.

8 Contributions of the Far East and Africa

Those of us who know not the secret of properly regulating our own existence on this tumultuous sea of foolish troubles which we call life are constantly in a state of misery while vainly trying to appear happy and contented. We stagger in the attempt to keep our moral equilibrium, and see forerunners of the tempest in every cloud that floats on the horizon. Yet there is joy and beauty in the roll of the billows as they sweep onward, toward eternity. Why not enter into their spirit, or, like Lieh Tsu, ride upon the hurricane itself? He only who has lived with the beautiful can die beautifully.[1]

Since the journeys and tales of Marco Polo aroused Western imaginations in the fourteenth century, the Far Eastern cultures have held a fascination for the West. In the seventeenth century the British East India Company and the *Companie des Indes* of France began importing quantities of silks, pottery, porcelain, wallpapers, and ivories from the Orient. As Eastern culture was disseminated into the Western world, new appreciations in design developed. Love for anything Oriental led to the creation of *chinoiseries*—designs for wall panels, fabrics, furniture, and screens in which Chinese motifs (mandarins, pagodas, parasols, and foliage) were given free and fanciful interpretations.

The Chinese civilization, from which the Europeans drew their chief design inspiration, was an ancient and highly developed one. The greatest bronze culture the world has ever known flowered during the Shang and Chou dynasties in China, beginning in 1523 B.C. Even at that early time bronze was being cast by the lost-wax process. By A.D. 618–908, the T'ang Dynasty of China was exporting designs to India, Persia, Arabia, the South Seas, and Japan.

---

[1] Kakuzo Okakura, *The Book of Tea* (New York: Dover, 1964), p. 63.

Because the contributions of the Far East are so varied and numerous, some of the outstanding ones are presented under these headings: philosophical systems and their influence upon Japanese design, the Japanese concept of beauty, known as *shibui*, and Eastern contributions to design.

Philosophical Systems and Their Influence on Japanese Design

Continuity in Oriental design was provided by Buddhism, which originated in India in the fifth century and made its impact upon the design of all Asian countries. The art of China reflected Indian Buddhism; the art of Korea reflected that of China; and the art of Japan reflected both Korea and China. Yet in no country were there persistent facsimiles. Designs were adapted and innovations made that eventually contributed to artistic discreteness.

Two philosophical systems that influenced Japanese design were the Shinto and the Zen Buddhist. In Shinto philosophy, anything recognizable as a thing has an essence, a divine vital force. This pantheistic attitude led to a great awareness of nature and love for natural objects, as expressed, for example, in these lines by a fifteenth-century poet:

> Manifesting Itself
> Is the awe-evoking Deity
> Even in a single leaf
> Or the weakest grass blade.
> Urabe-No-Kanekuni

The early art influenced by Buddhism was characterized by a high degree of refinement, which appealed to intellectual and aristocratic court circles. With the

8-1 Chinoiserie *print, red on white, copperplate print on cotton, design in the manner of famed* chinoiserie *designer Pillement, French, 18th century. Collection, The Metropolitan Museum of Art, New York.*

introduction of the Zen sect into Japan in the twelfth century, the emphasis upon intellectualism typical of the older, Chinese culture was replaced by attention to the spontaneous. In design, Zen stood for the astringent, strong, and economical. Modesty and understatement were valued.

The Japanese warrior class and the Zen monks are credited with developing the *shoin* style of architecture, characterized by strength, simplicity, precision, and freedom from clutter. It had many features that the West eventually adopted, including integration of the indoors

8-2 *Utamaro, Kitagawa (1753–1806). A young Japanese woman in the process of dressmaking, while a cat playfully entangles himself in the cloth. Collection, The Metropolitan Museum of Art, New York.*

the curved lines and the delicate shapes. A highly stylized set of shapes, *mon*, are based on geometric floral or animal forms. It is the *mon* that provides the motif that is transposed to fabric design and furniture design. The aesthetic differences from the East can be attributed not only to Buddhism but to all the religions of the Orient. Oriental thought, as expressed in several major religious traditions, suggests a different visual aesthetic than one finds in the Western world.

In the Paris International Exhibit of 1937, Junzo Sakokura, who had worked with Le Corbusier in France and was familiar with the technique of erecting structures on *pilotis*, provided a pavillion supported on steel posts whose framework constituted the exterior's only decorativeness. The exterior appearance paralleled the handling of the bare wooden framework in the interior of a typical Japanese home; thus, Western technology was combined with Japanese tradition. Startling at the time, this method has become common.

Frank Lloyd Wright was one architect who incorporated numerous elements of Oriental construction to provide for special domestic needs. He valued space moving through form with continuous flexibility. Among his adaptations was a handling of sliding partitions as separate panels under a continuous molding, thus making possible continuity in interior space. Further destruction of the box ("any box is more a coffin for the human spirit than an inspiration", as he put it) was accomplished by integrating the interior with the exterior by using sliding transparent doors. The provision of transitional areas to be shared by both interior and exterior, such as the terrace and the deck, allowed for spatial flow between inner and outer zones. The importance of oneness between the in and the out was expressed by Japanese philosopher Lzao Wou-Ki in a dialogue: "The purpose of a door is to enable one to get in and out. If you shut the door, nature is outside and we are inside. There is a difference. But if you leave the door open, there is no longer any difference."[2]

with the outdoors by treating the garden or patio as additional rooms; indirect lighting; the use of structural elements as decorations; provision of sliding doors or panels for interpenetration of space; and the directness of post and beam construction.

The outstanding principles of design that emerge from Eastern art are unity, balance, rhythm, and repetition. The elements of design that are most obvious are

[2]Claude Roy, *Zao Wou-Ki* (New York: Grove, 1960), p. 60.

However, Wright was not alone in incorporating elements of Japanese design. Walter Gropius strongly advised his students: "Young architects, forget Rome, go to Japan." Many have. Some of the finest architectural achievements in the world today show respect for the principles of Oriental design. It is well to keep in mind that the Japanese emulate the designs of China, but those continuous feudal wars that rent China and Japan's closed-door policy made access difficult for Westerners. Fortunately, many Chinese art works were brought back by Chinese travelers preserved in the Shoso in repositories. Today the world acknowledges the Chinese as our first great landscape painters. The Chinese were the fountainhead and source of ideas of Oriental art. The ideas moved to Korea, which was a separate Mongol civilization. The Koreans filtered and added dimensions and changed the art that had originated in China. The Koreans are known for their action, process, and spontaneity. They felt free to change and adapt Chinese design and were not tied to the Chinese tradition. The Japanese, in contrast, held precision, perfection, and fidelity to ancient tradition as aesthetic values.

The Japanese Concept of Beauty

Over the centuries, a standard of beauty had developed in Japan that the Japanese describe as *Shibui,* an adjective, and *Shibusa,* a noun, to denote the quintessence of beauty. *Shibusa* provides another set of criteria for determining good design. Dr. Lennox Tierney, Professor of Art History, University of Utah, and Curator of Japanese Art, San Diego Art Museum, has over the years translated the seven basic principles of Zen:

Fukinsei: Asymmetry or dissymmetry; suggesting things that are irregular. It is the opposite of geometric circles or squares.

Kanso: Simplicity; without gaudiness, not heavy or gross; clean, neat and fresh yet reserved, frank and truthful; not ornate.

Koko: Austerity, maturity, reduction to bare bones, basic essentials; lack of sensuousness. It refers to things that are aged, weathered, venerable.

Shizen: Naturalness, artlessness, absence of pretense and artificiality. It does not mean raw nature; it involves full creative intent but should not be forced. It is unself-consciousness; it is true naturalness that is a negation of the naive and accidental.

Yugen: Subtly profound; suggestion rather than total revelation; things not wholly revealed but partly hidden from view; shadow and darkness. Hence, *Yugen* involves the shadow areas of the garden.

Datsuzoku: Unworldliness; freedom from use of "compasses and rulers," freedom from worldly attachments, bondage and restrictive laws. It involves transcendence of conventional usage. It is often a surprise element or an astonishing characteristic.

Seijaku: Quietness, solitude, calmness, and silence, opposite of disturbance. In the Orient there is a saying that "Stillness is activity." This characteristic is strongly felt in a Japanese garden.[3]

The tea masters of Japan, Lennox Tierney feels, are the art critics for Japan. They are in contrast to art critics in the Western world who are not actively involved in the arts. In Japan art critics emphasize the nonvicarious experience, which is environmental and all-encompassing. The tea ceremony began in the fifteenth century and has been valued as a "social sacrament." It expresses the cult of the humble. The elements of rusticity are appreciated by many today. The materials used are characterized by the *Sabi,* a quality indicating nonassertiveness by the new, and by the *Wabi,* reticent simplicity. The stoneware tea pot that is used is usually brownish or muted in color to contrast with the greenness of the tea. The base

---

[3]Unpublished paper by Lennox Tierney, October 30, 1980.

must feel quietly rough in the palm, and the lip must be designed not to drip. Other utensils are selected for their textural contrast: an iron water kettle, a bamboo water dipper and whisk for mixing powdered tea and water, a lacquer caddy for tea, and a silk napkin to catch moisture. The guests sit on tatami mats of rice straw facing the *tokonoma,* a niche. The post that joins this niche to the interior wall is roughhewn and unfinished, the only treatment it has received is the stripping off of the outer bark. A vital part of the ceremony consists of appreciating the textures. Poetry is often hung on the wall and becomes part of the meditative quality of the surroundings and the experience of the tea ceremony.

Eastern Contributions to Design

Calligraphy

According to Lennox Tierney, calligraphy—that is, writing with a brush—maintains the art aesthetic in the East. He theorizes that a culture that maintains the brush for writing maintains the art aesthetic and that a culture that used the pen for writing becomes literate.

In Asian countries, calligraphy is considered art. It takes various forms. It can be precise and formal, slow-moving and semicursive, or rhythmic and organic, paralleling the movements of plants and animals. The "grass" or *So* script is a swiftly flowing line movement in which the brush dashes on from character to character in an unbroken rhythm.

The same cursive swiftness of *So* script is seen in

8-3 *Sesshū.* Landscape, *hanging scroll, "flung" ink on paper, Japanese, Muromachi period, height 30⅜". Sesshū was the greatest artist in Japan during the latter part of the 15th century; he developed* haboku, *the splashing style of painting. The calligraphy in the upper right-hand corner expresses the spiritualism resident in mountains. Eugene Fuller Memorial Collection, Seattle Art Museum.*

haboku, the flung ink style of painting developed by Sesshū, a Japanese Zen priest, who traveled to China in 1468 to gain mastery of the brush. The intent of *haboku* is to provide a direct and convincing impact through brush strokes that are as brusque as a sword cut, as immediate as intuition. If the painting is sensed in the Zen way, both visually and intuitively, one should feel emptied and calm. In a sense, Jackson Pollock was a *haboku* artist of the twentieth century with his tachist method of hurling paint on canvas. The abstract expressionists and action painters of the 1950s worked in a similar manner.

Woodblocks

The wood-block art of Japan, known as *ukiyo-e,* was enthusiastically supported by mid-nineteenth century Western painters: Van Gogh, Toulouse-Lautrec, Paul Klee, Matisse, Cézanne, and by Art Nouveau designers. The flat linear surfaces of rhythmical and decorative quality—simple, abstract, and colorful, with their pictorial content drawn from daily living—excited European artists, long accustomed to the formal academic approach to painting. It brought them a vision more suited to their temperament and served as a catalyst for furthering their creativity.

Architecture and Fine Arts

The influence of Japanese color prints and calligraphic expression was strongly felt in Western architecture and the decorative arts. Among those deeply influenced was Henry van de Velde. Like Hector Guimard, van de Velde was a multifaceted artist who designed not only the interior of a drawing room, but a dark velvet gown with an appliquéd back panel that matched the design of the Japanese panels on a door. Like the Japanese he designed asymmetrically, whether it was his desk or a cup and saucer.

Victor Horta also sought to unify man's environment through design. His door handles, which are remarkably

8-4 *Victor Horta. The door handle of the Hotel Solvay in Brussels, 1895–1900, is admirably designed for grasping action. Bolts become part of the total design. The rhythms are those characteristic of the Far Far East and Art Nouveau. Collection, The Museum of Modern Art, New York.*

8-6 *Georges Braque. The Table, 1928, oil on canvas, 70¾ x 28¾". As in Oriental design, one sees both an aerial and side profile, as though viewing a tilted table from above, a technique also employed by Picasso. Collection, The Museum of Modern Art, New York.*

8-5 *Panel: Taoist paradise, Canton-blue silk embroidered in colored silks in various stitches, Chinese, 12th century. Once again one travels gradually upward from the waterfalls of earth below to the high horizon with its translucent clouds of paradise. Collection, The Metropolitan Museum of Art, New York.*

suited to the grasping action of the hand, reflect Japanese influence. He developed the potential of iron in an interior of a residence in Brussels, making it flow like a vine. By leaving the hinges exposed in its construction, he showed how structure can contribute decoratively to a composition.

With respect to depicting space, the Oriental artist contributed varying means. Oriental landscapes are aerial views from which one can scan the grandeur of nature. One finds that Cézanne, Picasso, and Braque also used a similar technique and painted as though looking down upon a table of still objects. Foregrounds tend to be tilted and backgrounds flattened. The Japanese flaunt space. Through built-in alcoves, sliding panels, and tatami floor mats, objects are minimized and spaciousness lends serenity.

Time and movement are also important elements in both Chinese and Japanese design. These are particularly evident in their landscape designs. One walks through an Oriental landscape in time. The pathway lies around a bend—the view is never completely seen at one time. A short distance takes time to traverse because one may be distracted en route by a rock or stream. Space is also experienced psychologically in the design of an Oriental scroll. One walks through the design, arrested here and there by a stone, a flowering bough, a hillock—until one reaches the far and high horizon. The journey has been long, with time the fourth dimension.

The Chinese are recognized as our first great landscape painters, whose work the Japanese studied assiduously. To show Chinese sensitivity and preoccupation with nature, Louise Hackney wrote with respect to the bamboo, an inexhaustible subject:

The artist painted it in rain and sunshine, in wind and in calm. He studied the bamboo so assiduously and analyzed its leaves so minutely—as he did indeed every subject he portrayed—that he knew how they spread joyously in fine weather, hung down despondently in the rain, crossed one another confusedly in a wind, and pointed vigorously upward

8-7 *Mask of the Bwami secret society. Congo (Leopoldville), Warega. African art has inspired many contemporary artists. The style is often labeled primitive; visual forms are strong and decorative elements are applied to the human form. Collection, The Metropolitan Museum of Art, New York.*

in the dew of early morning. He portrayed it in small groups or groves, carrying a connotation of happiness—as single trees, or merely cross sections of its leaves and branches.[4]

The Japanese also made other significant contributions to floral and landscape design, which are considered in later chapters. But whatever their design medium, one finds the characteristics of naturalness, subtlety, simplicity, and understatement to be present.

African Design

As nations emerge from obscurity, their influence is felt not only politically but aesthetically. Though Africa has no designers of international reputation, in the 1960s

[4]Louise Wallace Hackney, *Guideposts to Chinese Painting* (Boston: Houghton Mifflin, 1929), p. 114.

8-8 *Nigerian print, mid-20th century, cassava paste resist, dyed in indigo. Courtesy of the Cooper-Hewitt Museum of Decorative Arts and Design, Smithsonian Institution, New York.*

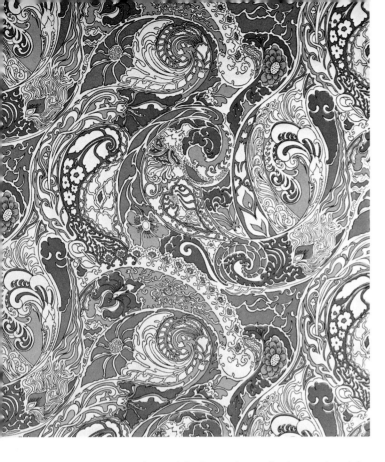

8-9 *Nils Anderson.* **Bagdad.** *A wallpaper design in a paisley tradition that has been used throughout much Western history. The paisley patterns were woven into paisley shawls in Paisley, Scotland, during the 1800s. They were adapted from fabrics previously produced in Kashmir, India. The Nils Anderson Studios, Inc., New York.*

8-10 **Tree of Life,** *cotton hanging, Indian, 18th century. This tree, rich in imagery, has been a continuous design inspiration through the centuries. Courtesy of the Cooper-Hewitt Museum of Decorative Arts and Design, Smithsonian Institution, New York.*

the African mood was felt throughout the home furnishings industry. Emphasis on the sensual elements of design was realized through "fondling" fabrics—pelts were used for rugs and pillows, and man-made fibers suggested not only animal textures but also their colors. Strong contrasts in values and colors were employed and designs were geometrically bold. The natural textures associated with the jungle were expressed through leather and rattan furniture. Even the plants used in interior design were not low but jungle- or tree-sized. In housing design, Jack Lenor Larsen was so inspired by the applied design on Ndebele homes in villages near Pretoria, South Africa, that he built himself a three-hut compound decorated with similar wall motifs at New Hampton, New York.

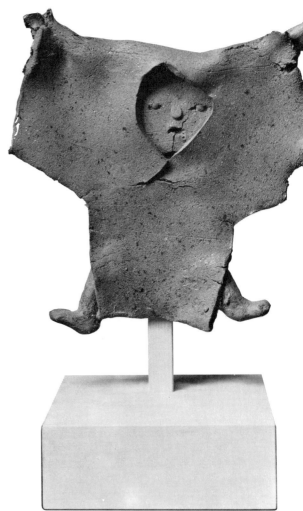

8-12 *Haniwa Woman. Japanese, mid-tumulus period, 3rd to 6th century, orange-red earthenware, height 30⅛". Haniwa means "clay cylinders." These were found at the margins of burial mounds, presumably to check soil erosion and to protect the mound from harm. Eugene Fuller Memorial Collection, Seattle Art Museum.*

8-13 *Isamu Noguchi. Big Boy, 1952, Karatsu ware, height 7⅞". Note the similarity in directness of treatment to the Haniwa woman. Collection, The Museum of Modern Art, New York.*

8-11 The Eavesdropper (*also called The Bathers*), *Persian miniature, late 16th century. In Middle Eastern and Far Eastern design, there is always a far horizon from which one looks down as though scanning the landscape from above. Collection, The Metropolitan Museum of Art, New York.*

Other Design Expressions

Designs from the Far East and Africa have influenced Western design style in interior spaces. They are expressions of cultures quite different from those of the Western world; yet, the timelessness of good design is appreciated around the world.

The primitive, the ancient, and folk cultures of the world have produced objects of art of perennial interest that are quite at home in twentieth-century interiors. Peruvian and Guatemalan textiles and fabrics with embroiderylike quality, African masks and wood sculptures, Mexican tinware, Indian paisley and the tree-of-life motif, Javanese batiks, the bark cloth of Hawaii and the South Seas, Persian miniatures, Spanish ceramic tile, Oaxacan pottery, and Japanese terra cotta are but a few examples of such designs.

That design can be for all time was pointed up concisely by John Gerald in *California Home* of September, 1966: "Timeless designs, old and new, depend upon constants: proportion, excellent workmanship, beautiful materials. That's why they endure and give us endless pleasure." Thus interior design may be consistent in the furnishings used from a certain period, or greater individuality can result from an eclectic selection of elements from various periods that are harmonious in form, color, texture, and spirit. Coordinating the whole becomes a creative adventure, as emphasis is placed upon visual relationships rather than styles.

9 Contributions of the United States

The American while adhering closely to his utilitarian and economical principles, has unwittingly, in some objects to which his heart equally with his hand has been devoted, developed a degree of beauty in them. . . . His clipper-ships, fire-engines, locomotives, and some of his machinery and tools combine that equilibrium of lines, proportions, and masses, which is among the fundamental causes of abstract beauty. Their success in producing broad general effects out of a few simple elements, and of admirable adaptations of means to ends, as nature evolves beauty out of the common and practical, covers these things with a certain atmosphere of poetry, and is an indication of what may happen to the rest of his work when he puts into it an equal amount of heart and knowledge.

James Jackson Jarvis (1864)

Immigrant Designers

A major contribution to design by the United States, that of outstanding functional and economical mass production, can be attributed in part to the country's traditional concepts of freedom and equality. Respect for individuals has not only provided a climate favorable to the creativity of native designers, but has encouraged the emigration of creative personnel from other lands. Where man has found his native climate limited to some extent, he has explored America.

The United States has benefited from such creative geniuses as Walter Gropius, who in 1937 became chairman of the Harvard School of Architecture. His approach to design influenced many students, who in turn have made their impact upon others. To the Harvard staff Gropius invited the German Marcel Breuer, who as a student had dreamed of an "invisible chair of compressed air," and whose chairs made of steel, aluminum, plastics, and bent and molded wood influenced designer Charles Eames, a native American. Eames has also acknowledged that he, as well as his contemporaries, drew much inspiration from the Scandinavian designer Alvar Aalto.

As early as 1933, the United States became home to Josef Albers, first at Black Mountain College, North Carolina, and later as chairman of the Art Department of Yale University. Since Bauhaus days Albers has made contributions to visual articulation. Through multiple series of paintings of squares nested within other squares, he demonstrated the relativity of values and intensities of colors, whose appearance is dependent upon their surroundings. His wife, Anni Albers, also born in Germany, not only made significant contributions to the art of weaving, but has been an articulate spokesman for the values of hand-craftsmanship in developing such rich human qualities as adventurousness, initiative, courage, and satisfactions from the creation of forms.

In 1938, Mies van der Rohe also left his native Germany to become head of the School of Architecture at the Illinois Institute of Technology. His clarity of structure, daring use of steel and glass, and exquisite feeling for space, proportion, and materials have become part of the tradition of modern architecture. There is little of nature's expression in his work; instead there are man-made materials exposed in logical structure to create beauty.

T. H. Robsjohn-Gibbings, born in England, arrived on the American scene in 1929 to create "total environments" of furniture and interiors. Through extensive writing he propounded his tenet that simplicity is beauty. As an antidote to the angular austerity of the Bauhaus, he invited a return to romanticism and the lyrically curved line. Through his chair, in a collection manufactured by the Widdicomb Company in 1946, he demonstrated his sense for refined proportions and considered restraint. His appreciation of Tiffany glass encouraged re-examination of the designs of Art Nouveau for the warmth of spirit they can contribute to interiors. Robsjohn-Gibbings also showed how emphasis and subordination can be achieved in interiors: "One color and one fabric throughout an entire house is the most successful way to create a beautiful background for individuals, their clothes, and their furniture."

Eliel Saarinen of Finland left his native shores in 1923 to design the forty school buildings and faculty houses for Cranbrook Academy in Bloomfield Hills, Michigan. He then imported the Danish sculptor Carl Milles, who served at Cranbrook for twenty-one years, creating some of America's most outstanding sculptures. By Saarinen's emigration, he brought to America his son Eero, who designed not only the St. Louis National Memorial noted in Chapter 2, but also such notable architectural structures as the Dulles Airport in Washington, D.C.; the striking CBS building in New York City; the General Motors Technical Center at Warren, Michigan; and the J. F. Kennedy air terminal in New York City.

Native Designers

On the home front, the United States has had its own great architects: among them Louis Sullivan, Frank Lloyd Wright, and Buckminster Fuller. Sullivan, as we have seen, provided the answer to the expanded city's spatial problem—build upward, build skyscrapers.

Wright's contribution has already been indicated: his organic approach to architecture, in which buildings take on the characteristics of growth patterns of natural organic life directed by intrinsic internal pressures. The needs and activities of a family determine the spaces to be created, the interior and exterior spaces are integrated, and the materials used reinforce the natural

9-1 *Frank Lloyd Wright.* Taliesen West. *The architecture is in harmony with the cactus, sand, stone, and spirit of the southwestern United States. Notice the texture of the stone combined with the wood and the architecture and how the light and shadow create their own unique supplement to the total design. Photograph by Julius Schulmann.*

elements of the environment—wood, brick, stucco, and stone.

Frank Lloyd Wright

Sullivan's dictum "Form follows function" has by now become a cliché in the design world. Wright, an apprentice of Sullivan, incorporated both it and Sulli-van's concept of organic architecture into his own work. Whereas Sullivan built civic and business edifices of classic formality for urban areas, Wright moved out to the prairies where his structures could flow with the terrain in dynamic asymmetrical space relationships. In his building of residential houses he brought the public to an intense awareness of Sullivan's theory made manifest.

Wright also educated the public to the architectural values he supported through his prolific and dramatic writing. His extension of space through the use of the diagonal line; the reciprocal flow of interior spaces; the integration of interiors with exterior and site; his low structures and extended roof lines; his use of identical

9-2 *Frank Lloyd Wright. Interior of Taliesin, East Wisconsin. Note the textural combination of wood, stone, Coromandel screen, Oriental rug, window glass (in the shape of the peace symbol), ceramics, leaves, metal, and painted Oriental scroll. Hedrich-Blessing photograph.*

113

exterior and interior wall surfaces; his breaking down of the box to spill out over the landscape—all these are now standard design elements. When determining spaces he also took into consideration the needs and activities of those who would inhabit a shelter. It is interesting to note that another nature lover, Emerson, once quoted a statement of the poet Coleridge that sounds like Wright himself speaking: "The organic form . . . is innate; it shapes, as it develops itself from within."

Wright saw the machine as a tool with which to make buildings into forms as organic as nature—skyscrapers like trees, houses like caves, and a museum like a shell.

In designing these, he utilized the natural materials of a locale—wood, fieldstone, volcanic rock, slate. His concept of organic design he considered not only as an aesthetic but as an ethic. It was based upon an inner need that dictated outer expression, just as an organism in nature such as a plant must grow from inner forces that impel it outward.

Mies van der Rohe

Wright's philosophy contrasts with that of the German architect Mies van der Rohe, who regarded iron and glass as independent elements, capable of expressing their own forms and needing the support of no other materials. He was a highly rational designer who believed in designing open spaces of impersonal character in which the individual can adjust his functions. To him structure had its own universal value, independent of any particularized function, site, climate, and materials. Materials were only important as they made possible a type of structure. But for the architectural composite he spared no perfection of detail, for to him, "God is in the details."

Of those materials that could aid in realizing his vision, iron and glass had existed as potential architectural elements as early as the middle of the nineteenth century, but it was Mies van der Rohe who gave them status. Instead of using glass as a precious ornament set into the stone façade of a building to serve as an adjunct to stone, he made glass, supported by geometric membranes of steel, into *the* architecture. The only decorativeness was integral, created by rectilinear mullions of steel. Thus by exposing the structural elements he created beauty. His interiors were open geometric

9-3 *Mies van der Rohe. 860 Lake Shore Drive Apartments, Chicago. "Greek temples, Roman basilicas, and medieval cathedrals are significant to us as creations of a whole epoch rather than as works of individual architects. Who asks for the names of these builders?"—A statement expressive of the philosophy of Mies van der Rohe. Hedrich-Blessing photograph.*

spaces, and the individual could wear his houses and structures like spectacles—to look out at the larger world. The nude interiors of unabashed simplicity permitted the furnishings to be seen dramatically. The simplicity and nonflowing quality of Mies furniture and buildings have an intensity of their own. With their clean-cut precise lines, they become a resting object of beauty. Beauty in this case is a product of simplicity, order, proportion, and texture.

R. Buckminster Fuller and Charles Eames

Buckminster Fuller, a dynamic designer, has dropped geodesic domes over the world like descending parachutes. They can be found in Southeast Asia, behind the Iron Curtain, and in Northern Alaska. At Montreal's "Expo 67," a dome housed the American exhibitions. Considered the most economical form to enclose the maximum of space, the dome bypasses conventional architectural plans by being built upon a system of triangles in contiguous tension with each other. The resulting strength of the structure proves the principle that the whole is greater than the sum of the parts. Fuller has predicted that in time an individual will be able to move to any geographical location and call by phone to have a dome delivered. Individuality in design will be made possible through personalized interiors.

The importing of architects, coupled with native genius and an economy of plenty in a land abundantly supplied with natural resources, has led to American pre-eminence both in modern architecture and to the production of industrial products for the home. Manufacturers and engineers in the United States have developed a machine craftsmanship and technical virtuosity that are admired the world over. The high standard of living, the wide range of consumer goods, and the buying potential of the masses are no doubt desirable. However, in some cases, designing for mass consumption has led to a leveling of taste by manufacturers who have placed profit above aesthetics.

9-4 *Buckminster Fuller. Carbondale Fuller Dome seen from outside through gate. Courtesy Buckminster Fuller and Leco Photo Service, Inc., New York.*

9-5 *Charles Eames. Exterior of the Eames house in Venice, California. Notice how machine-made components can be compatible in a setting of eucalyptus trees. Photograph by Julius Shulman.*

When the machine does produce aesthetically, as in the case of Charles Eames's fiberglass chair, it produces both quantitatively and qualitatively well so that many can enjoy the advantage. Eames's home in Pacific Palisades near Santa Monica also illustrates his exploration of the potential of the machine to create beauty. Its factory-made frame—trusses, sash, corrugated siding, and roof deck—is of painted steel. The gridlike wall sections are filled with prefabricated panels of clear and opaque glass and stucco. Across the black stucco panels white tension rods cross for further geometry of design. The house demonstrates the beauty and efficiency possible in machine-produced design when it is handled sensitively by an artist.

Today, good design is being encouraged by many industries and business for the interiors of their own plants. Just as the artists of Michelangelo's time were taken under the patronage of ruling families, so today corporations increasingly are playing the role of art patron. A notable example is the Columbia Broadcasting System building in New York, conceived by Eero Saarinen, who died shortly after completing his plans for the building in 1961. Every detail was superintended and passed upon by the management—from the surface texture of the granite and the gray tint of the window glass to the design of ashtrays and numbers on elevator buttons. Florence Knoll Bassett, former designer for Knoll Associates, devised the over-all furnishing plan, even to the selection of plants placed throughout the building to complement the color schemes of the rooms; and to the development of a year-round program for ordering flowers by hue and variety in order to preserve the unity of each color area. Contemporary paintings and sculpture were selected for hallways and for the offices of all employees. This is only one instance of an industry of the United States contributing to the psychology of environment. It has been recognized that visual surroundings that reflect concern for order and beauty can contribute to employees' morale, which in turn can lead to greater productivity.

The Look of Design

The over-all pattern of design in America today reflects the design of the machine itself. Just as there was beauty in the hand-crafted tools of yesterday—the ploughshare, the sickle, and the ax—so do the tools of today have a distinctive beauty. The revolution in power from push-and-pull, which required human and animal energy, to jet propulsion has enormously changed and influenced the design of man-made household articles, whose forms may now suggest the dynamics of precision and speed. They are often as clean and sculptured in appearance as a bullet-shaped jet engine. Likewise, just as new materials such as aluminum, plastic, and

9-6 *The forms of this German machinery exhibited at "Expo '70" are very rhythmic through repetition and suggest forms for sculpture. Photograph by Helen M. Evans.*

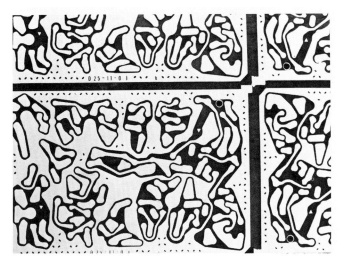

9-7 Printed Circuit, *1958, plastic sheet with copper foil bound to surface, 7⅜″ by 5″. Notice the similarity to Louis Gross's sculpture. Collection, The Museum of Modern Art, New York.*

stainless steel are introduced by industry for its machinery, so do manufacturers explore new contemporary materials for household utensils.

Take another example. The use of tubes in today's computers and electronic "brains" requires the arrangement of wires, tubes, and other elements. The same intricacy of design is reflected in some contemporary painting and in fabric and wallpaper design. The random design of a printed circuit board for TV sets, in which solder covers the thin copper foils, looks remarkably like a Mark Tobey painting. The patterns of a memory bank are repeated in contemporary variations in weave construction. The stainless-steel wares made by Ekco, the utensils coated with Teflon, the design of flatware—all have the calculated simple design of a machine. The vision of the artist appears to be unconsciously shaped to some extent by his environment.

To maintain an uncluttered look, George Nelson designed comprehensive storage units. In 1945, he devised the storage wall system, a flexible modular system of interchangeable sectional components, which treated

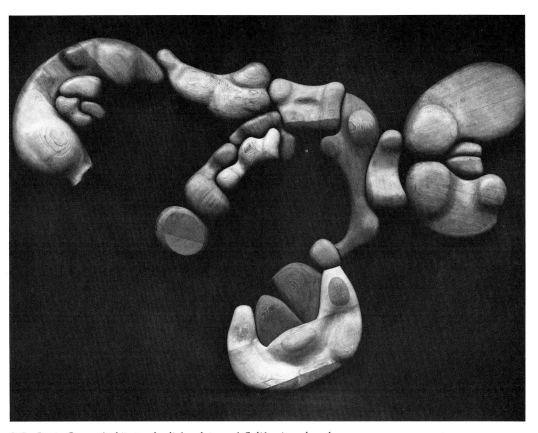

9-8 *Louis Gross. Architectural relief sculpture of California redwood, height 7′ 6″, length 11′ 6″. Biomorphic forms in sculpture parallel the variety in unity characteristic of nature's organization. The design suggests that inspiration may have derived from an appreciation of anatomy or from such contemporary man-made elements as the printed circuit.* California Design IX, *Pasadena Art Museum.*

storage as a decorative element. Television, stereo equipment, desk, and supplies were enclosed in a grid pattern. Open shelves were designed to house decorative accessories such as sculpture, ceramics, folk art, baskets of fruit, and books. In the years that have passed, the storage wall has become a standard system for organizing our multiple everyday objects into pleasing patterns.

Contribution of Artists and Sculptors

The experimental attitude fostered by the American climate has led to a breadth of artistic expression. David Smith brought the practical skill of welding to the production of sculpture, which he composed from such machine-made elements as wheels, disks, pipes, fittings, fenders, pistons, and rods. This welded linear sculpture departed from conventional sculpture in that it embraced rather than displaced space. It has led to further

9-9 *Robert Motherwell.* Elegy to the Spanish Republic XXXIV. *Albright-Knox Art Gallery, Buffalo, New York—Gift of Seymour H. Knox.*

9-10 *Benjamin F. Cunningham.* Equivocation, 1964. *Synthetic polymer paint on composition, 26 x 26". Because of sequential changes in spacing and size of units, a flat form becomes optically multi-faceted in depth with projecting and receding planes. Collection, The Museum of Modern Art, New York.*

appreciation of the design elements of machinery as having aesthetic vitality for artistic expression.

Willem de Kooning, Mark Rothko, Franz Kline, Robert Motherwell, and others opened up canvas to bursts of emotive and subjective representation. They were preceded, of course, by Jackson Pollock who had already hurled and dripped paint on lengths of canvas. In the 1950s the classical value placed upon form bounded by line almost vanished. Forcefully handled color became the dominant element. It was used to produced vibrations in depth and to evoke emotions within the viewer. The painting itself would evolve during the creative process with "a life of its own." By mid-century, energy,

acceleration through space, and the gamut of man's conscious and subconscious tensions had to a great extent displaced the more external aspects of familiar objects, which had previously been the subjects for painting. Interest now lay in developing a sense of kinesthesia, described by Hans Hoffman as "the push and pull on the picture plane." Artists' images were not static and limited, but active and inclusive.

On the surface of things, it looked so easy to the layman that many consumers had the courage to turn producer and the Sunday painter became an American phenomenon. Abstract expressionism and the controversy it provoked contributed toward greater aesthetic consciousness through active participation, too.

9-11 *Detail of a woven coverlet. Wool, United States, circa 1850. Note the similarity between this design and the one in 9-10; the dates of the designs span 100 years. The optical illusion created by rectangles of varying sizes is one of movement and volume. Collection, Cooper-Hewitt Museum of Design, Smithsonian Institution, New York.*

9-12 *Sam Maloof. Hand-finished walnut chairs with leather seats talking to each other. Structural dowels contribute to the design. Note the massing of chairs for a focal area and how the lines of the arms of the outer chairs direct the eye toward the center. Courtesy of Sam Maloof.*

After the Russian space advance, great pressure was felt in many educational institutions to place more emphasis on mathematics and science. In art, this more scientific approach was reflected in optical art, in which illusory visual effects were obtained through the use of line, color, and form. Interest became focused on the physics of vision. So pervasive a movement was optical art that it was reflected in several areas of design, including textiles, wallpaper, and fashions.

The artist also responded to American commercialism by turning to the images of a culture in which advertising, neons, cinema and graphic arts, photography, and a wide range of mundane objects assault our vision from dawn through darkness. Pop art was a frank confrontation with our daily environment, which included man-made objects. Artists Andy Warhol, Roy Lichtenstein, Jasper Johns, and many others translated this environment into visual drama. The banality of objects and their repetitive appearance were converted into design form. Popular visual forms were dramatized by the photographic technique of the blow-up. The simplest object, such as a plastic baby's bottle, the commonest object, such as the Coca-Cola bottle, and the most mundane object, such as a hamburger, all became subject matter for art. The range also included movie queens and plumbing fixtures, which were treated in a depersonalized and objective way, as opposed to the emotionally laden abstract expressionism. The entire environment of man became content for art, and increased our awareness of the blatancy of design that is so common in our daily lives.

Action and movement became not only a function of color and line direction but also of experienced fact. Alexander Calder had popularized the mobile, the moving art form that changes its spatial configurations with the air's currents. The new patterns of movement were constructions, some engineered by battery or electricity to present a changing kaleidoscope of hues, sounds, or movements. Thus movement, formerly expressed only psychologically by the elements of art, became an actuality.

Comprehensive design was further realized by the increased use of paper for disposable commodities. One could entertain in paper attire with paper accessories, plates, napkins, and tablecloths. A "Kleenex" culture, with emphasis on the expendable and disposable, was born. Man, who has long been trained and disciplined to save and preserve objects, now had to learn to throw them away. Because much of the design applied to paper articles was intended to be eye-catching and to satisfy an immediate need, it tended to be colorful and often flamboyant.

Textile Innovators

No greater advance has been made in industry in the United States than in the textile field, both in its structural and applied design areas. The new synthetic and the older natural fibers have been woven into blends and combinations of yarns, or used singly in combinations of colors and textures that at one time could only be achieved through hand-weaving techniques.

Dorothy Liebes became famed for the "Liebes look," for combining in her designs "a light, a dark, and a bright" (intense) color relationship. She greatly enriched weavings of age-old materials—cotton, wool, linen, and silk—by adding such original elements as jute, reed, and other grasses; strands of cellophane, ribbon, chenille, and plastic; lucite and variegated beads; copper and other metallic wires. She is credited with reintroducing metallic thread into weaving. Metallic yarns had been used for thousands of years, but being made of pure metal (lamé) they had always had the disadvantage of being heavy and brittle, and they tarnished easily. The new metallic yarns produced by American industry after 1946 were made by laminating a layer of aluminum foil between two sheets of plastic film. The sheets could be silvery, like aluminum, or colored before the laminating process with the metallic hues of red, gold, blue, green,

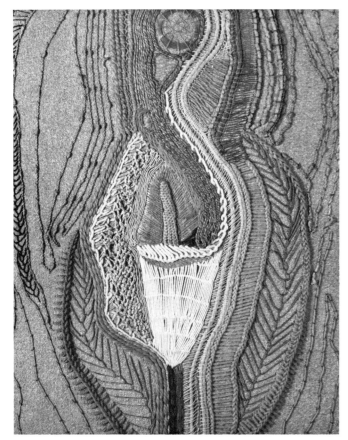

9-14 *Frances Robinson. Panel, black silk, machine-embroidered in white, pale blue, brown, and purple, 1962. Completed entirely by the sewing machine. Frances Robinson was a pioneer in showing how the machine can create beauty in stitchery. Courtesy of the Cooper-Hewitt Museum of Decorative Arts and Design, Smithsonian Institution, New York.*

9-15 *Jack Lenor Larsen. Waterlilies, from the Baedeker Collection. This fabric is described by his company as "Velvet batik, printed by means of a new method owned and operated by Jack Lenor Larsen Inc. The fine tracery caused by cracking the wax adds a patinalike chiaroscuro so that color burns through like glowing embers." The textile can be used for upholstery, drapery, or as wall covering. Jack Lenor Larsen Inc.*

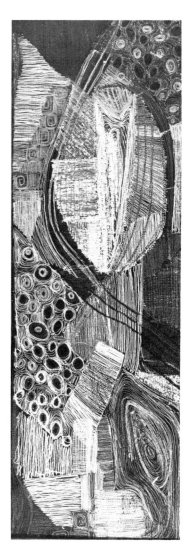

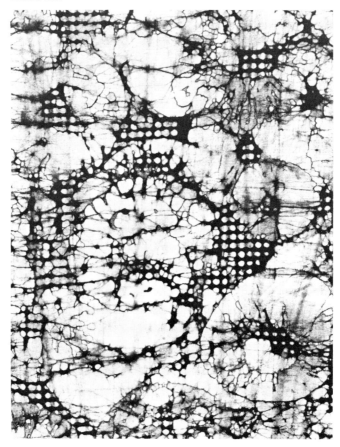

9-13 *Mariska Karasz.* Calla Lily, *panel, 1951. Courtesy of the Cooper-Hewitt Museum of Decorative Arts and Design, Smithsonian Institution, New York.*

and copper. The laminate could then be split into strips, $\frac{1}{120}$- to $\frac{1}{4}$-inch in width. Using these decorative elements, Dorothy Liebes wove exotic fabrics, directing her major effort to machine-produced fabrics for draperies and upholstery. Her range of products included rugs and blinds woven of many materials, colors, and textures. She introduced woven aluminum strips into window treatments for industry. She is also credited with developing correlation boards, which consist of carpet samples with matching or correlated fabrics, leather, wall coverings, and paint. Through these, the consumer can see how colors and textures will relate in a room.

Mariska Karasz, a needlework artist and designer, pionered in the art of creative embroidery in the 1950s. Seeing the advantage of incorporating a range of natural and man-made elements in embroideries, she used burlap, paper, wool, linen, and nylon netting as background surfaces, upon which she applied crewel stitchery. Instead of being limited to traditional embroidery floss—cotton, rayon, and woolen yarns—she utilized such elements as electric wiring, shoelaces, fishline, variegated hand-spun wools, hair, nylon cord, and string. Moss, shells, fish flies, beads, glass, and plastic disks were often interwoven for further textural enrichment. She also helped promote coordinated design in homes. In the Florida Pace Setter House of 1951, she embroidered a rug with a coral pattern, relating the interior to the exterior with its nearby coral reefs. Bathroom towels were also decorated with the coral motif. Subsequently, other designers became interested in coordinated design.

Not only did hand stitchery become popular, but the sewing machine, with its wide repertoire of stitchery variations, was found useful in the production of fine art. The machine has the capacity to produce visual effects that the hand cannot achieve.

An excellent designer of printed and woven fabrics is Alexander Girard. He has frequently incorporated into his work varied hues common to the design of other cultures, such as those of Mexico and Latin America. Through his varied use of color we have learned that magenta, cerise, pink, and orange can be beautiful in combination; so can greens, blues, and purples. As a result of exposure to a wide range of hues and unusual color combinations, our appreciation of color and design has been increased.

Another contemporary, Jack Lenor Larson, has also designed woven and printed fabrics; he has perfected manufacturing processes that duplicate the Javanese batik process of dying with wax resist. His designs can be applied to fabrics with multiple fiber content and varying textures—from heavy to light weights. After traveling to such diverse places as Africa, the Andes, and the Orient, Larson was inspired to produce warm, exotic designs. Fiber art has reached a level of excellence in the United States. Fiber Ten, a group of superb fiber artists in Pittsburgh, uses fiber as a medium for portraits, sculpture, and wall hangings in an infinite variety of textures. The creativity of Eloise Piper has raised batik to the level of fine art in America. Carol Lubove-Klein spins, dyes, and weaves fiber into garments that are functional works of art. Fiber, once the woman's work for clothing and linens, is now a powerful means of expression for creative artists throughout the United States.

Contributions of the Last Century 10

Contributions of Architects

Among the strongest influences on the modern design of articles for everyday use are those of the architect. He has not only created the visual evidence of impressive structures, but also has made declarations of philosophy that acquaint the public with his intentions.

The architect's role in designing furnishings is not new. For centuries before the Middle Ages, the carpenter was the craftsman who constructed not only dwellings, ships, and stockades around forts, but the necessary furnishings for these. Benches, chests, settles, and bedsteads were designed in relationship to the walls against which they were placed. Even after specialization evolved, the partnership between the furnishings and the walls persisted throughout the medieval period and the Renaissance that followed it. Furniture, though

sometimes crude, was structured through necessity and had an appeal resulting from man's honest use of materials.

With the Industrial Revolution of the eighteenth century, the machine replaced the human hand and simultaneously introduced uniformity and precision. Often using inferior materials, it produced in quantity forms and decoration that were imitative of hand processes. The workman, a commodity like the wood or leather upon which he labored, was deprived of any meaningful relationship to his work, because his judgment, imagination, and creative faculties were no longer enlisted. The machine itself was not regarded by most industrialists as a tool that could make a distinct contribution to design.

In England, however, as early as 1753, some responsible producers were directing their attention to the need for consideration of design in the manufacture of products. The Royal Society of Arts, orginally entitled The Society for the Encouragement of Arts, Manufactures, and Commerce, took as its objective the improvement of materials, techniques, and design. It held exhibitions of inventions and offered prizes for industrial products, called art manufactures, as well as for arts and crafts.

The Arts and Crafts Movement

In the nineteenth century among the voices of concern for preservation of the standards of excellence associated with the crafts was that of William Morris, who is credited with revolutionizing Victorian taste and being the first potent force in laying the foundations of modern design. He despised the ugly products produced by industry and took, as his ideal, art that should be made "by the people, for the people, as a joy to the maker and user." Although he never practiced as an architect, his architectural concepts gave unity and coherence to English craft activities of the later nineteenth century and influenced architects whose concern with the decorative or applied arts of wallpaper, furniture, fabrics, and stained glass paralleled their concern with the design of buildings. Though the Bauhaus on the European continent was the climax of the endeavor to integrate art and industry, Walter Gropius acknowledged the role played by Morris, and John Ruskin who inspired him, in initiating the concept of utility coupled with beauty for articles of everyday use:

Ruskin and Morris strove to find a means of reuniting the world of art with the world of work. Toward the end of the century their lead was followed by Van de Velde, Olbrich, Behrens, and others on the Continent.[1]

[1] Quoted in Ray Watkinson, *William Morris As Designer* (New York: Reinhold, 1967), p. 7.

Morris was at the center of the Arts and Crafts Movement when it developed in the 1880s and 1890s. Its participants' concern was with the role of man in an industrial world. They strongly believed that the designer should have equal status with the "fine" artist and architect, that art hallows work, and that all men are entitled to well-designed products. As the voice of the movement, Morris held many advanced ideas about the uses of the machine. He felt that its wise use would enable a man to work only four hours a day to produce his goods, thereby providing him with discretionary time for craft activities, which Morris considered "a vital mode of human activity and, what is more, a necessary underpinning for human freedom and autonomy." He believed that crafts are necessary to enrich human life and that they can serve as a pilot for fresh technological achievement. These tenets are just as valid today.

Among the designers of Morris's time was Owen Jones, an architect, who developed lithographs of the characteristic ornaments of most of the world's cultures, which he published in a handbook for architects and decorators entitled *The Grammar of Ornament.* In it he spelled out thirty-seven propositions, or principles of design, for architecture and the decorative arts. Of these, the first proposition, "The decorative arts should arise from, and should be properly attendant upon, Architecture," illustrates the significant role of architecture. Proposition 13, "Flowers or other natural objects should not be used as ornaments, but conventional representations founded upon them," shows Jones to be a proponent of stylized design, preferring to simplify and extract the essential geometry from a form rather than to represent it naturally. Three of Jones's other propositions also have relevance today:

Proposition 5: Construction should be decorated. Decoration should never be purposely constructed.
Proposition 3: As Architecture, so all works of the Decorative Arts should possess fitness, proportion, harmony, the result of all which is repose.

Proposition 37: No improvement can take place in the Art of the present generation until all classes, Artists, Manufacturers, and the Public, are better educated in Art, and the existence of general principles is more fully recognized.[2]

Charles Voysey, another contemporary, also echoed Owen Jones's sentiments. He believed that to go to nature is to go to the fountainhead of design, but that living forms have to be subjected to an elaborate mental and subjective process of analysis and selection, and at times be reduced to mere symbols, before the completed design can have aesthetic merit.

Art Nouveau

The English Arts and Crafts Movement had an impact on the continents of Europe and North America. Architects were the first to see that, with a transformation of the means of production, man had new needs and adjustments to make that could not be accomplished in outdated enclosures and surroundings. In Europe's visual revolt against traditional design, many painters—among them Peter Behrens, Bruno Paul, and Henry van de Velde—became architects who turned their attention to comprehensive design, including the design of objects for daily use.

Belgian Henry van de Velde took the lead in establishing a movement known as Art Nouveau, a name given the style by Samuel Bing, who commissioned van de Velde to design the interiors and furniture for his art galleries in Paris. Art Nouveau was an experiment in bringing harmony of form into the industrial age and in finding a new expression suitable for the approach of a new century. Designers were sated with the tradi-

tional use of Greco-Roman motifs, weary of the "long masquerade in period dress" of the Victorian era:

What do we see on every side? Wallpapers which wound the eye; against them, ornate furniture which wounds the eye; at intervals, a gaudily draped bay which wounds the eye; and every spare nook and cranny is hung with plates of spinach with decorative borders which wound the eye. Let the eye come to terms with all this as best it can. (Art Décoratif, 1899, No. 7)

Or again: The subjects chosen to enliven the dining room wallpaper are enough to put anyone off his food. The knives, forks, and glassware testify to a long and careful search to discover ugly and inconvenient shapes. The plates are either adorned with little punning devices calculated to neuropathological symptoms, or colored patterns of flowers and fruit created by schoolgirls who were taught porcelain painting as a genteel accomplishment to be sandwiched in between their sketching class and the piano lessons. Around the drawing room and bedroom mantels are clocks and wall sconces of indefinite shape, beds like gondolas, couches and sofas like instruments of torture, imitation gold frames and cardboard rose paneling are contemplated with serene satisfaction by the rent-paying occupant before settling down to sleep in this delightful setting. (Gustave Geffroy, 1900)[3]

In trying to create a more appropriate setting for modern life, the artists abolished the symbols of period styles—caryatids, lions, garlands, gryphons, swans, laurel wreaths, eagles, frets, the egg-and-dart motif. In several European countries, the new design took many expressions, based upon a pronounced linear quality. Many designers used the forms of nature as a protection against imitation of historical designs, adopting the long sinuous botanical forms of flowers and vines and the biological forms of octopuses, beetles, butterflies, peacocks, and serpents. They abhorred the straight line, found joy in the curvilinear. As classical art was based on the rational, Art Nouveau valued the poetically sensual and irrational and so anticipated the mood of

[2]Quoted in ibid, p. 32.

[3]Quoted by Maurice Rheims, *The Flowering of Art Nouveau*, (New York: Abrams, 1967), p. 212.

10-1 *Carlo Zen, Italian. Desk, with mother-of-pearl and brass inlay, circa 1902. Courtesy of the Cooper-Hewitt Museum of Decorative Arts and Design, Smithsonian Institution, New York.*

10-2 *Louis Tiffany. Hand mirror with peacock motif combining silver, enamel, sapphires, circa 1900, length 10¼''. The peacock was a favorite informal motif of Art Nouveau designers. The cricket, in the other frame, has its own formal design potential. Collection, The Museum of Modern Art, New York.*

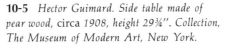

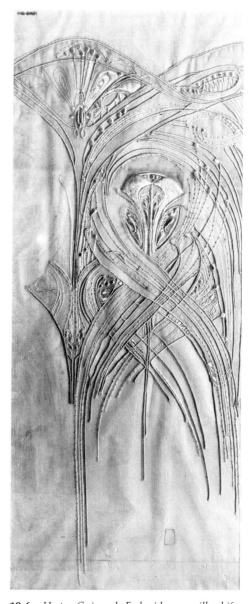

10-3 *Hector Guimard. Entrance gate to Paris subway station,* circa *1900, cast iron painted green with amber glass fixtures, height 15'. Collection, The Museum of Modern Art, New York.*

10-4 *Hector Guimard. Side chair of carved fruitwood, France, 1908. Courtesy of the Cooper-Hewitt Museum of Decorative Arts and Design, Smithsonian Institution, New York.*

10-5 *Hector Guimard. Side table made of pear wood,* circa *1908, height 29¾". Collection, The Museum of Modern Art, New York.*

10-6 *Hector Guimard. Embroidery on silk, chiffon, and net. Courtesy of the Cooper-Hewitt Museum of Decorative Arts and Design, Smithsonian Institution, New York.*

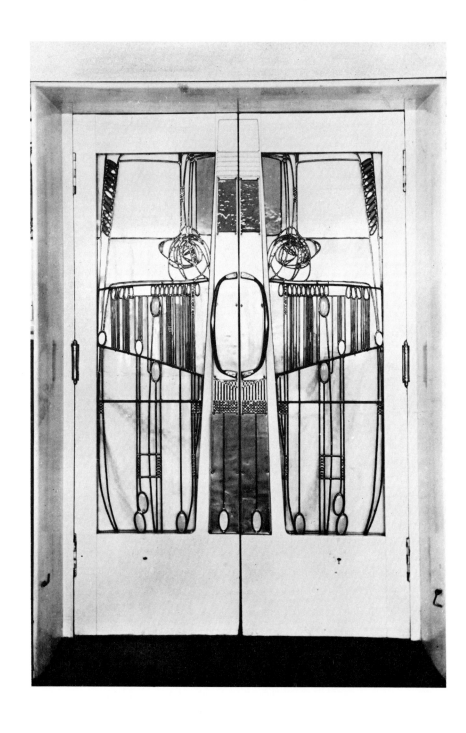

10-7 *Charles Rennie Mackintosh. Doors of leaded mirror glass in Miss Cranston's Willow Tea Room in Glasgow, Scotland. The University Art Collections, University of Glasgow, and Dalys, Glasgow.*

10-8 *Victor Horta. Van Eetvelde House, 1895, Brussels, Belgium. The union of glass with flowing iron membranes and supports suggests the realm of nature. Collection, The Museum of Modern Art, New York.*

Antoni Gaudí. Church of the Sagrada Familia, 1903–26, Barcelona, Spain. Gaudí borrowed from the High Victorian Gothic and used the native materials of Catalonia—ceramics, wrought iron, and stained glass. Collection, The Museum of Modern Art, New York.

surrealism. To insure the unity of all design, designers such as van de Velde and Hector Guimard designed comprehensively from exteriors to dress and embroidery.

In architecture, Art Nouveau took many directions. Among designers, the Scottish architect Charles Rennie Mackintosh, who built the Glasgow School of Art, had a strong feeling for linear network and spatial values, as can be seen in the slender uprights and elongated ovals set in the door that he designed for the Willow Tea Room in 1904. Their calculated proportions and restrained curves have continuous appeal and modernity. The Art Nouveau architects also recognized iron as both a decorative and structural material. The ease with which wrought iron could be bent and its ductility made it possible to create delicate stalklike filaments, in harmony with the spirit of the period. Art Nouveau is credited with being the first architectural expression to blend iron with glass aesthetically.

Among the most eccentric designers of the period was the Spaniard Antonio Gaudí. He experimented with a multitude of sculptural forms, creating fantastic architecture that did not reproduce nature literally, but suggested it metaphorically. In his first house, the Casa Vicens at Barcelona, built about 1880, he constructed a wrought-iron grille based on the design of palm fronds. His surrealistic quality, achieved through using metals and structural tile and cement stucco, constituted a definite break with former architecture. Later, Pier Nervi, Eric Mendelsohn, and Oscar Niemeyer would utilize molded and reinforced concrete, the major advance in twentieth-century architectural technology, to build sculpturally fluid forms.

Because the decorative curves of Art Nouveau were often on the surface and not structural, the movement was short-lived. However, it did lead to a harmony of design in all aspects of living, an appreciation of art as

10-10 Antoni Gaudí. Finial of a tower of the Sagrada Familia. Gaudí's use of mosaic with surrealistic overtones reflected his love of natural forms, which he converted into architectural stone analogies. Collection, The Museum of Modern Art, New York.

an integral part of life, and a heightened respect for craftmanship. It also led to a new cooperation between art and industry, with the Germans Peter Behrens and Richard Riemerschmid being recognized as the first *industrial designers,* as the term is now understood.

Thonet

There are a number of contemporary classics whose design quality entitles them to continued use and appreciation. By 1842, Austrian Michael Thonet, recognizing the inherent elasticity of wood, developed a steaming process whereby wood could be bent into curved forms to eliminate the necessity of joints and awkward construction. His inventiveness was preceded by the ancient Egyptians, who used bent plywood for mummy cases. Thonet's famous Vienna chair, designed in 1876, has been a longtime favorite for use in ice cream parlors and is still in production. This bent beechwood scroll chair of 1876—which in concept is very Art Nouveau—is still produced. A century after its appearance, this chair is still extremely popular in American interiors because it contributes an interesting variation of line to the angularity of other furnishings. By 1849 Thonet was considered the most important furniture designer in Austria and moved from Vienna to what is now Czechoslovakia. He built a new factory, whose structure, machines, and conveyor belt system he designed. In 1851, Thonet's furniture was displayed at the Crystal Palace in London.

10-11 *Michael Thonet. Reclining chaise of bent beechwood and caning, circa 1876. The strong curves contrast pleasingly with rectangular forms. Collection, The Museum of Modern Art, New York.*

10-12 *Michael Thonet. Armchair, left, circa 1870. Bent beechwood, height 31". This chair is still in popular use today.*
Michael Thonet. "Vienna" café chair, right, 1876, bent beechwood, 33½". Both, Collection, The Museum of Modern Art, New York.

The German *Werkbund*

In 1907, the German *Werkbund* was organized by industrialists and architects to improve the quality of Germany's industrial art. It was especially significant, for it paved the way for the later founding of the Bauhaus school. As in England, the German architects designed fabrics, wallpaper, glass, pottery, leather goods, and fur-

130

niture. The value placed upon common objects was emphasized by Adolf Loos, an Austrian architect, who admired the United States for its wholehearted adoption of the machine to produce articles for daily use. In his newspaper articles, written in the early twentieth century, he praised the new brand of humanism in America, which accorded significance to the functional design of everyday objects, such as spades and hammers, shoes and overalls. Walter Gropius, too, realized beauty of design in the mundane and taken-for-granted—the unproclaimed. He admired the American grain silo, describing it as possessing "monumental power," and as being "unacknowledged in majesty," on a par with the pyramids of Egypt.[4]

He himself devoted the same attention to the design of silver tablespoons and the door handles of mass-produced furniture that he bestowed upon buildings and railway cars. Objects do not have a hierarchy of status; the sincere designer has a democracy of vision.

The *de Stijl* Group

By the turn of the century the machine had made its impression on many artists and designers, in various countries, who were busy developing a new vision that would be consistent with machine precision. In Belgium, Theo van Doesburg led what came to be known as the *de Stijl* movement. The artists concerned were interested in creating a visual form that could be applicable to all the arts. Van Doesburg's painting *Rhythms of a Russian Dance* (1918) illustrated an organization of line, space, and form that had parallels in other visual expressions. One can see design relationships between it and George Vantongerloo's *Construction of Volume Relations*, 1921; the Gerrit Rietveld armchair, 1917; Frank

[4]James Marston Fitch, *Walter Gropius* (New York: Braziller, 1960), p. 21.

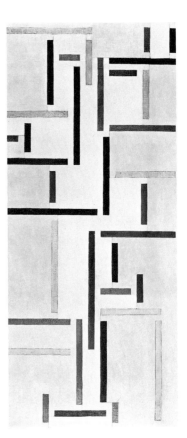

10-13 *Theo van Doesburg.* Rhythm of a Russian Dance, *1918, oil on canvas, 53½ x 24¼". van Doesburg's painting became the leitmotiv of* de Stijl, *recognized for unifying the diversity of arts. Collection, The Museum of Modern Art, New York.*

Lloyd Wright's Robie House, 1909 (Figure 4-22); and Mies van der Rohe's Farnsworth house, 1950 (Figure 7-12). In each of these there is evidence of *de Stijl* devices—asymmetry rather than axial balance, absence of a dominating point of interest to distribute the flow of movement over an entire area, and the bypassing of horizontal and vertical lines to extend space.

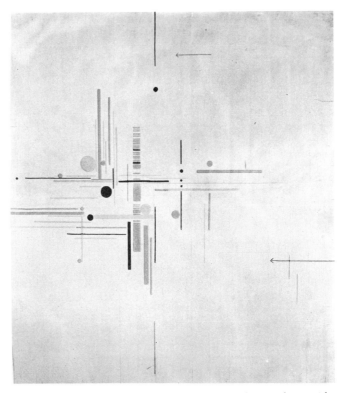

10-14 *Wallpaper, Germany, circa 1925. Planes bypass planes with well-planned distribution of spatial relations and color values. Courtesy of the Cooper-Hewitt Museum of Decorative Arts and Design, Smithsonian Institution, New York.*

10-15 *Georges Vantongerloo. Construction of Volume Relations, 1921, mahogany, height 16⅛". Collection, The Museum of Modern Art, New York.*

10-16 *Gerrit Rietveld. Armchair of painted wood, 1917. Collection, The Museum of Modern Art, New York.*

10-17 *Gunta Sharon-Stolzl. Tapestry of hand-woven black and white wool, silk, cotton, and metal thread, 1924, height 71". This hanging has a rich complexity of color values and spatial proportions. Collection, The Museum of Modern Art, New York.*

The Bauhaus and Walter Gropius

The German architect Walter Gropius is identified both with the leadership of the Bauhaus, a school of design founded in Weimar, Germany, in 1919, and as a leading spokesman for the social responsibilities of the architect. Gropius always stressed that "the satisfaction of emotional requirements is just as important as that of the material requirements and to which the goal of a new conception of space is more important than mere austerity and functional perfection." The intent of the Bauhaus was to promote interaction between art and industry, accepting the machine as a reality of the day and comprehensively exploring its potential in all fields of design: architecture and furniture; product design and ceramics; fabrics; painting; sculpture; graphics, typography, and advertising; photography, cinema, stagecraft, and ballet. All these branches were to be coordinated into a schematic whole, with architecture as the great unifier.

Bauhaus philosophy was opposed to "art for art's sake," and fostered the belief that every artist is first of all a craftsman. Its manifesto articulated its purposes:

1. "The Bauhaus believes the machine to be our modern medium of design and seeks to come to terms with it."
2. All design must recognize this fact of life and distill a new set of esthetic criteria from it. Such a process would, for architecture, lead to "clear, organic [form] whose inner logic will be radiant and naked, unencumbered by lying façades and trickeries."
3. The Bauhaus teaches "the common citizenship of all forms of creative work and their logical interdependence upon one another."
4. The scale and complexity of modern problems necessitates collaborative design. "Any industrially produced object is the result of countless experiments, of long systematic research." The design school must recognize this and equip the student with "the common basis on which many individuals are able to create together a superior unit of work."
5. The education of the designer "must include a thorough, practical manual training in workshops actively engaged in production, coupled with sound theoretical instruction in the laws of design."[5]

The Bauhaus designers placed great value on the machine ethic, which reflected the spirit of the century. This ethic was instrumental in creating a radical and unfamiliar beauty. Functionalism, simplicity, elimination of superfluous ornament, and clarity of uninterrupted planes characterized Bauhaus design. Whereas the architect and designer had formerly served the needs of the royal and affluent, who often preferred intricate ostentation, Bauhaus design was a minimal expression and an ode to democracy. Its designers had a social philosophy that mass production should serve the many and place emphasis upon the equality of human life. Buildings were not to be conceived of as monuments but as "receptacles for the flow of life which they have to serve."[6] The architect was to bring "inert materials to life by relating them to the human being. Thus conceived, his creation is an act of love."[7] Gropius's practicality is evident in the fact that he was a pioneer in making time-and-motion studies of labor-saving devices; these applied both to the design of a house and to the cabinetry inside it.

Bauhaus design, though hand-designed, had the quiet, impersonal, and efficient look of the machine. In time, this austerity failed to satisfy the needs of those designers who wished to incorporate their own subjective values and aesthetics. Today, designs produced by the Bauhaus seem to many people to be too geometrically angular, too functionally pure, too abstractly impersonal. Yet one must admire the courage with which the designers, in the face of much opposition from conservative resistance, cut the umbilical cords of the

[5] Fitch, op. cit., pp. 11–12.
[6] Ibid, p. 22.
[7] Ibid., p. 26.

past and held true to their determination to produce an original unadulterated design for this century.

The visual format they developed has served as a catalyst to designers of many nations. It freed them to discard old, outmoded expressions, to create forms consistent with their time, and to design more comprehensively for men's needs. It ranked the design of cutlery on a par with that of cars. As inheritors, we daily experience benefits from Bauhaus innovations:

the design of hand-crafted objects that could serve as prototypes for industrial mass production because of their simple geometric shapes.

the recognition by industrial management of the value of aesthetics in the manufacture of all articles of daily use, whether large or small; the employment of industrial designers.

freedom in the exterior design of our houses from the domination of an impressive façade.

freedom in the design of houses from massive load-bearing interior and exterior walls—instead, the use of steel and reinforced concrete to create taut walls, ribboned with glass, which permits a close linkage of interiors with exteriors and increases spaciousness and brightness.

the architectonic use of furniture—cabinets and storage built into walls; spacious interiors with furniture designed in partnership with the wall.

furniture of weightless appearance, employing tubular steel frames and structural elements under controlled tension; free-standing furniture designed to be seen from all sides—hence, the use of furniture as sculpture and furniture as walls or room dividers.

emphasis on functional and integral decorative design. According to Walter Gropius, "Beauty can only be achieved through complete harmony between technical-functional purpose and the proportions of the forms employed."

The Bauhaus purity of design led to uncluttered interiors of luxurious spaciousness. There is therapy and tranquillity in the simplicity and constraint of Bauhaus furnishings when contrasted with decorative saturation. Design quality can come from deliberately exposing structural members in the construction of an object. Decorativeness can also result from the interplay of spaces, created by horizontals and verticals used to support shelves, cabinets, or windows. Chairs can gain decorativeness from the texture of the material employed, such as wood grain, or through the process of manufacture, such as the interweaving of cane reeds to form structural elements.

The minimal design of the early twenties came to be known as the "International Look," because it crossed oceans and found expression in many lands. But no country need adopt ideas unconditionally, and by midcentury most designers had looked again to their own local and indigenous traditions. The "less is more"

10-18 *Ludwig Miles van der Rohe. House, Berlin Building Exposition, Berlin. 1931. Living Room. Photograph courtesy of Mies van der Rohe Archive, The Museum of Modern Art, New York.*

ideation of the Bauhaus under Mies van der Rohe's direction was questioned, and national aesthetics passed from adolescence into adulthood, with nations taking from the past and from other countries only those qualities that enhanced their own heritage and present.

The world had benefited from the Bauhaus, both rationally and aesthetically. Because of it, the consumer and his values has come into prominent consideration. Man must design for man—which means every man. How he sits, walks, stands, works, sleeps, and performs are equally important. His objects are tools or equipment to help him accomplish these activities with greater ease, grace, and dignity. As such, they should serve and free, not dominate, him. Bauhaus designers, by emphasizing functionalism, were being humane.

In 1933, the Bauhaus, which had been forced to move to Dessau and then to Berlin, was closed because of Nazi oppression. Though discontinued as a school, it continued to live as an ideational force and aesthetic reality through the work of the great designers who were imbued with its values or who had used it as a foil to test their ideas. Its designers and students migrated to other countries, where they continued to transmit Bauhaus values and to develop their creative talents. Bauhaus designers had shown man how to live with the machine. They had introduced a culture of the idealized commonplace. With these benefits it would seem men ought to be able to live comfortably with themselves and with others.

Le Corbusier and Others

Another pioneer who stimulated controversy in design was the Swiss architect-sculptor-painter Le Corbusier. He had some of the arrogance of Mies van der Rohe with respect to nature. He believed that man is man because he is civilized, "de-natural," and acculturated. Man has created himself; he has brought him-

10-19 *Le Corbusier, Villa Savoye, 1929–31, Poissy-sur-Seine, France. Collection, The Museum of Modern Art, New York.*

self up by his bootstraps and by conscious effort has achieved high levels of thought and discernment. On the other hand, nature *is*—it doesn't strive. Hence Le Corbusier did not support Wright's or the Japanese inclination to let nature penetrate the house so completely that one is not particularly aware of its definition. For Le Corbusier the house should assert man *in the face of* nature. It should exist as a superior reality, which imparts to the location a higher value and order than it previously held before man modified it.

His most commonly quoted expression, that the house is "a machine to live in," depicts Le Corbusier as a rigid rationalist supporting uncompromising functionalism. This is the hard view, taken out of context, for he also believed that the aim of architecture is to "establish emotional relationships out of raw materials." In his interest in Everyman he realized the machine would have to be enlisted if satisfactory housing were

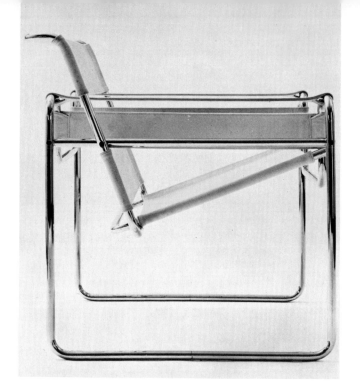

10-20 *Marcel Breuer. Chrome-plated steel tubular armchair with canvas, 1925. This chair is still in production and use. Knoll International, New York.*

look is not pleasant for those who value diversity, but Le Corbusier's proposed expression is realistic when viewed as an organized visual and spatial plan of a kind that our present haphazard development of urban structure ignores. In time, the value of Le Corbusier's vision may be more fully appreciated as the pressures upon us mount because of our own thoughtlessness, as evidenced in bulldozed landscapes, in the urban polyglot of forms, in the inconvenience that we endure in order to secure services for our daily functions, and in the random preservation of what is still undesecrated in nature's beauty.

Other architects have bridged science and art, designing consistently in the spirit of their time and utilizing the technology available. The Italian architect Pier Nervi used reinforced concrete and steel to create sculpturesque architecture that has both a highly structural and a highly poetic ornamental quality. In a similar fashion, Oscar Niemeyer, designing in Brazil, used the lyricism of hyperbolic-parabolic and spherical forms to create exciting contours in architecture. (See Figures 6-11 and 6-12.) Other architects who valued the softening of the contours of the original Bauhaus designs included Eero Saarinen, Marcel Breuer, Paul Rudolph, Minoru Yamasaki, and Eric Mendelsohn. Although Richard Neutra held to the straight line and the right angles of the post-and-beam construction, in his plot and sight plans he forsook them, recognizing that nature does not know a straight line.

Marcel Breuer's armchair of 1925, in which a chrome-plated steel tubing frame was combined with canvas, established a clear-cut distinction between the bearer and the borne and served as a prototype for much of the tubular steel furniture that has become so popular for dinette sets and lawn furniture. Breuer's chair carries an air of modernity, as does Mies van der Rohes's Barcelona chair of 1929. (See Figure 17-10.)

Eero Saarinen, son of architect Eliel, was born in Finland and came to the United States in 1923. He designed architecture and furnishings of outstanding beauty and individuality. (See Figure 23-6.)

to be the heritage of all. But he also valued nature. For materials, he used not only concrete but natural elements—wood, stone, and slate. These he enjoyed dramatizing by ordering them in calculated mathematical structures. His roofs and terraces not only permitted man to enjoy the sun, but served to structure and frame the landscape. He is most famed for his multiple-dwelling plans with their pillar foundations, *pilotis,* which project the house skyward and free the ground for its inhabitants' enjoyment of vegetation; for his roof solarium-terraces that bring people into contact with the sun; and for his glass walls, which further trap and distribute solar light.

He once proposed a utopian dwelling for universal man—a vertical city with apartments opening onto interior streets and all the human functions being cared for in a single complex dwelling, from automatic laundries to kindergartens, gymnasiums, and theaters. This future

Scandinavia

There are several factors that have contributed to the role of Scandinavian countries as design leaders. Recognizing those factors may help to understand the dynamics involved in producing high levels of national design.

The Scandinavians live close to nature. Sea and forest

10-21 *Alvar Aalto. The coffee table is of laminated birch plywood and plate glass, 17½" high. The stool of laminated ash plywood and leather is 18½" high. Both follow nature's accommodation to strain. Note that a branch becomes broader for reinforcement at the point where it takes its own life direction, remaining one with, but divergent from, the mother trunk. Collection, The Museum of Modern Art, New York.*

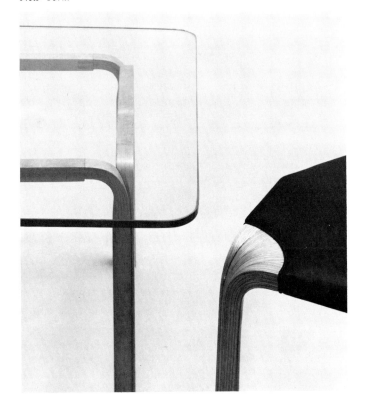

10-22 *Arne Jacobsen, architect. The Swan Chair. Fritz Hansen Inc., New York.*

are never far away. Because the people live intimately with nature, they incorporate its essence into their work. The sculptured leg of Alvar Aalto's chair (a trunk), where it branches to meet the seat (the boughs), parallels the organic growth of a tree.

Not only does communication with nature contribute to Scandinavian design; so also does communication with man. In Scandinavia, this exchange takes place on many levels. First, it exists among the peoples of the countries that compose the area. Scandinavia is a psychological entity of four nations that have become associated with a single name. The four countries have common racial origins. Furthermore, their affinities in

10-23 *Kaare Klint. Chair in oak or beech. Manufacturer: Fritz Hansen, Denmark. Courtesy World Pictures, Denmark.*

religion, law, and language have led to similarities in temperament and attitudes, the attitude toward the relationship of function and aesthetics in materials being a significant one.

The Scandinavian countries hold democratic views with respect to design. Design is not for *the* man—it is for *man*. Emphasis is placed upon creating products that are pleasing to all rather than objects that serve only a few. Unlike warm southern European countries where friends meet in outdoor cafés or local bistros, Nordics meet in their homes during the severe winter months. Objects that will be much lived with are carefully selected. In addition, a highly personalized setting is considered a necessary counterbalance to the standardization fostered by industrial life. Bourgeois comfort is not disdained, for it is felt that people regenerate themselves in the company of family and friends. The slogan "More beautiful things for everyday use," coined as a propaganda instrument in 1919, serves as an ideal. The goal of the designer is "to give each individual the possibility of a purposeful and happy life."

Because the Scandinavian countries were remote from the centers of industrialization, they clung longer to their hand-craft tradition and intimate ways of producing artifacts than other Western European nations. Their land helped develop a special solitude and serenity in its people—a patience and a rational outlook toward life and the production of goods. Valuing differences in folk traditions of craftsmanship have resulted in a rich heritage of design.

With the coming of the Industrial Revolution, a deliberate attempt was made in the Scandinavian countries to balance hand crafting with industrial production. The machine presented no problem to Kaare Klint, a Danish forerunner of the modern movement, who believed that the designer's function is to use materials honestly to solve human needs. He did not see slavish imitation of past forms in design as contributing to this end; but unlike the Bauhaus designer who rejected past designs, Klint studied them for adaptation in a contemporary idiom. He believed that certain old methods of construction cannot be improved. "An aversion for old things leads to a loss of perspective and excludes the best help one can get: building on experience acquired over hundreds of years. There are no problems that have not been solved many times before." To Klint, "The ancients were more modern than we." Modern to him did not mean conspicuous innovation—it meant a consistently well-done job.

Communication has not only taken place among the countries comprising Scandinavia, but also among the theoreticians, the designers, the technicians, the manufacturers, and the consumers, all of whom adopt one goal: excellence in the design of everyday things. The difference between fine and applied arts does not exist in Scandinavian countries. Design begins with a problem, which simply needs resolution in the most direct manner possible. There is an understanding between the Scandinavian producer and the designer regarding the value of their differing roles, and an appreciation of "handicraft as the laboratory of industry." Fathers still teach sons the arts of glassmaking, silversmithing, and furniture construction. The distinction between the hand-crafted and the machine-produced is a fluid one because craftsmen as well as industry possess efficient technical equipment to insure precision, and the machine product often has a hand-crafted look as a result of attention to significant details. Respect is mutual in the arts of production.

Exhibits and Societies

Exhibits have also served to promote communication and to educate the consumer. Each country has societies for industrial arts and design, whose functions include arranging exhibitions, encouraging competitions, promoting Scandinavian art abroad, conducting research studies concerning man's physical requirements, educating the public to appreciate the best in industrial design, and providing visual experiences to make the consumer more receptive to new ideas and to change. These societies also provide courses and lectures, secure scholarships, and work in cooperation with schools of design.

The Swedish Society of Industrial Design, founded in 1845, is an example. Its purpose is "to bring about improvements in the products of Swedish handicraft and industry through cooperation with artistic forces, to better the household culture, and work to raise the general level of taste." To advance its cause it publishes two magazines, *Form,* the leading magazine in Sweden for art hand-craft and industrial art, and *Kontur,* a similar publication written with special consideration for the foreign reader.

The Stockholm Exhibition of 1930 concentrated on display related to three aspects of modern man's everyday living: architecture and interior and exterior environments. Its theme was the application of the principle of functionalism to these aspects. As an educational device the exhibition was very successful. It led to violent discussions between traditionalists and functionalists and to contemplation of design by the general public. It provided an opportunity for the consumer to see products that broke with the handcraft tradition and were expressive of the inner convictions of designers seeking expression in new materials. It prepared people to accept change.

The New York World's Fair of 1939 offered further awareness of Scandinavian design through Sven Markelius' pavilion of furnishings, entitled "Swedish Modern," in which functional starkness was relieved by embryonic curves. The architectural critic Douglas Haskell commented at the time with respect to it, "None of the other artistic exhibits, not even the best, can measure itself in skill with that of the Swedish artists, who with the works of their hands tell what is moving in their hearts. The happy little Swedish pavilion is civilization." The slogan of the pavilion was "Swedish modern—a movement toward sanity in design."

This sanity was applied to the design of all Swedish objects, from pillowcases to automobiles. It stood for a level of high-quality merchandise for daily use, production for all consumers through modern technology, functional forms, honest treatment of materials, and aesthetic goods resulting from close cooperation between artist and manufacturer. At the time, this ethic of Swedish modern design elevated the design consciousness of the world.

Each Scandinavian country also has its society of arts and crafts, which works toward the protection of handcrafted designs, preserves the wealth of old patterns, stimulates the production of traditional designs, and encourages cooperation between art and industry.

Research Studies

The influence Scandinavian design has had upon the world is partly due to its rational approach. Functional

10-24 *Eero Aarnio. Lounge chair of polyester reinforced fiberglass. W. 36¾", D. 36¾", H. 21", seat ht. 12". Courtesy Stendig Inc., New York.*

studies have long been a part of the curriculum of schools and organized societies. Kaare Klint taught the necessity of analyzing all the demands that might be made upon a piece of furniture. His scope of inquiry included not only a study of the scale and functioning of the human body in order to accommodate it satisfactorily, but measurements of objects so as to provide suitably corresponding storage. In addition, testing machinery was devised to determine if furniture met established norms for the height and shape of the back of a chair, the inclination of its seat, the length and shape of the armrest, and the durability of its upholstery. The surfaces of tables were subjected to normal pressures to establish standards for resistance and durability.

The Swedish Society of Industrial Design sponsored functional studies of the daily habits of people. The eating, sleeping, and sitting practices of hundreds of people were carefully documented and furniture was built accordingly. As part of a consumer education program, the results of these studies were made available to all.

In the forties and fifties the Swedish Society of Industrial Design and the National Association of Swedish Architects also carried on massive research into the space requirements of the home and its furnishings. They concluded that the demands of habitation are interdependent. Cutlery cannot be completely separated from city planning. The smallest artifacts necessary for man's daily operations have relevance to a total design for living. Just as the poet Blake projected the whole in a grain of sand, so the design of cutlery can reflect the whole of man-made environment. It determines both the size of the drawer and the drawer's placement in relationship to other components in the kitchen. The kitchen, in turn, has a relationship to other rooms, the house to the organization of the neighborhood, and so on, in widening interdependent circles.

In the Scandinavian democratic ideal of providing for all people, the elderly and the young were not overlooked. The Swedish Society of Rural Communes encouraged the construction of furniture for older people with diminishing strength and agility. A complete line of furniture was designed for the aged by Carl Malmsten and his son Vidar. The Cooperative Society encouraged development of Sune Fromella's series of *Växa med Säxa* ("grow while learning") furniture for children. This furniture provided for expansion in dimension by raising or adding to accommodate the needs of a growing child. The child psychology department of the Pedagogical Institute of Stockholm University undertook a comprehensive study of children's body measurements and needs between the ages of two and six, which led to the manufacture of designer Stephan Gip's furniture for children. When durability tests were made on it, it was found that a chair could be teetered 87,000 times with an abnormal load of 154 pounds and show no sign of weakness.

Motivating Forces

In Scandinavia there are many motivating forces for creativity. One is the attitude of industrial leaders. Production in Scandinavia is not rushed. A good design is expected to stay in circulation as long as it functions well and meets the needs of consumers. The investment of time, thought, and expert technical craftsmanship are not considered compatible with the expendable and novel. Understanding the nature of creativity, the manufacturer provides an atmosphere in which new ideas can gestate. The bigger corporations have been known to keep a "stable of designers," who maintain the generative spirit behind design and work under no pressure from deadlines. Johan Beyer, president of the Orrefors Glass Corporation, defined the attitude of his industry:

"The requirements of our designers have been, since 1916, to make something beautiful, make something new, take all the time you wish, work when and how you wish. No work could have been more unrestricted. . . . As a result the demand for our glass is considerable, the supply insufficient."

A final influence upon design must be the individual designer's concepts and motivating forces. Scandinavian designers are extremely human. They are aware of design as expression and they are aware that objects assume qualities in common with people. Kay Bojesen, designer in silver and wood, has said: "Lines should be friendly. The things we make should have life and heart in them, and be a joy to hold. They must be human, vital, and warm." Indicative of this human closeness is his designing of rabbits, gymnastic monkeys, and bears in wood, which relate to the child in us as well as to the adult.

10-25 *Kay Bojesen. "Touch me" bears in oak and maple, elephants in oak. The Danish Society of Arts and Crafts and Industrial Design. Manufacturer, Kay Bojesen. Courtesy World Pictures, Denmark.*

We enjoy their fantasy and humor and receive tactile pleasure from stroking their smooth curvatures. The value of whimsy is also seen in Bjørn Wiinblad's droll designs in ceramics. Men and animals are both capricious in nature—objects can be symbols of this fact and remind us of our relationship to the animal kingdom and to youth.

Building on ancient traditions, the Scandinavians have adapted design to the contemporary spirit. Rya rugs, which originally date from ancient Viking days when they were used as hangings by day to shut out drafts and as coverlets by night, continue to delight the world through the designers' treatment of them as abstract

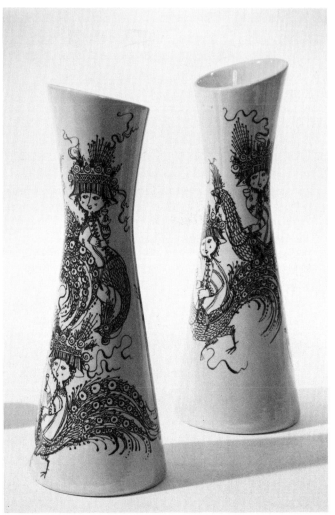

10-26 *Jacob E. Bang, architect. Vase/cocktail jug, with decoration by Bjørn Wiinblad, Denmark. Bjørn Wiinblad is famed for his droll humor, expressed delightfully and imaginatively on ceramic products. Manufacturer, Nymølle kunstfajance. Courtesy World Pictures, Denmark.*

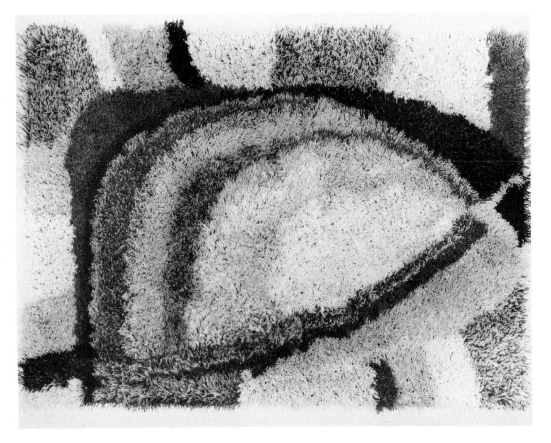

10-27 *Lofoten, rya rug. The deep pile and textured wool yarns are in the ancient tradition of rya rugmaking, brought to modern homes in contemporary design and colors. Egetaepper, Inc., New York.*

10-28 *Johannes Larsen. These foam chairs manufactured by Poul Cadovius in 1968 are forerunners to the present day foam furnishings often designed to double as beds, providing comfortable and economical seating and sleeping. The Danish Society of Arts and Crafts and Industrial Design. Courtesy, World Pictures, Denmark.*

10-29 *Eero Aarnio. Ball Chair. This upholstered fiberglass shell swivels on an enameled steel base. One can inhabit his own private orbit—on earth. Stendig Inc., New York City.*

10-30 *Gunnar Aagaard Andersen. Armchair, 1964. Urethane foam, height 30″. The designer exploits a material in order to discover its potential. Collection, The Museum of Modern Art, New York.*

paintings. The furniture designers—among them Kaare Klint, Borge Mogensen, Finn Juhl, and Hans Wegner—have also brought to the world well-designed pieces of timeless character. Their designs employ integral decoration through textures of wood, cane, and leather, the same beauty that was realized by American Shakers in the design of their homes and furnishings. Both have a purity of design that seems to spring from inspired idealism.

The lines employed by the Scandinavian designers often parallel those of contemporary architecture. The cantilevered arms of their chairs have a lightness and grace that suggest imminent flight, just as the slender posts or curving supports project a building upward in dynamic relation to the earth. Designers of objects for daily use in Scandinavia have frequently been architects who have brought a comprehensive vision to their craft.

The Scandinavian designer has taught the world the meaning of texture and of the beauty inherent in natural materials. Sweden's Bota Glass Works exploit the molten, blown, bubbly qualities of the medium. In working with wood, textures are enhanced in the finishing processes. The dark stains and the glossy varnishes that change the natural textures and color of the wood to flat, gleaming, or ruddy surfaces have been avoided by Scandinavians. Instead, they apply oil to wood and then rub and buff the surface until it has the desired depth and beauty. The surfaces of tables that are not oiled increase in beauty as they are washed and used. That natural textures can be attractive is evident from the use of unpolished leathers and of pottery glazes that resemble lichen.

Practicality and beauty are concerns of the Scandinavian designer who wants to develop transportable, exportable, or institutional furniture. Lightweight, collapsible, stackable, and screwless furnishings whose members are held together under tension have been developed. Rocking cushions of plastic foam covered in wool, designed by Danish artist Jonannes Larsen, can be stored as compact cylinders when not in use. Danish Eero Aarnio designed a famous "ball" and "gyro" chairs

in plastic. A great departure from conventional form was made by Denmark's Aagaard Anderson, whose surrealistic chair is formed by polyester foam ejected through a nozzle. Where technology has been adopted by the Scandinavian designer it has exploited innovative and aesthetically pleasing design to the fullest. To sum up, then, the factors that have contributed to Scandinavian design have included the geographic and the cultural heritage; a centuries-old tradition of craftsmanship; a climate of mutual respect between designer, producer, and consumer; design based on research; consumer education programs; and exhibitions and competitions. More importantly perhaps, there is an idealistic approach to design by those who create: an understanding of materials, a willingness to experiment, and a capacity to transform raw materials into products that both serve human needs and provide interest.

The 1960s

The new movement in design in the late 1960s, labelled postmodern by the English art historian Nikolaus Pevsner, was consistent with the period's social and technological changes. Among the directive forces were man's recognition of the potential of design and production elements with laws as yet undictated—of establishing precedents in the design possibilities of plastics, light manipulators, movement, electronics, and computers. There existed a youth culture that wished to incorporate into its environment a richness of sound and vision above considerations of restraint and "good taste." The need for flexibility and change in life patterns was reflected in the design of "breakdown" furniture, based on modular and component parts used singly as stools or linked to form chairs, sofas, and tables to fit into any space. Organic forms and furniture were built on the circle, the cylinder, and the cube, which could be divided into successive parts.

Design in the 1960s was characterized by adventurous experimentation with forms and materials and by an increased appeal to man's total sensory capacity. By contrast, design in the 1980s relies on social and behavioral issues and other human factors.

Italy

Italy's international success in design is attributed to many factors, not the least of which is the Italians' willingness to experiment and their appreciation of the

10-32 *Tobia Scarpa. Grande Pigreco armchair. The frame is of solid wood with a lacquer finish. The upholstery is foam rubber over plywood. Knoll International, New York.*

10-33 *Joe C. Colombo. Seggio stack/gang chair, made of molded plastic. These chairs can be stacked on each other or joined to create greater horizontal width. Hank Loewenstein, Inc., Ft. Lauderdale, Florida.*

10-31 *Gruppo Architetti Urbanisti Citta Nuova. Lamp, 1966, orange fiberglass, diameter 21". The Italians were recognized in the 1970s as great experimenters in light and its potential. Collection, The Museum of Modern Art, New York.*

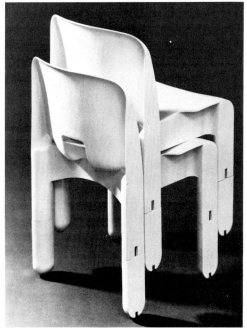

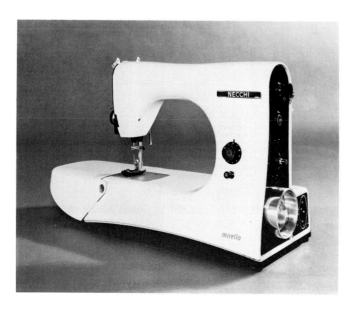

10-34 *Marcello Nizzoli. Necchi electric sewing machine, 1956, metal housing, enameled ivory, and black. Manufacturer: Villorio Necchi. Collection, The Museum of Modern Art, New York.*

aesthetically expressive. The Italians have a long heritage of artistic appreciation and creativity, which dates back to Leonardo da Vinci's versatility in the application of the principles of art to the many designs of objects for man's use. While never losing sight of the fact that function determines form, the Italians have become skilled at combining art with technology. To encourage creativity, Italy has a number of medium-sized industries that can afford to experiment with revolutionary designs and serve as pilots for those factories engaged in mass production. Their designers are often architects, who, in Italy's recession in 1962, brought their comprehensive view to the design of objects for daily use.

Furthermore, the design magazine *Domus* has not only informed the world about the direction of Italian design, but has sponsored international exhibitions to promote excellence in design, to facilitate communi-

10-35 *Sebastian Matta. Malitte lounge chair of foam polyurethane upholstered blocks. Knoll International, New York.*

10-36 *Sebastian Matta. Malitte lounge chair assembled for shipping or storing. Knoll International, New York.*

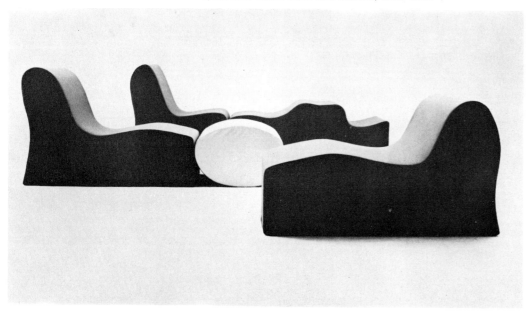

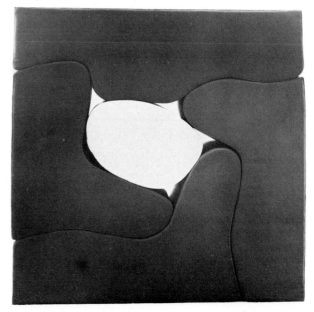

cation among designers, and to encourage innovation. These exhibitions have served to bring the design potential of modern materials—metals, glass, and plastics—to the awareness of the world.

There are many media the Italians have brought to a high point of development. These include light, wicker, glass, ceramics, furniture, fabrics, automobiles, typewriters, vacuum cleaners, and domestic wares of all kinds. Recognized not only for the utility of its products but also for their beauty of design, Italy has earned the title of "exporter of good taste."

Among the well-known products that have become familiar to many world markets are Olivetti typewriters, Necchi sewing machines, Gucci handbags, Paolo Lomazzi inflatable plastic chairs, Ferragamo shoes, Joe Colombo plastic chairs, Gae Aulenti lamps, Venini glass, and Emilio Pucci fabrics and costume designs. The Italian approach is fresh and exploratory, as indicated by the instruction given the designers by a prominent manufacturer. His recommendation for designing a new machine was: "Restudy the whole problem of this machine; then determine how it ought to look in a modern world, ignoring all previous concepts." As a result, Italian design is often unconventional, as in Fabio Lenci's chair with its multiroll leather upholstery, with wide side supports of glass, or Sebastian Matta's lounge set, which can be assembled for shipping like a jigsaw puzzle.

The Italians' approach to design also takes into consideration man's sensuous self: colors are vibrant, daring, and bright. Rattan is widely used for its particular congeniality and warmth; it lends itself well to baroque and rococo forms, which contrast with the harder lines and angularity other materials provide. Ceramics and glass allow for subtle nuances in color and texture. Marco Zanuso, feeling the ringing of a telephone should sound pleasant to the ear, created a "singing cricket" telephone that, with the turn of a small knob, can sing anything from soprano to low bass to accommodate one's mood. Italian design is both varied and amusing, reflecting the people's versatility and their particular zest for living.

Britain

Britain's interest and leadership in industrial design has already been noted by the concern felt by the Royal Society of Arts in the eighteenth century and by leaders of the Arts and Crafts movement in the nineteenth. The painters Dante Gabriel Rossetti, Edward Burne-Jones, William Morris, and James Whistler took such interest in all objects of daily use that they set out to create beauty in man's total environment and to bring all aspects of living into harmony. Since their time, not only nostalgia for the excellent designs of that period but a sentimental attachment to Victorianism in general and a dependence upon design from Scandinavia and Italy had to be overcome before a native English design reflecting vivacity and imagination could emerge. With the end of World War II, which had drained Britain's creative productivity for wartime purposes, and with the 1951 Festival of Britain (which is now being recognized as a great turning point in the development of postwar British design, despite the lack of quantity of well-designed articles from which to present selections), the creative talents of British designers began to find release from their long suppression. Expression developed so fast that by the 1960s the design revolution in furnishings was as forceful as the fashion upheaval on Carnaby Street. Chrome, plastic, plywood, chipboard, glass, and paper became the media for design of lively, experimental furnishings.

At the same time that the Festival increased public awareness of modern design, the Design Centre was established in London by the Council of Industrial Design. Here the Council maintains a continuously changing exhibition of durable consumer goods to acquaint consumers and buyers with the best of contemporary British design. The Council also maintains the Design Index, a reference catalog of British consumer products that are selected for their high standard of design. The Council has contributed to the public's design-consciousness by promulgating high standards,

prodding manufacturers, engaging in propaganda for good design, and launching numerous exhibitions. The Council of Industrial Design's Scottish Committee functions in a parallel manner at the Scottish Design Centre in Glasgow.

Educationally, Britain's continued interest is also reflected in her recognition of the need for an interdisciplinary study of design, *ergonomics,* in which evaluation of the design of objects produced by the machine is made by both psychologists and designers. In recognition of a need for coordinated color in interiors to aid homemakers and interior designers in making unified selections, the British Standard 2660, Colors for Building and Decorative Arts, was adopted. Based upon the Munsell interval scale, it serves as a guide for manufacturers of plastics, ceramic tile, linoleum, and vitreous enamel. Its creation is indicative of Britains continuing concern and responsibility for quality design.

Britain's young designers are many, and they take the same freedom in working with materials as the Italians. Among the nation's growing list of acknowledged designers are Peter Murdock, David Hicks, William Plunkett, Terence Conran, and Peter Hoyte. David Hicks has not only created some of the most distinctive interiors of our time, but also has given expression to the process of creation in such publications as *David Hicks on Decoration* and *David Hicks on Living—With Taste.*

One of the most innovative recent designs for the homemaker is that created for a design competition organized by Birds-Eye Foods and Britain's Council of Industrial Design by the young British designer Ilana Henderson, while she was still a student at the Royal College of Art. In her proposal for a cylindrical space-age design, the motorized work areas were designed to be rotated clockwise or counterclockwise and moved up and down to suit an individual's height, thus making it possible for one to perform work while sitting or

10-37 *David Hicks.* Jagged Diamond. *Connaissance Fabrics, Inc., New York.*

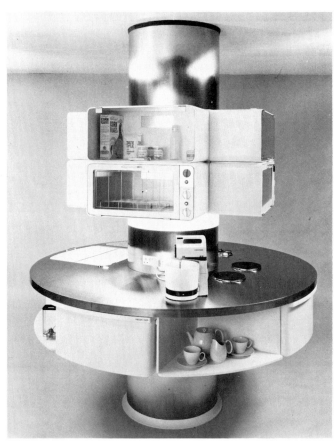

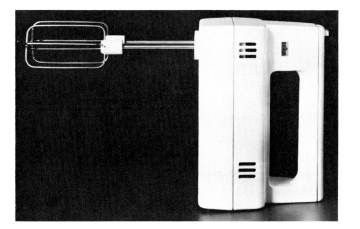

10-39 *Braun M 12 (hand mixer) with stainless steel attachments, Germany, 1963. Manufacturer, Braun AG, Germany. Braun AG of Germany designs some of the most functional and arresting designs in domestic housewares. Collection, The Museum of Modern Art, New York.*

10-38 *Ilana Henderson. Award-winning mock-up for kitchen design competition organized by Bird's Eye Foods and England's Council of Industrial Design; microwave oven with storage cupboard above and freezer drawer below work top. The design is a flexible kitchen system suitable for the kind of conditions that are expected in ten to twenty years' time. The Council of Industrial Design, London, and The Design Centre.*

10-40 *Walter Pabst.* Kinder *juvenile furniture series: chair, rocking horse, game table, swing. The polypropylene chair shells have white vinyl steel legs. Hank Loewenstein, Inc., Ft. Lauderdale, Florida.*

standing in one position. The full size mock-up of the kitchen illustrated her ideas for including electric and gas burners, microwave and gas ovens, refrigerator, freezer, two sinks, chopping block, garbage disposal, storage cabinets, and a work counter in a single compact unit.

Part Three
Inorganic Materials: Media for Design

Foreword

In the third and fourth parts of this text, man's use of materials is explored. Attention is directed to the nature of materials and to the high points in man's aesthetic development of them. The philosophical and aesthetic approaches of some leading designers who employ the various media are presented, in order to encourage an appreciation of the creative process. Preceding this discussion is an analysis of the relationship of creativity, which is the essence of design, to the production process and to differing expressions of design activity.

Creativity and Production 11

The Nature of Creativity

Creativity is a universal quality that has many facets. It is given not to the few, but to all. One facet we all experience is the one we call upon in solving our daily problems. Each person is faced with complexities in his environment, juxtapositions of events that exist and need resolving before further progress in life can take place. The more highly creative person welcomes these, not as problems of a negative character, but as challenges that provide an opportunity to use himself, his mind, and his emotions in some form of action.

Yet everyone is to some degree creative, because the task of living requires making decisions. Selecting one's clothing in the morning is a creative act. It involves taking stock of an available wardrobe, interpreting the needs of the day, determining the image one wishes to project, relating his feelings and emotions to the colors and characteristics of the various items of apparel available for expressing himself, and then selecting the garment that most nearly satisfies these multiple demands. When one has put it on, he may find that it is not functioning in the way anticipated, so the process is repeated. Unless a person wears a uniform or unless his wardrobe is extremely limited, there are no known or given answers as to what the final selection will be.

In simple decisions such as these, the individual engages in both the scientific and the creative act. He takes into consideration the various data, relates these as best he can, mentally explores the possibilities, projects an outcome, and then takes action. The relating of all relevant data and the trying out of something new is creative. As no one faces the same complex of data or brings an identical backlog of experiences to an event each day, each person creates his life in a myriad individual and unique ways. Even impulsive behavior, though it takes all the available factors into less consideration, has its dynamics in past thought and reflection or feelings of need. Although the behavior seems precipitate, it is not without antecedents.

There are some who are more creative than others and who are more open to all their experiences in making decisions. They do not shut out or repress the negative, but allow both the positive and negative full play. They are more inclined to value their irrational impulses, their fantasies, their dreams, their miasmic, free-flowing, unrelated thoughts before wakening, their ambiguities, and the ambiguities of others. They delight in paradoxes and placing events and ideas in chesslike positions to explore the potential of many plays. These are the people that the psychologist Alexander Maslow refers to as self-actualizing. He says of them:

Their ease of penetration to reality, their closer approach to an animal-like or childlike acceptance and spontaneity imply a superior awareness of their own impulses, desires, opinions, and subjective reactions in general.[1]

Or, in another instance,

Self-actualizing people have the wonderful capacity to appreciate again and again, freshly and naively, the basic goods of life, with awe, pleasure, wonder, and even ecstasy, however stale these experiences may have become to others.[2]

Creativity thus seems related to the acceptance of all one's human responses as worthy of consideration in decision making and to appreciating with savor the smallest event in daily living.

To better understand the production of design, we will take a look at the differing production levels that influence the quality and character of consumer goods.

Folk Art

On the most elementary level of artistic production is folk art. Once a prevalent form of world design, today it has largely disappeared and can only be found in pockets widely scattered geographically. Its milieu is undeveloped, from the standpoint of modern culture. Historically, the tea masters were the first to recognize the simple natural beauty of the rice bowls used by Korean laborers, and the masters adopted the native designs for the cups they used in the tea ceremonies. Appreciation of folk art is still evident today. Japan has a folk art organization whose purpose is to create in the manner of the earlier peasant tradition. Pennsylvania Dutch and other folk arts of early America are found in museums all along the eastern seaboard of the United States.

What are the characteristics of this design that man often misses today and feels he must preserve or emulate?

1. Folk art is an indigenous creation of ordinary people living in rural or village environments, especially those cut off from the mainstream of urban civilization. It is traditional, often remaining unchanged for generations, and reflects ancestral experience and wisdom. Designs have been perfected and refined over a long period of time, and so the artisan executes those that have stood the test of time.
2. It is utilitarian and ordinary; objects are designed to be functional and practical for daily use. They are sturdy enough to stand up under frequent use and they can be easily reproduced. Beauty is not a goal, but is the end product when an object is sincerely

[1] A. H. Maslow, *Motivation and Personality* (New York: Harper, 1954), p. 210.
[2] Ibid., p. 214.

11-1 Nativity Show, *New Mexico, American folk art. Courtesy Charles Eames.*

conceived and executed with respect to function and materials.

3. Wherever the Industrial Revolution has not yet changed lives, mores, and traditions, folk art is produced in quantity at low cost in the family factory where all hands can be employed. Being a family or clan-centered activity, the production process may be held in secret. Therefore wares take on a local or regional color, because the materials and techniques become the unwritten possession of a group. One comes to identify the goods with a particular geographical locale or people.

4. The works are unsigned and collective in spirit. They are not consciously made to impose the image of one person, because they have evolved over a period of time with many people contributing to their refinement of form, and their design quality in fact derives from critical refinement. They are not spontaneous, but collective in spirit.

Alexander Girard has been extremely interested in real folk art and particularly in folk toys and objects related to them. He and his wife have collected toys and other objects of simple beauty produced by unsophisticated artisans wherever and whenever they could on their travels. They have collected more than 65,000 individual pieces, which now belong to the Girard Foundation Collection and are housed in its warehouse. Mr. Girard has designed and installed various exhibitions employing objects from the Girard Foundation Collection, notably the very large special exhibition "The Magic of a People," which was housed in a Girard-designed building at the Texas World's Fair "Hemisfair" of 1968.

While "The Magic of a People" had approximately 10,000 toys and objects that came exclusively from Latin America, the collection itself covers the world, and includes such articles as a large group of shadow puppets from China, Java, and Turkey; pottery toys from Russia and Japan; masks from numerous countries; rag dolls from Rajasthan and the United States; figures and paintings from Ethiopia; Victorian toys from Western Europe; numerous candles; and other charming and expressive objects. The characteristics all these objects have in common are, in Girard's words, that they are "unsophisticated or naive in character; ingenious in concept; direct in expression; sincere in creation; bounded by vigorous limitation of a tool, a material, and handcraft, or a machine process."[3]

This is art of simpler technologies from the past. In countries all over the world, recognition of the validity of this design is leading to a concerted effort to preserve traditional designs and hand-crafting processes. But according to Girard: "As soon as efforts are made to arti-

[3]"Artless Art," *Horizon,* **VII:2,** (Spring 1966), p. 72.

ficially preserve traditional designs and hand-crafting processes, it regretfully but surely becomes a conscious activity, thereby initiating the decline to early extinction. When the traditional reasons and social climate are degenerated or tampered with, so is the folk art equally degenerated and changed."[4] (See Figure 11-1).

Primitive Art

Primitive art is also created by preurban societies, but it is generally more closely associated with the art produced by a number of unrelated cultures that lie close to the equator, such as Africa and Oceania. For the most part, the art is non-Western in spirit and is not produced in temperate zones, except for that of British Columbia and some pre-Columbian art. No distinction is made between fine and applied art by the primitive artist because objects created in the service of the community to express family and tribal values and feelings must also have intangible expressive qualities and beauty. The primitive craftsman makes household objects for his daily use, and just as the folk artist may make sophisticated products for his princes and maharajas, so may the primitive artist produce sophisticated products for his chieftains and their ceremonies. These objects range from sculpture, masks, shields, boats, weapons, utensils, votive objects, and ceremonial dress to ancestral poles. Objects are produced not only to function, as a spear to kill, but are embellished and decorated in such a way as to convey delight and awe. It was the expressive sculpture of certain Congo tribes that so impressed Picasso and Matisse that their subsequent art reflected reminiscences of African images. The late Nelson Rockefeller had one of the world's greatest collections of primitive art, which is housed in The Metropolitan Mu-

[4] Ibid.

seum of Art. These art objects were equally appreciated by his son Michael, who lost his life off the coast of New Guinea in 1961 while on an expedition to study and collect these exotic artifacts.

The Individual Artist

There are those who direct their efforts toward the specific purpose of creating objects known as fine art. Their motivation is self-expression and their ends are aesthetic rather than utilitarian. They impress an individual stamp upon their work. The difference between a work of fine art and that of craft and commercial design is not absolute, but a matter of emphasis and degree. The painter or sculptor has the same need as the designer to understand the potentials and limitations of his materials, to be familiar with the tools and techniques for working them, and to order the elements into a unified whole. Ideally, the artist maintains his integrity and does not compromise his aesthetic values for such considerations as profit, prestige, and mass appeal. Having less need to please society, he can be more self-assertive and can express his idealism, his inner drives, and his positive or negative reactions to society through visual media.

The Artist-Craftsman

On another level is the artist-craftsman who designs and makes objects in his own studio or workshop and thus perpetuates the tradition of the preindustrial craftsman. He is his own producer, remaining free from the pressures of conformity and creative frustration that one may experience with industry. His values demand a sense of personal freedom and the hand-crafted look and vitality of the individual product. The ceramists

11-2 *Joan of Arc. Toile de Jouy. This French print on fabric comes from a small factory operation in Jouy, France, where quality artists were employed to produce fabrics,* circa 1800. *Courtesy, The University of Connecticut, Storrs, Connecticut. Photographed by Carla Davis Dumesnil.*

Gertrud and Otto Natzler, woodcraftsman Sam Maloof, weaver Anni Albers, and furniture maker George Nakashima fall into this category.

Small Factory Operation

Heath Ceramics is an example of small factory operation that fuses art, technology, and business. Edith Heath began her career as an artist-craftsman producing hand-thrown pottery. Later, she moved into small factory production with her husband and began operating Heath Ceramics for the manufacture of quality dinnerware. George Nakashima has hand-crafted furniture, but he has also used machinery for that part of the production process where no aesthetic advantage is gained through manual work.

In former times, the owner or co-owner of a business was the designer-technician responsible for the design of the company's products. But gradually business began to realize the value of an industrial designer who was an artist-craftsman with the business acuity and ability necessary to coordinate the efforts of technicians, craftsmen, and salesmen. In Scandinavia, Kay Bojesen was one of the first hand-craftsmen to develop this role by designing a series of kitchen and table knives for the Universal Steel Company and setting a model for the role of industrial designer. Herman Miller, Inc., by employing Charles Eames and George Nelson as furniture designers, and Alexander Girard as furniture and fabric designer, has shown how production, quality, and aesthetics can simultaneously benefit from using the specialized talents of industrial designers.

The Industrial Designer

Unlike the fine artist, who produces primarily for self-expression, the industrial designer produces goods for others. The best in industrial design reflects the unity of vision between the designer and those responsible for producing the finished product. This end is not realized by unilateral action on the part of the designer, but from his relating a projected design to the total manufacturing complex: the management, the die and toolmakers, the materials to be employed, the employees who will put the design into production, the distributive resources, and the needs and desires of the consumer public.

As such, the individual designer has a role different from that of the artist working in a studio, who is responsible only to his own inner drives. The designer's role is no less creative; it is merely more complex. Instead of pouring into the mix his own feelings, expression, knowledge, and skill without consideration of others, he must bring to the proposed design an interpretation of many variables. His role may be more tenuous, because he must creatively project and evaluate

11-3 *Guitar. Wood with ebony and ivory inlay. German, 18th century. Such specialized and decorative instruments were often made in small factory operations, as they still are. Collection, The Metropolitan Museum of Art, New York.*

people. . . . My work isn't *avant garde*. On the contrary, it's simply made, with care for people". Buckminister Fuller professed: "The greatest fact of the twentieth century is that we can make life on earth a general success for all men." These designers live constructively in their society in much the same way as the psychologist Carl Rogers described the well-balanced person who is "in as much harmony with his culture as a balanced satisfaction of needs demands." Being welfare-oriented, they secure pleasure from relating their aesthetic faculties to producing goods that not only fulfill their own creative urges and reflect their personal selves, but that simultaneously satisfy the needs of the larger society.

Today, teamwork is considered such a vital part of industrial design that the distinction between the industrial designer and design engineers is becoming obsolete. During the stages of design—conception, development, and production—the designer may still be the moving spirit of the production team, but realization is growing that the cooperation of all employees is so necessary and their efforts are so interrelated in producing the final product that credit should go to the entire team. Hence, designing a cooperative and competent team is becoming the objective of many industries.

Other Industrial Design

Not all the well-designed products on the market today can be attributed to the work of a designer. Very often the technicians of a plant, such as the engineers, the die makers or the mold makers, or some other long-time employees develop a feeling for form and contribute to the design of a product. To some extent, in their anonymous artistry, developed through time and experience, they function in the folk art tradition of creating design. Some of the kitchen tools of Ekco Housewares company are the product of design by their designers, engineers, and model makers. The digital

these variables in trying to arrive at a design that will respect not only his own valid concerns but also those of others. The most successful commercial designers are those who are motivated to produce by the needs of mankind and who empathize with man in general.

For example, Charles Eames stated his objective as "the simple one of getting the most of the best to the greatest number of people for the least." Likewise, Terence Conran aimed to create "well-designed merchandise at modest prices for the maximum number of

clock that was designed by the staff of the Howard Miller Clock Company of Zeeland, Michigan, is also a fine example of a staff-designed product.

Today hand-craftsmanship and industrial production are both recognized as having contributive roles in design. The high cost of industrial operation requires that innovative design be tested in the smaller laboratory. The studio can be used for this experimentation. For instance, Dorothy Liebes maintains her hand loom to develop experimental weaves and prototypes for production on power looms. Charles Eames experiments with materials and techniques in a workshop directly under his control. Even if a studio is strictly private and does not serve as an adjunct to industry, the designs created by the artist-craftsman become visually disseminated and may inspire or stimulate the industrial designer by fertilizing his vision.

Hand craftsmanship preserves integrity of design and quality workmanship in the ordinary objects used in daily living. Industrial design makes possible the production of goods in sufficient quantity that they can be purchased by the average consumer, thereby adding enrichment to many lives. The best in industrial design fuses technical skill with aesthetic sensitivity.

12 Rocks and Earth

Colors which you can hear with ears,
Sounds to see with eyes,
The void you touch with your elbows,
The taste of space on your tongue,
The fragrance of dimensions
The juice of stone.

Marcel Breuer

An Introduction to Inorganic Materials

Man's development from a nomadic to a pastoral culture began with the domestication of plants and animals. With domestication came a release of time and human energy for other activities. The period between 4000 and 3000 B.C. was a dynamic millennium in which much of the foundation for the modern world was laid. Knowledge of metallurgy was a tremendous catalyst in advancing man from his Stone Age activity into highly sophisticated working with metals of copper, bronze, iron, brass, pewter, and silver.

The entire millennium was one of spectacular achievement, in which various peoples reached unprecedented levels of utilitarian and aesthetic productivity. In addition to metallurgy, the basic principles of weaving were developed. The plow was in use and the wheel was employed both for transportation and for turning pottery. Writing was developed and man started recording his history on clay tablets. Almost every known human civilized activity is traceable to that early era. Concomitantly with these advances came urbanization, religious organization, and the development of government and commerce.

The Sumerians, who occupied the region between the Tigris and the Euphrates, are credited with being among the first peoples to engage in those arts and practices associated with civilized life. By the middle of the fourth millennium B.C. they had created a literary and technological culture that included pictographic writing on clay tablets and the use of copper and cast bronze for tools and weapons. They may have had some influence upon the civilization of the Indus River valley circa 2500 B.C. Paralleling, yet independent of, the Sumerian culture in its advanced civilization and sophisticated use of materials was the Egyptian. The Near East functioned as the diffuser of early technology, because it constituted the international highway linking the continents of Africa, Europe, and Asia.

Though it is common practice to indicate the ages of man in terms of his use of materials, such as the Stone, Copper, Bronze, and Iron Ages, these labels merely signify that a specific culture had reached a certain stage of development. Developmental patterns tended to be similar, but there was no universal evolutionary scheme or sequence common to all cultures. For instance, while the technological use of stone seems to have preceded the use of metals, anthropologist Ralph Linton points out[1] that though no metals were being used at the time of Europeans' discovery of the Melanesian Islands, the stone and wooden objects that were in use there bore marks imitative of metalworking details. Hence he assumed that metalwork may have preceded working with wood and stone. Because of European contacts, Melanesia passed directly from stone to iron usage in the latter half of the nineteenth century. We also find that, unlike many other cultures, Africans did not experience a Copper or Bronze Age. America also bypassed the Bronze Age by going directly from the Copper to the Iron Age. Egypt passed through Stone

[1] Ralph Linton, *The Tree of Culture* (New York: Knopf, 1964), p. 53.

and Bronze Ages to the Iron Age while Britons were still stone-oriented. The Chinese were making extensive use of iron while Mediterranean cultures were operating at the bronze level.

Moreover, according to Linton, in the ages ascribed to man's technology of materials, the designation of an age by a material is merely indicative that occasional artifacts have survived. In the ancient days of Stone Age culture, articles of stone were supplemented by extensive use of organic materials—wood, skin, antlers, bone, and grasses. In that age these were as vital to man as stone, but they were more subject to decomposition. Thus the ages of man denote the introductory use of a new material with survival structure and not necessarily the materials that in reality were found most useful in that period.

The inorganic materials man first used included stone, meteoric iron, glass in the form of obsidian, and gold and copper in native unencumbered states. Technological advance came with the arts of smelting copper and tin from their associated ores to produce the alloys of bronze, brass, and pewter. The history of man evolved around these coveted resource materials. Copper, iron, and tin were abundant in the ores of Asia Minor and the countries surrounding the Caspian and Mediterranean seas. The value of these resources and the advantages they yielded to those who could secure them led to ceaseless conflicts among ancient peoples and to the rise and fall of civilizations contending for control of mineral abundance.

In the parts that follows, merely as a means to organization, the writer will present man's use of inorganic materials before the organic.

Stone

Man has recorded his history in terms of his relation to stone and minerals, and later through the industrial

and scientific technology made possible through use of these same materials. He has learned about his Stone Age self by studying artifacts of flint, stone, bone, and antlers found in caves or buried in layers of the earth's crust. He has learned about himself through metals in utilitarian and decorative form deposited in ancient tombs or burial mounds and through radio-carbon tests of buried fabrics and potteries recovered from dried lake beds.

Of all these materials, stone and bone have been used by man through the millennia. More than a million years ago, primitive Zinjanthropus walked erect and made pebble tools. Later man learned to shape flint and bone implements. During the later Paleolithic period, man further developed stone implements from the crude hand axes and flake tools of former periods into finely crafted and diversified tools designed for specialized purposes. Of these the graver, or burin, was a highly significant invention, for it not only facilitated the extensive working of bone but also aided the development of art. Art began as engravings made with a burin on the walls of caves, which presumably served as religious symbols to promote benefits during the hunt. Upper Paleolithic art was mural art—tracings and engravings, bas-reliefs, and paintings on walls of caves and rock shelters, such as are seen at Lascaux, France, and Altimira, Spain.

It is understandable that stone should have been widely used by prehistoric man because it was abundantly present for immediate use. Its use preceded the knowledge of fire making. Stone required no smelting or refining, as did the metals that came into use later, and no knowledge of chemicals or electricity, as did the aluminum of the nineteenth century or the plastics of the twentieth. That man could accomplish the highest

12-1 *Marble statuette of a woman. Cycladic, 3000–2000 B.C. Note that at this early age, designers were able to achieve expression through emphasizing the portions of the body considered most significant and through dramatizing basic vertical and horizontal rhythms. Collection, The Metropolitan Museum of Art, New York.*

levels of art using only his hands and stone implements is evident in the forming of stone sculptures and relief carvings on architecture during the medieval or pre-Columbian period of American civilization in Mexico, the southern United States, and Central and South America.

Among the oldest evidences of stone being used for architectural purposes are the granite pyramids of Gizeh, built about 3700 B.C., near Cairo, Egypt. Their simplicity of structure exemplifies the power inherent in minimal elaboration. Their abiding presence is testimony to the endurance of granite, which has in fact become symbolic of timelessness. The acts of transporting the granite from distant areas and hoisting it to unprecedented heights without the use of machinery must rank among man's greatest engineering feats. The pyramids are matched by the granite buildings of Peru; without benefit of machines, horses, or oxen for transportation the Incas performed the same feat as the Egyptians, though at a much later date.

An advance in technological application is exemplified in the construction of the hypostyle hall in the temple of Karnak on the Upper Nile, with its forest of closely set columns that support a stone roof. It exemplifies the architectural knowledge of the day concerning the use of materials and appropriate construction techniques. With stone as the principal building material for palaces and temples, the bearing posts were necessarily heavy and closely set in order to support the stone roof. Columns were frequently made of limestone because it was easily carved or incised to depict events. Entire walls were also accented by a surface covering of hieroglyphics, which resulted in a textural pattern. (See Figure 4-11).

The Greek Parthenon of the fifth century B.C. survives as a triumph in marble. The decorativeness of the friezes is kept subordinate to the structural design. Human figures are sculptured to accommodate the geometric spaces they occupy. The technological advancement of truss construction permitted greater spanning of space and greater variation in spatial proportions than the post-and-lintel construction employed by the Egyptians.

Marble was extensively used for palaces in India, the most famous being the Taj Mahal at Agra, which was built between 1632 and 1653 from pure white Majarana marble by Shah Jehan as a memorial to his wife. Its aesthetic distinction is a consequence of simplification of line, perfection of form, and rhythmic repetition, with secondary ornamentation that consists of delicate carvings and inlaid stones. Like other marble palaces of India, the Taj Mahal is surrounded by a reflecting pool of water, which acts much as a mounting to a jewel, mirroring the colors and forms in softened images. Thus the edifice gradually becomes related to the earth. It blends the dream with reality in much the same way as Indian sculpture blends the sensuous with the spiritual. The interior of the Hagia Sophia in Istanbul is also like a stone gem because of its many-faceted mosaic columns.

Stone has also been used for recording history. In Romanesque architecture stone capitals were sculptured to narrate biblical events. Similarly, Gothic cathedrals were religious documents written in stone, with human figures elongated, curved, and ordered to reinforce and correspond to the architectural rhythms.

Stone has been used by all cultures for enduring sculptures of gods and men. The Greeks showed great respect for the qualities of stone, giving greater emphasis to structural form than to decorativeness. Buddhas and Hindu gods were immortalized in stone with monumental dignity and force. On the other hand, there are examples of stone being intricately sculptured; some of the sensuous gowns of Siva Indian dancers simulate elaborate feathery plumage, which is inconsistent with the nature of a hard material. The Cambodian ruins at Angkor-Wat, built during the early twelfth century, are so monumental and exalted that they fill us with awe. So do the Assyrian stone reliefs on the palace walls at Nimrud, circa 883–859 B.C.

Ancient sculptors from the Mezcala river basin in Mexico, using only stone and obsidian drills, created stone statuary that is only three to fifteen inches high,

but which looms massive and powerful because only the essential details were included. A modern sculptor who worked with the same respect for stone and its potential was Constantin Brancusi. To him the sculptor's function was not to impose form upon stone but to release the form within it. In attempting to free the "inner life" of materials, he chipped away the stone until the essential form emerged as a powerful symbol.

Today the beauty of stone—its intrinsic naturalness, strength, and solidity—makes it as a valued material in the exterior and interior design of buildings. Fieldstone, marble, granite, flagstone, and slate lend inviting textural contrasts to wood, stucco, brick, and cement. (See, for example, Figure 9-1 of Taliesin West.)

Gemstones

As the first igneous rocks, such as limestone and granite, were being formed within the earth by tremendous heat and pressure, certain minerals within them were combining and crystallizing into varying shapes. The rocks, then torn by violent volcanic disturbances, were forced upward through layers of sediment toward the surface of the earth. Eventually, exposed to rain and frost, the rocks were worn down and gem stones were exposed. These special minerals made up of chemical elements have been classified as precious and semi-precious stones because of their beauty, hardness, and rarity. In the crystalline form in which they are recovered from the earth, few gem stones are attractive, however; they depend upon the cutting and refining processes performed by a gem cutter for their beauty.

Of the 2,000 known organic materials, the *Encyclopaedia Britannica* recognizes many gemstones, among them diamonds, jade, lapis lazuli, opal, quartz, topaz, tourmaline, turquoise, ruby, sapphire, zircon, emerald, and amethyst. Of these, the diamond, ruby, emerald, and blue sapphire are recognized as among the most precious. The pearl though a quasi-mineral is also recognized as a precious stone.

The gem minerals are colorless and translucent when

12-2 *Constantin Brancusi.* Mlle. Pogany, *1931, marble on limestone base, height without base, 19". Throughout his life, Brancusi valued three qualities: extreme simplification of forms, emphasis on materials, and lucid emphatic rhythms. Note the rhythmic S shape and his elimination of all extraneous detail to capture the "essence" of woman. Philadelphia Museum of Art; The Louis and Walter Arensberg Collection.*

pure, their color depending upon the pigmentation from impurities they contain. The opal is the only important mineral not found in the crystalline but in an amorphous state. Because of its other unusual properties, such as exceeding brilliance and hardness, the diamond is the only gem valued for its lack of color.

These gems were known to ancient man and fascinated him by their mysterious qualities, their brilliance, and lasting beauty. A science grew up concerning their nature and miraculous properties, a tradition that still persists in the modern practice of wearing a birthstone. Gems were reputed to provide the wearer with such

12-3 *Green stone tiki, New Zealand (enlargement). This expressive stone was worn to charm away evil spirits. Courtesy of The American Museum of Natural History, New York.*

properties as love and happiness, with the ability to prophesy, with wisdom, and with protection from accidents, disease, and snake bites. Until the eighteenth century, pulverized gems played a role in the cure of diseases, and in all major civilizations they were in some way associated with the splendor of the deity, as in the jade castle attributed to the Chinese ruler of the heavens, or the heavenly city in the Revelation of St. John, which rests on precious stones and has walls of jasper and gates of pearl.

Traditionally, man has also concentrated his wealth in gems because they are easily portable and find a ready market in all parts of the world. Pliny expressed Roman enthusiasm for beautiful stones by stating they are "beyond any price and even beyond human estimation, so that to many men one gem suffices for the contemplation of all nature." Because of their size and beauty they have always been associated with intrigue and historic significance. Some particularly famous gems are the Hope Diamond, which is thought to be a recut from the "Tavernier Blue" diamond once in Louis XVI's possession and which, since 1958, resides in the Smithsonian Institution; the Kohinoor Diamond ("Mountain of Light"), which has been recorded in Indian legends for a thousand years; the "Star of Africa," the world's largest diamond, weighing 530 carats, which is set in the scepter of the British sovereign and kept in the Tower of London; the "Star of India" sapphire, weighing 563.35 carats, and the "Black Prince's Ruby," which Henry V wore in his helmet at the Battle of Agincourt, and which is now the centerpiece of the British Imperial State Crown.

Brilliance and Cutting

The brilliance of a gem depends upon the amount of incident light reflected from the surface and from the interior of a stone—that is, its index of refraction. The greater the index of refraction the greater the amount of light reflected. To increase the brilliance by refraction and reflection of light, stones are cut into facets. Until the Middle Ages gems were cut either *en cabochon,* rounded with a flat underside, or into flat platelets for encrusting such articles as sword hilts. The cabochon method continues to be used for opaque, translucent, and some transparent stones, such as the opal; but for most transparent gems faceted cutting is employed to increase their brilliance. The four most common cuts are the "brilliant" and "rose" cuts used for diamonds, the "step" or "trap" cut used for emeralds, and the "baguette" used for flat stones.

To provide the common man with the beauty of gems, synthetic, chemical, and glass stones have been produced since ancient days. Today plastic stones are also widely used. These have the advantages of providing color and textural variation to costume and furnishings and of being readily available and replaceable. However, they lack the aura of preciousness, mystery, and charm long associated with precious stones. Of the gem stones jade will be given further consideration for its special functional and decorative usefulness to man.

Jade

Jade, which today is considered a semiprecious stone associated with the ornament, wealth, and luxury of ancient China, was used before metals were for both functional and decorative purposes by primitive neolithic man. The Alaskan Indians and the Aztec and Mayan carvers used jadestone not only for decoration but for tools and weapons. Even as late as 1769 Captain James Cook found the Maoris of New Zealand, who were ignorant of metals, using tools, weapons, and ornaments made from wood, shell, whalebone, and jadestone.

Definition
The jadestones are jadeite and nephrite, with nephrite being the more common. Jadeite is a silicate of sodium and aluminum; nephrite a silicate of calcium and magnesium. Dependent upon such mineral contents as iron, chromium, and manganese, both are similar in color, ranging from near white or colorless to yellow, green,

mauve, red-brown, and gray-black. Both have wide variations in translucency, although jadeite is more frequently translucent than is nephrite. The luster and texture of the two stones differ. Jadeite is composed of masses of interlocking grain which provide vitreous hardness and the capacity for high polish and brilliance. Nephrite consists of closely matted fibers; when polished it has an oily texture that is more mattelike than reflective.

Jade is a very hard substance that is unfusable at high temperatures. Unlike most stones it cannot be sculptured by chipping or flaking but must be drilled or ground into form. Drilling is an arduous process which makes great demands upon a craftsman's time and patience. Incision into the stone was formerly made by the use of wood, hollow bones, or bamboo staves carrying wet sand, which were rotated like primitive firemaking tools. Later, metals, crushed garnets, carborundum, and diamonds facilitated drilling.

Jadestones are valued for their color. The light colors of nephrite, such as *yang chih* ("congealed mutton fat") and *chi-ku pai* ("chicken-bone white") are considered select. In nephrite, the green *Fei-ts'ui,* ("plumage of the kingfisher") is most cherished for its likeness to the brilliant plumage of that bird. Central American jades range from apple, pea, and celadon green to green-gray. Their emerald green is called *quetzalchalchihuitl* after the brilliant plumage of the prized quetzal bird.

Historical Background
Jade is intimately tied into the life of the Chinese. As gold and silver were to the Westerner, so was jade to Eastern man. From neolithic days onward the Chinese used jade and bronze for tools and cult objects. After the introduction of iron for tools in 500 B.C., jade was the material used for religious vessels, swords, scabbards, and sculpture. Jade craft reached maturity during the Chou dynasty about 256 B.C.

Of all materials jade had a special significance to the Chinese, for they believed it to be a product of heaven itself. As such it was endowed with powers of healing, preserving, and conferring immortality. Merely possessing and contemplating objects of jade, especially those that were white or whitish in coloration, diverted evil thoughts. Jade amulets buried with the dead helped to preserve the corpse. The most sacred symbol of the Supreme Deity, which paralleled the Cross of Christendom, was a jade disk with a central circular perforation. As indicative of the esteem in which jade was held, the word *yü,* "jade," was employed in Chinese metaphor as symbolic of nobility, purity, and beauty.

For a long time the Chinese definition of jade had simply been "a stone that is beautiful." In the second century A.D. a Confucian scholar added further qualifications to include those values attributed to it by the Chinese:

It has five virtues; there is warmth in its lustre and brilliancy, this is the manner of kindness; its soft interior may be viewed from outside revealing (the goodness) within, this is the matter of rectitude; its note is tranquil and high and carries far and wide, this is the way of wisdom; it may be broken but cannot be twisted, this is the manner of bravery; its sharp edges are not intended for violence, this is the way of purity.[2]

The Chinese regarded art as a servant to the divine. To be worthy of the deity, craftsmanship had to be as perfect as humanly possible. As with much art produced by man in honoring his god, or gods, intricate and fastidious detail have been considered indicative of an attitude of reverence. A parallel can be noted in India and Persia of the sixteenth century. The Moghul emperors had hilts of swords and daggers made from jade, but, not content with the stone's simple beauty, they added inlays of gold, diamonds, emeralds, and rubies. As a result, many objects have more emphasis placed upon man's wealth and upon the ingenuity, patience, and skill necessary to work materials than upon the intrinsic beauty and eloquence of a material.

[2] Peter C. Swann, *Art of China, Korea, and Japan* (New York: Praeger, 1963), p. 33.

To the Aztecs of the twelfth and thirteenth centuries, jade also played a significant role functionally and symbolically. It was used for ornaments, amulets, vessels, and badges of rank. As with the Chinese, the Aztecs believed that jade could help in the afterlife. A piece of jade, representing the heart, was inserted into the mouth of the deceased to assure his continuous and successful functioning. The Aztecs valued jade above gold. In presenting Cortez with gifts of jade, Montezuma assumed he was conferring upon him the highest possible honor. He was surprised to find that after the glint of gold, jade seemed dull to the Spaniard.

The beauty of jade and its rarity assures that it will remain a precious medium for man's aesthetic expression.

Ceramics

As primitive man viewed his environment for means of accommodation and survival, the natural elements most obviously present were grasses, wood, stone and the earth upon which he walked. Baskets were woven into receptacles for carrying; lined with clay and then filled with water and hot stones, they also served as utensils for cooking. It is conjectured that technological advance came through accident, when a basket lined with clay was left too close to a fire, and burned. Man observed the first product to be more stonelike than air-dried clay. The same discovery was made by numerous early civilizations.

Pottery artifacts from ancient Egypt, Mesopotamia, and the Mediterranean and Aegean regions are found in most of the museums of the world. Their preservation results from the belief by men of all these cultures that not only should the body of the deceased be preserved but that, since afterlife is a continuation of natural life, similar provisions would be required. Unwittingly, ancient man left valuable visual testimonials to his way of life.

Although clay has been considered a fragile medium, its long survival attests not only to its endurance but to its ruggedness. The early uses of clay during the neolithic periods of Asian and American cultures include the fashioning of images of gods by adding pellets to a base form to build up anatomical features, such as eyes, ears, nose, and breasts. In ancient Mesopotamia everything man needed for his daily living came from the earth's clay—fishing sinkers, spindles, seals to establish property rights or to record one's beliefs, vessels—and even axes and sickles.

The use of clay for man's multiple purposes from these early times and on through the centuries makes it possible to record man's entire history through the study of clay artifacts. A sufficient number of vases are extant to allow archaeologists to make chronological reconstructions of obscure civilizations. The capacity of baked earth to preserve traces of terrestrial magnetism that are indicative of earth's geographic origin makes it possible for geologists to formulate theories of the earth's past.

As the supply of bronze became short during China's Shang and Chou dynasties, pottery vessels replaced those of bronze for exalted burials. Forms of the pottery duplicated those of bronze, and even a glaze of red and green earthenware was developed to give the same irridescent patina as was formed on the bronzes during burial. Burial objects included all the anticipated needs of man in an afterlife—from clay cooking stoves and food to pleasure pavilions, granaries, pigsties, and chicken runs. A high-fire stoneware with a greenish blown glaze, the ancestor of the long line of Chinese celadon wares, was also developed at this time.

During the brilliant Shang period (A.D. 618–907) Chinese artistry reached a zenith of influence among Far Eastern countries. As Greek and Roman art was to the West, so was that of China to the East. Plastic clay lent itself well to multiple functions such as serving as a medium for portraying the majesty of Buddha and for

12-4 *Figure of hippopotamus superimposed on photograph of real lotuses in plant form in the Ornament Exhibition of 1933. Egyptian faïence, 12th Dynasty. Collection, The Metropolitan Museum of Art, New York.*

caricaturing the ire and ferocity of the guardians to temples. The culminating achievement of the T'ang period at the turn of the tenth century was the development of pure porcelain, antedating the West's similar discovery by seven hundred years. Porcelain is produced from kaolin, a white clay fired at high temperatures. During the Sung dynasty, the manufacture of porcelain achieved a degree of aesthetic and technical perfection characterized by an elegance and delicacy which has never been surpassed by any succeeding cultures.

In the Yuan dynasty a departure from Sung ware came with the discovery of the effect of a blue cobalt underglaze. Dramatic contrasts of brilliant white were contrasted with dark intense blue in overall designs of pictorial content. These were further developed under Ming and Ch'ing rule. Blue and white ware became the prevailing style and flooded European markets in the eighteenth century. The taste for Eastern tea and other beverages produced a parallel desire for service from Chinese porcelains. With the development of European porcelain manufacturers, the designs of China continued to serve as models. The purity of Chinese white glazes, their exquisite modeling of figurines, and the gemlike color of the *famille verte* and *famille rose* ware were in the spirit valued by the rococo designers who attempted to duplicate their charm.

Japanese Ceramics

In neolithic Japan's Jōmon period, clay vessels were formed not on the wheel, as in China, but built up in coils by hand and decorated with cord markings, again evocative of basketry twining. Haniwan clay figures, strong in design, were used by the Yayoi culture of the third and second centuries B.C. to surround huge man-made mounds used for burials. These figures consisted of clay models of humans, animals, houses, or boats inserted into the tops of long cylinders (*Haniwa* means "cylinder") pressed into the earth around the tomb so the figures rested on the ground. Though much of Japanese art that followed aspired to the Chinese example,

the Haniwan figures attest to an independent Japanese inspiration. They continue to hold much charm for today's ceramists.

During much of their long ceramic history the Chinese sought to transform clay from its earthy crudeness to a heightened refinement by creating delicate forms and high-fired glasslike glazes. Technical perfection and exquisiteness were prized. Japanese potters, on

12-5 *Ewer, Oribe ware with "tortoiseshell" decoration, Japanese, Momoyama period, 17th century, height 7⅝". Stoneware with green and transparent glazes over painted decoration in brown slip. It has been hypothesized that the beautiful tracery of tortoise shells suggested the character of Chinese calligraphy. Eugene Fuller Memorial Collection, Seattle Art Museum, Washington.*

the other hand, tended to emphasize clay's natural, unassuming qualities by creating sturdy sculptural forms and using subtle earth-tone glazes, as is evident in their Shino and Oribe ware. Freedom, vitality, daring, and abandon are communicated by Japanese design. The understated beauty of Japanese ware was recognized and promoted by the tea ceremony master Sen-no-Rikyū in the sixteenth century, who encouraged the creation of beautiful but unpretentious low-fired tea bowls of rough lustrous glaze for the ceremony.

Near East Ceramics

Its culture dating from 3400 B.C., Southern Mesopotamia was one of the early cradles of civilization. It was the pivotal core of the Near East, which extended from Turkey (Anatolia) through Iran and from the Caucasus to the Gulf of Aden. During the ancient millennia, all the arts of gold, silver, copper, bronze, pottery, glass, and precious stones were developed to a high degree of excellence. The Sumerians used clay to construct thick brick walls for temple architecture. By 3100 B.C. they had recorded pictographic signs on tablets of stone and clay.

The most profound influence upon the more recent art of the Near East has been the religion of Islam, founded in the seventh century A.D., which consists chiefly of the Revelations of God as expressed by Mohammed the Prophet in the Koran. The calligrapher of that day held an exalted position above that of all other artists, for he had the sacred responsibility of enhancing the meaning of God's word through the beauty of his script. Hence the linear characters served as decorative elements on metal vessels, rugs, textiles, wood carvings, paintings, and ceramics.

Because the representation of human and animal forms was prohibited by Islamic religion, the impetus toward abstraction was reinforced by spiritual belief. Frequently, the entire surface of a material was decorated with abstract vegetative and geometric forms intertwined symmetrically in arabesques, in a lacelike,

12-6 *Water jar. E-Shino ware (brush-marked Shino), Japanese, Momoyama period, 1573–1615, height 7". Stoneware with finely pitted ash-gray glaze and painted decoration in red-brown iron oxide. The primitive character of this vessel was highly prized and still serves as inspiration to contemporary ceramists. Eugene Fuller Memorial Collection, Seattle Art Museum, Washington.*

textural pattern, with the palmetto and the Greco-Roman acanthus serving as favorite curvilinear symbols.

Under the Abbasid Caliphs (750–1258) exotic lusterware was developed. Pottery was first fired with a thick white glaze, then decorated with solutions containing metal oxides, and refired to precipitate the metals on the surface. The resulting metallic shades of gold, red, and brown contrasted richly with the white ground.

The height of Islamic decorativeness was achieved by the Seljuk Turks under the Mongol régime (1256–1393). They developed the arabesque to a classic form, and laced such elements as inscriptions and a variety of human and other animated forms into a rhythmic and integrated whole. They also developed faïence mosaic, small tessarae of glazed earthenware ordered to a pattern and secured with plaster.

Mediterranean Pottery

Between 2000 and 1500 B.C., on the island of Crete, the maritime Minoans, named after their legendary King Minos, built the first major civilization of Europe. Their technological knowledge is thought to have been gained from the Near East. Through them the dominant mainland city of Mycenae gave its name to the age and culture. The *Iliad* and the *Odyssey* are believed to have been written in late Mycenean times. Though their civilization collapsed when the main center of Knossos was

12-7 *Bottle, pear-shaped faïence, Persian, 17th century, height 11". For beauty, decoration may be simple, ornate, textural, formally geometrical and stylized, or naturalistic. The design may be so organized as to produce unity with variety, as evident in the design of this bottle. Collection, The Metropolitan Museum of Art, New York.*

destroyed in 1500 B.C. by earthquake and inundation, the Minoans laid the foundations of Greek culture, for it was the Minoan artist and craftsman who set the standards of pottery and metalwork for the entire Aegean world. Furthermore, it was from their Mycenean precursors that the Greeks acquired their heroic code, their outlook, and reverence for *arete*, the pursuit of personal excellence.

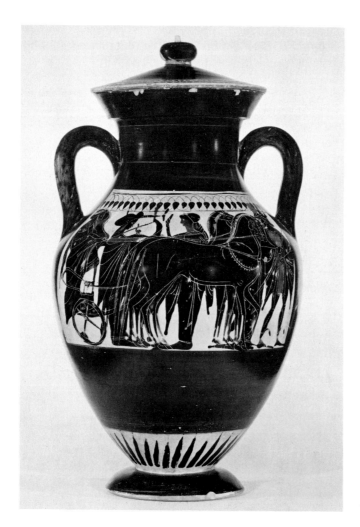

12-8 *Black-figured amphora with cover, Athenian, 6th century* B.C. *Through decoration ancient peoples recorded their history. The decoration is ordered to correspond with the structure of the vessel. Collection, The Metropolitan Museum of Art, New York.*

The great palaces built by the Minoan kings at Knossos and Phaistos have yielded knowledge of that ancient culture. The bull was adopted as the symbol of Minoan life. Ceramic vessels decorated with abstract geometrical designs—bulls, flowers, plants, creatures of the sea, and war scenes—convey the ebullient spirit and animation of these early people. The vessels remain today as informative picture books without texts.

The Greeks recorded the events in their lives on ceramic vases. Two major styles of their drinking and storage vessels are recognized: those with black figures upon a light background and those with light colors upon dark. Working with a black glaze on a light background necessarily requires greater simplification and stylizing, because shadow effects are not as readily attainable. For this reason, the black-figured wares are considered more aesthetically pleasing, because of their relatively flat patterns and greater integration of decorativeness with structural design, than are the pictorially treated light characters upon a darker ground.

Ceramics of America

Although the Aztecs of Middle America knew neither the potter's wheel nor the art of glazing, their ceramics had great vitality and artistry. The Spaniards found the Aztec culture highly advanced in ceramic production. Throughout Central and South America a variety of designs were used for statuettes and vessels. Each region produced designs characteristic of its locale. A few will be cited to indicate the artistic achievement of a civilization that did not know the use of common metals or machinery, but which succeeded in creating monumental architecture and fine sculpture.

From the site of Monte Alban come burnished jars which have the strength and vigor associated with early Chinese bronzes. In the Teotihuacan area was discovered a jar of baked clay with a polychrome pattern on a stucco ground that incorporates in its design the motif of a monster mask similar to that of the Chinese, and which is reminiscent of early Asiatic cloisonné. The

12-9 *Pre-Columbian pottery head, Vera Cruz, Mexico, height 6½".
Known as "Totanic laughing face," the design is carefully structured,
even to the headdress extending to the ears. The smile seems to emanate over the whole, lending* expressiveness. *Photograph courtesy of
The Museum of the American Indian, New York.*

ramics with a thin layer of stucco, which could then
be highly decorated. The applied design showed great
respect for the verticality of the cylinders, whereas horizontal movements provided linear contrast. Their bowls,
sculptured in relief, exhibit sophisticated handling of
material and integration of design. Outstanding also in
form and applied decoration is work from Code, Panama, which parallels the ceramic wares of the Indian
culture of the southwestern United States in whimsy
and idea and in their stylization of plant and animal
forms to conform to geometric areas. Alligator-ware jars
from Brazil are outstanding in form and conception,
resembling the bronzes of ancient China.

In North America the prehistoric American Indians
had progressed to high levels of artistry in basketry,
textile weaving, mural painting, ceramics, and sculpture.
They had a keen appreciation of three-dimensional
plastic form and an equally great concern with two-

long-headed flat-bodied Tarascan figurines, discovered
in the region known today as Michoacan, exhibit a
variety of expressions and attitudes that are universally
appealing. In the Colima region on the west coast of
Mexico, squat, plump dogs were placed in graves to
serve as guides in the afterworld; these are geometrically
bold. The Totonac square, laughing faces from Vera
Cruz, which resemble the Etruscan in conception, show
a high degree of organization, with caplike headdresses
extending to the ears, repeated frets, and geometric
delineation of features.

The Mayas developed fresco painting by coating ce-

12-10 *Pre-Columbian alligator-
ware burial jar, Brazil, height 2'.
The conventionalized reptile and fret-
like background area parallel to some
extent the decorative design conventions of Chinese bronze vessels. The
University Museum of the University of Pennsylvania, Philadelphia.*

12-11 *Pueblo jar, or olla, New Mexico, 13th century. The decoration of zigzags in frets, checkerboards, triangles, and rectangles is characteristic. Forms of white on black, with striated areas, add nuances in texture and color values. School of American Research, Santa Fe, New Mexico.*

dimensional decorative design to reinforce that form. The abstraction and geometry of their decorative design may have resulted from a long visual association with weaving, in which the warp and weft are necessarily juxtaposed at right angles in the fabrication process to create decorative pattern.

In North America, the two great pottery regions, as indicated by findings in burial mounds, were that just east of the Mississippi and the Southwest. The cultures of the East did not survive the impact of white civilization, while in the Southwest there has been no break in ceramic development. The Hohokam culture of 2,000 years ago survives today with the Pima and Papago Indians. Their pottery is buff in color, with painted red geometric designs of iron oxide arranged in complex patterns.

The earlier Pueblo culture of New Mexico developed a black-on-white pattern, inspired by basketry designs. Their most familiar pottery today is polished black ware, produced by firing the pots in a kiln made of dried cakes of animal manure, which is consumed in the process. Carbon from the fuel smoke is deposited on the pottery. Polish is secured, not through glazing, but by rubbing with smooth stones before the firing.

The Indians of the Mimbres river valley in southern New Mexico developed a style of silhouetting whimsical human and animal forms in black on the white-slipped matte surface of their wares. The ceramics of the Hopis and other southwestern United States Indians are also of high quality. Patterns of birds, thunder, corn, lightning, and other natural elements are highly conventionalized and ordered to integrate with the form of their vessels. The desert's sienna and umber tones—the colors of sand and earth—are repeated on their sturdy forms.

Ceramics Today

There are several eminent ceramists today, among them Marguerite Wildenhain, Otto and Gertrud Natzler, Peter Voulkos, John Mason, and Nicolas Vergette. Don

12-12 *Marguerite Wildenhain. Broad vase with textured flattened circles. Gray and black, 1968, height 11". Courtesy of Marguerite Wildenhain. Photograph by Fran Ortiz.*

12-13 *Gertrud and Otto Natzler. Bowl, verdigris crater glaze. Collection, The Museum of Modern Art, New York. Photograph by Hella Hammid.*

12-14 *Gertrud and Otto Natzler. Spherical pot with blue crystalline glaze. Courtesy of Gertrud and Otto Natzler. Photograph by Hella Hammid.*

Wallance in *Shaping America's Products* credits Marguerite Wildenhain with contributing much to the advanced state of ceramic development today, not only through the excellence of her ceramic art but through her articulation of the values of craftsmanship. She professes that crafts serve a number of functions: personal development, cultivation of taste, manual dexterity, a feeling for materials, and the preservation of human and creative values. She assigns to the artist the task of being "the conscience of his time." To the ma-

chine she assigns responsibility for making products of beauty and integrity.

Otto and Gertrud Natzler, innovators of a wide range of glazes and ceramic expressions, take the rudimentary elements of earth, water, and fire and scientifically control them to evolve forms of elementary simplicity, reminiscent of Zen stringency. Their control of ceramic elements has reached such a refined state that they not only can impose their own volition upon a form but can "let the medium speak its own language freely—the language of nature." Earth contains minerals and chemicals which in glazes create their own indigenous movements. By overfiring, craters are formed by emanating gases to produce lavalike flows. Variations of color, texture, and movement are created by subtle manipulations of glaze content, moisture, temperature, drafts, and smoke. For Otto Natzler, it is man's "creative emotional force that produces the form, and it is the creative in-

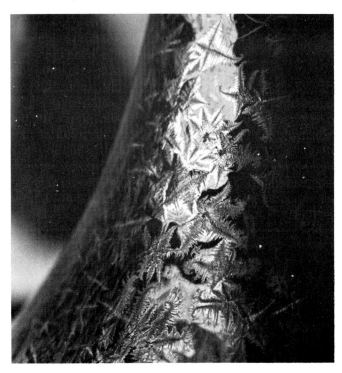

12-15 *Gertrud and Otto Natzler. Detail of a crystalline glaze. Courtesy of Gertrud and Otto Natzler. Photograph by Hella Hammid.*

12-16 *Nicolas Vergette. Garden sculpture (See Figure 4-30, for detail.) Courtesy of Nicolas Vergette.*

12-17 *Residence in New Mexico, made from adobe (earthen clay dried in the sun in desert regions). Note the timber horizontal beams and the element of light enhancing the design through cast shadows. Photograph by Julius Shulman.*

tellectual force that relates it to the natural forces of the fire, and thus the medium. . . . Enough knowledge of the complete technology of a glaze will enable us to achieve a considerable control over the accidental by willfully inducing and exploiting it. . . . Only the pot that is true to the essence of the medium, both as to form and execution, will retain the timelessness inherent in the best of ceramic art."[3]

In 1954, Peter Voulkos started a "clay movement" with John Mason in California. Influenced by abstract expression in painting, Voulkos' ceramics were dramatic and gritty, with strong color applied to large sections. He became known as the "action potter," and is credited with changing the concept of a pot that functions as a container into that of a pot as an assembled sculpture whose function is complete when it is expressive.

The versatility of ceramics is demonstrated by its use for sculpture and for interior and exterior ceramic-clad walls. In the southwest United States, earthen clay in the form of adobe is used for shelter, as seen in Figure 12-17. Suki Graef's *The Cocktail Party* speaks for itself.

Concrete and Its Decorative Uses

Concrete is one of the oldest and most useful of man-made materials. Being of rocklike composition, it was formerly used mainly to imitate stone. Only in recent decades has man developed concrete reinforced with steel to extend its tensile strength so that forms are now freed from their former massive bulkiness and can assume graceful lyrical contours. Not only has the range of concrete construction been extended structurally, but concrete has been made into a diversity of decorative forms to beautify architecture. Sculptors also have found it a valuable plastic medium for expression.

[3]Otto Natzler, "Direction: Penetration of a New Medium." *Craft Horizons*, Vol. 24, July/August, 1964, pp. 24–27.

12-18 *Suki Graef.* The Cocktail Party, *stoneware, 6′ x 3′, 200 lb. Design for whimsy.* California Design XI, *Pasadena Art Museum.*

Composition

Concrete is a generic term that includes any hard insoluble material composed of an aggregate—crushed stone or gravel—mixed with sand, water, and a cementing material. In ancient times clay and bitumen were the cementing materials used; the use of burned gypsum and lime dates back to the Egyptians. Lime was used extensively by the Romans to create imposing

12-19 *Herbert Goldman.* The Henge, *of Gunnite concrete sprayed over welded steel pipe frames, is a monumental sculptural structure, 100' long and rising 15' above the surrounding landscape in New Mexico. It extends underground in a labyrinth of passageways, galleries, spiraling staircases, and caverns. The hillock on which it stands is also a part of the sculptural entity. Courtesy of Herbert Goldman.*

12-20 *Frank Lloyd Wright.* George Millard House, *Pasadena, California, 1906. The surrounding landscaping embraces and the pool mirrors the star-studded house of concrete blocks. Photograph courtesy of The Museum of Modern Art, New York.*

masonry structures of great length and span—aqueducts, bridges, and great public baths.

Today two types of cement are recognized: Portland cement, which is composed of calcium aluminum silicate and so named for its resemblance to the Portland stone found in Great Britain and an alumina cement, identified as such because of its high content of alumina, nature's hardest mineral, except for the diamond. These raw materials are ground to a powder, and, with the addition of water, a chemical reaction occurs. The mass becomes plastic, and gradually solidification takes place. Because of the many varieties of aggregates that may be used for additional color and texture, and also because of its original plasticity, concrete can be made into unlimited decorative forms by the designer. Moreover, though originally only white or drab gray in hue, cement can now be colored to include a palette of red, buff, khaki, and black. The variety of finishing processes that are possible further increase the decorative potential and appeal of the medium.

Structural Decorative Design

Until the 1960s the wide use of concrete in the United States was generally considered to be of inferior aesthetic quality, whereas on the European continent architects were employing concrete for a range of structures in which decorativeness as well as function were given thoughtful consideration. Because the concrete used for architectural purposes is usually contained in forms made from wood, the pattern and texture of the forming boards and the bolts securing them are impressed upon the concrete and constitute an important part of the final aesthetic. Hence, if the concrete does not have its surface modified by additional treatment after solidifying, it is essential that the preliminary architectural drawings include the position of the construction joints and the bolts securing the forms that will contain the cement.

A very well-planned design is the UNESCO Congress Hall in Paris, where construction joints and bolt holes

12-21a, 12-21b *Group of two. Cast concrete blocks for architectural design come in a variety of patterns, two of which are shown here. These weigh 12 lb per unit. They may also come in Nova-Stone, weighing approximately 1½ lb per unit. Arts for Architecture, Inc., a division of James Seeman Studios, Inc.*

were carefully planned and treated as part of the building's ultimate design. Because they were not possible to conceal, a splayed timber fillet was attached to the framework at the joints to create a recessed groove that accentuated the design. The bolts were likewise ordered into the total design pattern.

In the United States in 1923 Frank Lloyd Wright was building cement homes in California in which he developed the aesthetic potential of concrete. Using machine techniques, he created richly patterned decorative blocks that could be used for both interiors and exteriors. His last structure, the Guggenheim Museum of Non-Objective Art in New York City, is a daring exploration of concrete to simulate the continuous spiral flow of a nautilus shell.

A few other decorative devices for making blocks or a framework that contains the concrete should be noted. Overlapping the forming boards or using circular tree trunks creates interesting striations. Attaching regular or irregular pieces of lumber to the basic framework creates a bas-relief, an incised pattern in the face of the concrete. Thus walls of concrete can have an interesting play of light and shadow that varies throughout the day. Thermoplastic sheeting can be used on areas to provide smooth eggshell finishes that contrast with the more complex ones to offer more variety.

Other design manipulations include those that deteriorate the surface to expose the aggregate. Washing, brushing, rubbing with abrasives, using hydrochloric acid, or sandblasting over a stencil of engraved lines will reveal the texture of coarse aggregates in patterns that contrast with that of smooth cement. Plastic molds can also be used for creating intricate designs in concrete blocks. The apertures created by the mold can be filled with glass, ceramics, or plastics to make decorative walls, dividers, and panels.

Structural Design

With the development of reinforced concrete, that is, the embedding of steel bars or mesh in the concrete for added tensile strength, the structural design of buildings changed. The rigidity of the right angle in architecture was supplemented by elliptical forms. Buildings no longer rested on broad supportive bases but were cantilevered in winglike aerial postures. (These are particularly evident in some of Eero Saarinen's architecture.) As buildings were constructed with more rhythmic contours, man could contemplate his architecture not only as shelter but as sculpture.

Another technical advance that permitted engineers and architects to design lighter and more graceful structures without sacrificing strength was the development of prestressed concrete. By reinforcement with high-strength steel wire or rods that had been subjected to tension, a concrete was developed that could span wider distances and bear heavier loads, thus further liberating space. The new lyricism achieved by these means has already been noted in the works of Pier Nervi and Oscar Niemeyer.

Copper and Alloys 13

Copper

Copper in its pure stage was one of man's first metals, dating back to the late Stone Age. Perhaps, seated around his campfire, man accidentally found that fire could melt copper and permit its reshaping. It was then used for ornamental purposes and for making hammers, weapons, and utensils. It combines with other metals to produce the alloys of bronze and brass.

The island of Cyprus was highly prized for its abundance of copper. Hence it passed into the successive control of Egyptions, Assyrians, Phoenicians, Greeks, Persians, and Romans. Copper was known as *Cyprium aes,* "ore of Cyprus," which the Romans later abbreviated to *cuprum,* giving us our chemical symbol Cu.

Copper has been valued through the ages for its warm reddish texture, its gleaming reflection of light, and its conductivity. Domestic vessels dating back to the fourth millennium B.C. have been found in Sumer and Egypt. In the eighteenth century, collections of copper and brass would be the pride of a household. Well-equipped kitchens were agleam with burnished copper and brass, which were displayed for visual enjoyment as well as for accessibility. Large establishments might have as many as five hundred vessels, requiring the full-time service of a polisher for household metals. Today Revere ware utilizes copper in the bottom portion of utensils for rapid heat conduction. The contrast of two metals enhances the aesthetic qualities of each: the warm copper tone is complemented by the cool color of stainless steel.

Copper is also being used in furnishings, in combination with other materials such as brass, slate, and wood,

13-1 *Revere Ware. Copper-clad stainless steel, which dates to 1801, has become a familiar household word. Courtesy Revere Copper and Brass Incorporated, New York.*

13-2 *The New Imperial Palace, Tokyo, 1968, with copper roof. The eye delights in the lines and proportion. Japan Information Service, Tokyo.*

13-3 *Detail of the New Imperial Palace, Tokyo, 1968, with copper roof. Japan Information Service, Tokyo.*

for its color and textural contribution. Thin-gauge copper is being laminated to plywood to extend the range of architectural materials. Copper combines a dramatic color and sheen with functional durability. The Sports Palace constructed for the 1968 Olympics in Mexico City has an all-copper roof of 121 pyramidal shapes that echo the shapes of the nearby Aztec pyramids.

Another unique and beautiful structure is Japan's new Imperial Palace in Tokyo, completed in 1968. The amount of copper needed for its sensational roof and for pillars and eaves exceeded 700 tons. Other facets of its exterior construction, in which modern technology was adapted to carry on classic styles, are also noteworthy. In traditional Japanese architecture, the exterior walls of a structure require a plaster finish. However, the same color sense as a plaster finish was achieved by using aluminum plates on which white acrylic plastic was fused. On the interior, tradition is preserved through the use of the finest grains of cryptomeria wood and specially woven brocade and hand-woven tapestries.

Bronze

Bronze, an alloy of approximately 90 percent copper and 10 percent tin, is thought to be the first alloy to have been created. Preceding its development, man had to learn the art of refining copper and tin from their associated ores. The resistance of bronze to corrosion has earned it the descriptive label of "the eternal metal." Its textural variations, gained through atmospheric exposure, increase its beauty. After centuries of burial in the earth, a shifting patina of greens, cobalt blues, sepias, and browns develops on the surface of objects. The sculptor and metal worker today attempt to duplicate the enviable weathered texture of ancient objects by the use of chemicals. The enhancement of bronze

13-4 *Mirror back of late Celtic period art, end of 1st century* B.C., *height 13¾". The mirror is of incised and patinated bronze, its handle of linked, soldered iron rings. By permission of the Trustees of the British Museum, London.*

through weathering has made it through the ages a favored material for outdoor sculptures.

In Europe the Etruscans were first to employ bronze for multiple purposes. Cast or beaten bronze was used for votive vessels and statues of gods and heroes, for swords and helmets, furniture and candelabras, and even for chariots. The Metropolitan Museum houses a chariot of circa 600 B.C., whose sheathing is of bronze inlaid with silver and gold. Circles of polished bronze, silver, and copper served as hand mirrors to ancient peoples.

13-5 *Bronze statuette of a horse, Greek, 8th century B.C., height 6 5/16". Ancient sculptures capture some dynamic rhythms and intriguing proportions in stylized designs. Collection, The Metropolitan Museum of Art, New York.*

13-6 *French commode, 1750–1775. A highly decorative rococo commode with veneer and marquetry of rosewood, tulipwood, and other woods on oak. The mounts are of gilt bronze and the top is of marble. André Charles Boulle and other 18th-century ébénistes designed in this spirit. Courtesy of the Cooper-Hewitt Museum of Decorative Arts and Design, Smithsonian Institution.*

Metallurgy was so highly respected during the Renaissance that learning metalcraft was considered a prerequisite for working in other media. At the Florentine school, sculpture in bronze flourished. Bronze was used for the doors of the Spanish palace at Cordoba, the Roman Pantheon, the Hagia Sophia in Constantinople, St. Mark's in Venice, and the Florentine Baptistry. It served as a mounting for jewels and sword blades and was used for ecclesiastical items such as reliquaries, crucifixes, medals, and vases. Donatello's equestrian statue of Gallamelata at Padua, designed in 1453, is one of the first great bronzes. Domestic use of bronze during the Renaissance included door knockers and handles, inkstands, and candleholders.

In the seventeenth and eighteenth centuries, French *ébénistes* worked in ormolu (gilt applied to bronze or to a baser metal) in order to produce furniture mountings of intricate and unparalleled workmanship. André Charles Boulle inlaid copper and brass on tortoiseshell and sculptured bronze mounts on the sumptuous cabinetry he designed for Louis XIV for furnishing the palace of Versailles. With industrialization, the use of bronze declined.

Bronze in the Far East

The most extensive use of bronze occurred during the eighteenth to the third centuries B.C., in China under the Shang and Chou dynasties. So voluminous was the production of bronze vessels and weapons, and so enduring the metal, that today thousands of bronze artifacts provide testimony to that great aesthetic achievement. Regarded as a status metal connoting luxury, the supply was monopolized by the ruling classes of China who reserved its use for lofty purposes.

Objects most frequently designed from bronze were vessels. Ritual vessels were used in ancestral worship. Ceremonial vessels aided in deifying Buddha. A variety of vessel forms was developed, each with a characteristic design and specific function. For instance, *ting* vessels were used for cooking sacrificial food; sacrificial

13-7 *Chinese ritual food vessel of the Shang dynasty, 1523–1028 B.C., bronze, height 9½". The vessel is formally balanced and illustrates characteristics of the monster mask. The patina and encrustation developed through the centuries is a prized part of its total aesthetic. Gift of Mrs. Donald E. Frederick, Seattle Art Museum, Washington.*

wine was served in *taun* vessels. Vessels were also employed in the celebration of great events such as granting a fiefdom to a king or commemorating important events in the lives of the owners. Bronze also served as heirlooms for the Chinese, with such inscriptions chased on vessels as, "Let sons and grandsons for a myriad years cherish and use." Being associated with divine or sacred usage, vessels were not only functional but highly decorative. Abstract patterns of silver, jade,

or turquoise were often inlaid in them to further enhance the luster of the bronze.

Character of Decorative Design of Chinese Vessels

Both the forms and the decorative design of Chinese bronzes were uniquely different from those of early Greek cultures. The Oriental functions at a lower eye level than does Western man. This closeness to the earth is reflected in the design of bronze vessels as well as in low furniture and the more prevalent use of floor pillows. Chinese vessels tend to be squat and substantially bellied, establishing a close spatial tension with the surface on which they are placed. They have feet instead of legs, ears instead of handles.

The cast decorative designs, though sculptural, are basically compact, two-dimensional, and linear. The most common geometric motif is the squared spiral *lei wen*, the "thunder" pattern. Animal forms of dragons, serpents, tigers, and mythical beasts are highly stylized and ordered to relate to the form of the vessel they decorate. Fascinating design results from the frequent metamorphosis of one creature into another on the same vessel, such as a tiger changing to an owl, who in turn metamorphoses into another bird.

The chief animal motif of the Shang was the "ogre or gluttonous mask," the *t'ao t'ieh*, which consists of two animals—either serpents, bulls, tigers, or deer—seen in profile facing each other. Their forms are flattened to create a masklike quality similar to the carvings of the Indians of the American Northwest and of the Mayan Indians in Mexico and Central America.

Bronze Today

In the 1950s and 1960s there was a renaissance in bronze casting as the lost-wax process of casting, used by many ancient civilizations, was revitalized. The foundry became a classroom as enthusiasm for the lost art grew in the art classes of colleges, universities, and art schools. Some artists have chosen to revive traditional methods which have fallen into disuse. Such artists are aware that throughout the history of mankind,

13-8 *Omi (King) of Ife, Nigeria, 13th to 14th century, height 14½"—lifesize. The bronze was cast by the lost-wax process. The Omi has a proud mien. The scarification of his face reiterates the rhythmic decorativeness of the bust. By permission of the Trustees of the British Museum, London.*

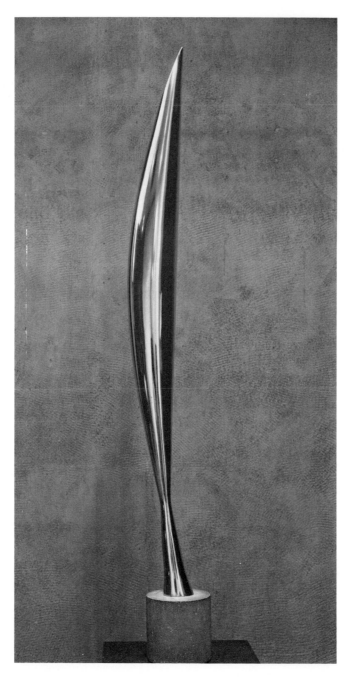

some art forms have been irretrievably lost. When a culture fails to pass on such knowledge, the loss becomes a form of cultural extinction.

Brass

Brass is an alloy consisting mainly of copper and zinc. Like bronze, it was probably discovered accidentally, because copper often occurs in ores containing zinc as well as tin, and hence at first it was not differentiated from bronze.

The decorative use of brass does not go back to as ancient an age as other metals, because its production occurred later; nevertheless, it is one of the most highly developed craft metals of ancient civilizations. It first came into European prominence during the closing years of the Roman republic. In India, crafts have long been used symbolically to express the emotional urges of the people and so their art has not only practical but religious and philosophical significance. The importance of handicrafts was established in the Indian scriptures in these words: *Atma Sams Kritir Vaba Shilpani* (Handicrafts are the surest means of the salvation of our souls). Hence it is not unusual to find metalcraft, including the use of gold, silver, tin, and brass, developed extensively there. One of the skills is that of damascening. This art of decorating metals by inserting and hammering metal wires into the grooves of a receiving metal, originally received its name from Damascus, where it is still widely practiced today. The Indian designs are often very intricate lacy arabesques of conventionalized natural forms.

Brass is prized for its goldlike luster. Benares is especially famed for its brass wares, including trays, cups, shields, and betel nut holders. Tin is often soldered to the brass and then incised to reveal the color beneath. The creation of dolls and toys, which are used for decoration, for festivals and acts of worship, and as play-

13-10 *Brass bowl inlaid with gold and silver, Persian, second half of the 14th century (Mongol period), diameter 7¼". Brass was frequently used in conjunction with other metals for richness of texture and for vivid visual contrasts. Collection, The Metropolitan Museum of Art, New York.*

things for children, has had a long and continuous history in India. Little terra-cotta figurines and playthings have been found at all the archaeological sites inhabited by the Indus people. Ivory and polished brass are favored materials for toys—or: temples, chariots, bullock carts, scenes from Hindu mythology, and figures of ani-

mals. Little girls often have a complete set of pots and other household utensils made from clay or metal.

In Western cultures, brass came to marked attention when it was used to decorate French furniture of the early eighteenth century, and it was much used in the period styles that followed both in France and England. Its rich color and the ease with which it can be worked have contributed to a range of decorative household uses.

13-11 *Brass chandelier, Netherlands, second half of the 17th century, height 71". This is an example of beauty in design that can be created by respect for the nature of a material. Collection, The Metropolitan Museum of Art, New York.*

13-12 *Brass-plated funerary figure of Bagota tribe, Africa. Notice how striated rhythmic lines dramatize certain areas and the repetitive use of similar forms create unity. By permission of the Trustees of the British Museum, London.*

In home furnishings today brass is not as extensively used as in past decades, because stainless steel and glass have replaced it to a great extent. However, its gleaming color and contrast with the cooler hues of other metals will no doubt assure it a unique role in the home. Just as copper is frequently used in combination with other materials, so brass is used for its contribution to the ensemble. It still remains a popular material for door-knobs, lamps, lighting fixtures, candlesticks, bowls, and vases. In Japan, China, and Thailand it is a common medium for flatware. It has long been used by primitive people for masks, because of its textural quality and color and the ease with which it can be plated to other materials. These days, contemporary artists and crafts-men are pounding brass to produce many objects, in-cluding sculptures.

Pewter

Metals, like people, can assume a hierarchy of status. Those that are rarest and most precious, such as gold and silver, have long associations with the aristocracy and royalty. Pewter is an inverse alloy to bronze, being basically 90 per cent tin and 10 per cent copper. It is softer than bronze and does not have its rich patina. Widely used by a broad populace, it has not been con-sidered a luxury metal; its soft gray color has earned it the epithet of "poor man's silver." However, it has its own subtle qualities and a quiet sophistication that is cherished and preferred by many.

Types of Pewter

Two kinds of pewter may be differentiated—antique and modern. Pewter used by the Orientals two thou-sand years ago and by the Romans contained sufficient lead to cause the surface to develop a dark satiny sheen. Pewter of this antique formula was crafted by the mas-ters of Williamsburg, Virginia. Reproductions are still popular today, some of them being cast from the origi-nal molds. Ancient pewter has subdued luster, neutral color quality, and a sensuous tactile surface unlike that of silver or polished chromium. Its quiet reticence, warmth, and unassuming character make it congenial in a variety of interiors.

Modern pewter contains 91 per cent tin, 7.5 per cent antimony for whiteness and hardness, and 1.5 per cent copper. With machine polishing, its surface develops a whitish, crisp, bright sheen. It lacks the mellow quality of the ancient metal, but relates well to contemporary materials.

Other Properties

Pewter was considered the plastic of its day because it is highly fluid, malleable, and ductile. Unlike many other metals it does not harden or stiffen with cold working by tools, so it requires no annealing. The fact that it melts at 425–440°F. makes possible the conversion of old pewter objects into new. This quality gave rise to the "traveling tinker" of colonial America who travel-ed on horseback or afoot carrying his molds with him. He repaired, bought, sold, melted, and recast old pewter.

The same techniques of metalcraft apply to pewter as to other metals. An additional frequent treatment of pewter is *appliqué,* in which several layers of metal are built up by soldering. Many pewter pieces are charac-terized by moldings of Greek columns at the base and mouth. Enrichment comes from the simple moldings, which are terminal to broad surface areas that have been planished to smoothness with hammer blows.

Historic Uses

Like bronze, pewter, with its composition of copper and tin, was well known to ancient civilizations. The Orientals used it for temple decoration, sculpture, and religious accessories, often inlaying it with other metals or precious stone for greater enrichment. Romans are credited with the first practical use of pewter for utensils, coins, and seals of office. Their supply came from the extensive tin mines of Cornwall and Devon in England. Pewter objects made by the Roman legions have been excavated from English soil.

English smiths, who knew its use since Anglo-Saxon times, made extensive use of pewter for both church and domestic purposes during the Renaissance. A high quality of pewter metalcraft was maintained by the guild system. The guilds required a long apprenticeship before allowing a craftsman to practice independently, and they maintained strict supervision and regulation in the production of pewterware in order to assure its quality and merit. Pride of workmanship was generated by the use of "touch plates," which indicated membership in the guild, the Worshipful Company of Pewterers, which was chartered in 1348 by Edward III. The touch plate was a decorative steel die with the initials of the craftsman, which he could impress on his work for identification. "Touches" were recorded on a collective plate at Pewterers' Hall and displayed on the premises of each craftsman.

So prevalent was the use of pewter in Europe during the Renaissance that it has been called the Pewter Age. While the peasants used wooden platters and the nobles gold and silver plate, the middle and upper classes and the clergy dined on pewter. With the extraction of tin from the mines of the Dutch East Indies, pewter was very widely used by the Dutch for household wares. The popularity of pewterware can be noted in Dutch genre oil paintings in which pewter flagons and plates form an integral part of the composition.

In America the brazier, blacksmith, tinsmith, and pewterer were indispensable personnel in a new land. Metalcraft was an important industry in Colonial America; it ranked only behind farming and merchandising in importance to everyday life. Pewterers from England carried the tradition of quality craftsmanship to America, where the American colonist developed its use to high levels.

13-13 *German pewter pitcher, about 1770. Rhythm of fluid lines and well-planned spatial relationships predominate and contribute to the success of this design. Courtesy of the Cooper-Hewitt Museum of Decorative Arts and Design, Smithsonian Institution, New York.*

Pewter was being made as early as 1630, but an English embargo was placed upon tin, so the colonies did not make extensive use of it until the period between 1700 and 1850, which is known as the golden age of American pewter. Pewter was then used for every conceivable purpose—from mustard pots to shoe buckles. The list includes porringers, candlesticks, chandeliers, buttons, snuffboxes, flagons, and church chalices. During this time almost half the dishes manufactured were

13-14 *Frances Felton, Pewter pitcher, height 15". "Pewter is such an ideal metal to live with—so clean! . . . the absence of lead in modern pewter makes it absolutely sanitary," says Frances Felton. Compare the design merit of this contemporary pewter vessel with that of the early German one. Though hand-crafted, does not the Felton vessel reflect some of the beauty, precision, and simplicity of contemporary industrial machinery? The Museum of Contemporary Crafts, New York.*

made of pewter. The colonist could select from a wide range of sizes. On an early Georgian list of "Pewterer's Goods," dishes came in eighteen sizes, varying from 28 to 10¾ inches in diameter. Soup dishes and plates came in a corresponding range.

So important was the New York Pewterers' Society at this time that its members marched in the parade celebrating ratification of the United States Constitution in 1788. However, with the increasing supply of pottery, glass, and tinware, the use of pewter gradually diminished and only coffeepots remained as the mainstay of the industry. After 1850, as pewter work became a business and not a craft, pride in workmanship declined and inspiration was lacking. A few companies survived by supplementing their pewter production with the silver-plated wares which were much in demand.

Recently interest in pewter has been regenerated as designers look to the past for evidence of significant form, design, and use of materials. Pewter has many of those intrinsic qualities that are valued by today's artist-craftsmen and currently fine examples are mass-marketed.

Common Metals 14.

Iron and Steel

When the temple in Jerusalem was completed, Solomon invited to a feast all the artificers who had been engaged in its construction. As the throne was unveiled, the guests were outraged to see that the seat of honor on the king's right, as yet unawarded, had been usurped by the ironworker. Whereupon the people in one voice cried out against him and the guards rushed forward to cut him down.

The king silenced their protests and, turning to the stonecutter, said: "Who made the tools with which you carve?"

"The ironworker," was the reply.

To the artificer of gold and silver, Solomon said: "Who made your instruments?"

"The ironworker," they answered.

To the carpenter, Solomon said, "Who forged the tools with which you hewed the cedars of Lebanon?"

"The ironworker," was again the answer.

Then Solomon turned to the ironworker: "Thou are all men's father in art. Go, wash the sweat of the forge from thy face and sit at my right hand."

An Old Hebrew Legend

Historic Uses

Iron is the most useful metal known to man. It has traditionally been the chief material for instruments of war. With iron swords, nations made conquests that altered empires and upset geographical distributions of population. As a result, new tribes who came into power placed their stamp upon the direction of future civilizations. Iron has contributed to man's development from ancient to present times.

The earliest recorded artifacts of iron are some beads

14-1 *José de Rivera. Steel Century Two (Construction 73), 1960–65. The total diameter embraced by this motorized stainless steel construction is 11'8". It is one of the joyous sculptures to be experienced in the garden of The Museum of Modern Art. Collection, The Museum of Modern Art, New York.*

14-2 *Railway switch. Mechanical objects can have their own sculpturesque affinities. This photograph also illustrates the illusion of space that can be achieved by lines directed to a distant vanishing point. Photograph by Vincent Bernucci.*

14-3 *Long and short sword (daisho) with 15th-century blades. Japanese. Collection, The Metropolitan Museum of Art, New York.*

found at Gizeh, Egypt, that were made from meteorite iron dating from 3500 B.C. or earlier. In China by the second century A.D., the Bronze Age culture had given way to iron for the manufacture of weapons, utensils, sculpture, and temple furniture. Pagodas were cast in iron in the tenth and eleventh centuries. In the seventeenth century, the Chinese developed iron pictures to imitate ink sketches. However, iron vessels still remained imitative of those made from bronze, the traditionally prized material of China.

The Japanese were freer developing iron as an expressive material in its own right. It reached a high artistic development with the establishment of the *samurai* class after the wars of the twelfth century. The art of using the sword, which then became part of every warrior's costume, led to artistic concentration on the design of that instrument. The mountings of the blade were made highly decorative, not only by casting and hammering but by tooling, inlaying with other metals, and incrustation with precious stones. When the Edict of 1876 prohibited the wearing of swords, more emphasis was placed upon small decorative objects of iron.

In medieval Europe, when cathedrals were often subject to attack, iron was used for protective doors and windows and for screens to shield shrines, treasuries, and tombs from pillage. The ironwork of the west doors of Notre Dame in Paris was so superbly wrought that they were assessed as being of divine workmanship. Under the rule of Louis XIV, iron was highly favored as a metal. Everywhere there was iron—at the entrances of gates and gardens, in staircases for mansions and palaces, and in the screens built for churches and cathedrals. The tradition continued with the rococo style of Louis XV. Iron, being extremely manipulable, lent itself to the creation of swirling arabesques and luxurious

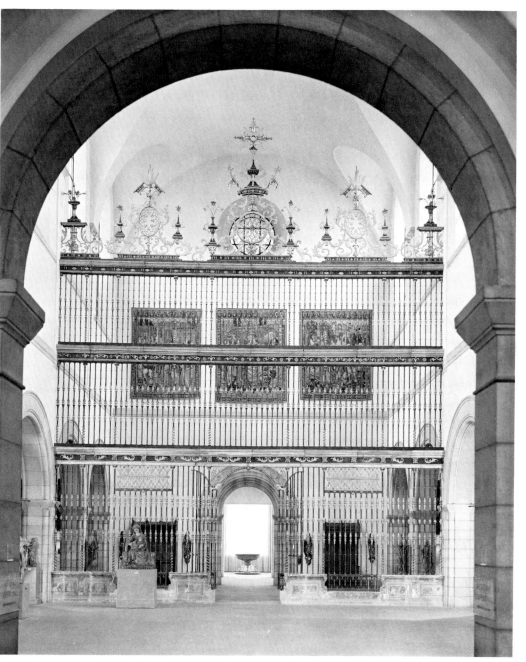

14-4 *Pedro Juan, master ironworker. Spanish* reja *of iron and limestone in the Cathedral of Valladolid, Spain, 1668, height 52', width 42'. Iron* rejas *were used to protect the wealth of the altars from robbery by invaders. Collection, The Metropolitan Museum of Art, New York.*

embellishments. Fortunately, the artists of the day preserved quality in their work by not letting the curvilinear get out of hand; they incorporated enough verticals and horizontals to preserve a sense of stability.

Until the sixteenth century, Italy is credited with preserving the character of iron by developing only those forms that could be wrought with hammer and anvil. Spain also accepted limitations of tools in order to create a tradition of superior ironwork; screens of monumental size, twenty-foot- to thirty-foot-high *rejas,* were constructed for cathedrals to shut off the high altar of the church from the nave.

Iron was widely used in colonial America. The blacksmith was an artist who designed functional objects of aesthetic merit, which varied from door knockers, weather vanes, three-legged trivets for the fireplace to keep food warm, andirons, and skillets, to hitching posts. The smith was regarded as a man of status, whose desirability is noted in the numerous surnames of Smith in the United States. He was immortalized as a colonial superman by Longfellow in the poem "The Village Smithy."

In later eras in America, iron was used to embellish architecture by means of railings, fences, grilles, gates, and balconies. The French tradition of ironwork is particularly evident in the South, which was French territory until 1803. New Orleans has the reputation for having more ironwork in balconies and porches than any other city of the United States. Preservation of the old French Quarter shows recognition of the historic artistry of an earlier era. The designs of Louisiana served in many foundries as models for smiths, who not only wrought or forged iron into intricate forms but cast and pierced it into panels for grilles, screens, and treillage.

The use of iron continued in the Victorian Gothic Revival period with its luxuriant detail. In the Art Nouveau period that followed, iron was used because it was particularly amenable to being wrought into the tendrillar decorative forms so popular at that time. Louis Sullivan made extensive use of ornament with iron in his architecture.

Contemporary Uses

Steel is a commercial derivative of iron; it can contain up to approximately two per cent carbon, which is less than does iron. The more carbon, the more brittle and the less strength. In 1856 steel was produced from iron with Bessemer converters and in 1864 by the open-hearth process. Today steel is extensively used in the construction of both residential and commercial buildings. Steel framing of housing exteriors has changed heavy massive load-bearing walls to slim columnar posts of steel that support ribbons of glass. Steel beams, because of their strength, can span vast areas, and steel reinforcement in concrete makes it possible to develop new forms to challenge the centuries-old rectilinear format. Steel cables are increasingly used to support interior balconies and to free space. Many uses of this metal are shown in the Chicago Museum of Science and Industry's permanent exhibit of the steel components that go into houses. Among these are casement windows, garden screens, stainless steel wall tiles, ribbons of enameled steel to serve as curtains or room dividers, and circular stairs.

In addition, one finds that iron and steel are much used for sculpture. A high tensile steel has been developed which when left unpainted rusts to a beautiful cinnamon brown. The rust does not develop beyond a certain point and acts as a protective skin over the steel. In Picasso's recent sculpture for Chicago's new Civic Center, the metal was deliberately allowed to rust so that its color becomes a dominant element in the design. The famous Iron Pillar of Delhi, which still stands, bears witness that the craftsmen of India were familiar with the process of making an enduring steel in the fourth century A.D.

David Smith, one of America's most important sculptors, had a particular fascination with iron. In his words: "My reverence for iron is in function before technique. It is the cheapest metal. It conceptually is within the scale of my life. And most important, before I knew what art was I was an ironmonger. The iron element

I hold in high respect. I consider it eidetic in property. The metal particularly possesses no art craft. What it can do in arriving at form economically—no other element can do."[1]

In stainless steel, iron is alloyed with chrome to prevent rusting. There are many attractive contemporary designs in stainless steel flatware, which make it a popular metal that can compete with silver for beauty. Not only is it widely used for flatware and houseware items, but today stainless steel is also being used in furniture design.

Lead

Lead is a bluish-gray metal known to everyone through the common lead pencil. Being readily reducible, with a low melting point, it was probably one of the first metals used by prehistoric man. Its utilitarian function has superceded the aesthetic, but it is not without the latter. During the eighteenth century, Germany and Austria produced lead garden sculpture of aesthetic merit. Some sculptors have favored lead in sculpture, abandoning the grander materials such as marble, wood, and bronze for lead's stark, dramatic quality. Dark, nonreflecting, and dramatic in color, it has been valued for these characteristics by sculptor Aristide Maillol in his works *The Three Nymphs* and *The River* and by Jacob Epstein for his *Virgin and Child* in Cavendish Square, London.

Like that of other metals, lead's use is ancient. Lead coins have been found in the ruins of Egypt and lead votive figures in Mycenae. The Romans made much use of lead for urns and sarcophagi. In medieval times small badges and medallions of lead were sold to pilgrims at

[1]David Smith, *Vogue*, "The Private Thoughts of David Smith," November 15, 1968, p. 136.

14-5 *Donald Wallance, industrial designer. Vantage, Lauffer stainless steel, 1966. Lauffer stainless steel incorporates the finest in form, balance, and quality. Composed with 18% chrome and 8% nickel, it is highly resistant to corrosion. H. E. Lauffer Co., Inc., New York.*

14-6 *Rex A. Stevens. Stainless steel mixing bowls,* circa 1940. *Light illuminates form by scintillating reflection to lend beauty to bowls that in their simplicity have a beauty similar to a Brancusi or Prestini sculpture. Collection, The Museum of Modern Art, New York.*

14-7 *Arne Jacobsen. Cylinda-Line hollow ware, Lauffer stainless steel, 1968. This Cylinda-line is one of the finest examples of the classic geometry of the cylinder. It has also been engineered for maximum efficiency. H. E. Lauffer Co., Inc., New York.*

religious shrines. Lead fonts dating from the twelfth century are still in existence in England. The use of lead for fonts is particularly appropriate because water does not cause the metal to rust or corrode.

Though not as highly prized as bronze and precious metals, lead was often used as a substitute for them because of its ease of workmanship and its availability. In the fourteenth century, caskets were covered with lead tracery, which was gilded to look like precious metal. During the Renaissance, replicas of bronze medals and plaques were made of lead to satisfy man's passion for collecting these items. Goldsmiths made lead molds in which to cast gold objects, because they could not model in gold as finely as they could in lead.

Because lead is immune to corrosion and weathering, it is ideal for outdoor use. It is used today for reflecting pools, bird baths, decorative door locks, and plant tubs. With its soft gray color, it is a foil for colorful flowers or for bright foliage and provides a pleasing textural contrast to cut stone, rocks, bricks, and wood.

Tin

Tin has been associated for so long with bronze that the isolation of metallic tin as an independent metal is unknown. In the Iliad, Homer refers to both tin and bronze, and Pliny the Elder establishes a difference between tin and lead by referring to tin as white lead and to lead as black lead. The earliest known objects of unalloyed tin are a ring and bottle from an Egyptian tomb dating from the Eighteenth Dynasty (1580–1350 B.C.). Generally it would seem, however, that tin was

14-9 *Tole tray, Pontypool, Wales, 1760–1770. Courtesy of the Cooper-Hewitt Museum of Decorative Arts and Design, Smithsonian Institution, New York.*

combined chiefly as an alloy with copper to make bronze.

The South American Indians of Peru were employing tin to make bronze before the advent of the Europeans. In 1519, Cortez found the natives of Taxco, Mexico, using tin for money. Tin is still widely used in Mexico for masks, chandeliers, and candleholders.

Though today the tin can is almost as disposable as facial tissue, in early America tin was much more highly cherished. At first the colonists relied solely upon wood, pewter, and ironware for their utensils and tableware. Wooden objects were bulky; both pewter and iron were comparatively dark and dull; and ironware was heavy to lift and carry. Tinware, imported from England, provided a welcome relief, because it was shiny, light in weight, and looked warm and gay when painted. About 1700, English tinsmiths had commenced the painting of tinware, known as toleware, to resemble the lacquered pieces imported from China. The structural design of tole was stable and unpretentious. Containers were created with sturdy broad bases and handles that could be gripped easily. Decorative design was bold and stylized with a lasting beauty.

Today tin is predominantly used for practical, undecorated objects. The design of the tin-faced food can is so sound, functional, and adequate that it has required no great change in design.

Aluminum

The history of aluminum is comparatively contemporary, dating from 1825. Unlike other common metals, pure aluminum cannot be produced by direct smelting

14-10 *Aluminum garden rake. Manufacturer, Kenco Products Company. Can you relate the design of this common tool to the principles of design? Collection, The Museum of Modern Art, New York.*

14-11 *Extruded aluminum forms interlocked for external architectural embellishment. Kaiser Hospital, San Jose, California. Photograph by Vincent Bernucci.*

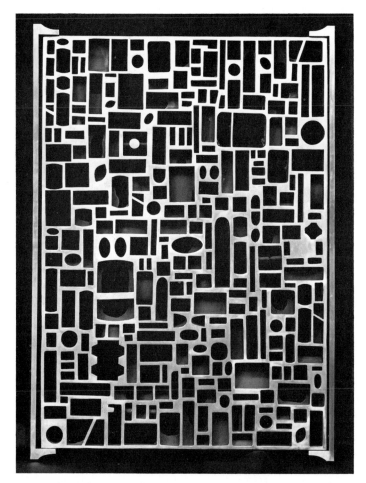

14-12 *Gene Thompson. This cast aluminum gate, 5′ x 7′, is hung on massive hinges. The face is polished, the rest unpolished. What principles and elements of design predominate?* California Design X. *Pasadena Art Museum. Photograph by Richard Gross.*

14-13 *This beach house of glass and aluminum, which rotates on a turntable to follow the sun, was designed by Robert Fitzpatrick, of the architectural firm of Harrison and Abramovitz. Built around a central aluminum column, the house features a peaked aluminum roof and glass walls that swing open. Aluminum Company of America's FORE-CAST Collection.*

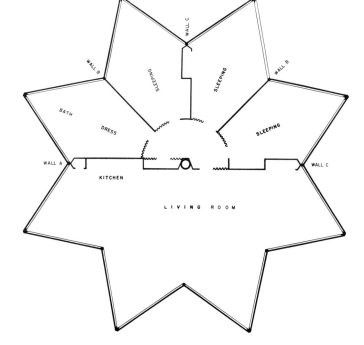

14-14 *Floor plan of Robert Fitzpatrick's beach house of aluminum and glass. Dividing walls radiate from the central area like spokes from a wheel (radial rhythm or balance). The beach house is based on a circle 37 feet in diameter and features a large living and dining area, three bedrooms, and a spacious bathroom. Aluminum Company of America's FORECAST Collection.*

of its ores; it requires chemical refining. With other metals man can trace their development and use back to ancient times. Aluminum is the end product of modern man's inventiveness; its production constitutes one of the greatest technical achievements of the nineteenth century. Today aluminum plays a leading role in domestic and architectural uses and also lends itself to decorative and sculptural forms.

Although not employed as a metal in prehistoric times, crude salts of alum were used as astringents and mordants by the fifth century B.C. Aluminum derived its name from the Latin *alumen,* which signified a sulphate of alum, probably potash. By the thirteenth century man had converted the crude salts to crystalline form. That this had a metallic base was proved in 1809 by Sir Humphry Davy, who suggested the name "aluminum" for this metal. In 1825, Hans Christian Oersted produced aluminum by amalgamation. The modern electrolytic method of producing aluminum was discovered simultaneously in 1886 by Charles M. Hall of the United States and Paul Hirault of France. This advance in technological means, the development of a dynamo that produced currents of several hundred amperes to facilitate separation of elements, was responsible for the subsequent rapid development of commercial aluminum.

Aluminum has had what might be called a displacement history. In the 1890s it displaced cast iron for tea kettles, with aluminum ones being cast from the same molds. During World Wars I and II aluminum replaced wood in the construction of airplanes. Today anodyzed aluminum is replacing chrome-plated steel for appliances and automobiles. Because of its lighter weight, high strength, and low cost, aluminum foil has replaced tin foil as a wrapping material for foodstuffs. The tin beer can has been displaced by the aluminum one.

Because of aluminum's special properties, it has been used widely in the architectural industry since 1926. By 1960, the building and construction industry had become the largest consumer of aluminum. Its intrinsic texture and color may be retained for its own luminous gray beauty, or it can be modified through painting,

14-15   *Charles Eames. Aluminum group, soft pad swivel lounge chair. Courtesy of Charles Eames.*

14-16   *Charles Eames. Solar Toy, aluminum. Energy is provided by solar rays, which set the toy in motion. Courtesy of Charles Eames.*

enamelling, anodyzing (application of pigment by electrolic action) or coating with acrylic plastic. Harrison and Abramovitz produced the Alcoa house, in Pittsburg, Pennsylvania, the first aluminum-clad building (thirty stories). Robert Fitzpatrick, on their staff, won Alcoa's *Forecast* competition with his summer house in the form of an eight-pointed star, described as "a crown jewel on the land that wears it." His house is unique in that he approached the use of aluminum with no preconceived ideas except that the form be congruent with its ultimate function—to provide an intimate environment for rest and relaxation. He disposed of the traditional post-and-beam and also the relatively new concept of curtain walls for an aluminum starlike form, cut, as it seemed, from folded origami paper with alternating planes of aluminum and glass.

A dramatic use of aluminum in home furnishings is in furniture design. Aluminum can express qualities of sophistication, lightness, and grace. Its reflective texture of inorganic composition contrasts with the organic composition of fabrics, leathers, and plastics. Designers Charles Eames, George Nelson, Eero Saarinen, Paul McCobb, and Edward Wormley very early capitalized upon the potential of aluminum by employing it in furnishings, pedestal bases, and seating frames.

In the fine arts, sculptures of aluminum are increasingly numerous. Charles Eames created one of the first aluminum kinetic sculptures, a solar toy employing the power of the sun, which, from 93 million miles away, acts as a fuel source to rotate reflecting disks of aluminum. His objective was to demonstrate the availability of one of our natural resources, solar energy; he made a highly imaginative toy sculpture utilizing the sun's energy to put motors, wheels, and pistons into action and to cause colors to flash and blink. It is delightful as sculpture as well as illustrative of nature's omnipresent resources, which can be utilized constructively—if for no other purpose than to charm man.

Precious Metals 15

Gold

Unlike most other metals, which are combined in ores with various minerals, pure gold can occur in the form of nuggets, flakes, and specks. Hence, it is thought to have been the first metal used by primitive man. Because of its beauty and rarity, it is considered the most precious of man's metals. It has been the symbol of wealth in all great civilizations. Men have fought, died, and pirated for it. Whereas other metals have been melted and remelted in critical historic times, gold and gold artifacts such as jewelry and vessels have been so valued that all the known quantities extracted in the last ten thousand years have been accumulated in banks, government vaults, and museums throughout the world. Since 1493 all the gold that is mined goes through countinghouses and mints. No other material has been so zealously hoarded and guarded.

During the Middle Ages the fascination with gold led alchemists, who considered it the very elixir of life, to try to create it from baser metals. Even today gold engages the efforts of chemists, who attempt to transmute base metals into golden isotopes.

In ethics as well as beauty, gold has been employed metaphorically as the symbol of excellence. The golden rule, "Whatever you would that men should do to you, do ye even so to them," is a concept whose name implies the superseding of all other rules. The golden mean and golden section of the Greeks signified the ultimate in divisions of space. In the Old Testament, Aaron made a golden calf for the Israelites to worship during Moses' absence on Mount Sinai. From the eleventh century onward, each year the pope has sent a golden rose

15-1 *Gold necklace with plaited strap and bud and amphora-shaped pendants, thought to be from Asia Minor, 4th to 3rd century* B.C. *Notice the rhythm through gradation in the size of the amphorae. Could the necklace be worn with today's costumes? Collection, The Metropolitan Museum of Art, New York.*

America, the Spaniards were dazzled by the gold of Mexico and South America. So greedy were they that Montezuma is reported to have remarked, "The Christian must have a strange disease that can only be cured with gold." To the Indian, gold was valued not as a medium of exchange, but as one of the most satisfying materials for man's religious expression. His possession and enjoyment of it was in the form of ceremonial and decorative objects. The Spaniards lacked this appreciation and, though they retained some articles that were small enough to be carried on their bodies, even converting some to body chains, vast amounts were stockpiled, melted down into ingots and bars, and stamped with the royal arms of Spain. Cortez is reported to have had a cannon made of gold and silver alloy.

Pizarro found gold so abundant in Peru that he ordered golden shoes for his troops' horses as the iron ones wore away. He found the Incas employing gold and silver not only for the goblets, ewers, vases, and ornaments they used in their temples and palaces, but for roofing their Temple of the Sun. To the Incas gold was the tears of the sun. So great a quantity of gold was being brought from the New World to Spain during the sixteenth and seventeenth centuries that it served as further motivation for England to seize Spanish ships.

The discovery of gold in California in 1848 led American pioneers westward over the Rocky Mountains and to the Pacific in the "Gold Rush" years. Another transmigration took place between 1890 and 1915 when gold was discovered in the Alaskan Yukon. The lure of gold has always caused men to give up the comforts of the known and secure to brave dangers and deprivation, in the hope of enjoying its luster, touch, and possession.

Artistic Uses of Gold

Gold leaf is gold beaten to the thinness of a leaf. As such, it is translucent, and so delicate that it can be moved or straightened with a slight breath. Its use was known in ancient Egypt and Rome. Egyptian furniture and mummy cases were gilded with gold. Roman capi-

set with gems to a meritorious individual or ecclesiastical body as an expression of highest honor.

Gold supposedly became known in the Aegean area during the early Bronze Age. Continuous military ferment in the countries bounding the sea resulted from attempts by early civilizations to gain control of the gold-producing regions of the Aegean and of Thrace and Macedonia. Gold artifacts have been found in Egyptian, Minoan, Assyrian, Etruscan, Greek, and Roman remains. Burials dating from medieval North and South American civilizations have also yielded objects of gold.

In other continents, gold was also the motivation that spurred men on to conquer other civilizations and unknown wildernesses. Following the discovery of

15-2 *Two-handled Greek-Mycenean* kanthoros *of gold, 1450–110 B.C. Collection, The Metropolitan Museum of Art, New York, Rogers Fund, 1907.*

15-3 *Daniel Smith and Robert Sharp, London, 1785. Gold teapot and stand, height 9⅝". The cylindrical simple elegance of this teapot compares with that of a classic column. The spout, knob, and handles are of wood: the tray protects polished table tops. Beaded mouldings are echoed at many structural points for unity and rhythm. Courtesy of The Barber Institute of Fine Arts, The University of Birmingham, England.*

15-4 *Jack Lenor Larsen.* Bagdad. *Casement cloth of golden fiber. Jack Lenor Larsen Inc.*

tals and temples gleamed in the sun with gold leaf. It still remains the principal material for gilding wood, paper, textiles, metals, ceramics, and glass.

Gold, silver, and bronze were used in the ancient Minoan and Mycenean cultures. Though silver and bronze were frequently used for vases, gold was used more exclusively for cups, small phials, boxes, and funeral furniture. The classical form of the *kantharos,* a drinking vessel of reverse concave and convex curvature, was developed by the Myceneans.

During the classical period, gold and silver were used by the Greeks for a variety of vessels. These served as an enrichment to shrines and sanctuaries, as offerings to the gods, as evidence of gratitude to them for athletic successes, and as expressions of human atonement. At Delos in the fourth century B.C., sixty different kinds of vessels appeared on the treasure list. Stored in boxes, these required the employment of an official inventory clerk for their cataloging and surveillance.

The comparative rarity of gold led to the development of basic forms that were retained for extended periods of time. Fortunately the Minoans, Myceneans, and the archaic and classic Greeks had a refined sense of proportion and an intuitive sense for the potential of materials. Their timeless forms served as prototypes for the Romans and later European cultures. They continue to serve as inspiration to ceramists today.

Today gold is not as widely used as in the eras before controls restricted its circulation. However, gold leaf, with its luminosity and gleam, is still widely employed in decorating the altars of cathedrals in order to suggest divinity and glory. Small quantities are also frequently used by today's artists to enhance contemporary paintings. Exquisite pieces of jewelry are wrought in gold by contemporary designers. To extend the range in fabric design, Jack Lenor Larsen designed a gold casement textile inspired by the cloths of the court of Kublai Khan. Flatware in gold tones is being increasingly used for table service. Its warmth of tone may have greater consistency with the color ranges of food than does the coolness of silver and stainless steel. Through electrolysis, gold can be deposited upon a base metal, with the range varying from 12K to 23K, the depth of gold increasing with the increase in karats. Such flatware is called vermeil. Dirilyte, invented by two Swedish engineers more than forty years ago and manufactured in the United States, is an alloy of a golden color. Being a solid metal, the gold is consistent throughout the depth of the ware and so will not wear through. However, the range of dirilyte designs, though select and of excellent quality, are limited—unlike that of vermeil, which can be applied to the multiple variety of silver patterns on the market and whose greater range of ornateness of design may appeal to many.

Silver

The use of silver can be traced back to the beginnings of civilization in the Egyptian, Greek, Celtic, Saxon, and Roman worlds. Even then wealth was measured by man in terms of the precious metals. From the early Bronze Age throughout ancient times, silver was obtained by smelting lead ores and then separating the silver. Asia Minor, from which silver was exported as early as 3000 B.C., is considered the home of silver. By 800 B.C. both gold and silver were used as currency in all the countries between the Indus and the Nile.

Silver has had a long history of association with the romantic and with the mysterious appeal of the moon. A silver coin broken in half, each partner retaining a part, preceded the use of a wedding ring. The tradition of a parental gift of silver flatware to the bride is thought to have begun in the Golden Age of Greece, when a father endowed his daughter with part of his wealth, including silver utensils. The association of silver with luminosity and the enchantment of the moon is reflected in the poetry of man's daily speech. Lovers meet "by the light of the silvery moon." Clouds have silver linings. Orators are silver-tongued. Moonbeams are silvery. According to Roman records, before the use of the word *argentum*, from which the chemical symbol of silver, Ag, is derived, *luna* and a crescent moon were symbols of silver.

Spanish silver was used by the Greeks in 650 B.C. and by the Romans after Hannibal acquired the silver mines as a result of the Second Punic War. During the Aegean Bronze Age, almost all the basic skills in producing gold and silver were already known, except for casting and spinning. Gold and silver were in the possession of the wealthy, so no smith was permitted to work independently. Silver, like gold, was used for multiple lofty purposes: as gifts to the gods, for the decorative enrichment of shrines, as diplomatic gifts of exchange, as thank offerings for athletic victories, and as memorials of events. As with all Greek design, the vessels were in excellent proportion, decoration was restrained, and objects had a universal and perennial appeal.

Although the Greeks used silver vessels almost exclusively for serving liquids, the Romans brought silver into extensive use and production for domestic as well as ritualistic purposes. Frequent conquests led to their exploitation of the rich silver mines of Macedonia, making silver available for private individuals as well as rulers. The acquisition and appreciation of silver approached the proportion of a cult. Wealthy businessmen used gold and silver as collateral. Collecting expensive tableware was commonly practiced. Silver was used not only for vessels and plates, ladles and strainers, but for furniture, bathtubs, mirrors, and even ear picks. Because food was brought in ready-cut portions to the table, knives were not necessary. Cereal spoons with pointed handles doubled for the extraction of shellfish. Large households had to employ several slaves to care for the gold and silver wares.

The variety of vessels used by the Romans for serving and pouring wine paralleled the Greek, but the silver designs copied from Greek models lacked the simple elegance of the archaic Greek pieces. The decoration of Roman vessels consisted of mythological creatures, naturalistic flowers and foliage, wreaths, animals and birds, masks of Bacchus, flutings, and gadroons. Both silver and gold plate were also inlaid with precious stones or with niello.

With the coming of troubled times during the first century A.D., silver was buried by the Roman owners in a desperate measure to save it from the invading barbarians. Large deposits have been found in such remote places as Ireland, Denmark, and Switzerland. In A.D. 79 the burial of Campania beneath the lava and ashes of Vesuvius preserved much Roman silver. In 1895, the Treasure of Boscoreale, consisting of 108 pieces of silver hidden in a wine vat, was discovered; in 1930, 118 pieces were found stowed in a bronze chest buried beneath the ruins of Pompeii.

Silver continued to be used in Europe through succeeding ages for ceremonial, commemorative, and ecclesiastical purposes. As the degree of religious fervor was equated with ostentatiousness of design, the early simplicity and quality of Greek archaic design was soon lost. Silversmiths vied with each other in elaborate and intricate workmanship.

With Renaissance affluence, collections of silver plate became common, and silver was used not only as an

15-5 *Pear-shaped teapot, 1718. The teapot has the forthright simplicity and solidity common to much of the design during the Queen Anne era. Victoria and Albert Museum, London. Crown Copyright.*

15-6 *Paul Lamerie, English silversmith. Silver tea kettle, with stand, 1744–1745, height with handle down 11½". Although Lamerie designed objects of greater simplicity, this one demonstrates his undeniable expertise in intricate workmanship. Compare with Figure 15-5 for enjoying the intrinsic beauty of a material. Collection, The Metropolitan Museum of Art, New York.*

203

15-7 *Christopher Dresser. Soup tureen and ladle. 1880. Silver with wooden handles and knobs; tureen, 8½" x 9¼", ladle, 12⅜" long. Manufacturer, Hukin & Heath, London and Birmingham. Many so-called modern-looking designs were developed before the 1900s. These pieces make a simple statement and utilize the reflective quality of silver. Note the handles and their reflections. Collection, The Museum of Modern Art, New York. Gift of Mrs. John D. Rockefeller, 3rd.*

index of wealth, but as portable capital. During the reign of Henry VIII, silver was more valuable than currency because it retained its standard of purity, whereas the currency was debased in an attempt to rectify the king's faltering financial policies. The basic design of Renaissance plate was a free adaptation of classical ornamental detail rather than an emphasis on classical form. Models for workmanship were the great Florentine metallurgists, such as Benvenuto Cellini, who displayed virtuosity through complicated, elaborate design. Silver was also sumptuously enriched with enamels and gems.

The introduction of tea, chocolate, and coffee during the seventeenth century necessitated the introduction of a variety of serving utensils. There is a refreshing relief from decorativeness and a respect for form and material in the designs of teapots and coffeepots made during the Queen Anne period. Under the Georges, design at first succumbed to increased use of classical ornamentation and then to the vivacity of the rococo. Paul de Lamerie, known as the finest goldsmith in England between 1703 and 1751, received numerous commissions for elaborately worked ceremonial or presentation plate. His florid style of ornamentation was deplored by William Hogarth, who had been trained as an engraver on silver and who regretted the serpentine line that "leads the eye a wanton sort of chase."

In 1742, the process of silver-plating or fusing a sheet of silver to a thicker one of copper, which could then be worked in the same way as silver sheet, was developed by Thomas Boulsaver, a Sheffield cutler. Design became less imposing in consequence, because the method of mechanical manufacture required simpler lines and ornamentation that could be easily repeated. Silver plate, along with pewter, became the poor man's silver.

To assure the purity of silver, which is easily alloyed with or adhered to other metals, various measures have been taken by reigning monarchs. For example, in 1300 it was decreed in England that the fineness of silver be the same as for coin—92.5 parts of silver to 1,000 parts of metal. If so tested by the Goldsmith's Hall in London, it was marked or "touched" with a leopard's head. Various additional hallmarks were devised subsequently. These have included identification of the craftsman, the town, the year, or commemorative markings such as the crowned head of Queen Elizabeth II, which has been used on British silver since her coronation. The stamp "Sterl," first used on Irish silver during the eighteenth century, became "sterling," the obligatory designation for American silver of standard quality.

In America, far from the court circles of England, the colonists designed silver of rhythmic lines, satisfying proportions, and restrained ornamentation. Many excellent silversmiths were working at that time, the best known being Paul Revere of Revolutionary War fame. Today many consumers continue to prefer silver for flatware, hollow ware, and jewelry.

15-8 *Pre-Columbian silver alpaca, Peru. Rhythmic striations and facial mien suggest hauteur—which is expressiveness. Courtesy of The American Museum of Natural History, New York.*

Georg Jensen of Denmark

The name Georg Jensen of Denmark has become internationally synonymous with silver of fine craftsmanship. Originally trained as a sculptor, Jensen turned his attention in 1904 to silversmithing and to designing jewelry. It was the era of Art Nouveau, and he employed elements of nature—clusters of grapes and intertwining leaves—as ornamentation on basic simple forms of objects for daily use. He contrasted decorative organized masses with smooth planished surfaces. His designs of the 1920s and 1930s, which were based not on fashion but on empathy with material and respect for form, have endured. The aesthetic vitality of his firm has been maintained through his employment of gifted architects, sculptors, and artists with similar psychological and aesthetic sensitivity. They continue to give reality to Jensen's dream: "To create beautiful and functional silver for everyday use in the homes of our time."

Johan Rohde, a painter, gave great impetus to the Jensen philosophy through his craft and teaching. Rejecting ornamentation that lacked organic justification, he emphasized form and quality in materials. The design of his coffee service, executed by Georg Jensen in 1906, has become a classic. He is credited by Åke Stavenow, director of Sweden's School for Industrial Arts and Crafts, as being a "functionalist before functionalism was a conscious program." (See also Figure 6–17.)

After Jensen's death, Harold Nielsen guided the efforts of younger designers in carrying out the founder's intent. As a guide to the use of ornament, he said, "The ornament must never dominate. It is subservient to the

15-9 *This coffee service, designed by Johan Rohde and executed by Georg Jensen in 1906, has become a classic. The handles are of ebony and the surfaces of the silver set are subtly hammered. Courtesy Georg Jensen, New York City.*

harmony of the whole and does not exist for its own sake. It can stress the quietness and simpleness of outline but must never distract. . . . Seeing the thing in its wholeness through simplifying and balancing ornament against plain surface is my basic principle in carrying farther the spirit of Georg Jensen."[1]

[1]Charlotte Hathaway, *Tradition In Danish Silver,* pamphlet; *Craft Horizons:*3 (Aug. 1952).

The beauty of Jensen's silver is not only in form but in finish. Instead of polishing silverware, Jensen let it remain matte, with its own gray-white tone. He also preserved the subtle traces of hammering as a sign of life and as an indication of the manner of creation. Darker oxidation was used in areas of relief to increase depth and to further accentuate the design. More recent designers use mirror surface and brush satin effects for textural interest.

Glass and Related Art 16

Glass

Glass, with its special characteristics, flowing dynamically alive, fascinates me. The fragile air bubble—the massive lump of crystal, a sparkling air of estivity—a simple clearness. It is the material which bridges extremes and challenges the designer to work with all its attributes.

Edvin Öhrström[1]

Though it occurs as obsidian, which is black glass fused from rocks and sands by lightning or volcanic eruption, glass is otherwise a miracle of man's ingenuity. It is the means whereby he has succeeded in extending his vision to better see himself and the world about him. The glass windows of our shelters make it possible for

us to relate to our surrounding environment, whether it be land, sea, mountain, or cityscape. While enjoying the protection that glass permits us, we can sensuously enjoy the impact of natural phenomena: rain, snow, wind, sun, and shadow.

Glass has been an educative aesthetic, an inspirational medium for telling the story of man and his salvation. The windows of Chartres and other European cathedrals depict scenes from the Old and New Testaments. Stained glass provides a warm, glowing, jeweled depth of atmosphere conducive to meditation and reflection. In contemporary times the potential of glass as a medium for communicating man's relationship to his universe has found continued expression with George Rouault, Henri Matisse, and Fernand Léger designing stained-glass windows for churches in Europe. In 1960, Marc Chagall designed twelve glass windows depicting

[1]Edvin Öhrström. *Design Quarterly*, No. 34 (1956), p. 10.

207

the tribes of Israel for the synagogue of the Hadassah Hospital at the Hebrew University Medical Center near Jerusalem.

Properties of Glass

Special consideration is given to the properties of glass in order to appreciate its varied potential. It is composed of the following raw materials: silica in the form of sand, flint, or quartz; alkalies such as soda, potash, and lime; and red lead or litharge, which acts as a flux in the melting of the ingredients. Color is added through metallic oxides such as manganese, cobalt, and copper.

The versatility of glass through the ages—its use for windows, ornament, lenses, eyeglasses, and assorted vessels—stems from its plasticity and range of characteristics. It can be spun into thread finer than cobwebs. Though fragile and delicate, when combined with plastic into the form known as fiberglas, it becomes as

16-1 *Bowl,* Millefiori *glass in a pattern of the cross, Roman, 1st century* A.D. *Collection, The Metropolitan Museum of Art, New York.*

strong as steel. Though glass can be shattered, it can also be made into flameware, which is resistant to heat and breakage. Its great strength is also indicated by the fact that the lenses of landing lights set into airport runways can withstand the repeated impacts of landing airplanes. Glass may serve as simple table crystal or as ornately etched and jewel-encrusted sacramental chalices. It can take the form of a minute glass bead, or it can be molded into telescopes weighing several tons.

History of Glass

Ancient and primitive man used native glass in the form of obsidian for his tools and ornaments. Vase-shaped vessels of polished green glass, cut from a solid mass as though from stone, have been found in Mesopotamia. Glass also appeared there about 3500 B.C. as a colored glaze for ceramic vessels. Egypt extended the use of glass to small perfume and unguent vessels and beakers and to inlay on sarcophagi and thrones. A sandstone or clay model, affixed to a metal rod, was dipped into molten glass, and when the model was removed, a hollow glass vessel would remain. Egyptians made glass in imitation of jasper, onyx, and agate. Various feathery, zigzag, and striated decorative patterns were achieved by dragging glass thread over a hot base of unsolidified glass, which was then embedded by marvering, that is, rolling on a flat stone. Glass rods arranged in bundles were melted, cut across, restructured, and melted again to produce starry flowerlike designs known as *millefiori,* "thousand flowers."

The most dramatic and exciting innovation that gave tremendous impetus to the glass industry was the discovery that liquid glass at the end of a blowpipe could be shaped spontaneously to any form desired, and handles, feet, and other decorative appendages could then be added. The blowpipe is thought to have originated with Syrian glassworkers, some of whom migrated to Italy during the first century A.D. The advent of blown glass accounted for the phenomenal growth in the glass industry in the Mediterranean and Near

Eastern countries, which took place at this time. Glass, previously regarded as on a par with jewels and in the sole possession of the nobility, came into such common use that the first four centuries were considered its golden age. Glass was blown, molded, enameled, engraved, and gilded. The technique of grinding through an opaque white overlay to a darker ground, known as cameo glass, was developed. The Portland vase shown in Figure 16-2, with its nuances from white to blue, remains the classic example of this art of the Roman Empire. It later served as motivation to Josiah Wedgwood, the English ceramist, for his famous blue and white porcelains.

By the time of the Crusades, an elaborate guild system of glassworkers had been developed, and the exalted and prevalent use of glass led to its second golden age. In France, stained-glass windows reached a height of perfection. In Italy, Venetian glassworks were transferred to the island of Murano to protect Venice from the danger of fires caused by the high temperatures needed to power the glass furnaces and to confine and isolate the workers so that their secrets of glassmaking would not become common knowledge. Murano's fame was based upon the development of a colorless, clear glass that could be blown to extreme lightness and transparency in almost any shape and complexity. Because of its resemblance to natural crystal, it was called *cristallo*. Effecting the delicacy of lace, *latticino* glass was made by laying delicate threads of opaque white glass over the surface of a bubble and letting them form varying patterns of integral design as the bubble was further blown and spun. The classical period of Venetian design admitted no decoration considered foreign to the native material—no painting, cutting, or engraving. Design was integral, and resulted from the manipulation of materials during the furnacing process. The resulting beauty of Venetian glass is indicated by Jean Cocteau's reference to Murano as "the Foundry of the Angels."

The renown of the Venetian glassmakers spread. Though their earlier pieces retained the beauty of form and decoration characteristic of ancient Egyptian,

Islamic, and Roman glass, the export trade to the kings and nobles of other European countries led to progressively more complex forms and heightened decorativeness. Though each country adapted the style to its own milieu, materials, and expertise, design became excessively engraved, enameled, and gilded, in order to indicate its owners' wealth and rank. Germanic lands, particularly Bohemia, became famed for their expert enameling and engraving. During the eighteenth century, glass became the form for commemorative goblets, showpieces for ducal tables and collectors' cabinets, as well as a medium for portraits and literary illustration.

16-2 *Portland vase. This vase in blue and white was designed by the cameo technique of carving through layers of glass to reveal the desired figures. It is thought to date to Rome, either the 1st century* B.C. *or* A.D. *It served as the classical inspiration for Josiah Wedgwood's famous ware. By permission of the Trustees of the British Museum, London.*

16-3 *A latticino and filigree goblet, probably* Façon de Venise, *actually made in Germany or the Netherlands, late 16th or early 17th century, height 21 cm. Compare this plate with Figure 18-4 for unity, rhythm, and respect for the special attributes of glass. The Corning Museum of Glass, Corning, New York.*

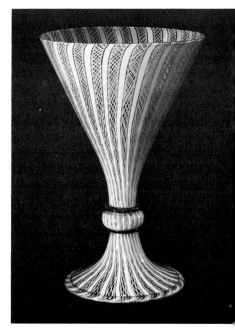

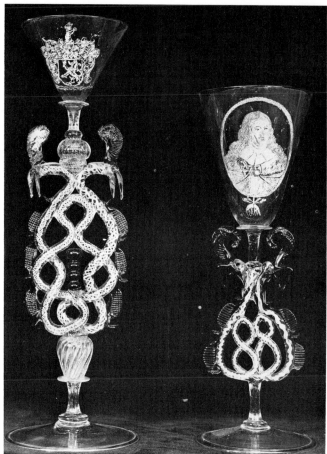

One marvels at the intricate craftsmanship of the period, but seldom do the wares elicit genuine aesthetic pleasure. They are historic documents that exploit a material in order to communicate hierarchy and affluence. Today they constitute museum items, to be appreciated as part of man's status symbolism and consummate craftsmanship.

Though ordinarily the English followed the Venetian style, in 1675 George Ravencraft introduced lead oxide as a flux in producing glass. The resultant glass, more solid and durable than the Venetian, was also more readily engraved and cut. Its brilliance and depth of shadow produced a greater refraction of light rays. The fragile, delicate Venetian idiom was abandoned for the simple native style of Queen Anne. The proportions of pear-shaped bulbous stems to funnel-shaped bowls were pleasing, and the sturdy bases of wineglasses served a functional purpose as well—they could withstand loud, boisterous rapping on the table in response to toasts.

Though English glassmakers adopted the arts of engraving and enameling, they initiated an international style with the ornamental technique of cut glass. The period of 1745 to 1770 became England's golden age of glass cutting. At this time shallow cuts in the form of diamonds, hexagons, and flutes appeared in low relief, which retained the basic character of the glass. By the second quarter of the nineteenth century, however, fascination with cutting led designers to cut ever more deeply and produce increasingly complex patterns, labelled by some as "prickly monstrosities." When seen at the Great Exhibition of 1851, "death by a thousand wounds" was the phrase applied by the discerning to much of England's glass.

William Morris's promotion of the Arts and Crafts movement encouraged the simplicity of all applied design, including glass. He employed Philip Webb to design tableware that in its restraint and dignity set the spirit for England's later work.

During the Art Nouveau period, the spirit of the time was expressed through the plasticity of glass, which could readily assume the fluid quality of vegetation. The French glassmakers Eugène Rousseau, Emile Gallé, and René Lalique produced the first of what has come to be known as art glass, which qualifies as fine art as well as serving domestic uses. Like other artistic products of that era, decoration was poetic, linear, and evocative of nature. Lalique became a leading advocate for using glass in architectural design and for lighting equipment. Gallé cut and etched ornamental designs from casings of glass. He established the practice of signing his name to his work as one would to other artistic productions.

Later, Maurice Marinot was the first to exploit the aesthetic possibilities of heavy, massive glass to trap impressions of bark, moss, running water, and clouds of air bubbles.

Baccarat Glass

The Baccarat Company, founded in 1765 by the Bishop of Metz at Baccarat, France, is the largest and most diversified lead crystal factory in the world. Earning the title "Crystal of Kings," Baccarat glass adorned the tables of the czar of Russia, the emperor of Japan, the Ethiopian emperor Haile Selassie; the kings of France, Egypt, Greece, Portugal, and Spain; and nearly all the maharajahs of India. It is France's oldest and finest glass-manufacturing company, producing a range of glassware from candelabras and chandeliers to dainty stemware, cameo portraits, and paperweights. Replicas of historically famous glass and special designs to coordinate with other furnishings are also made.

American Historic Glass

Though in ancient times and in early American colonial days glass was regarded as being as valuable as jewelry, its commonness today has resulted in dispensable containers. The value of glass was realized by American colonists, whose first successful glassworks was started in 1739 by Caspar Wistar of Salem County, New Jersey. He established what became known as the South Jersey tradition—making simple utilitarian wares out of ordinary window glass. Crown or bull's-eye windowpane, much valued today, was made by twirling a large bubble until flat against a pontil rod which left a scar in the shape of a crown when broken off. Wistar also originated the lily-pad design, in which a hot gather of glass at the base of the bowl provided the material from which the sides could then be drawn up.

Among other well-designed glassware was that produced by William Henry Stiegel from 1763 to 1774, who worked clear and colored glass in subtly attractive mold-blown patterns of daisies, diamonds, and hexagons. Workmen blew the glass into a small mold of iron or wood to give it the desired pattern; then, upon its removal, continued to blow and rotate it to the desired shape and size. Patterns of swirled ribbings or quiltings, much softer than hard-edged cut glass, appeared as integral design.

By 1815, inventors had perfected molds that made flasks in exact pint and quart sizes. This led to the production of flasks in hundreds of designs, including portraits of national heroes, political slogans, eagles, and flags—not outstandingly aesthetic but delightful. Advertisements listing half-pint flat drum bottles as "suitable to carry the comfort of life into the field," and a log-cabin flask used by a Philadelphia distiller named Booz added the now common noun to American vocabulary.

The glasshouse of Bakewell, established in Pittsburg in 1808, was the scene of a number of "firsts" in American glassmaking history. It was the first to use coal for fuel in glassmaking, the first company to supply the White House (President James Monroe) with glass, and

16-6 *Maurice Marinot. Bottle and stopper of glass with deeply etched decoration and grayish bubbles. The treatment is in unity with the potential of glass to trap air in order to create its own unique textural quality. Victoria and Albert Museum, London. Crown Copyright.*

16-7 *Pressed and cut compote dish, Cristalleries de Baccarat, France, circa 1840–50, height 17.8 cm. Ornateness can contribute to beauty. The Corning Museum of Glass, Corning, New York.*

the first to hold a patent, in 1825, for mechanical pressing of glass. Subsequently, Deming Jarvis, founder of the Boston and Sandwich Glass Company, produced pressed glass, which he advertised so widely that "Sandwich" became a generic term for any American pressed glass.

In 1858, John L. Mason of New York patented the screw-type Mason jar for home canning—a masterpiece of functional design. During the Art Nouveau period, Louis Comfort Tiffany's work stands out as America's greatest achievement in glass. His objective was to produce glass as an artistic expression and to provide a variety of quality designs for use in the American home. To this end he had long been fascinated with the brilliant and iridescent patina of antique Roman and Persian vases, developed through burial for long centuries in humid soil. After assiduously studying chemistry, he succeeded in imparting the rich luster of ancient glass to his flower-form wares by exposing colored glass rods to the fumes of vaporized metals during the firing process. These were absorbed by the glass in a succession of delicate films to refract light as do the nacreous layers in a sea shell. He claimed to have made a careful study of the natural decay of glass and to have reversed the action in order to achieve desired effects. His patent claim reads:

The metallic luster is produced by forming a film of a metal or its oxide, or a compound of a metal, on or in the glass, either by exposing it to vapors or gases or by direct application. It may also be produced by corroding the surface of the glass, such processes being well known to glass-manufacturers.[2]

The Corning Glass Works

Because of the universal use of glass, there are several outstanding contemporary glass manufacturers. The

[2]Robert Koch, *Louis C. Tiffany, Rebel in Glass* (New York: Crown, 1964), pp. 121–122.

16-8 *L. C. Tiffany. circa 1900, height 12⅝". The stemmed favrile glass (favrile means belonging to a trade or craft) is a delightful blossom. Its fluted lip and green and gold swirls with white are typical of Tiffany's sensitivity to elements and principles. The Corning Museum of Glass, Corning, New York.*

production of glass as both fine and applied art has been accomplished by the Corning Glass Works of New York. With sixty-two plants, it produces fifty thousand different technical products to satisfy modern needs. For example, Pyrex brand dishes are common household objects, that not only function practically, but also provide visual satisfaction through their clarity of design. Steuben art glass is appreciated for its incarnate

16-9 *Corning glass containers for food service. Unity of idea is expressed through the use of mushrooms, not only stuffed for food but also in the centerpiece and for holding cocktail picks. Corning Glass Works, Corning, New York.*

16-10 *The original battery jar that was used experimentally by an employee's wife to bake a cake—an event that led Corning Glass Works into the manufacture of housewares. Corning Glass Works, Corning, New York.*

beauty of crystal and purity of line and form. These designs are the result of careful consideration, study, and experimentation by many individuals and agencies.

Corning has long been concerned with the social, psychological, and economic roles of art in industry. Its directors firmly believe that the usefulness and longevity of a product is increased by giving objects both aesthetic and utilitarian dimensions.

The discovery of a flameproof heat-resistant glass began as a casual coincidence in an imaginative new use of an old product. Glass had been used all through recorded history, but not until 1913 was it successfully used for baking. It occurred to the wife of a young Corning research scientist to bake a cake in the cut-off bottom of a battery jar made of heat-resistant borosilicate glass. Her success led to the production of Pyrex laboratory glass and baking ware.

To maintain quality design and sales, in 1948 Arthur A. Houghton, a company director, enlisted the coopera-

tion of Boston's Institute of Contemporary Art in an experimental training program. Twelve young designers—painters, sculptors, architects—were given extensive training in glass technology, research manufacturing, and marketing. The designers were free in their use of time to consult and converse with home economists, model makers, engineers, and market researchers. Because household products are not subject to change with fashion cycles but are used over extended periods of time, they warrant this concerted effort. The experiment resulted in the production of high-quality design as a result of the team approach.

Steuben Glass

Steuben Glass, named after Steuben County, New York, was founded in 1903 by Frederick Cardner, an English glassmaker and artist, for the production of art and table glass. In 1918 the neighboring Corning Glass Works purchased the smaller factory, which thereafter became its Steuben division, producing handmade glass in a broad variety of shapes and colors.

In 1933, young Arthur A. Houghton, Jr., great-grandson of the founder of Corning Glass Works, took over the by then faltering Steuben division and applied his talents to a careful analysis of its potential. Two major assets were at hand—a fine corps of skilled glassmakers and a newly discovered formula for an exceptionally pure and transparent crystal. But traditionally the master craftsman had come to fill the role of designer as well as maker. Houghton believed that this approach led too often to haphazard design and too rarely to works of art. Design, creative and integrated, must dictate the course of his company.

He enlisted the help of an architect, John M. Gates, and a sculptor, Sidney Waugh, and together they set their goal: to produce clear crystal glass to standards of design, material, and workmanship that would rank it with the finest art the world has seen.

The team's efforts were rewarded: Steuben gained an international reputation for its fluid forms and intaglio

16-11 *Sidney Waugh.* **The Merry-Go-Round Bowl,** *height 10". This engraved crystal bowl was presented to H.R.H. The Princess Elizabeth on the occasion of her marriage, November 1947, by the President of the United States and Mrs. Truman. Expert craftsmanship can express motion in glass. Steuben Glass, Steubenville, Ohio.*

16-12 *Lloyd Atkins. An interpretation of Melville Cane's poem, "To Build a Fire," height 12". An abstract flame form is cut from a solid block of clear crystal. The flames curl upward around an open center. Compare this illustration with the former. What different values are expressed by each? Which would you choose as a gift for a queen? Steuben Glass, Steubenville, Ohio.*

ings from internationally known painters and sculptors. A unique experiment occurred in the "Poetry and Crystal" project of 1963, which was carried out in collaboration with the Poetry Society of America. Themes of poems, commissioned from distinguished contemporary poets, were interpreted into abstract crystal forms by Steuben. Lloyd Atkins's interpretation of "To Build a Fire," by Melville Cane, is shown as Figure 6-12.

The hearth waits,
Clean and bare and ready.

First:
To lay the paper,
A bed of prose to start with.

Then:
Artfully, bit by bit,
Add shavings,
Curling phrases,
Kindling symbols.

Contrive a rhythmic nest of sticks
And crown it with symmetric logs.

Finally:
Loosen and unclog,
That air may flow
And flame may catch.[3]

engravings. The respect in which Steuben glass is held is indicated by the fact that it serves as a medium for diplomatic exchange. In 1981 President Reagan gave the Prince and Princess of Wales an engraved crystal Steuben bowl, "The Crusaders," on the occasion of their marriage. State gifts now number in the hundreds. Though Steuben designs have longevity of design merit, and hence of production, they are supplemented with experiments and commissions for designs and engrav-

Orrefors Glass

The Orrefors works took the lead in developing modern glass in Sweden immediately after World War I. With artist-designers Simon Gate and Edward Hald as managing directors, the industry has held to high levels of aesthetic production. Cooperation and integration between all facets of the industry have been stressed by Hald in his credo: "To make glass a swiftly flowing drama which cannot be played in any other material. There are no extras. Everyone has a main part, with the

[3]Melville Cane, "To Build a Fire," from *Poetry in Crystal* (New York: Spiral Press, 1963), p. 22.

artist as the director. Successful or not, it is the intensity in the ensemble which stimulates to new exertions."[4]

The ensemble of workers is important because blueprints do not exist for glass blowers to follow. The form of the object is complete when it comes from the oven. If an artist-designer is employed, he indicates his intention orally or by a simple sketch. Only after an individual piece of glassware is successfully created is a guide drawn to serve as the model for continued production.

Orrefors has contributed to the glass industry the technique known as Graal glass. As in Emile Gallé's work, patterns are cut into layers of casings, but they are then subjected to further firings to regain the intrinsic fluidity of glass, another example of integral decorative design. "Ariel" glass is glass in which patterns are created by sandblasting into the core of the glass and laying a casing over the forms to enclose channels of air.

Among other Orrefors designers' responses to the production of glass is that of Ingeborg Lundin, who believes a drinking glass to be the most difficult object to design. Nils Landberg enjoys glass as a medium because "one gets an idea, goes down to the foundry, and gets it transformed into immediate reality—no other material has such possibilities. Bull's-eye or flop—it is the spontaneity in work with glass which gives me the greatest satisfaction. Form gives suspense by itself, but often one gets a feeling that something must happen to a flat polished surface, and so one adds enrichment."[5]

There seems to be an enjoyable spontaneity present in Orrefors glass. A master's work is unlabelled and gives the impression of being easily produced. Excellence gives no evidence of the long, tedious hours of apprenticeship, the trial and error that contribute to its attainment, or to the philosophies that direct the designers' activity. Yet behind the production are the motivating mottoes of various units of the industry—the voices of

[4]*Design Quarterly*, No. 34, 1956, p. 5.
[5]Ibid., p. 16.

an ensemble. Management says: "Trust the artists." The workmen claim: "You never end your apprenticeship." Artists warn: "The glass must congeal at its most beautiful—but never let your ideas congeal."

Contemporary Free-Blown Glass

Many glass blowers today are exploring the capacity of glass to evolve into unique sculptural forms through control of the blowing process. Among them is Robert Fritz, an American who blows glass into free innovative forms of mysterious and unfathomable depths. Purples, blues, greens, smoky golds, iridescent blacks, and occasionally silvers for the interiors of his vessels contribute to the beauty and abstruse quality of his art.

16-13 *Orrefors crystal Ariel vase. Courtesy Fisher, Bruce and Co., Philadelphia.*

16-14 *Robert C. Fritz. Free-blown contemporary glass on right, height 18". Free-blown glass sculpture on left, height 14". Courtesy of Robert C. Fritz.*

Mosaic

Either light was born here, or,
imprisoned here, it reigns supreme.
—Lines on vestibule walls of Ravenna chapel
by unknown poet.

Mosaic is the combination of separate pieces of material, the classical ones being marble and stone pebbles or glass, cut into segments called tesserae. These are assembled and adhered with mortar to form a unified composition. Seen from close at hand, the design may appear as a random collection; with distance they take on form and relationship. The ordering of geometrically cut tesserae results in a degree of abstraction that invites the viewer to use his own imagination to fill in the whole, provided the artist has not attempted to duplicate painting by employing minute tesserae and polishing them to a smooth plane. The ideal mosaic is not, as Vasari, the Renaissance writer, described it to be, "indistinguishable from painting," but has its own unique character. Colored tesserae, each set at differing angles with respect to light, not only have an increased intensity of hue but the reflected light makes their color seem more scintillating and vibrant. The heightened combination of light and color that can be achieved has made mosaic a favored medium in churches for evoking emotion and arousing religious sentiment.

In the fourth century, with Emperor Constantine's transfer of the imperial court from Rome, Byzantium (Constantinople) became the center of civic and reli-

16-15 Empress Theodora and Her Attendants. *Portion of a mosaic about 547 A.D. in the Church of San Vitale, Ravenna. Here is a highly structured Byzantine mosaic in which the small almond-shaped faces are dominated by huge staring eyes. There is a staid frontality and immobility in the characters' stance. The gold and jewel-colored tesserae suggest associations with the celestial rather thanf the secular. Alinari-Art Reference Bureau.*

gious life. Technical developments led to greater skills in glassmaking. These included producing variously colored tesserae, making gold tesserae (gold leaf fused between two layers of clear glass), which had formerly been imported from Egypt, and perfecting a light mortar strong enough to secure mosaics to walls and ceilings. Mosaics then could rise from floor to ceiling to become the great spiritual art of the Byzantine world. The use of mosaic spread to the Balkans, Asia Minor, Italy, Sicily, South Russia, and Spain. Knowledge of the Hebrew Bible and the life of Christ was spread by mosaics throughout the entire Aegean and Mediterranean area.

Advances in the technology of architecture also encouraged mosaic artists. Early christian religious fervor was high and was reflected in the construction of churches. Development of the pendentive, a rectangular span topped by a dome, and the architectural devices of vaults and apses provided expansive surfaces that invited enrichment. Flat geometric design was encouraged because the dogma of the Eastern Orthodox Church forbade statuary design, which was associated with idolatry. Under Eastern spiritual influences, the classical design of the West became luminous, exotic, and abstract.

Byzantine artists took into consideration the interrelationship of architectural design and the materials and techniques of production used in creating mosaics. The ability of glass tesserae to magnify and add to the poetry of light if they are set opportunely, the use of flat design in harmony with a flat surface, and the structuring of decorative elements to relate to spatial divisions of walls and ceilings can be observed in their work. Unlike the Roman and Renaissance ideal of mosaic as "painting for eternity," the Byzantine artist simulated the splendor of heaven through his manipulation of light reflectance and color. In this respect he anticipated both the pointillists and the cubists of later centuries, who also fragmented reality into prismatic semblance.

The art of mosaic declined with the Renaissance bias for painting. During the seventeenth and eighteenth centuries, it was kept alive in Italian workshops by the orders of popes who favored reproduction of paintings through mosaic. Today the Vatican operates one of the largest mosaic workshops, supplying tesserae and filling church orders for clients all over the world.

In the late nineteenth century, the Catalan architect Antonio Gaudí set another precedent for mosaic as an integral part of architecture with his lavish use of the medium for the spire of his Cathedral of the Sagrada Familia in Barcelona. The Mexican architect Juan O'Gorman astonished the world in 1952 by his use of mosaic for the four walls of the library of the University of Mexico in Mexico City. Each wall carries a record in tesserae of the history of Mexico. Since then not only Mexico but the United States and Europe have recognized that mosaics have a logical and legitimate place in contributing to the aesthetics of architecture. Today's craftsmen, responsive to all media, not only work in mosaic in the traditional manner, but also employ other means in order to create textural enrichment for the flat surfaces of table tops and counters and of both exterior and interior walls.

16-16 *Jeanne Reynal. The Blizzard of '88, 1965, mosaic in the State Capitol, Lincoln, Nebraska. The lavalike flow of mosaic creates its own rhythms. Miss Reynal observed that "the art of mosaic is not painting with stone, but a medium, the character of which is texture, and the esthetic, light. A wall clothed in mosaic becomes a presence." Courtesy of Jeanne Reynal.*

16-17 *Margaret Montgomery Barlow.* Bird Vendors, *enamel.* California Design VIII. *Pasadena Art Museum. Photograph by Richard Gross.*

16-18 *June Schwarcz.* Fibers, *enamel, 9⅛ x 6″. Various levels of etched panels are built up by electroforming. Other art forms, such as textiles, can provide inspiration to the designer. Courtesy of June Schwarcz. Photograph by Kenneth Reichard.*

Enamel

Enamelling is a method of fusing a vitreous glaze onto a metallic surface for decorative purposes. Along with illuminated manuscripts and stained glass, it was one of the chief means of gaining brilliance of color during the Middle Ages. Its practice required applying a glass

silicate that became fluid at fairly low temperatures to a metal that would not. Hence one does not find it as extensively practiced as other arts. Evidence exists that enamelling was known to the Myceneans, to the Egyptians at the time of Alexander the Great, and to the Romans of the Celtic area of the Roman Empire.

The art of enamelling, though its origin is obscure, is believed to have been introduced to China by way of Western traders or traveling craftsmen by the third century B.C. Chinese artifacts of bronze inlaid with glass beads indicate a knowledge of cloisonné effect; however, the art was not practiced extensively until the T'ang period (A.D. 618–906). A silver mirror from that period deposited in the Japanese Shōsō-in warehouse is decorated in a cloisonné design created by glazes fused between carved grooves of metal or thin strips of brass. The Japanese court followed the Chinese example of maintaining enamel artists in the seventh century. The Katsura Palace has enameled metal bands decorating its sliding doors and lintels. Commencing in the tenth century, Byzantine artists achieved a high level of enamelling artistry. In Saint Mark's in Venice, the altar screen known as Pola d'Oro is believed to have been brought from Constantinople to Italy in about 1105; it ranks as a masterpiece of this period.

In the twelfth and thirteenth centuries, the Limoges school of enamelling in central France produced cloisonné, which deteriorated in merit, copying in Italian paintings and engravings. On the other hand, splendid decoratively enamelled reliquaries, chalices, and processional crosses were designed by Italian artists, including the Duccio of Siena and Giovanni Pisoni. In the fifteenth century, enamel colors were applied by Venetian artisans to glass.

Though the art of enamelling continued through the Renaissance, like that of mosaic it became directed more by the art of the painter than by the nature of the medium itself. Today it is again enjoyed by those artist-craftsmen who recognize its unique decorative character and who enjoy intensity of color. (See Figures 7-3 and 16-18.)

Part Four

Organic Materials: Media for Design

Materials Close at Hand 17

Ivory

Ivory is the material of tusks of the upper incisor teeth of mammoths, elephants, hippopotamuses, narwhals, and walruses. Before the use of metals, bones and ivory were among man's most available and valuable materials. During the Aurignacian period, twenty thousand years ago, man was making such extensive use of ivory, bone, and horn for utilitarian, religious, and decorative purposes that the era is referred to as the Ivory period.

Ivory is familiar to us through the expressions "tickling the ivories" of the piano and the "ivory tower tradition." The latter phrase suggests man's past regard for ivory when its rarity, beauty, and color symbolized purity and so led him to rank ivory with gold, jade, and other precious stones.

Historic Uses

The Egyptians used ivory in decorating utilitarian objects, such as inlay for furniture and knife handles carved with hunting, fishing, or warring scenes in bas relief. The Phoenicians employed ivory, often inlaid with gold and lapis lazuli, in bas-relief for caskets, furniture, and assorted boxes. The familiar Cretan snake goddess was made of ivory, as were the figures of acrobats from Knossos, Crete.

In the days of dynasties and monarchs, the efforts of artisans were channeled into making objects that were considered worthy of their masters. The whiteness and purity of ivory was considered particularly appropriate for thrones. The Bible says of King Solomon, "Moreover the king made a great throne of ivory, and overlaid it with the best gold" (I Kings, 10:18). The entire surface

silver, precious stones, and mosaics. During the Middle Ages the art of ivory carving reached a high point of development. Ivory statuettes and diptychs (hinged tablets) are thought to have served as visual models for sculptors working in stone on the Gothic cathedrals.

From the fourteenth century through the Baroque period, artists were so enamored of ivory that they attempted to convert everything that had originally been made of other materials to ivory. Such works as Michelangelo's sculptures and Rubens's paintings were copied in ivory bas-reliefs on plaques, goblets, and vases. As ivories became imitative of other media, they declined in aesthetic character.

of a Danish coronation chair, dating from the seventeenth century, is decorated with narwhal ivory inlay. Sword hilts, scabbards, and musical instruments might include ivory in their design, or ivory inlaid with gold and precious stones.

Ivory was also used instead of parchment; carved ivory diptychs were issued by Roman emperors and consuls upon their taking office and for proclamations; patrician families used ivory for commemorating marriages; litanies for the imperial welfare were written on ivory. Ivory chairs became gifts of religious and political diplomacy with Cyril of Alexandria and Justinian of Constantinople. The splendor of the Byzantine regime was reflected by prolific use of ivory as well as of gold,

Far Eastern Ivories

The first Chinese script to survive is recorded on bone. China has always ranked ivory on a par with gold and jade. Artifacts found in the tombs of the Shang kings at An-Yang, North Honan, suggest an ivory tradition dating back to prehistoric times. Ivory served the imperial court, from chopsticks, which were invented by the last Shang king, to a chariot of ivory owned by a Chou sovereign. During the Han dynasty, high officials wore ivory memorandum tablets as girdle pendants, whereas the lower classes wore tablets of wood.

Ivory workshops flourished under imperial patronage. The highest quality of ivory workmanship was that of

17-2 *Pair of doors, Egypto-Arabic, late 13th, early 14th century. Of brown wood inlaid with panels of carved ivory and strips of lighter wood, they are radial in rhythm and formally balanced. The Metropolitan Museum of Art, New York.*

that invited stroking and rubbing, much as one enjoys fondling beads, the ivories for export were often hard-edged, and lacked the tactile quality that might provide sensuous pleasure.

It is not possible to establish any great antiquity for carving ivory objects in Japan until the Tokugawa Period (1603–1867). At that time, because the traditional costume had no pockets, a belt was used from which hung the pipe and tobacco pouch, a medicine flask for sake, and a purse for keys and money. To secure these to the belt *netsuke*, or toggles, were developed. The *netsuke*, sometimes not more than an inch in length and diameter, were miniature sculptures of remarkable quality and rhythmic fluidity that felt like sleek, washed stones. These fulfilled men's desire for adornment, because members of the newly risen middle class who ranked below the samurai were not allowed to wear jewelry.

Netsuke designs included an infinite number of themes: human and mythological figures; masks; wild, domestic, and fantastic imaginary animals; fruit; and objects of daily use. Though they were carved from wood, bone, metals, coral and semiprecious stones, ivory was the favorite material. As costume changed toward the end of the Tokugawa regime of 1876 and cigarettes replaced the pipe, *netsuke* were no longer required to hold the pipe and tobacco pouch and they became obsolete. The ivory carvers of Canton then turned to satisfying the European Victorian taste for ivory jewelry, jewel boxes, fans, brooches, buttons, and chessmen.

Ivories of the North American Indians

The Eskimo tribes who inhabit the Arctic and sub-Arctic regions have also developed the carving of functional and decorative objects from ivory to a high art. They, too, made toggles—toggles for dog harnesses and harpoon heads. Needlecases, made from hollow cylinders of bone or ivory to carry bone or copper needles and dating back a thousand years, have been found in ruins from Alaska to the Labrador peninsula.

the Ming dynasty, when ivory was not stained, painted, or elaborately carved, but worked into simple forms, retaining its own natural mellowness of color. A decline in aesthetic production commenced during the Ching dynasty, when lack of imperial support brought increased catering to foreign markets and tourists' desire for novelties. Whereas the ivories carved for the nobility and scholars of the Orient were worked to a smoothness

The Grasses

Grass is earth's carpet, covering the sod wherever the climate permits. It is a rejuvenating force in life for whenever the earth has been gouged and scarred by man's war against man, grass rises, covers, and heals like new skin. Even slag heaps eventually grass over as though in defiance of man's despoiling the good earth.

It is to be expected that grass, distributed over the face of the earth, should be utilized by man for both functional and aesthetic purposes, because man lives by converting nature's bounty to his uses. Reeds, rushes, sedges, wheat straw, flax stems, rye grass, and corn husks have been used since ancient times. Dorothy Hales Gary describes the growth of papyrus along the Nile:

For countless ages these banks have been crowded with generous thickets of dark green papyrus sometimes rising to a height of twenty feet, eternally rustling and creaking, eternally in motion. The waterfowl nested in the shadows of the papyrus forests, which gave shade to men and beasts. Out of those long slender grasses the ancient Egyptians made nearly everything they wanted. The roots were food and sustenance. From the stalks they made boats, mats, ropes, sandals and cloth. Bound together, they made posts; woven, they produced roofs. Cut into fine strips, laid crisscross and pressed together, papyrus became paper. Cradles and coffins were made of it. These tough fibers were the supreme gift of the Nile.[1]

The member of the grass family most prevalent and universally used today in the construction of household articles is cane. Cane is a generic name that includes the species rattan and bamboo. Rush, reed, and willow are also used for basketry and in furniture construction. Concentration in this text will be limited to cane because it is used most extensively and can serve as an example of man's ingenuity in converting plant material to constructive uses.

Rattan is the long trailing stem of climbing palms

[1]Dorothy Hales Gary, *Sun, Stones and Silence* (New York: Simon and Schuster, 1963), p. 10.

found at low altitudes in tropical areas such as the Malay Archipelago. As a fiber it is strong, tough, and elastic, varying in diameter from an eighth of an inch to arm width and in length from a few feet to six hundred feet. It clings by hooklike spines to the supporting jungle vegetation, from which it must be pulled for domestic use. The outer portion, which is hard and tough, is converted into mats, baskets, and seats; the inner, which is porous and softer, is made into rope, cables, and furniture. The term *wicker* is used for split rattan.

Bamboo is the largest member of the grass family and may grow as high as 120 feet. It is extremely strong, supple, and light in weight because of its hollow interior. Like rattan it can be split and woven into window blinds, furniture, and baskets. Unlike rattan, it receives color well. In the cultures of the Orient bamboo has a centuries-old tradition. It has served almost every Oriental need from food (bamboo shoots) and drink (beer made from its seeds) to clothing (woven hats and footgear); it has provided furniture, housing construction, and landscaping; not least, it has provided inspiration for poetry, religion, and fine art.

Historic Background

Grasses have been used by primitive men since prehistoric times. Basketry and weaving with grasses antedate the ancient craft of pottery making. Grasses have not only been used by societies in the early stages of civilization but advanced work in construction with grasses has been performed by peoples in a much more rudimentary developmental stage. Basketmaking is considered one of Neolithic man's contributions to culture.

Grasses served as the construction element of early shelters, and were incorporated in basketry to serve almost all of man's religious and secular functions. They have been used in the construction of hunting and fishing equipment, vehicles of transportation, instruments of warfare, musical instruments, ceremonial and cult objects, storage granaries, furniture, and toys. The

Hupa Indians of California perfected a cooking basket twined so closely that they could boil soup or acorn mush by filling it with liquid and lowering hot stones into it. Basketry jars, coated by a layer of crushed Parinarium nuts, which harden to imperviability, were used by the Admiralty Islanders to store coconut oil.

Although a highly perishable material, some vegetable fiber has been preserved in the arid sands and dry caves of both hemispheres. The age of grass specimens dating from 7000 B.C. in Danger Cave, Utah, and of twined baskets dating from 5000 B.C. found along the coast of Peru has been determined by the use of radiocarbon tests. Basket-lined corn granaries in Fayum, Egypt, have been found to date from 4784–3929 B.C. In Europe the Swiss lake dwellers used coiled and twined techniques for basket making circa 2500 B.C. What is traditionally considered to be the first Christian church of Britain was erected at Glastonbury in Somerset, England, in the first century A.D. It is a thatched-roof structure with walls of wickerwork. In the first seven centuries A.D., the southwestern United States enjoyed a simple hunting culture known as Basket Maker because of the fine cooking, storage, and burden baskets produced during that period.

The art of basketry construction, a manual operation that cannot be duplicated by machinery, has declined with the industrial manufacture of functional objects of pottery, wood, metals, plastics, and paper. However, the ancient twining technique still persists in the construction of such household articles as waste receptacles, clothes hampers, bread and laundry baskets, and wicker furniture. In the industrially undeveloped areas of the world, professional basketmakers still produce fine basketry. Physically handicapped persons also make a special contribution in this area.

Cane in Furniture Construction

Although the art of basketry has declined to an appreciable extent, the use of caning for furniture construction persists. As designers use woods and metals

17-3 *Armchair, bamboo. China, made for export about 1815. This chair demonstrates the potential of bamboo to be bent into fanciful design relationships. Courtesy of the Cooper-Hewitt Museum of Decorative Arts and Design, Smithsonian Institution, New York.*

as the unyielding bearers of furniture skeletons, the borne or upholstering element is frequently flexible cane, which gives with the plastic contours of the human body. The juxtaposition of wood textures with grass fiber and of unresilient inorganic metal with organic molecular structures provides a textural range that can be pleasing aesthetically. Light reflection from the differing compositions provides visual enjoyment.

Historic evidence of the use of grasses in chair construction can be seen in the sculptured chair from a sepulchral monument of the late second or third century A.D., now in the Archaeological Museum at York,

17-4 *Fancy side chair. Made by L. Hitchcock. Hitchcocksville, Connecticut, circa 1830. Maple, hickory, ash. The back of this chair is stenciled with the maker's name and address. Hitchcock chairs are still made and sold. Typically they are painted black and decorated with colored and gilt stenciled paintings. The seats are generally rush, a hollow-stem grasslike marshplant, or cane. This chair design has become a symbol of the early history of the United States. Collection, Greenfield Village and Henry Ford Museum, Dearborn, Michigan.*

England. The fact that professional basketmakers made chairs out of wicker in medieval times is recorded graphically in thirteenth-century illustrated manuscripts in the Bodleian Library at Oxford, England. Basketmakers were listed among the craftsmen of London as early as 1422 and restricted to plying their trade in only one section of that city because of fear of fire from their readily inflammable material. Almost a century later they were accorded official recognition as the Company of Basketmakers of the City of London by a court order of the Lord Mayor and aldermen.

The tradition of using cane in seats and chair backs dates to Chinese influence during the eleventh and twelfth centuries, when establishing trade with the Far East led to Europeans becoming acquainted with the versatility of grass fiber in combination with wood framing. Samuel Pepys mentioned the popularity of cane chairs in his diary written in the 1660s when he quoted from the Cane Chair-Makers Petition: "Cane chairs . . . gave so much satisfaction to all the Nobility, Gentry and Commonality of this Kingdom . . . ". Cane remained a favored medium in England from the Restoration through the subsequent reigns of William and Mary and Queen Anne. Slat-back and Windsor chairs had seats made of rush. In the second half of the eighteenth century, interest in Chinese designs became avid and intensified both in England and on the European continent. Rattan caning was employed in the classic works of Adam, Sheraton, and Hepplewhite, and in the French furniture of Louis XV and Louis XVI. In America, the colonists used rush for the seats of their Hitchcock and Shaker chairs.

Designers with Cane

Cane is used today not only for informal patio or leisure-time furniture but in sophisticated interiors. Hans Wegner's famous chair (figure 6-15) combined the textures of smooth teak for the framing with an open cane-woven seat and a cane-wrapped back rest. Naana and Jørgen Ditzel of Denmark have created chair de-

17-5 *Elinor McGuire. High-back Italian willow chairs, setting by Arthur Elrod. Courtesy The McGuire Company. Photograph by Leland Y. Lee.*

signs in traditional basketwork. Their hanging basket chair is a novel addition to leisure-time furniture. The Dane Kaare Klint, in designing a chair for Grundtvig's Church, used the woven rush seat found in the simple folk-type chairs of French and Italian churches. Michael Thonet's popular steam-molded scroll chair employed cane in both seat and back. Marcel Breuer and Mies van der Rohe juxtaposed the colder reflectant textures of chrome-plated steel tubing with the warmer matte textures of caning.

Italian designers make extensive use of cane in the design of furniture and containers. Danny Ho Fong in the United States designs a range of rattan furnishings for Tropi-Cal. The McGuire Company in San Francisco designs some of the world's most distinguished wicker furniture which is hand-crafted in Italy of sleek willow whips woven onto sturdy cane framing.

Thus it appears that man, whether rudimentary in his human development or at the zenith of his culture, has responded to nature's grasses by converting them to multiple uses for his practical and aesthetic enjoyment.

Fur and Leather

Among man's most intimate materials from the beginning of time have been furs and leather. During Europe's last glacial period, more than 75,000 years ago, Paleolithic man found within his dwelling caves the hibernating bear, which supplied him with pelts for cold-weather garments. Since then leather has provided man not only with material for his clothing but for his shelter. It has fastened his arrowheads to their shafts; it has formed his saddles, sails, shields, armor, water bags, and bows; it has also served as money for the exchange of other material goods.

Leather has been particularly important in pastoral and hunting economies. In the Sudan and Guinea states of Africa, leatherworking is a highly skilled art, and the trading of leather goods an important business. Products include leather bags, harnesses, cushions, ornamental daggers, powder horns, quivers, hats, and shoes. These may be lavishly decorated with fringes, beads, and cowrie shells. Hair and hide are also used decoratively on wooden ceremonial masks.

To this day furs and leather provide warmth in cool climates and add textural variety to costume and interiors. These materials have an elemental quality that modern men enjoy in combination with such techno-

logical products as aluminum and plastics. An increased interest in leather is indicated by its use today for bedspreads, café curtains, wall coverings, pillows, and upholstery. Polyurethane-coated fabrics that look like soft leather have been developed by many plastics firms for covering furnishings or making clothes and shoes. In the fashion world, furs and leather have provided many exotic costumes—embroidered goatskin jackets from Afghanistan, *chaparajos* made of curly lamb, and embroidered pigskin dresses and jackets with matching boots.

Historic Uses

Well-preserved leather articles have been found in Egyptian tombs. Leather was always used for the seats of ancient Egyptian camp chairs. Greeks, Anglo-Saxons, Tartars, and Chinese used leather for armor—leg-guards, shirts, boots, and helmets. In medieval times leather was almost as popular as were knotted tapestries for wall coverings. Leather's beauty is suggested by the writer of the catalog of the Deutsches-Tapeten Museum at Kassel, Germany, a museum devoted exclusively to the study of mural hangings.

These leather hangings may be looked upon as the first "wallpapers" in our sense of the word: they soon banished the Gobelins and other tapestries from the castles . . . and even today the brilliantly coloured specimens gleam with gold and silver in spite of the patina of centuries.[2]

With the advent of papermaking in the seventeenth century, the leather gilders, who had made decorated

[2]E. A. Entwisle, *The Book of Wallpaper* (London: Barker, 1954), p. 32.

leather hangings for rooms, turned to the making of wallpaper, a less expensive substitute.

The Moors introduced a great variety of leathers into Europe. Moroccan leather was highly prized for its fine quality and for its beautiful grain and color. Both the Spaniards and the English used leathers extensively for court furniture during the Renaissance period. Leather is particularly associated with the sixteenth- and seventeenth-century Spanish craftsmen who used it to cover chests, chairs, desks, tables, and screens. In finish, it could be plain, embossed, gilded with gold leaf, or decorated with nail heads. Oxhide, calf, and fine goat skin were used in the later years of Louis XIV's reign and also by Chippendale and other eighteenth-century designers.

The American colonists found that the Indians on the North American continent were skilled in tanning leather and used it extensively (particularly buckskin) for their clothing, tepees, and canoes. Leather, like wood, played a very significant role in the lives of the early settlers. The fur trader was the first resident on every pioneer front from the Atlantic seaboard to the Pacific Northwest. Traders made their livelihood by exchanging the craft and factory products of the colonists—guns, scalping knives, iron tomahawks, alcohol, beads, and bracelets—for the skins of deer, buffalo, and beaver. From these the colonists made knee breeches, jackets, coats, and boots. Coaches were upholstered in leather, and wide slings of supportive leather served as springs. Mail was carried between the colonies and westward in the nineteenth century with the Pony Express in pouches of leather, which were flexible and resistant to weathering.

Designers in Leather

There are a number of excellent contemporary designers of furnishings where leather is used in combination with wood and metal. One of the most understated and effective designs utilizing metal and leather is that designed by Katavolos, Littell, and Kelley, which is pro-

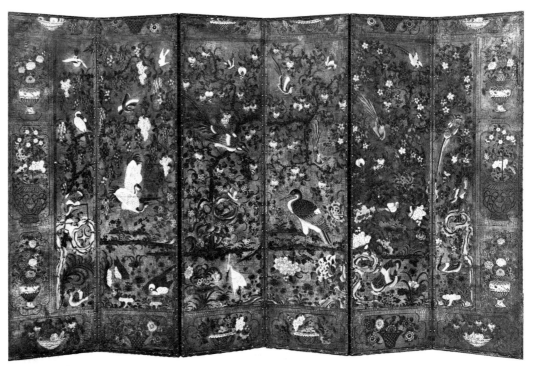

17-8 *Leather screen with lively* chinoiserie *design. Victoria and Albert Museum, London. Crown Copyright.*

17-9 *Tooled illuminated leather, from Flanders, style about 1780. Courtesy of the Cooper-Hewitt Museum of Decorative Arts and Design, Smithsonian Institution, New York.*

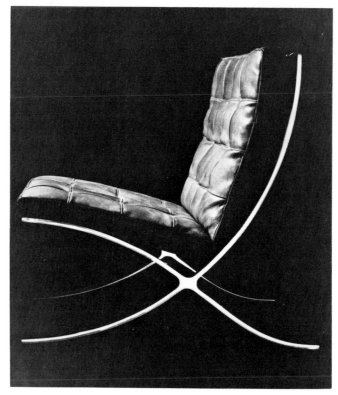

17-10 *Mies van der Rohe. Lounge chair. This chair of metal frame and leather upholstery was first shown at the Barcelona Fair of 1929. It has survived through time because of its quality design. Knoll International, New York.*

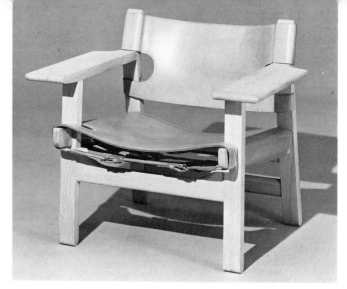

17-11 *Børge Mogensen. Chair in oak, with seat and back in uncolored stretched hide, designed in 1958. The chair is sturdy, unpretentious, and masculine in character. The leather would support while adapting to the body's physical strain. Note the undisguised assemblage of the chair. Courtesy World Pictures, Denmark.*

17-12 *Meret Oppenheim. Object. Fur-covered cup, saucer, and spoon, 1936; diameter of saucer 9⅜". Our regular expectations may suffer some affront, which was an objective of Dada art of the early 1920s and funk art of the 1960s. Our sense of vision is provoked into awareness, and the logical use of materials for particular functions is dramatically told. Collection, The Museum of Modern Art, New York.*

duced by Laverne Originals. It consists of a single sling of glove-textured leather suspended securely on a three-legged frame of chrome-finished steel. It is a lesson in economy of means, which when well-directed can achieve the beauty of form.

A Danish designer who has used leather with great effectiveness is Børge Mogensen. His sturdy oak chair, designed in 1958, with its seat and back made of uncolored stretched hide, suggests Spanish design with its saddle stitching and buckles. Its unpretentiousness results from Mogensen's use of untreated wood and uncolored oxhide. He believes in using quality materials whose texture is not modified by any finishing processes. These materials will not be affected by sunlight and fading, and daily use and wear will actually improve their warmth and depth of color.

Feathers

Historic Uses

Primitive man used the materials close at hand to design with ingenuity. The Maori of New Zealand used

17-13 *Poncho shirt, cotton, tabby weave with feather application. Chimu culture, Peru, 1000–1300* A.D., *33¼ x 33¼". Courtesy of The Art Institute of Chicago.*

either dog skins or bird skins for protection from the cold. Polynesian chiefs wore feather headdresses or helmets. Also they used human hair, supporting a whale's tooth or pearl shell, as adornment to indicate rank. Of all these materials, feathers were used most decoratively. Just as the male bird is equipped with beautiful plumage to attract the female, so primitive man adopted feathers for his personal beautification. The volcanic glass obsidian, another available material, was shaped into blades for cutting and trimming the feathers to the required design. With the help of a bone blade or copper knife the feathers were then set in position. The art of featherwork reached its culmination in Peru and

17-14 *Lenore Tawney.* Bird, *hanging of silk and feathers with a brass support, 30" x 25". The Museum of Contemporary Crafts, New York.*

the Polynesian islands scattered over the eastern Pacific Ocean within the vast triangle formed by Hawaii to the north, New Zealand to the south, and the Easter Islands to the east.

At the time of the Spanish conquest not only in Peru but also in the Aztec society of Mexico the feather worker and feather merchant ranked high in societal status. In Mexico featherworking was a hereditary craft, with workers occupying their own section of the community and worshiping their own special gods. Montezuma, the Aztec emperor, had featherworkers employed in his palace to make colorful dance costumes—head ornaments, bracelets, fans, covers for shields, and banners. The birds most prized for their color of plumage were the quetzal bird and blue cotinga. Plumage also came from the hummingbird, red spoonbill, troupial, crested guan, and parrot. The feathers were fastened to each other with glue or maguey thread.

Feather capes and cloaks were also made in New Zealand, Tahiti, and Hawaii. Feather ponchos and skirts have also been found in Peru. In New Zealand feathers were attached to each other by a form of finger weaving that employed paired interlocking weft threads to secure them. Tahitians fastened bunches of feathers to a long cord by means of knots, and Hawaiians tied bunches of feathers to a foundation of netting. In Hawaii red and yellow feathers, obtained from parrots and other local birds, were the symbolic colors of high chiefs and gods. Domestic fowl, the long-tailed tropic bird and the man-of-war hawk or frigate bird provided large feathers which were used to form a base to which others could be secured.

In Hawaii the feather cape and cloak were reserved as the attire of chiefs. Men were the only ones allowed to construct the garments, and professional bird hunters were employed to study the habits and find the roosting places of the forest birds. The nests they used for trapping birds may be seen today in the Bishop Museum in Honolulu.

Current Uses

With our increased interest in tactile and textural covering for both costume and home furnishings, it is not surprising that the plumage of birds is again being generously used in exotic clothes for women. An entire dress may be made of deep green coq feathers or of ostrich curls. Earrings and wigs have been made of peacock feathers. For high style the designer Scaasi even created gaucho trousers in speckled guinea-hen feathers. Whatever her fancy, the woman of means can adapt the plumage of birds to suit her mood and so capture some of birds' fleeting and tantalizing qualities. Today's weavers, such as Lenore Tawney, inspired by Peruvian and Polynesian artifacts, have incorporated feathers into their woven sculptures and wall hangings.

Textiles 18

In most of the world's prehistoric cultures, nomadic tribesmen, who used to wander about in search of food, settled in one area once they acquired sufficient knowledge to bring wild plants under cultivation. When man had learned how to utilize cotton and flax to make fabrics to cover his body, he had less need to gain comfort by changing environments. The ability to control plant life has been a significant factor in the spontaneous development of societies and of art. Without knowledge of scientific principles, primitive man attributed plant growth to mystic and magical forces. Man's early art was a by-product of devotion and a means of propitiation. He would use symbolic art objects, which he had made, in ritualistic events to influence his god or gods. Through the manipulation of these objects, he disposed the gods to cure his diseases, bring rain to his crops, provide safety and success during the hunt, or curtail floods. Thus an integration between life, religion, and art was established.

Textile design was one of the early symbolic media used by spiritual leaders for affecting the temper of the gods. It was then only a short step to the use of fabric design and decoration to establish political and class differentiation, because those persons in authority who held godlike powers were often revered as deities by the humble. Thus the use of clothing for social distinction and communication was established. Its contribution was recognized and succinctly expressed by Thomas Carlyle: "Society is founded on cloth."

Fabrics have served many other purposes, too. They have shielded man from the elements and provided him with whatever form of modesty his culture requires. They have also served significantly as a medium for personal aesthetic expression. Man has always used himself as a portable canvas upon which he designs daily. He has never stopped exploring novel forms of self-decoration by which to communicate, express, and project himself. His early environment provided furs, skins, and feathers for coverings; grasses and reeds, cotton, flax, and wool for woven constructions; roots, berries, bark, flowers, leaves, insects, and marine animals for dyes with which to paint himself and his fabrics. Today the dye and textile industries continue the search to provide a palette and a range of materials that make dressing oneself and designing one's immediate environment among the most engrossing arts of our time.

The tools and materials for weaving and decorating fabrics—spindles, looms, needles, and dyes—have been common in several widely separated cultures without benefit of intercommunication. Excavations made in 1853–54 of dried lake beds in Switzerland revealed that the art of weaving was known to the lake dwellers of the Old Stone Age by uncovering bales of flax ready for spinning, spindle whorls (weights for warp threads), yarns, and fabrics of linen and wool. By the Bronze Age, looms were in use. Depictions of the entire sequence of textile production, from raising sheep to spinning yarn and weaving it into fabric, can be found carved in stone on the walls of Nineveh, Babylon, and Thebes, among the ruins of Assyrian and ancient Persian towns, and at archeological sites in Peru and Mexico.

In the Swiss lake dwellings were also found sewing needles made from mammoth bones. The needle—a small uncomplicated object—has been one of mankind's most significant tools. It has been constructed from almost every known material—bone, ivory, walrus tusks, wood, copper, bronze, silver, gold, and thorns. Not only the lake dwellers but the Chinese of the Shang dynasty and the Indians of prehistoric Peru used it. Some of the finest Peruvian textiles were thought to have been constructed by the needle rather than the loom. Needles have been found in excavations at the archeological sites of Harappa and of Mohenjo-Daro in India. In the Vedic hymns the role of plying the needle is put on a parallel plane with that of bearing a son:

"With never-breaking needle may she sew her work and give her a son most wealthy, meet for praise." Nothing has been added to the needle's basic principle of operation since its conception. Its use had permitted the development of protective clothing, which has allowed man to expand his environment to other climates and even into space. Today the needle is also recognized as a tool for the fine arts of machine- and hand-stitchery.

A history of the world could be written focusing upon textiles and their design, so we will present only a limited number of textile developments here, to include the most decorative forms.

Contributions to Textile Design

Egypt and India

Although no exact date can be clearly established for the arts of weaving, painting, dyeing, and embroidering textiles, Egypt and India both have a long and continuous record of producing fabrics of unparalleled beauty and fineness. There is evidence of a stamping technique being used in Egypt as early as 2500 B.C. Mummies have also been found wrapped in cotton, native or imported, with a thread count of 540, surpassing any we produce today.

The Egyptians were also familiar with a complicated coloring process. Pliny the Elder, a Roman writer who lived in the first century A.D., described Egyptians' dyeing fabrics in his *Natural History:*

Moreover in Egypt they have a device to stain cloths . . . which they besmear not with colours but with certain drugs that are apt to drink and take colour: when they have so done, there is no appearance in them at all of any dye or tincture. These clothes they cast into a lead or cauldron of some colour that is seething and scalding hot: where, after they have remained a pretty while, they take them forth again, all stained and painted in sundry colours. An admirable

Indian silks and muslins, under the name of *textilis ventalis* (woven air), were imported by the Romans, who prized them highly. Chintzes, whose name is derived from the Hindu word *chint,* meaning "variegated in color," dates back to 400 B.C. Indian cottons became known in other countries through the conquests of Alexander the Great, through Arab trading, and through Vasco da Gama's establishment of a sea route to India in the sixteenth century. In the seventeenth century the establishment of the British East India Company brought the romance of the East to the European market. Calicoes, named for the seaport Calicut in southwest Madras from which they were exported in quantity,

18-2 *Indian calico print,* circa *1780. Courtesy of the Cooper-Hewitt Museum of Decorative Arts and Design, Smithsonian Institution, New York.*

18-1 *Funerary model of a weaving shop from upper Egypt during the Middle Kingdom period; wood, stucco, and paint. The history of the craft of weaving parallels the history of man's development. Collection, The Metropolitan Museum of Art, New York.*

thing, that there being in the said cauldron but only one kind of tincture, yet out of it the cloth should be stained with this and that colour, and the foresaid boiling liquor change so as it doth, according to the quality and nature of the drugs which were laid upon the white first. And verily, these stains or colours are set so sure, as they can never be washed off afterwards.[1]

[1]Quoted by Meda Johnson and Glen Kaufman in *Design for Fabrics* (New York: Reinhold, 1967), p. 9, from Philemon Holland (trans.), *The Natural History of C. Plinius Secundus* (Carbondale, Ill. 1962), p. 427.

18-3 *Cotton block print with birds, England, 18th century. The design emulates the Indian crewels, hand-embroidered designs of fanciful birds and flowers in wool on a beige-colored linen ground. Courtesy of the Cooper-Hewitt Museum of Decorative Arts and Design, Smithsonian Institution, New York.*

became a great favorite with Europeans and served as a catalyst for their textile development.

The beauty of Indian textiles has been attributed by some to India's topography. India is a lush tropical country in which man's relation to nature is much more intimate than in cooler climates. Dense jungles and vegetation abound, filled with insects, flowers, birds, and animal life. A sense of mystery, of warmth and passion, of languor, and of religious mysticism pervades the atmosphere and evokes a sensuousness that the Indians weave into their cottons; these are as fine and lustrous as silk. Designs traditionally have been symbolic, with religious connotations. Allegedly, when Buddah attained nirvana, the state of eternal rest, his body was wrapped in a Benares fabric that shot radiant flashes of red, yellow, and blue hues. In the old sculptures and paintings, Buddhas were draped with

brocades and with muslins so filmy and transparent that only the lines of folds and borders indicate that the figures are clothed. Fine muslins, requiring five to six months to complete half a length of approximately six to seven yards, have been woven for royalty. Names given to these muslins suggest their elemental textures— *abrawan,* "running water"; *bafthawa,* "woven air"; *shabnam,* "evening dew."

Because Indian fabrics are generally uncut, selvage to selvage, and require little sewing, the needle is most generously employed in the art of embroidering. Pearls, and silver and gold wire add an exotic quality to fabrics. Indian workmanship has served as a model for this art from an early date. The use of decorative gold cloths is very old; in the *Rig Veda,* reference is made to *hiranya-drapi,* or "shining gold woven cloak" and in the *Mahabharata* to *manichira,* a fabric with pearl-woven borders.

India is also famous for its batiks. The fineness of the Indian batiks, in which a wax resist is used, results from the long bleaching and softening processes to which the fabrics are subjected. The Indians' expert knowledge of dyeing techniques contributes further to their beauty. Originally developed as a folk art, cotton batik has been used for the daily dress of peasants and is also highly prized by royal personages, because Indian batiks rank with silk in their elegance and richness.

Color is a very important element in Indian fabric both for its emotional and for its symbolic content. Every mood has its color association and each religious sect its color preference. In the sari, the national dress, rhythm in color is employed to reinforce the rhythmic flow of line. Gradations in value and intensity diminish any strident effects that might result from the juxtaposing of vibrant colors. Diagonal stripes, formed in arranging the sari, produce a feeling of movement to correspond with the rhythmic sway of the wearer's body. Borders create contrasts of plain to patterned fabric to relieve monotony. The Indians have brought border art to a high level of artistic expression.

In India, embroidery is the work of children and men

and women of all ages. The subdued elegance of their fabrics is the result of expertise developed through years of experience in manipulating the needle. Cultural tradition reinforces the use of motifs taken from nature—peacocks, lotus, elephants, wind-blown cypress (the form of the paisley design), mangoes, pomegranates, dogs, horses, and bird forms. The Indian tree-of-life pattern was adapted from ancient Persian designs.

When very minute, Indian embroidery is almost indistinguishable from weaving. Several stitchery designs can be identified. The running, darning, satin, chain, and herringbone stitches are basic. In chain-stitch rugs, the chain stitch is used to cover the entire ground. In *gabba*

work, the chain stitch is used to appliqué together old shawls and other worn-out woolen garments to form couch covers or bedspreads. Kathiawar and Sind embroidery make lavish use of small mirrors, held down by circles of buttonhole stitches of bright color. In *phulkari,* threads are counted very accurately so as to produce geometrical designs which cover the entire background. Embroidery is done from the reverse side of the cloth so that the work simulates tapestry. In *chikan* white embroidery, a satin stitch floated on the back of a very fine transparent fabric creates an outline on the front and gives the fabric an opaque, shadowy effect. French knots are produced by minute satin

18-4 An Indian woman's garment (chadar), with cloth of gold and silk threads, 18th century. Note the flow of the material with the body's natural elegance. Collection, The Metropolitan Museum of Art, New York.

18-5 A woolen shawl from Kashmir, India, 18th–19th century. Courtesy of the Cooper-Hewitt Museum of Decorative Arts and Design, Smithsonian Institution, New York.

stitches. The Kashmir *namda,* a pressed felt rug colorfully chain-stitched with floral motifs, is necessarily bold in design because of the rug's thickness.

The design quality of Indian work is high. The Indians are masters of the ornamental and miniature in which much is included to produce a rich effect on a close field. Design becomes textural because of the flatness and closeness of the motifs. Animals, birds, and flowers are conventionalized with no shading of color, so that designs rest in a bed of mosaic. Balanced symmetry produces a feeling of order.

The Indian government is concerned that the ancient arts of Indian fabric production should not be lost to mechanization. Craftsmanship in weaving plays a very important role in India's economy and in maintaining her national image. The All India Handicrafts Board and the All India Hand-Loom Board attempt to preserve a balance between hand-loomed textiles and mill products. They also function to maintain the traditional regional and national characteristics of Indian textiles and to discourage the production of stereotypes in mass-produced goods. The importance of the sari as a national and social symbol is recognized by reference to it as "a fashioner of personality and a mirror of social life."

The *khadi* movement, the home production of cotton fabrics, was encouraged by Gandhi to eliminate the necessity of imports from English mills. Its importance to India's *esprit de corps* was pointed up by Shri Nanda, a supporter of the movement, who felt that hand-spun cloth is "precious to the nation as a symbol and a concept." This kind of national concern with preservation of the cultural heritage of a people is necessary if we are to save the beautiful and ancient arts on a worldwide level.

Recognition of the beauty of Indian fabrics is indicated by the fact that thousands of yards of gold-threaded and brilliantly hued yards of sari fabric are imported yearly into the United States and are designed in a Western mode to satisfy American women's desire to experience the utmost in exotic body covering.

China

Marco Polo, the first Western man to visit China, described China as a land of exotic spices, exquisite jewels, strange dress, and beautiful fabrics. By then, silk culture was an old industry in China, dating back to circa 2700 B.C.

Whereas cotton had always been India's chief textile fiber, sericulture flourished in China. Its use is attributed to the Empress Hsi Ling Shi, wife of Wuang Ti, whom

18-6 *Emperor Hui Tsung.* Chinese Lady Sewing Silk. *Silk is our heritage from China, and even emperors found fulfillment through artistically depicting seamstresses at work. Courtesy, The Museum of Fine Arts, Boston.*

18-7 *Chinese mandarin square: K'o-ssu (silk tapestry) with gilt thread in the background. Ming Dynasty 1368–1644. The mythological beast was probably a* hsieh ch'ai, *the emblem worn by a censor. Many Chinese motifs were symbolic. The whiplash line of the Art Nouveau period may have been influenced by the Oriental use of back-lashed curves. Collection, The Metropolitan Museum of Art, New York.*

legend states discovered silk when a cocoon fell from a mulberry tree into her teacup. Spooning it out, she noticed that it trailed an endless filament; later she became deified as the goddess of silkworms. So significant was her contribution to China's development that through the centuries a ceremony for feeding silkworms and rendering homage to the Empress has been held. China maintained a world monopoly in silk, successfully guarding knowledge of its production until the sixth century when two Persian monks, assigned by Emperor Justinian of Constantinople to visit China and discover the secret, concealed the seeds of the mulberry tree and some silkworm eggs in the hollow staves they carried.

Subsequently luxuriant Byzantine fabrics were developed; silks were woven with gold thread and encrusted with jewels to glow like mosaics.

There have been many fabrics developed in China. Among them are rich brocades, satins, damasks, tapestries, embroideries, and silks—crepe de Chine and pongee. Like Indian fabrics, those of the Chinese have been rich in symbolism, reflecting their belief in an elaborate system of forces that affect human life and existence. In the past the symbols have served many functions. They indicated the virtues the wearer wished to acquire or marked his office and rank in the hierarchy of Chinese society. Among the familiar symbols is the circle divided by an S-line into dark and light halves.

18-8 *Jack Lenor Larsen.* Happiness. *The hand-printed fabric from Larsen's Kublai Khan Collection is suited for draperies and upholstery in rooms of various periods. Notice his inclusion of Chinese omens for good—clouds, waves, and rainbows. Jack Lenor Larsen, Inc.*

This symbolizes the dualism in the world, entities not conflicting but complementing. Yang is the male component: his are the sky and sun, fire and noon, light and warmth. Yin, the female, has the earth and moon, water and evening, darkness and cold. Systems of personality and philosophy have been built upon these two complementary structures.

Because the Chinese live close to the soil and the elements, it is natural that their textiles should include many plant and floral designs. The plum tree is especially esteemed in China, because it is believed that beneath it the great philosopher Lao-Tze was born. The peach, favorite fruit of the people, is the fruit of their tree of life, which signifies longevity. The peony is the emblem of love and affection, the symbol of feminine loveliness. The lotus is a sacred symbol; hence Buddha and Buddhist priests are often represented seated on the lotus blossom. The chrysanthemum signifies joviality and ease.

The natural elements also have associated colors. Water is black; metal is white; wood is green; and earth is yellow. Because earth was believed to be the center of the universe and dominated by the emperor, yellow is the imperial color.

The bamboo was the symbol of gracefulness and enduring strength, and being hollow symbolized open-mindedness and willingness to accept change and good advice. The willow, symbol of spring, is familiar to us through its design on the blue and white chinaware of China. In 1780 the English potter Minton engraved the willow pattern on copper for use in England. Since then the design has become popular in other countries as well.

Japan

Whereas the Chinese were master weavers, an art they taught the Japanese, the Japanese excelled in the field of dyeing fabrics. In the Western world, the line of dress and its potential for variation have engaged the creative talents of the costume designer. The Japanese kimono, however, has remained relatively static in design over the centuries—a square-cut body with square-cut sleeves. Diversity has been realized through decoration. In integrating decorative design with structural design the Japanese have made dress a fine as well as an applied art. The No dramas, for which costumes were expressly designed, led to further integration of the arts.

The study of Japanese textiles and those of other cultures has been made possible by the existence of the world's most ancient museum, the Shōsō-in, built at Nara in the middle of the eighth century to house the imperial treasures. Among the diversity of its Asian artifacts are 61,000 textile samples, which were thus preserved and protected from the ravages of wars and floods that tore the continent apart and otherwise destroyed the best of ancient Oriental artifacts.

The Japanese revere their textiles as they do nature, and give them symbolic and poetic names. As with the Chinese, such motifs as flowers and flowering trees, flowing water and waves, and the crane and the tortoise are employed, reflecting the Japanese sense of oneness with nature and intimacy with its many forms. For instance, the design of a crane combined with a pine tree or branch became the conventional symbol in conveying wishes for everlasting happiness to brides, because the crane symbolized life for a thousand years.

The Japanese also made much use of crests, developed during the Heian period (794–1185); these heraldic devices were borne hereditarily by the nobility of the imperial court. Family crests became popular during feudal times when the samurai class adopted them, and later, during the Edo period, it was customary for every family to have its emblem. The crest is a simple geometric device that suggests, within a small area, subtle nuances between the elements of nature. Although the crest has lost its significance with respect to family identity, its stylized motifs continue to be used as decorative devices by Japan and other nations in designing fabrics, chinaware, and wallpaper.

The Japanese innovations in textile design were mainly in the arts of dyeing, because the development

18-9 *A cotton* sumba, *detail of a shroud from the Dutch East Indies, late 19th century. Like the Japanese* ikat *technique, the yarns are tied and dyed in various colors before weaving to give a blurred effect. Collection, The Metropolitan Museum of Art, New York.*

18-10 *Kimono fragment, Mountains, Clouds, and Phoenix, Japanese, Momoyama period, 1573–1615, height 28¼". This silk is decorated by employing* Kanoko *and* Shibori *techniques. Eugene Fuller Memorial Collection, Seattle Art Museum.*

of batik, stencil, tie-and-dye, and wood-block printing techniques were learned from other cultures, mainly the Chinese. A few of their dyeing techniques are

Rokechi, the batik process using wax as a resist.

Kasuri, a tie-and-dye process in which the yarns are tied and dyed before weaving to create a splashed pattern (also known as *ikat* in Indonesia).

Kokechi, tie-dyeing to produce an eye or a dot pattern. The small dot, associated with the eye of the deer or the markings on his flank, is produced by wrapping thread tightly around small tufts of material caught up by the fingernails or by a small hook. Tying a gathered bunch of fabric produces the sunburst or spiderweb effect. Tying smaller areas makes possible a dimpled texture, which can then be appliquéd into other motifs and arrangements in the kimono. *Kanoko-kokechi* (*kanoko* means "fish egg") refers to knots so small and fine that the resulting pattern resembles the roe of a fish.

Tsujigahana, later called *shibori,* is one of the most complex forms of tie-and-dye work, because it is usually combined with embroidery and employs floral designs. In *shibori,* the outlines of a design are care-

a visual impact from a distance. By allowing the float yarns of a brocade to float on the surface instead of the reverse side, strong vigorous color resulted.

Many of the techniques used by the Japanese are finding favor among today's experimental artists. These old processes are being revitalized and used in a contemporary idiom. Students of all ages are finding the arts of the ancients inspirational for their own creative development and design interpretation.

Europe

Tapestries

The Bayeux tapestry is the most celebrated embroidered tapestry in the Western world. It was completed in the later twelfth century to portray the invasion of England by William the Conqueror. Nineteen inches high and two hundred feet long, embroidered with wor-

18-12 *Coptic tapestry, Egypt, 7th–9th century. Courtesy of the Cooper-Hewitt Museum of Decorative Arts and Design, Smithsonian Institution, New York.*

fully basted with fine stitches and drawn up tightly. The puckered part is then wrapped in a sheath of bamboo to resist the dye. When the ties are released, the design is delineated by the shirred outline and can be further hand-shaped by painting.

Kirigane, a technique imitating the Chinese *kinran,* in which gold leaf is applied to damp lacquer.

Katatsuke, the use of fine rice-paste resist in stencil-resist dying.

One inventive contribution Japan made to weaving was the *kara-ori* brocade. The costume desired by the priests and the No dramatists was one that would create

18-13 A Hawking Party: *Flemish wool tapestry made at the beginning of the 16th century with a* **millefleurs** *background. Collection, The Metropolitan Museum of Art, New York.*

sted thread on linen, it commemorates a turning point in history.

France's outstanding contribution to textile manufacture during the fourteenth and fifteenth centuries was the development of Gothic tapestries. Tapestries were known in Egypt as early as 1500 B.C., and tapestries of such outstanding beauty were produced by the Copts (the Egyptian Christians) in the fifth and sixth centuries A.D. that they still provide inspiration to contemporary weavers. The Crusaders brought back the knowledge of tapestries from Constantinople and the Holy Land. As hangings, they proved particularly useful in reducing the cold of stone-walled medieval halls. Their decorative structure suggested the Persian miniature in which the eye, without benefit of perspective, is allowed to roam over a richly detailed scene and to arrive at a high hori-

zon where one can take a bird's-eye view over a pano-rama of flat masses.

The subject matter of Gothic tapestries was religious, allegorical, and mythical, or it might be pastoral, courtly, or hunting. Like the Oriental rug, it often had a *millefleurs* theme (many flowers arranged in a repeat design). In designing the tapestries, objects were not reduced in size to show distance. There were no grada-tions or rounding of forms, nor were colors atmospheric in order to produce depth—instead, the ground seemed to rise up to meet the viewer, bringing him face to face with a high horizon. Figures were not treated realisti-cally but distorted to create the design effect desired. The material was treated as a fabric, not as an oil paint-ing, and had a flatness consistent with the wall's surface. Later Renaissance tapestries became increasingly realis-tic and imitative of oil paintings, even to having scenes enclosed in widely woven frames.

Velvets, Damasks, and Brocades

Outstanding for their beauty among European textiles are the Spanish and Italian silk velvets and damasks of the Renaissance period, and French eighteenth-century brocades. The designs of the Renaissance fabrics re-flected a Byzantine influence. In eighth-century Con-stantinople, known in those days as Byzantium, the representation of human or animal forms was consid-ered idolatrous because it violated the second com-mandment concerning the use of graven images. As a result, fabric designs become geometrical and abstract, orderly, and symmetrical, an influence upon design which was far-reaching and long-lasting.

The rococo line that so fittingly expressed the spirit of eighteenth-century France under Louis XV is evident in the beautiful silken brocades of his time. Then during the classical revival under Louis XVI, fabrics reflected

18-14 *Velvet panel, cut and uncut, woven of silk and metal, Italy, 17th century. Courtesy of the Cooper-Hewitt Museum of Decorative Arts and Design, Smithsonian Institution, New York.*

18-15 *Silk damask, Italian Florentine, 16th century. Courtesy of the Cooper-Hewitt Museum of Decorative Arts and Design, Smithsonian Institution, New York.*

18-16 *Silk brocaded with floral sprays in serpentines, Louis XV period. Courtesy of the Cooper-Hewitt Museum of Decorative Arts and Design, Smithsonian Institution, New York.*

the delicate, straight, slender lines and modest ornamentation of design in excavated classical Pompeii.

The Toile de Jouy

A German, Christophe-Philippe Oberkampf, was actually responsible for the design of the fabric known as *toile de Jouy,* manufactured at Jouy in France. The toile is a cotton fabric whose design consists of a single hue on a beige background. Oberkampf had been sent abroad by his father, who owned a large dyeworks in Germany, to study foreign methods of textile production. He was so impressed with the gay and colorful *indiennes,* as the cotton prints of India were called in France, that he translated his impressions of them into a European idiom. He used a wide gamut of designs, among them millers, reapers, hunters, sailors, American Indians; the playful gambols and idyls of the rococo era; architectural vistas; literary, allegorical, and historic scenes.

So valued was Oberkampf that King Louis XVI be-

18-17 *Jean-Baptiste Huet. Offrande a l' Amour, France, late 18th century. Note the inscription at the base of the toile, "Manufacture de Oberkampf A Jouy Près Versailles Bon Teint." Courtesy of the Cooper-Hewitt Museum of Decorative Arts and Designs, Smithsonian Institution, New York.*

Chinoiseries

Chinoiserie is an all-embracing term for things designed to imitate the Far Eastern arts of India, China, and Japan, but which often miss in authenticity. The manufacture of *chinoiseries* began during the reign of Louis XIV as French interpretations of imaginary Chinese motifs and scenes, but as they subsequently developed in France and England, elements of French rococo and classical design were introduced, which imparted a uniquely whimsical quality. The design was widely used for numerous objects including fabrics, wallpaper, the wood inlay of china cabinets, panels of decorative lacquer on screens and cupboards, and mirror frames. The English furniture designer Thomas Chippendale was especially enamored of Chinese color and motifs.

The Islands

Tapa Cloth

Tapa is a decorative textile that is much used for furnishings and for clothing by Oceanic peoples. Long ago, they domesticated the paper mulberry tree for the making of fabric from its bark. Just as the ancient Egyptians pounded reeds together to make papyrus for writing paper, so did island people pound the spongy bark of the mulberry tree into tapa.

To prepare the mulberry bark for the felting process, it is first steeped in a river bed until thoroughly pliable. Three layers, with the grain at right angles, are laid on top of each other and placed on a stone or prostrate trunk of a coconut tree. They are then beaten with a heavy mallet until the fibers are matted together tightly and the desired thickness is achieved. After bleaching in the sun, the cloth is impregnated with vegetable dyes—usually hues of yellow, orange, and brown—in bold abstract patterns.

Tapa is much like felt. Because it cannot be draped like woven fabrics, it is most serviceable for apparel in warm climates where close-fitting garments are not required and a sarong suffices. Tapa has been brought into the American market largely by way of Hawaii. It is used

stowed upon his factory the title *Manufacture Royal* and permitted Oberkampf to use the arms of the king as a trademark. With the coming of the French Revolution, the stigma of royal association led to abandonment of the title for protective reasons, but later Napoleon again honored the designer, conferring upon him the Cross of the Legion of Honor.

Toiles have continued to be used to this day in fabrics and wallpapers. They found their way into many colonial interiors—and into twentieth-century dress design. Part of their perennial appeal lies in the restricted use of only two colors, which do not contrast highly in value. However realistic the motifs, their fineness of line always contributes an etched textural quality.

18-18 *Tapa cloth, Samoa, late 19th century or early 20th century. Courtesy of the Cooper-Hewitt Museum of Decorative Arts and Design, Smithsonian Institution, New York.*

The San Blas Mola

The *mola* is a highly respected folk art of the Indian women who inhabit the San Blas Islands off the Atlantic coast of Panama. These San Blas women prize their *molas* just as the American colonial women prized their quilts and the Javanese women their batiks, because each forms part of the marriage dowry. In many cultures, needlework has had a long tradition of symbolizing feminine virtue.

To the Indians, *mola* signifies a blouse or shirt, but to the collector it has become identified as a technique of appliqué. To make a *mola*, three or more layers of colored fabrics are placed upon each other to form a sandwich, as in making plywood. Just as in the tech-

18-19 *San blas mola, 20th century. Courtesy of the Cooper-Hewitt Museum of Decorative Arts and Design, Smithsonian Institution, New York.*

here for decorative place mats, which are treated with plastic to resist staining, for decorative wall hangings, and for background design in displaying resort clothing. Many large cities have "tropical island" cocktail lounges where walls and ceilings are papered with tapa. Tapa's individuality of style, impersonality of design, abstraction of form, and warm but limited color range contribute to its decorative versatility.

nique of intarsia one cuts back to expose the different grains and colors of wood, the Indian cuts into the bed of fabrics to expose variations in color and texture. In constructing these, the edges of the cuts of fabric are carefully folded under and stitched. Thus the background area, the negative space, is so integrated with the foreground that at times the two may appear equivocal. The motifs used in earlier times were abstractions of people, animals, fish, plants, and the heavens, but Western influences have brought the use of motifs such as airplanes and "pop" art, to emulate foreign culture.

Today the older *molas* have the freshness and fascination of design that the primitive sculptures of Africa once held for the Western collector. They are being hung as wall hangings, framed as pictures, and made into exotic sports costume. They illustrate that the needle can be as creative and sophisticated a tool as the brush.

18-20 Wool garden carpet, Persian, 18th century. Note the divisions laid out like pools and beds of flowers. Motifs are small and generously floral. Collection, The Metropolitan Museum of Art, New York.

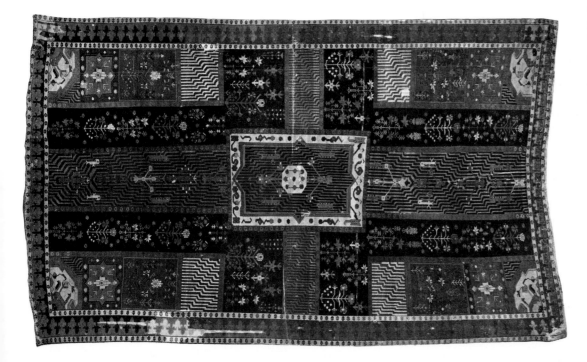

Other Decorative Textile Design Forms and Designers

Rugs

Oriental Rugs

Of all Eastern textile designs and artifacts, the Oriental rug has had the most continuous appeal through the centuries. The earliest known carpet, dating back to the fifth century B.C., was discovered in 1949 in a Scythian burial site at Pazyryk, close to the Outer Mongolian border. This ancient rug, now in the Hermitage Museum in Leningrad, is tied with 225 knots per square inch, indicating that the art of knotting was already well developed long before the Christian era.

The rug was the quintessence of Persian art, and the sixteenth and seventeenth centuries are considered the golden age of carpetmaking in Persia. Rugs gave an air of elegance to the court and were the chief objects of goodwill and gift exchange with foreign embassies. Rugs were used to hang from balconies, to span bare façades, and as prayer mats. Being a portable item, the rug constituted a form of travelling wealth and was found in tents of such warring conquerors as Alexander the Great, Genghis Khan, and Tamerlane. Its beauty was noted by the Greek philosopher Themistocles, who likened man's discourse to a "rich Persian carpet, the beautiful figure and pattern of which can be shown only by spreading and extending out."

There are many classifications of Oriental rugs, depending upon the design motifs and organization of the field. Among these are Indian, Turkoman, Caucasian, Turkish, and Chinese. There are many similarities in design between all these rugs, except the Chinese. Persian craftsmen, the recognized experts in the field, were employed to work in other Asian courts, where they adapted Persian design to the usage of the country. Chinese carpets, being of more recent origin, have less of an overlap with Persian motifs. Chinese Oriental rugs tend to be restrained in color, the positive design frequently being rendered in blue. The same motifs are used that appear in Chinese fabrics—stylized peonies, waves, clouds of eternity, the mythical dragon, the butterfly, and Taoist symbols.

The Persians' love of pools and gardens is reflected in the pattern of their rugs, where the central medallion found in many of these designs may be likened to a courtyard pool, surrounded by borders of flowers and foliage, which extend to the walls of the garden. In both Persian and Indian rugs, the favorite motifs are birds, animals, and plants; these are somewhat delicate and

18-21 *Wool carpet, Indian, period of Jahangir (1605–1627). Collection, The Metropolitan Museum of Art, New York.*

18-22 *Wool prayer rug, Turkish, from Bergama, Asia Minor, early 17th century. Collection, The Metropolitan Museum of Art, New York.*

18-23 *Wool rug, Caucasian, 19th century. Collection, The Metropolitan Museum of Art, New York.*

hammed's wisdom and by its continuous line movement to contrast with the all-over design of the main field.

The motif we know as paisley is called *botek* in Persian, meaning "leaf" or "bunch of leaves." A popular symbol all over the world, it occurs in the form of a pear, a pine cone, a lozenge, an almond, or a cypress tree swaying in the wind. The motif varies in size and shape and is often filled with tiny flowers. It is a design much used in fabrics for men's and women's clothes and in interior design for draperies and wall paper.

The Turkish, the Turkoman, and the Caucasian designs reflect greater masculinity, angularity, and boldness. The Turkish rug resembles the Persian and the Indian but has the precision of line associated with a ruler's edge. The Turkoman is composed of linear geometric designs —squares, diamonds, octagons, stars, and crosses. The background wool that is used is dyed the color of blood. The medallions of the Caucasian rug have jagged step edges similar to the blanket designs of the American Navaho and other Indians of the Southwest. Contrasting colors are combined with lightning lines to produce the sensation of being present in nature's elements.

Rya Rugs

One of the most powerful statements of Finnish art is the rya rug. Rug knotting, which is related to tapestry weaving, is an ancient technique in both Sweden and Finland. Woolen or linen wool yarns of varied length and density are knotted and secured into the warp yarns to produce deep shaggy rugs in which the pattern becomes blurred and expressionistic as the pile moves backward and forward. With the pile worn next to the skin the older rya rugs were worn by the Vikings and also by seal hunters, and deep-sea fishermen. Rya has also served as coverlets, wall hangings, bench and chair coverings, and carpeting. (See figure 10-27.)

By the eighteenth and nineteenth centuries, instead of being woven in a single color as formerly, the ryas duplicated colorful tapestries and constituted a valuable part of a girl's dowry. The designers of rya rugs have

small in scale and are depicted with curvilinear lines. Many have all-over textural patterns, similar to the *millefleurs* of French Gothic tapestries. Although the symbols are natural, they are flattened, flowing, and stylized. Flowery Arabic calligraphy is frequently used in the borders of Persian rugs to quote some of Mo-

18-24 *V'Soske. Tiffany, 8'8" circle, 1968, in the tradition of Art Nouveau, with gradation of values, and a central focal point. Courtesy of V'Soske.*

heights of pile was employed. After World War II, they set up shop in Puerto Rico to take advantage of the quality of wool produced there and the availability of Puerto Ricans with the ability to do fine craftsmanship.

Color and texture are dominant elements in the design of V'Soske rugs. With respect to color, the V'Soske collection contains at least 100,000 dye formulas. One rug may have as many as fifty-six different dyes. Textural interest is not only achieved by differing densities and heights of pile, but by shearing, carving, and embossing.

The rug designs range from the traditional to contemporary. Patterns of any exacting specification, from a Picasso or Mondrian to an eighteenth-century French

18-25 *V'Soske. Shadow of Time, 1961, 6' x 7'9", is an interpretation of an Abbot Pattison abstract. Courtesy of V'Soske.*

tended to adapt their patterns to the changing spirit of the time. Cubistic and abstractly expressionistic designs have been developed. Today's designs are extravagant in color and ruggedly bold in design. In Finland they provide the cheer and color needed in a severe climate, and in other countries they coordinate well with modern furnishings.

V'Soske Rugs

Great versatility and beauty in rug designs for wall hangings or floor treatment have been achieved by V'Soske. During the 1920s a group of craftsmen brothers from Grand Rapids, Michigan, the V'Soske, conceived of making handmade rugs and carpets by tufting wool yarns through a strong cotton base. For this purpose, a needle that could produce varying densities and

18-26 *Detail of mantle of woolen cloth with borders embroidered with human figures. Peruvian embroidery of early Nazca culture. circa 600. Collection, The Metropolitan Museum of Art, New York.*

Savonnerie, are designed to order. A client can have a custom-made rug woven to accommodate any area and to integrate with the pattern of wallpaper, upholstery fabric, or any other interior element of his choice. Each rug is considered a work of art and is constructed in the finest craftsman tradition. The beauty of V'Soske rugs has led to their being exhibited on the walls of both the Metropolitan Museum and the Museum of Modern Art in New York.

Weaving

Peruvian Weavers

Exploring fresh means of creative expression, contemporary weavers study the weaving techniques of ancient cultures, particularly those of Peru, where textile weaving is four thousand years old. The materials used by the ancient Peruvian were fibers from cotton, wool, hemp, cactus, and grass. Seeds, shells, feathers, and gem stones served for decoration. With very simple equipment, the natives for centuries have produced textiles of excellent quality, fineness, and distinction of design. The earliest spinning was done with the fingers. Later, they used twigs, and, finally, spindles with pottery or bone whorls. Their needles were made from metal, wood, fishbones, or thorns. Without benefit of association with other civilizations, they developed a consummate textile art. Their techniques included twining, plaiting, braiding, knotting, looping in a figure eight, coiling, netting, embroidering, and the weaving of tapestries, gauze, feather mosaics, brocades, double cloth, velvets, and openwork designs. The Peruvian women were never idle, but spun as they walked or tended their flocks. The more elaborate Inca shirts were woven of vicuna and adorned with gold, emeralds, and other precious stones. Tapestries, into which feathers were woven, were given as gifts to members of the nobility.

Lenore Tawney

Among weavers, Lenore Tawney has drawn particular inspiration and knowledge from the study of Peruvian

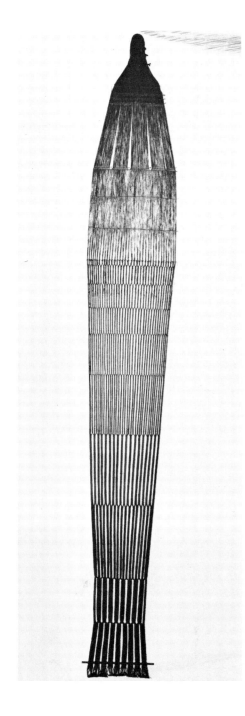

18-27 *Lenore Tawney.* The River, *1961, black weaving, length 13'.*
Collection, The Museum of Modern Art, New York.

18-28 *Lenore Tawney. Detail 1 of* The River. *Collection, The*
Museum of Modern Art, New York.

18-29 *Lenore Tawney. Detail 2 of* The River. *Collection,*
The Museum of Modern Art, New York.

textiles. Lenore Tawney was originally a sculptress, studying with Alexander Archipenko. Her valuing of form led her to weaving "hangings in space," which often extend from ceiling to floor. These are suspended transparent pieces in which groupings of warps form geometric columnar forms. She has defined her work as "Bound weaving . . . instead of one weft thread going through from one side to the other, there are two threads, one from each side. These separate and the separate parts again separate, and perhaps again. . . . It is like breathing; it expands and contracts. . . . That is what gives it form."

Like the Incas, Lenore Tawney uses feathers in her weaving (although she gathers them in the parks of New York) and yarns of natural undyed color, which range from white to tan, sepia, brown, and black. Form, line, and texture are her most valued elements; these appear more dramatic if color remains restrained and subtle. Of her weaving she says:

The work takes its form through its own inner necessity. . . .

The techniques are bound weaving, twining, knotting, braiding, twisting.

All the pieces are constructed as expanding, contracting, aspiring forms—sometimes expanding at the edges while contracting in the center. Some, like "Dark River," expand while dividing and separating, then gather in.

When I looked at my "River," it looked to me like the river. The changing ways, the current, the surface. I knew what it was going to be, and I think I knew it was the river. I had it inside and I think that when it is there on the inside it seeps through to your mind. It is an inner landscape that I am doing.[2]

Navaho Weavers

The Navaho tribe of Native Americans learned weaving from the ancient Pueblo tribe. Weavings were used by tribes for blankets and clothing. Each individual trading post featured different designs for sale. Those designs are still symbols for various geographic areas. Navahos not only weave the rug on the vertical loom, but also raise the sheep and spin the yarns. Navaho rugs are highly prized and collector's items.

Boris Kroll

Among commercial weavers of outstanding quality is Boris Kroll, who is respected as one of the world's greatest weavers. Mr. Kroll's forte has been in applying the Jacquard power loom to produce tapestry-type upholstery fabrics. His training began in his family's furniture factory, where he learned the structural considerations a manufacturer needs with respect to fabrics. He supplemented this practical education with six years of concentrated schooling in the aesthetics of hand

18-30 *Navaho rug. Collection, Utah Museum of Fine Arts, Salt Lake City, Utah. Two Grey Hills. Gift from Judge Willis W. Ritter.*

[2]Rose Slivka, "The New Tapestry." *Craft Horizons,* **23**:2 (Mar.-Apr. 1963), p. 18.

weaving, after which he began designing hand-woven fabrics for the upholstery and drapery industry. Now power looms multiply his ideas; he believes technology is a design agent, like the brush and the pencil, but believes in "creative automation." He credits 50 per cent of his work to technology and 50 per cent to artistic sense. Of himself he says: "I am adventurous. I concentrate on new approaches to the use of the loom and new fibers. I am . . . like Hindemith, Ravel, Shostakovich, Bartok."

Like Jack Lenor Larsen, who drew his design inspiration from such diverse areas as Africa and the Andes, Boris Kroll developed a Caribbean series of fabrics that captured the color of the foliage and fruits of those islands. Later he designed an exotic Oriental series, a vibrantly colored Mediterranean series, an Etruscan series ranging from natural colors of fibers to the jewel-like tones of ancient precious gems, a Florentine series, and a Transitional collection. He considers the element of color to be the most critical of the creative tools of the designer. He is credited with influencing and elevating the aesthetic of the entire home furnishings area. Here is his recommendation for creative design, which he himself has followed and that has led to his pre-eminence in the field:

Fabric designers should concentrate more on the history of design in every possible phase. Creative design does not come from the atmosphere. Creative design comes from a reservoir of studying, seeing, and absorbing which is directed by intuitive drives.[3]

Batiks

With our extended interest in the cultures of Indonesia, India, Polynesia, and Africa comes a renewed awareness of the design potential of the art of batik dyeing known to many ancient cultures. The name *batik*

[3]"Boris Kroll: Creative Force in the World of Weaving," *American Fabrics*, No. 48, (Winter 1960), p. 82.

18-31 *Indonesian batik with* **wayang-kulit** *figures, 19th century. The Malayans of Indonesia absorbed Indian elements to develop their own indigenous folk art in the form of the* **wayang-kulit,** *or shadow plays, in which puppets in the guise of heroes or mythological and religious figures dressed in batik patterns, performed in theatrical scenes. Courtesy of the Cooper-Hewitt Museum of Decorative Arts and Design, Smithsonian Institution, New York.*

derives from the Javanese word *tik*, meaning "a fine point," or "a point of light in the dark." Batik printing was practiced in ancient Egypt and is thought to have been brought by the Hindus from Turkey and Persia to Java, where it reached a zenith in development. Traditionally in Java, it was an aristocratic occupation practiced only in the homes of wealthy and leisured women, who spent months producing designs of great beauty and intricacy. Today, commercial batik printing has become an organized village industry.

The "point in the dark" is aptly descriptive of batik,

for by using a *tjanting* tool (a long narrow pipe) filled with hot dye-resisting substances, such as melted beeswax, rosin, or paraffin, small beadlike or trailing designs can be created. Multicolor effects can be achieved by applying additional areas of wax and immersing the fabric in a succession of dyebaths in a light-to-dark color sequence. Crackling the hardened wax to allow the dye to flow between the fissures creates the weblike texture characteristic of many batiks. There are many contemporary artist-craftsmen who employ the medium to create textile designs for clothing and for decorative hangings in interiors. Vaki is well known in Mexico for producing designs that echo the arts of ancient cultures, such as the wayang-kulit shadow puppets of Java, the Aztec and Mayan designs of Mexico, and Oriental and Persian themes. Otto and Peggy Holbein produce decorative hangings for banks, hotels, and homes in Florida and the Caribbean. Even the Pentagon showed appreciation of batik in its purchase for the permanent collection of the Air Force Museum of an eagle carrying bolts of lightning in its beak, which was designed by the Holbeins.

Stitchery

It has been noted that embroidery is an ancient art that was already being practiced in the Orient many centuries ago for the embellishment of court costume. With the establishment of trade routes to the Orient and through the exposure to Eastern influences resulting from the Crusades, Europeans became enamored of the art. English crewel designs of Indian floral inspiration, embroidered in wool yarns on natural backgrounds, evolved from this exposure. Embroidery, at first the occupational art of court ladies, became the work of the people. To record the kinds of stitches, samplers became popular. The sampler was a personal record, an encyclopedia of stitches that served as a reference book to the embroiderer. Samplers were handed down from mother to daughter, each adding her own newly invented or acquired stitches. In this way the values and spirit of the time were subtly reflected, as the sampler recorded changes between generations. Later, working a sampler became a discipline and chore for young girls, who were required to reproduce the alphabet and morality verses in cross-stitch, and the sampler lost its imaginative appeal.

Mariska Karasz

Recently, there has been an increased appreciation of the art of stitchery. In the 1950s, Hungarian-born Mariska Karasz pioneered with new abstract expressions to reflect our time. Since then several artists have taken up the needle and stitchery is now recognized as an expressive aesthetic medium.

Mariska Karasz' work showed an evolutionary development from the hackneyed images of the past to the more highly imaginative and abstracted ones of today. The explanation of her growth is one that is common to many artists who at first express themselves through designing familiar images, but with time and experience find more satisfying personal expressions. She wrote of her style:

By stopping frequently to evaluate I remain free to change my attitude and to grow. I feel that it is this growing that explains the changing of my style. The break from the pictorial came to me naturally. The change from the traditional and representational level was gradual, a growing upward rather than a jumping from one level of work to another. Moving into the abstract was an inner development.[4]

[4]Karasz, Mariska, "Abstract Stitches," *Craft Horizons* **XIII:2** (Mar.-Apr. 1953), p. 11.

18-33 *An English sampler, mid-17th century, using colored silk, human hair, and metal thread on linen. The cross borders show people (perhaps in a religious scene), floral designs, verse, and a signature. The stitches used are satin, cross, double running, rococo, stem, and chain. Courtesy of the Cooper-Hewitt Museum of Decorative Arts and Design, Smithsonian Institution, New York.*

18-32 *Batik square, Java, cotton, 19th century. Batik patterns depict emblems of happiness, long life, flora, and fauna. Batik was so highly prized that it served as the material of the lowliest citizen as well as the courtly raiment of princes. Courtesy of the Cooper-Hewitt Museum of Decorative Arts and Design, Smithsonian Institution, New York.*

18-34 *Nik Krevitsky.* Voodoo. *The stitchery's design, applied to black wool suiting, 27" x 32", and using mohair, linen, cotton, wool, and silk fibers as well as tussah silk and wool appliqué, suggests voodoo sorcery. Courtesy of Nik Krevitsky. Photograph by Peter Balestrero.*

Nik Krevitsky

The person engaged in creative stitchery today uses far more than floss and fabric. Any materials that can be secured or held together with thread or yarn or wire are employed. These may include beads, plastic disks, feathers, shells, straw, raffia, reeds, ringed beer-can lifts, or any found object. Nik Krevitsky, a designer in stitchery, states his procedure thus: "Assembling these materials is a constant venture, and I doubt that I could work with the restriction of going shopping for the ingredi-

ents for a particular stitchery in advance of doing it. I find it easier to work with a wide selection at my immediate disposal."[5]

Anna Ballarian

Anna Ballarian, a West-coast artist, encourages people to experiment with creative stitchery because it is a medium of expression that permits one to "move the colors, shapes, and lines around easily, to achieve a design that pleases one without muddying the colors. This gives a feeling of success."[6]

Some of her work is a fascinating textural collage of batik, appliqué, tie-and-dye, needle embroidery, and machine-stitchery. These she often manipulates into a single composition to achieve varying depths, rhythms, nuances of color, and textures, which recreate images of seascapes, outer space, or canyoned ravines. To her, as to many artists, nature is the great repository of design from which one can continuously draw inspiration.

Macramé

Macramé, meaning embroidered veil in French, according to Webster, is an ancient art that is currently being rediscovered. Its art was practiced in Spain, France, and Italy between the fourteenth and sixteenth centuries. Author-designer Virginia Harvey, in her book *Macramé, the Art of Creative Knotting*, points out that the art probably began when man used a knot to attach two vines together, this act antedating the spinning and weaving of textiles. Evidence of man's early uses of knotted designs are gamebags and nets used for catching wild beasts; some of these are preserved in the Kircheriano Museum, Rome. With advances in civilization, knotting was used decoratively by many societies for the fringes of garments and household linen, be-

[5] Nik Krevitsky, "On Stitchery," *Craft Horizons* Nov.-Dec. 1963), pp. 18–20.
[6] "A Talk with Anna Ballarian," *Creative Crafts* **III:1,** (May-June 1962), pp. 10-13.

cause it eliminated the visual abruptness of a hem. Among those who practiced knotting were members of religious orders who made knotting trim for religious garments. Sailors also spent long hours during sea voyages knotting cords, twine, and ropes into practical and decorative objects. Today's macramé is used for screens and dividers, wall sculptures, bags, and placemats. Beautiful objects can be made from a ball of string by employing variations of only two basic stitches.

Other Printed Fabrics and Their Designers

The silk-screen process for producing decorative textiles, developed in the twentieth century, has made possible a wide range of creative and original designs. In the 1960s, a revolution occurred with respect to visual expectancy in textile design, as a result of utilizing the silk screen process to its fullest. In apparel fabrics, designers had held to a great extent to the familiar visual images, which were built upon hand wood-blocked patterns with small repeats. According to Helen Giambruni:

This was partly owing to conservatism and lack of imagination but also (at least in the case of apparel fabrics) to a belief that fabric design should be subservient both to the lines of the body and to the needs of the clothing designer. (Complex cut and fit are difficult when large, spaced prints must be considered.)[7]

But with the coming of the 1960s, ordering of a design to a repeat pattern consistent with the warp and filling of a fabric was no longer considered essential. The entire individual with his clothing design became part of a total image in which body and dress were not clearly defined but appeared as a single image; this image could in turn merge as one with the background. Fashion designers turned to making their own single-image designs, avoiding "the tyranny of the repeat" in order to integrate design with the shape of a dress. The artists employed bold design, using the body itself as a canvas; the fabric design simulated a painting with movement over the entire surface. Thus distinctions formerly made between fine and applied art became further blurred.

Among these bold designers were Emilio Pucci, Tzaims Luksus, Jack Lenor Larsen, Julian Tomchin, Maija Isola for Marimekko, Jean Sibert and Leon Hecht for Print Directors, Timo and Pi Sarpeneva, and Vera. Bold, brilliant prints dominated the scene, while the design inspiration could come from anywhere. Emilio Pucci used the blazing colors and geometries from Italian Renaissance guild flags and the banners of Italian districts; he also drew inspiration from Indian fabrics, from the cathedral stained glass, and from Chinese embroideries. Finnish Armi Ratio in her Marimekko prints drew her inspiration from sources as diverse as the contrasting designs in nature, Russian folk art, architecture, calicoes, and baroque tapestries. Her palette included combinations of red and hot pink with bittersweet, gold and fiery orange, navy with royal or cerulean blue, black with cranberry, chartreuse with violet or rust, and magenta with brick and orange.

For intensity of color, Finnish designers Timo Sarpeneva and his wife Pi perfected a new technique called "Ambiente" for printing by use of machinery but without engraved rollers and with no use of the silk screen and no repeats. By this process both sides of the fabric are colored simultaneously to produce intense color effects.

Vera, well known through her fabric design for apparel and household linens, is recognized for fusing expert handicraft with mass production. She married a textile manufacturing expert, George Neumann, a descendant of an old Hungarian textile printing family and head of the Printex screen print plant in Ossining, New York. The facilities of the plant make possible the entire processing of a design in one day, from the conception of an idea to the finished product.

Since her husband's death in 1962, Vera functions not

[7] Helen Giambruni, "Color Scale and Body Scale," *Craft Horizons* **28**:3 (May-June 1968), p. 47.

only as chief designer and generator of ideas, but as head of the Printex firm. Her idealism with respect to design has contributed to elevating consumer taste. F. Werner Hamm, joint founder of the firm, says of Vera:

I have never known Vera to design down to a price group nor would anyone think of asking her to do so. We began in the belief that there is a mass market for good taste in America. Fortunately for us, it has proven to be so, and each year the market has grown as our own salesmen, together with buyers, retail salespeople and the consumer herself, have become more and more educated to Vera's design aesthetic.[8]

Vera's design technique parallels that of the *sumi* brushwork of Japanese painters. Simplicity and abstraction are present, with subtle variations in value and line. Detail is minimal, sufficient only to recreate the essence of a form. Her designs, spontaneous and ingenuous, nevertheless convey an air of sophistication.

[8] "Vera," *American Fabrics,* No. 63 (Winter-Spring 1964) p. 89.

Tree Products and Related Art 19

Behold the wood
where life has drawn
Lengthwise a river
Crosswise an island, surrounded
by concentric years.
Behold the darkening knots
Like shadows of birds' eggs
in the nests that have tumbled
from living towers that have fallen.[1]

Harry Martinson

Wood

From ancient times to the present day, wood has been one of man's cherished and most intimate materials, appealing to him not only for its functional purposes, but also for the sensuous and spiritual responses it evokes. By the hearth of his home man, watching the flames of wood and dying embers, dreams his silent dreams. Wood assaults his olfactory sense. Newly sawn lumber has a pungent odor, and woods such as cedar, sassafras, pine, and redwood retain some of the scent of the forest for an extended period of time. That wood appeals to man spiritually is indicated by Bryant's lines in *Hymn to a Forest:* "The groves were God's first temples."

Wood is extremely functional in helping man adapt to his environment. The forest was his first home, because prehistoric man lived in trees. Trees have provided

[1] Quoted by Ulf Hård af Segerstad, *Modern Scandinavian Furniture* (New Jersey: Bedminster Press, 1963) p. 26.

19-1 *Oak panel, Gothic tracery. Courtesy of the Cooper-Hewitt Museum of Decorative Arts and Design, Smithsonian Institution, New York.*

19-2 *Edward Livingston, recognizing that primitive man reclined in grass hammocks and sat on hewn tree stumps, designs structures around this concept. His cradle with reedlike frame provides integral beauty as well as comfort. Courtesy of Edward Livingston. Photograph by Bob Lopez.*

262

him with the material for constructing his shelters. The Hebrew Bible informs us that Noah's ark, which was the early home of both man and animal, was built of acacia wood. The Buddhas of the Far East were sculpted from wood as well as stone. Wooden artifacts, such as veneered boxes of intricate design, were discovered in King Tutankhamen's tomb.

As early as the seventeenth century B.C., Egyptians and Babylonians were using ebony in combination with gold, silver, and ivory for court furniture. In the Shōsō-in are treasured ancient wooden objects from Japan, Persia, India, and China. The Greeks and Romans used cherry for inlay, as did the *ébénistes* in the Louis XVI period. In medieval times, lords and ladies sat around great oak tables. Five hundred years before the beginnings of the Christian era, the Persian emperors Darius and Xerxes carried the first walnuts into eastern Europe. The Romans expressed their esteem for walnuts by calling them "nuts of Jove" after Jupiter, or Jove, their top-ranking deity. So popular was walnut in both the William and Mary and the Queen Anne periods in England that the entire era has sometimes been labelled the Age of Walnut.

Cortez, on his journeys of conquest, discovered mahogany in Central America and built his ships from it during the first half of the sixteenth century. During his explorations of the New World, Sir Walter Raleigh repaired his ships with mahogany, and Queen Elizabeth was so fascinated with the wood that she had it introduced into furniture design. Later, mahogany was to become the favorite wood of the Georgian designer Chippendale. Rosewood was used for the elaborate and extravagant court furniture during the reigns of Louis XV and Louis XVI.

In America, the colonists had to clear the wilderness of wood before they could build a home or till the land. Here men used wood for practically all the necessities of life. It provided them with shelter and furniture. Early American utensils were made of "dish timber," poplar and white basswood. Spinning wheels were constructed of wood; so were the first sewing machines. Wood served for ax handles, barrel staves, and farm machinery. The wooden bow, arrow, and harpoon made it possible for men to secure food for their survival.

Men used constructions of wood as means of transportation. On land, buggies, shays, covered wagons, and prairie schooners were all wooden. Later, even the first automobiles and airplanes were constructed at least partially from wood. For transportation on water, men used bark canoes, rafts, flatboats, and sailing vessels from tiny fishing boats up to clipper ships and whalers—all built from wood. Through fortitude and the efficient use of wood men were able to survive in the New World.

Although it has been forecast that by the turn of the century wood will have been replaced by paper, plastic, and metals, wood has so long a tradition of satisfying our aesthetic, spiritual, and utilitarian needs that it is unlikely we will ever completely sever these ties.

Japanese Use of Wood

Almost all cultures have used wood—for the hunt, architecture, household furnishings, sculpture, masks, beads, and decoration.

The Japanese from the eighth century onward developed outstanding palace and temple architecture and sculptures from wood. The Ise Shrine, temple to the sun goddess, is a masterpiece of architectural design. First built in the eighth century, it is tradition to rebuild it every twenty years. The Japanese adopted the drapery pattern, thin as a string, of the Indian stone Buddhas. Their drapery in wood has a rhythm like that of waves of the sea, alternating with deeper and shallower falls and varying crests.

Laminated wood was used during the Japanese Fujiwara Period (897–1185) and developed to a high degree in the Kamakura (1185–1333). The use of this technique permitted large statues to be built without splitting and cracking and allowed for great characterization and facial expressiveness through carving. The sculptures maintained the structural character of a tree

19-3 *Wooden Akua Iba dolls, Ashanti art, Africa, 19th–20th century, height 11¾". The paintings of German-Swiss painter Paul Klee have a similar simplicity in their childlike whimsical imagery. Notice how the eyebrows, eyes, lips, and neck are repetitive in form, creating unity. By permission of the Trustees of the British Museum, London.*

trunk while the folds of the drapery imparted a swaying rhythmic motion.

In the sculpture of the intensely realistic *kongorikishi*, who were the guardians of the temple and the frighteners of evil spirits, the style took on the aspect of force and agitation to the point of grotesque caricature. Using wood as his medium, the sculptor would exaggerate the muscular structure, and create bulging tendons and veins, as well as ferocious miens.

African Use of Wood

Wood has also been used as part of the simple technology of African societies. Although their sculpture is intended to serve religious, medical, and social purposes and is not conceived of as conscious art, it has long been recognized as one of the world's most powerful aesthetic expressions.

For people who have not learned to write, such as African primitives, communication is often through sculpture and much concentration and thought are involved in order to communicate swiftly and incisively. In these societies, religion tends to be the nourishing mother of art. Because religion is an abstract concept, many of their art forms convey such abstract ideas as invisible and transcendental power, tranquility, composure, and death. To do so, the sculptor employs various symbolic forms to express spiritual and emotive qualities. These do not correspond to the proportions of human anatomy as we experience them in our culture, but they emphasize those areas most closely associated with supernatural forces to the African: the head, mouth, eyes, and genitals. These are given "proportions of significance."

The appeal of the primitive to the Western artist lies in the African's ability to coordinate naturalistic and abstract elements into an unfamiliar unity, very different from that fostered by the Greek ideal, but one that also respects the principles of art. The test of a principle is removing it from the particular to see if it still holds. African art reflects an intuitive application of the aesthetic principles.

Emphasis upon proportion is very obvious in some African tribal art. The design is frequently upon an elongated central axis, which corresponds with the character of the tree's structure. The sculpture has a bold frontal and monumental aspect with pronounced horizontal divisions at significant changes in the anatomy. Incised areas may be deeply cut and clearly articulated in geometric and cubic forms to provide strong contrasts in light and shadow. Detail is minimized in order to elicit viewer response through dynamic and concentrated form.

The techniques employed to bring about a unity in the design are quite evident. An eye may be emphasized by repeated encirclement, either by incision or painting. Rhythm is achieved through repetition and radiation.

The triangularity of an eye may be repeated in the triangular shape of the lips, the ear lobe, the breast, and the pubic region, thus gaining harmony through repetition of related forms and simultaneously establishing rhythm through the repetitious beat of that form.

The Colonial American

Primitive man, working with simple tools, first studied his material intensively, relating it to his capacities and to that of his implements. The result was a sense of fitness of material, of process, and of form that gave aesthetic distinction to work motivated by functional considerations. This same fitness is found in the American colonial artisan who, as a pioneer and homesteader, was engaged in endless training and retraining in craftsmanship. Artisans composed the third largest class in colonial America, exceeded only by farmers and merchants. They had to design almost all the articles for daily use. Surrounded by forests of oak, hickory, ash, maple, cherry, walnut, and pine, they converted these into objects for survival in a new world. The colonial era in America might well be called the Wooden Age of America.

Here the colonial carpenter and the artist were one. Immediacy of need did not permit any distinction between fine and applied art. With limited materials and limited time at his disposal and with his efforts directed to combatting a wilderness and maintaining survival, the pioneer made sturdy objects that were simple and economical of means.

Wood was the most plentiful medium for instant use. Log cabins were the pioneer's first home, and eventually the great log barns that housed the livestock became the architectural symbols of progressive America and rural affluence. By 1753, Lewis Evans made the comment used in evaluating the rural countryside of the colonies: "It is pretty to behold our back settlements, where the barns are large as palaces, while the owners live in log huts; a sign of thriving farmers."

Wood served as a material for utensils as well as shel-

ter. Bowls, ladles, plates, egg beaters, spoon racks, drinking mugs, and butter and dough molds were masterpieces of wood design. Wood composed nearly all man's furnishings—his trestle table, his captain's and ladder-back chairs, his storage boxes and chests. It was used to make his clocks, some of which, although they are one hundred to one hundred fifty years old, are still running. Other utilitarian works of art are the carved wooden roosters that served as weather vanes of the Lutheran and Reformed churches of Pennsylvania German settlers.

The use of wood for transportation was immortalized by Oliver Wendell Holmes in a poem, *The One Hoss Shay,* in which he described his shay in its sturdy wood construction as threatening to last forever, but finally falling apart in November of 1855. He stated the construction as spokes, floors, and sills of oak, thills of lancewood, crossbands of ash, and panels of whitewood that lasts like iron.

Wood made possible America's expansion to the Pacific. By covered wagon and prairie schooners the settlers moved westward. Forts, mining camps, saloons, gambling halls, sidewalks—all were constructed of wood. In New Mexico and California, Spanish friars won the West for Christianity. Although the missions were constructed of adobe, they were furnished with wood. Mission furniture, of fumed or natural oak, paralleled the design of the William Morris chair. Indian folk artists carved *santos,* "saints," of wood for the missions. These continue to be produced by Mexican artisans.

The Woodcut

In contemporary times, the hand crafting of wood is still a valid activity in both the fine and applied arts. Sculpting in wood engages the artist today, but not as it did yesterday. The twelve-hundred-year-old art of the woodcut has enjoyed a revival during the past few decades. The Chinese made the first woodcuts in the eighth century; later the Europeans used woodcuts to illustrate printed books, and then replaced them with more dura-

19-4 *Karl Schmidt-Rottluff.* Christ on the Road to Emmaus, *1884. This particular wood cut shows strong definitive forms, and an expressiveness unique to the material and process of creation. Courtesy, Museum of Fine Arts, Boston, Massachusetts.*

19-5 *Pamela Weir.* Rocky reindeer and uni-rock (rocking unicorn). *Walnut and maple.* California Design, XI, *Pasadena Art Museum.*

ble metal line engravings. Today, woodcuts are again popular, not only because of their unique contribution to design, but because they provide an economical means of securing original works of art; as many as two hundred prints can be made from a single block of wood.

Designers in Wood

Many contemporary commercial designers have used plywood, which can be subjected to heat and pressure, to make curved shells that accommodate the human body. Others are working as designer-craftsmen and enjoying the facility with which wood can be carved, lathed, or laminated. Pamela Weir, Louise Nevelson, and Marisol Escobar have created unique sculptures from wood. Among the most beautiful objects of the 1951 Triennale were Finnish Tapio Wirkkala's dishes of aircraft plywood, which resembled nature's abalone shells in form. Textural interest was achieved by cutting through layers of laminated wood. The German designer Ernst Röttger and Denmark's Kay Bojesen have each used this same technique to produce engaging "touch" toys.

Some outstanding American designers of furniture, interiors, and household objects who have cherished and preserved the hand-crafting heritage are George Nakashima, James Prestini, Wendell Castle, Pedro Friedeberg, Wharton Esherick, and Sam Maloof.

George Nakashima is a skilled craftsman who discovered that the most satisfactory way of life for him lay not with architecture and the drafting board, but in hand crafting wood for household furnishings. He believes that one maintains integrity between work and life by remaining close to the material with which he works and with its process of construction. Cutting, planing, and sanding to bring out the inherent grain of wood are rewarding acts of creation to him. Part of his love of wood he attributes to his inherited Japanese reverence for wood and gentleness toward nature. Whereas, to the extent they can, the Japanese leave a piece of wood alone to be valued for its natural appear-

Wendell Castle designs furniture in laminated wood whose surrealistic sculptural forms seem organically to be "plant, human, animal, shell, bone, at once." His rhythmic designs appear to be constructed from a single wooden member. Like many Scandinavian designers, and the Koreans, too, Castle welcomes the effects of normal wear on a material's surface, because he believes watermarks, scratches, and cracks are natural to wood and increase its beauty. Among his innovations is suspending furniture from the ceiling, thus freeing the floor from a forest of chair legs.

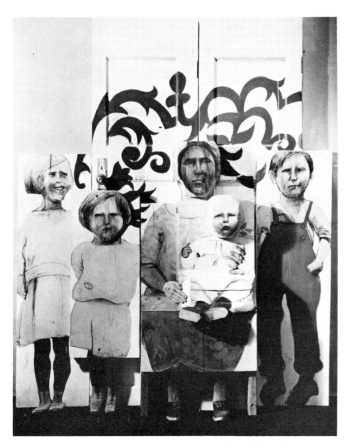

19-6 *Marisol, (Marisol Escobar). The Family, 1962. The assemblage is of painted wood in three sections, 82⅝ x 65½". Collection, The Museum of Modern Art, New York.*

ance and form, even to its knots, the French "will take a magnificent piece of wood, carve it to death and then gild it."² To match his ideas, Nakashima discriminately seeks out boards that many commercial companies would reject for their defects, but that, for him, challenge and provide "the core of our . . . madness, I guess, and also our business."³

²"George Nakashima the Craftsman," *Life* **68**:74 (June 12, 1970), p. 78.
³Ibid., p. 77.

19-7 Shawabty Figures of Yuya. *Egyptian, 18th dynasty, circa 1400 B.C. Sculpture in wood that has been partially painted. The texture and the grain of the wood are visible and enhance the total form of these two figures. Collection, The Metropolitan Museum of Art, New York.*

19-8 *Wharton Esherick. Treelike stairway hewn from solid logs.
"The sculptor's free form could easily be used more often with the
mathematical straight lines and right angles of architecture. The spiral
stair was created from my studio in 1930. When the New York
World's Fair came around in 1939, George Howe, as architect, and I,
as furniture designer and builder, were called to do a room. We lifted
the stair out of my studio and built the room around it." Wharton
Esherick. Renwick Gallery, Smithsonian Institution, and* House
Beautiful. *Photograph by William Howland.*

19-9 *Entry and staircase from the Samual Wentworth House, Ports-
mouth, New Hampshire,* circa *1710. A turn staircase and wood panelling on the walls create a warm, elevated interior. The play of light
is enhanced by the turnings on the balustrade. Collection, The Metropolitan Museum of Art, New York.*

Pedro Friedeberg sculpts wood unconventionally with a sense of humor, such as a chair's seat and arms shaped like a hand supported by a foot for its base. Of his response to life he says, "I was born in Italy during the era of Mussolini, who made all trains run on time. Immediately thereafter I moved to Mexico where the trains are never on time, but where once they start moving they pass pyramids."

The late Wharton Esherick aimed to elevate furniture to the category of sculpture. His work in wood ranged from small pieces such as bowls to individual pieces of furniture and sculpture, in which the latter became part of an organic totality. An important acknowledgement of his position among contemporaries came in 1939, with the New York World's Fair, for which he designed one of the sixteen interiors in the "America at Home" exhibition. This contribution featured the stairwell from his own studio.

Sam Maloof has perfected form and finish in distinctive furnishings. His articulation of the role of the craftsman in today's world echoes values held by the members of the Arts and Crafts Movement and illustrates the continuity of man's thought:

As long as there are men who have not forgotten how to work with their hands, there will remain for the heritage of the craftsman a bright light of hope that began at the dawn of civilization.

In this generation of automation and numbers the individual as such is rapidly diminishing. The majority of designers today design for the machine and not for man. I find that designing for man as an individual is more satisfying and rewarding. The craftsmen throughout the world, individually and collectively, are making a stand for the choice of working and maintaining a way of life that is too often apart from our materialistic present way of living.

The designer and craftsman cannot, *should* not, be separated. Not only should man be a designer on paper, but he should also be able to use his hands to create that which he has designed. The end result is more convincing and gratifying when the same person is both designer and builder.

Man must have faith in himself, faith in his work, and faith in God who gives each one of us whatever talents we may have. These talents are not ours alone but ours to share with our fellow men. Emerson said, "I look on the man as happy who, when there is a question of success, looks into his work for a reply."[4]

Lacquer

The lacquer to be discussed here is the artistic lacquer ware of China, Japan, and Korea. Lacquer of the Far East is a natural product derived from the whitish-gray sap of a sumac tree, *Rhus verniciflua,* that is indigenous to China and has been cultivated in Japan since the sixth century A.D.

While Europeans were enchanted with the glow and the satiny subdued sheen of finely polished Oriental wares, few realized the time-consuming art involved. Evenly grained pine was primed with a film of sticky lacquer and then hempen cloth was stuck to it to make a base. After drying for from twelve to twenty-four hours, the piece was polished by whetstone and hand rubbing until it reflected like a mirror. This procedure might be repeated as many as thirty times, preferably with the piece maturing in a damp cave between applications and rubbings, in order for the lacquer to age properly. Lacquer colors range from a deep, bottomless black to olive green and *aubergine,* the plum color of eggplant. The addition of cinnabar, red mercuric sulphide, produced the highly prized red hue associated with China and its imperial throne. Although most frequently applied to a wooden base, lacquer can be made to adhere to porcelain and brass as well. Objects can also be carved out of solid lacquer.

Lacquer work, which began as early as the Shang dynasty, as a means of decorating bronze, became a major industry under Han rule. Painting in lacquer on bowls or plaques was the step that preceded the devel-

4 Personal communication.

significant feature of a floral design, splash it in gay abandon over the surface, and often continue it rhythmically to the underside. Contrasting colors of gold on black, asymmetry of balance, and stylization of blossom and leaf were characteristic features.

Lacquering became a favored medium throughout Western Europe for *chinoiseries* made to satisfy the

19-10 *Imperial Chinese throne in carved red lacquer. Victoria and Albert Museum, London. Crown Copyright.*

19-11 *Writing box of black lacquer on wood, design of gold paint with birds of inlaid lead and pewter, width 8½"; Japanese, Edo period. The playful treatment of equivocal spatial relationships, where the body of one bird may be behind the body of another yet his feet project in front of the first, was a device used in the decorative screen paintings of the 16th and 17th century. This ambiguity in spatial treatment predated similar primitive work by early 20th-century European artists, as well as the work of more recent artists. Gift of Mrs. Donald E. Frederick, Seattle Art Museum, Washington.*

opment of painting proper. Lacquer was used for writing on bamboo strips, for utensils, ceremonial vessels, decoration on carriages and architecture, and even for payment of taxes. The virtuosity with which it could be worked is evident in the design of Chinese musical instruments in the Shōsō-in repository. Figures of gold and silver, inserted on the surface of the instruments, were covered with lacquer, which was then rubbed down to expose the metals.

The Japanese brought lacquer work to its consummate level, paralleling the development of porcelain in China. So widely was lacquer used that in A.D. 905 a sumptuary edict regulated the quantities and size of lacquered domestic utensils. Its range of use extended from lacquered *netsuke* and sake cups to temple walls. Even portraits were sculptured from dry lacquer.

The Japanese sense of design, most clearly expressed through lacquer, reached a height during the Mamoyami period. The lacquer artist would select a small

New York City Subway tile: *Canal Street BMT Station.*

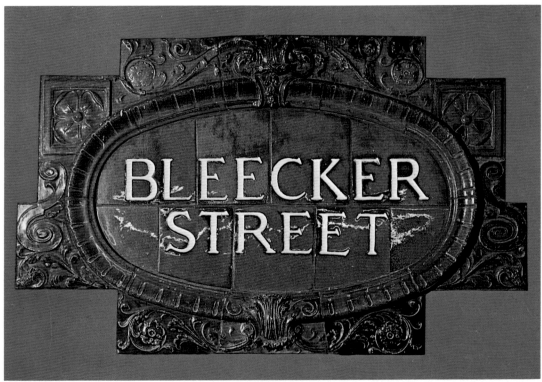

New York City Subway tile: *Bleecker Street IRT Station.* The decorative and informative elements of the durable ceramic tile were once used in the New York Subway System. They are good examples of immovable objects that used symbols for the public. Cooper-Hewitt Museum, Smithsonian Institute.

Heath dinnerware, at home with sand and sea, native elements of its composition. Balance is asymmetrical on the plate, equivalent on the cup and saucer. Photograph by Vincent Bernucci.

Food served in a pleasant surrounding enhances the meal. Photograph by Borge B. Andersen for *Lion House Recipes*, (Salt Lake City: Deseret Book Company, 1980), p. 31.

19-12 *Mexican spirit papers, approximate height 6". These were made from folded hand-made bark paper by the Otomi Indians. They were used in sorcery to gain good luck. The paper, folded in half for cutting, automatically resulted in bisymmetry. Museum of Contemporary Crafts, New York.*

rococo taste—cabinets, tea tables, clocks, bookcases, leather wall hangings, and sometimes entire walls were lacquered. Chippendale set the mode with whole sets of furniture in lacquer of Oriental design. Lacquer was applied to metal (tôle ware) and papier-mâché throughout the eighteenth century. The term *japanning* came from the English recognition of the superiority of Japanese lacquer. It was considered "in goodness of black and stateliness of draught . . . more rich, grave and majestic" than the lacquer from other areas.

The Coromandel screen, which takes its name from India's Coromandel coast where it was produced, is as respected aesthetically today as it was in Europe during the eighteenth century. These black lacquered screens, some of which are as long as twenty feet and eight feet high with twelve leaves, have incised flat designs cut in intaglio, which are finished with gold and varied colors or with inlay of shell or porcelain to add to their beauty.

Paper

Paper is an expression of the fleeting moment, the fleeting thought, and most importantly, an expression of evolving reality.[5]

John Massey
Director of the Container Corporation of America

The 1960s ushered in the use of paper for a variety of articles unprecedented in man's history and an ex-

[5] *Made with Paper,* Museum of Contemporary Crafts, New York City, 1967.

19-13 *Traditional horse carried in religious processions, from Bengal, India. The paper is glued to a bamboo frame, 57" x 13" x 39". Museum of Contemporary Crafts, New York.*

perimentation with paper paralleling that of plastics. The international exhibit *Made with Paper,* premiered at New York's Museum of Contemporary Crafts and organized by the museum and the Container Corporation of America in 1967, displayed more than four hundred contemporary objects made of paper and paperboard. These consisted of traditional articles from many parts of the world—sculptural forms, toys, and apparel—and unconventional uses of paper for furnishings: tables, stools, chairs, lamps, wall coverings, and rugs. The

paper poster has enjoyed a renewal of appreciation with particular appeal to youth for its strong vibrating colors and low cost.

Historical Uses

The use of paper began so early as not to be fully known. The Chinese are credited with inventing paper from flax, rags, and vegetable fibers about the first century A.D. They kept their invention a secret until Chinese prisoners captured by the Arabs at a battle near Samarkand in 751 disseminated the knowledge. With the Arab occupation of Sicily and the Moorish seizure of Spain, papermaking was introduced to the European continent; it became an established art by the latter part of the fifteenth century. Paper was used decoratively for linings of boxes, chests, cupboards, and for hangings on walls.

Toward the end of the sixteenth century French *dominotiers* were printing small decorated sheets (known as domino papers), playing cards, and covers for books. Papier-mâché was used in France in the eighteenth century as an economy of precious paper. The nightly discarded playbills of the French theater were converted into snuff boxes. In the nineteenth century, Toulouse-Lautrec brought paper poster art to a high level of aesthetic achievement.

Paper has been generously used for costume as well as for furnishings. Here, too, its use is not new. According to Lenore Hershey[6] men and women of Hawaii were wearing paper apparel in 500 A.D.—the men a loincloth, the women a wrap-around skirt. Garments were waterproofed with coconut oil and decorated with natural dyes.

Contemporary Uses

Paper was used for numerous functional purposes during the 60s. Among companies which used paper was

[6]Lenore Hershey, "Paper Wrap-Up." *McCall's* (April 1967) Vol. 94, p. 10.

Hallmark Cards, which manufactured a complete paper party kit. The kit includes a flower-printed hostess shift and matching cups, plates, place mats, napkins, matches, invitations, tablecloths, nut cups, fruit bowls, bridge tallies, and centerpieces. (One is invited to assess whether complete unity may create a need for variety.) Many companies produced coordinated paper designs such as bedspreads, draperies, lamp shades, sheets, and pillowcases, thus promoting unity in design.

Other items produced in the 60s were tables and chairs for children and adults, storage bins and boxes, playthings, rugs, sculptures, fabrics, and wearing apparel. The basic material of the furniture was a heavy grade of corrugated cardboard surfaced with a plasticized paper to resist soil and dampness, just as papier-mâché furniture was strengthened by resins and glues. Apparel fabrics were usually a loosely woven nylon or rayon scrim, bonded to several layers of cellulose wadding, a wood pulp fiber.

The value of these objects lay in their brightness, gaiety, low cost, and disposability. They satisfied the human desire for change, variety, and whim. They were particularly appropriate for occasional costumes. Designer Elisa Daggs predicted a revolution in dressmaking techniques and the wide use of paper for apparel. "Paper needs its own architecture," she says. "Sealing machines will replace sewing machines."[7] This has yet to come about.

Others view the "instant decorating" paper makes possible as being especially suitable for second homes at the beach or in the mountains, first temporary homes for young married couples and students, nursery rooms where paper furniture will last the length of time desired, homes for campers, and temporary housing for migrant farm workers. However, the building industry in its experimentation with new materials does not see the paper wall as temporary. The limitations of one material can be overcome by combining it with others,

as the textile industry has so well demonstrated. A paper wall is described in *Architectural Forum* thus:

a sandwich panel was created consisting of an egg-crate "filler" of corrugated paperboard impregnated and bonded to two thin slices of veneer plywood, finished on the exterior with a clear, transparent film of du Pont's polyester plastic that will last the life of the building. This panel withstood test loads exceeding 3,000 pounds per square foot, far above the peak load of many ordinary curtain wall panels.[8]

Papier-Mâché

The art of papier-mâché involves laminating several layers of pulped paper, followed by lacquering or illuminating the surface. Being a craft related to ceramics, plastics, and stucco in its potential to be formed, it can be used to create very sensitive designs. The art is thought to have originated in China as a way to reuse paper—a scarce and valuable product. In China, Japan, and India, where papier-mâché was used extensively for screens, trays, caskets, and vases, the art was perfected to such an extent that it became difficult to distinguish papier-mâché from lacquered wood. During Ptolemaic times, coffins of papier-mâché, painted and gilded to resemble the wooden coffins of the Pharaohs, were used by wealthy Egyptians.

The use of papier-mâché for furniture in Europe is thought to have resulted from the Eastern trading companies' inability to meet the heavy demand for imported Oriental objects. European craftsmen did not understand the process of using layers of slowly dried sap from sumac and so used layers of stove enameling on wood to get the dark finish they desired. To hasten the process, heat was applied, which resulted in the wood's

[7]Elisa Daggs, "The Wastebasket Dress Has Arrived," *Life* **61**:22 (Nov. 25, 1966), p. 132.

[8]"Building with Paper and Plywood," *Architectural Forum* (Feb. 1959) Vol. 110, pp. 132–133.

warping. It was discovered that a japanned finish could be applied with greater speed and with more satisfactory results on papier-mâché than on wood.

The highest aesthetic development of the art came in 1772 with Henry Clay's production of wares in Birmingham, England. He invented a heat-resisting paperware, so hard that it could be carved, dovetailed, and screwed like wood. His paper was made from cotton rags in a mixture of glue, resin, and flour, which made an unusually strong product. The processes he then used were laborious and painstaking. The sheets of paper were pasted on forms to the desired thickness. These were then oiled or varnished, oven-dried at fairly high temperatures, smoothed by pumice stone, and rubbed and polished with chamois leather. A japanning process followed, in which several coats of lampblack, turpentine, balsam, drying oils, pitch, resin, and wax were applied. In turn, each coat was allowed to dry and then polished to glassy perfection by hand. Painting or gilding with gold leaf to contrast with the glowing depth of the black lacquer followed. His production included trays and panels for carriages and sedan chairs, for rooms and doors, and for cabins of ships, cabinets, bookcases, screens, and tea tables. Clay's firm in Birmingham was later taken over by Jennens and Bettridge, who continued in the Clay tradition of superior craftsmanship. The use of papier-mâché was extended to the construction of drawing-room chairs, sofas, and the casings of pianofortes. Jennens and Bettridge also patented a process of mother-of-pearl inlay, in which the pearl was adhered to the surface and lacquer built up to secure it. Bettridge invented a method of using papier-mâché in combination with stove-dried wood. Benjamin Cook applied papier-mâché to metal.

Eighteenth-century English architects also made much use of papier-mâché to decorate ceilings and walls with relief sculpturing. During the seventeenth century, similar effects had been achieved by the use of a plaster made from hay, straw, and wood bark, which was applied to woodwork and ceilings to form cornices, scrolls, rosettes, and architectural elaborations. Papier-mâché

19-14 *Victorian papier-mâché side chair with curvilinear lines. England, 1844. The chair reflects the Victorian flair for embellishment with paint, gilding, and mother of pearl. Courtesy of the Cooper-Hewitt Museum of Decorative Arts and Design, Smithsonian Institution, New York.*

was lighter than plaster, however, and its extreme plasticity allowed the exuberance of design that was currently in vogue.

Papier-mâché was put to a new use in England during the 1830s: to make wall panels for housing construction. These panels, prefabricated on a modular system, were hooked into place to construct a village of small houses. These are reported to have withstood a flood that rose to two feet.[9]

The English firm of Jennens and Bettridge exported papier-mâché goods to America, and emigrants brought the art of its production to the states. The Litchfield Manufacturing Company, operating at Litchfield, Connecticut, between 1850 and 1854, produced clock cases decorated with a single rose with inlaid mother-of-pearl petals and gilt leaves and stem. The Litchfield Historical Association has preserved many fine pieces of that day.

In Britain, the use of papier-mâché for home furnishings reached its zenith during the Victorian era. Furniture was designed with *chinoiserie* patterns, classical motifs, and floral bouquets. Ornamentation knew no restraint. All kinds of objects, including spectacle cases and buttons, were made from paper.

The art of papier-mâché eventually declined. By the 1870s, stamped tin sheets had replaced lacquered papier-mâché for making England's tea trays. The long, painstaking papier-mâché operation had required not only hand craftsmanship but the craftsmanship attitude. Britain's economy was moving toward increased mechanical production and a larger export trade, in which speedy construction and low cost were important considerations. With hasty production techniques, the structural design, workmanship, and applied decoration of papier-mâché goods all suffered, because the beauty of the medium had been in its precision of design and jewel-like refinement of finish and decoration.

Another factor that is thought to have contributed to decline in its use was the change in women's fashions from the slim skirts of filmy fabrics worn in the Empire period to Victorian styles, with their crinolines supported by heavy hoops. The lightweight papier-mâché tables and chairs were easily toppled as women moved about, which necessitated the use of heavier furnishings.

Today papier-mâché is largely relegated to the making

of masks, puppets, small statues, toys, stage props, objects for window display, decorative boxes, and jewelry. Many of these items come from India, the Orient, or Mexico, where labor costs are not high and the craft remains a cottage industry.

Paper Folding

Paper folding is the art of creasing paper into forms without recourse to cutting, pasting, or decorating. It reached its highest development in Japan where it is referred to as *origami*. The Japanese have developed hundreds of traditional folds and a corresponding literature. Among the objects they make are *no shi,* folded decorations attached to gifts. The Japanese are ingenious in imparting the kinetic to their forms: a bird can flap its wings when its tail is pulled; a frog can jump when its back is tapped.

The art was introduced by Friedrich Froebel into the kindergarten movement that he initiated in Germany in the nineteenth century. As a child, Frank Lloyd Wright played with the Froebel construction blocks, made of colored papers, which may have contributed to his feeling for slabs of planes and volumes. Although considered by some to be nursery school art, paper folding has been a discipline engaged in by sophisticated artists, philosophers, and architects.

The appeal of paper folding lies in its simplicity and in the contrasts that are produced through light and shadow, elevation and depression, valley and ridge. With only paper as material and his hands for tools, man is challenged to design. Paper's restrictions and possibilities were particularly realized by Joseph Albers of the Bauhaus, who used paper in a *vorkurs,* or introductory course, not for students to create decorative or functional objects, but as an instructional prototype to create an awareness of the problem of designing and to develop an appreciation of the basic character and potential of a material. In his words written for the *Made*

[9]Jane Toller, *Papier-Mâché in Great Britain and America* (Newton, Mass.: Charles T. Branford, 1962), pp. 32–35.

with Paper exhibit in New York's Museum of Contemporary Crafts: "Saving is virtuous, everything must be used. . . . No tools, no glue, no tacks, only two hands to start with. Discover for yourself what each surface or edge can do. . . . For each medium there is a *materialgerecht*—what is honest and right in paper cannot be imitated in wood."

Wallpaper

Wherever a plain surface exists, it would seem that man has felt compelled to modify it. During the seventeenth century brocades, velvets, and damasks were used. Wallpaper manufacture originated in England and the European countries as a less expensive substitute for these. It is believed to have been begun by letterpress printers who, in their experimentation, extended the use of the press to make decorated sheets using black printer's ink carried on wood blocks. One such sheet, printed on the back of a proclamation made by Henry VIII circa 1509 and used as a decorative frieze, was discovered during restoration work in 1911 in Christ's College, Cambridge, England. It illustrates the early parallel between the design motif of textiles and wallpapers: the design on the paper is a highly conventionalized pomegranate, a common motif on medieval Italian velvets and a traditionally favorite pattern for damasks. Early designs were also copied from embroideries, such as Tudor "black-work," (Spanish embroidery in black and silver thread) and from printed linens. Flocked papers were also made to duplicate textile designs. To produce these, a design simulating the pattern of a fabric was printed on the paper, and a drying adhesive was then applied, followed by a powdered wool flock. An advertisement published in 1560 by Edward Butling, a stationer in London who dealt in wallpapers, illustrates wallpaper's dependence upon inspiration from fabric design. According to the *Encyclopaedia Britannica* Butling stated in the advertisement that he

19-15 *Flocked paper, probably from England, late 18th century. Courtesy of the Cooper-Hewitt Museum of Decorative Arts and Design, Smithsonian Institution, New York.*

19-16 *Wallpaper border. A highly imitative paper, with a design of swagged fabric and lace printed from woodblocks, France, 1805–15. Courtesy of the Cooper-Hewitt Museum of Decorative Arts and Design, Smithsonian Institution, New York.*

19-17 *Chinese paper for export, late 18th century. This is among the more aesthetic forms of* chinoiserie. *Courtesy of the Cooper-Hewitt Museum of Decorative Arts and Design, Smithsonian Institution, New York.*

19-18 *Walter Crane,* Peacock Garden, *block-printed wallpaper, 1889. Courtesy of the Cooper-Hewitt Museum of Decorative Arts and Design, Smithsonian Institution, New York.*

19-19 *William Morris Wallpaper,* Pimpernel *copy, England, reprinted in 1934 from a design of 1876. Courtesy of the Cooper-Hewitt Museum of Decorative Arts and Design, Smithsonian Institution, New York.*

maketh and selleth all sorts of Hangings for Rooms in Lengths or in Sheets, Frosted or Plain: also a sort of Paper in Imitation of Irish Stich and several other sorts, viz: Flockwork, Wainscot, Marble, Damask.[10]

It is believed Samuel Pepys was referring to wallpaper when he wrote in his diary of the hangings in his wife's closet as "counterfeit damask."

With the growth of the East Indian trade, Western Europe became familiar with Eastern design. The imported Chinese papers of the seventeenth century, having no repeats or repetition of detail, were highly prized. Perennially beautiful, they are treasured art in today's museums and historic mansions. During the latter years of the eighteenth century, the Frenchmen Jean Zuber and Joseph Dufour became famous for their scenic papers, some of which were made in eighteen- to twenty-one-inch strips with twenty-four to thirty-five strips to a scene, requiring as long as two years to complete.

With the invention of a roller printing machine in 1839, emphasis changed from quality to quantity production of papers, which were considered a short-lived and expendable item. Consequently, artists preferred to focus their efforts on less ephemeral media. Manufacturers produced designs to appeal to the masses, who for the most part had little appreciation of any but highly naturalistic designs. In England during the latter nineteenth century, William Morris, Charles Voysey, and Heywood Sumner concentrated on improving wallpaper design. In the Art Nouveau and Bauhaus periods, with attention being given to total design, wallpaper was considered an aesthetic medium. Otherwise, throughout the first half of this century its design was largely neglected.

Today's industry has not only given more thought to wallpaper design, employing such well-known artists as Salvador Dali, Miro, and Picasso to design papers, but industrial research has extended paper's properties. Paper compounded with melamine has wet strength and when impregnated or coated with plastic is wash-

¹⁰*Encyclopaedia Britannica*, Vol. 23, p. 310.

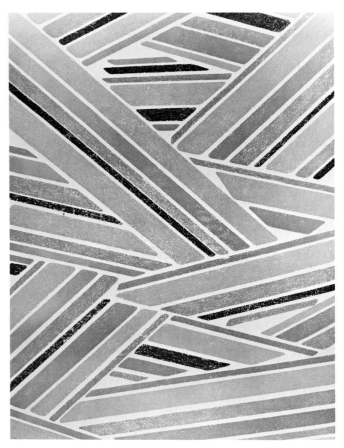

19-20 New Era. *Silver, off-white, and beige are combined in a contemporary wallpaper design. Note the depth, multiple planes, and movement achieved through diagonals. C. W. Stockwell Company, Los Angeles.*

able. Prepasted wallpaper, in which adhesive is dried to the back, ready to be softened by wetting, makes papering walls a simple operation.

Wallpaper's contribution to design lies in its endless variety and relative economy, which permits one to add beauty and to change the mood of his immediate environment. Anything that can be drawn, painted, etched, engraved, embossed, blueprinted, or photographed can be reproduced on paper by machine or silk-screen printing. The range includes grass cloths, gilt foil papers textured with spots of oxidation, murals, documentary reproductions of early historic designs, silk fabric adhered to paper, marbleized patterns, photographic murals, novelty and fun papers, and graphic papers.

Whether quiet or exciting, wallpapers can serve man's need for ephemeral expression and for change of pace in his decorating. They can be to interior design as change of dress is to body costume—instant and relatively temporary.

20 Plastics

In the 1960s plastics emerged as a new synthetic man-made material favored by experimenters, and the term *plaesthetics* was suggested as an addition to our vocabulary. The word *plastics* is derived from the Latin *plasticus* and Greek *plastikos,* from the Greek verb *plassein,* "to form, or mold"—and the material lent itself to unlimited processes and appearances. Plastics could be poured, sprayed, molded, foamed, inflated, and deflated. They could be hard and geometrically angular or soft and undulant. They could be as transparent as the finest optical glass, or opaque; colored, textured, and patterned; matte or shiny; lightweight or heavy with materials imbedded between laminated layers; and tearable, or as indestructible as steel when reinforced with fiberglass. No other medium has provided man the designer with greater creative potential and challenge.

As many designers searched for the unique aesthetics of plastics, they no longer used them to imitate other more highly respected materials, and many innovations resulted. In the design of everyday objects, emphasis was placed upon the elements of form and space so that furnishings could provide enjoyment as sculptures when they were not in use to satisfy physical needs. In recent years Italian artist Carlos Sansegundo expanded the aesthetic of plastics not only to objects but to space itself—a room. Using transparent acrylics, he designed an entire room and its furnishings in plastic. Plastics became the medium for a "room within a room . . . a sculpture when not in use, a dining room when used."

In the 1970s the ecologically minded have called attention to plastics' potential to help conserve our ecosystems. Substituting plastics for furs, fibers, leathers, and feathers would conserve animal species; substi-

20-1 *Ben Gurule. Plastic chandelier. The convolutions create shadows and spatial depth. Modeline Company of California, Inc.*

tuting plastics in furniture and implements would conserve timber; and substituting plastic for equipment, ornaments, and paints would conserve our mineral resources.

Historical Background

The decimation of the African elephant herds that took place in the second half of the nineteenth century meant that the great "ivory floors" of Europe's warehouses were standing empty. With business suffering from the diminished supply, in 1863 Phelan and Collander, manufacturers of ivory billiard balls in Albany, New York, offered an award of $10,000 for an ivory substitute. Working with his brother Isaiah John Hyatt

discovered cellulose nitrate, later to be called by the trade name "celluloid," which has been acknowledged as man's first plastic. In 1908, Dr. Leo H. Baekeland developed bakelite, first of the thermosets (those plastics which, having attained rigidity, cannot be remelted or reformed, in contrast to thermoplastics, which regain their pliability with heating). There then followed a phenomenal increase in the manufacture of plastics for multiple functions.

The use of plastics in home furnishings can be traced to Bauhaus experiments, for although Bauhaus designers did not use plastics in the design of furniture, the use of new materials and manufacturing processes was encouraged. It has been noted that László Moholy-Nagy employed plastics and glass in his sculpture in order to develop the potential of light as an aesthetic element.

Experimentation by other designers led to development of plastic and plywood seats for chairs which could be stamped out in the same manner as an automobile body from a die press. Plastics, by making traditional joinery unnecessary, permit a fluid line that is characteristic of sculpture and a greater resemblance of man-made objects to biomorphic forms. Chairs can be molded and upholstered with the back, arms, and seat as one, cradling the occupant as in Eero Saarinen's 1946 "womb chair," a contemporary classic shown in Figure 23-6, the interior of Charles Eames home; Danish Arne Jacobsen's "Egg" and "Swan" chairs, Figure 10-22, and Finnish Eerio Aarnio's "Ball" chair, Figure 10-29.

Composition and Kinds of Plastics

Although the term *plastics* can be applied to all materials while in a plastic state, such as wax, glass, and clay, it is usually limited to the family of synthetic materials that have large molecules made up of chains of atoms

20-2 *Serving dish. A Thermo-Serv double-wall insulated serving dish that is both functional and attractive. Thermo-Serv, Anoka, Minnesota.*

20-3 *Mr. and Mrs. Karl H. Wenzlaff's Fold'n Pour dust pan. Mrs. Wenzlaff conceived the idea of the dust pan one day when she heard the women in a beauty parlor complaining about sweeping up and disposing of hair and waste. Mr. Wenzlaff, a toolmaker, developed and made the tools for the dust pan. Courtesy Foley Manufacturing Company, Minneapolis.*

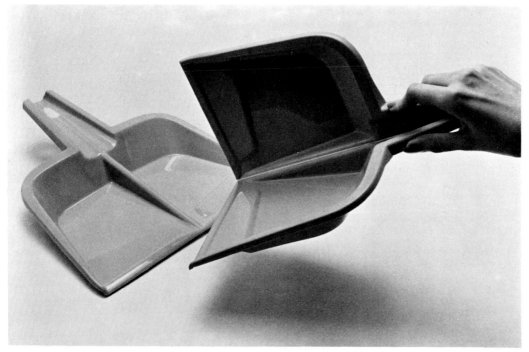

that are soft and moldable during manufacture but that eventually solidify. The elements of their composition include water, air, coal, petroleum, salt, and natural gases. Combined in varying proportions these make possible plastics' great diversity of properties. Plastics are considered not a single entity but a family of materials. Among the family members in common daily use are these:

acrylics: dome lights, decorative panels, fabrics
nylon: tumblers, dinnerware, rugs, fabrics
polyethylene: squeeze bottles, kitchenware
vinyl: floors, wall coverings, window and lamp shades, tablecloths, upholstery
melamine: counter and table tops, dinnerware
polyester: carpets, chairs, panels for walls, ceilings, partitions reinforced with fiberglas
polyurethane: bedding, furniture cushions, urethane foam spray to cover the surface of furniture
polypropylene: indoor and outdoor carpets

Functional Uses of Plastics

Plastics for Household Wares

The engineering and designing of outstanding products is assumed by such companies as the Dow Chemical Company, which maintains extensive technical service facilities to help manufacturers solve specific molding and designing problems and to aid them in their color styling. The design of plastic articles for everyday use is frequently of high quality; dustpans, irons, and vacuum cleaners have become aesthetically pleasing objects. Dinnerware of excellent design quality is found in many melamine wares.

Plastic Molded Components and Surface Laminates

Molded plastic components of polystyrene and polyurethane are used extensively today. These can be solid, contoured, and hollow; nailed, screwed, or doweled; and grained in the mold to achieve the texture and feel of genuine wood. This is a significant development for the furniture industry, because intricate carvings, molding, rosettes, overlay, and frets of wood, which previously were processed manually with costly machine and sanding operations, can now be mass produced.

Another dominant functional use of plastic is as a decorative surface laminate. Because of their ease of care and resistance to stain and scratching, melamine and vinyl are used for the surfaces of domestic and

20-4 *Baby toilette. An object used daily can have a sculpturesque quality and can help in the development of a child's aesthetic sensitivity by his being exposed to well-designed products.*

commercial counter tops, cabinets, and other furnishings. These may be given the matte satin finish of wood or have a low-sheen finish that can be oiled like standard wood surfaces. Good workmanship and design and high quality have contributed to the use of plastics not only for low-priced lines of furniture but also for quality custom lines.

In using plastics whose texture and color so duplicate those of wood as to defy ready differentiation, one recognizes that the material makes a decorative contribution. Moreover, some designers see plastics philosophically as an answer to a moral problem. This is the position of Quasar Khanh, a Vietnamese designer. To him plastics mean "an end to the destruction of nature, of woods and forests." For many, however, where cost, care, and mass production are not considerations, the textural quality of the genuine material is preferable. It has been suggested that the great increase in craft production in recent years may be the result of man's need, in a world becoming increasingly synthetic, to work directly with his hands and to feel the tactile quality of natural materials.

Other Uses of Plastics

Various plastic coating materials protect furnishings from scuffing by shoes, chipping by vacuum cleaners, and from general impact and abrasion. Sprayed-on silicone and polyester films give stain resistance to woven fabrics. Vinyl fabrics with a "wet" look provide textural contrasts in home furnishings. Naugahyde's brilliant range of colors has vitalized the interiors of homes and public buildings. Coordinated vinyl wallpapers, fabrics, and window shades contribute unity to household interiors. Matching kitchen table tops and upholstery fabrics of vinyl are being produced for coordination and unity of design.

Plastics underfoot may be of varied synthetics. Nylon and acrilan are used for interior design. Indoor-outdoor carpeting of polypropylene now makes possible the cushioning of man's foot out-of-doors as well. Polyurethane has been designed as grass for roof-top gardens and as turf for track and football fields.

Contemporary Furnishings

On the international scene during the 1960s, designers of many countries experimented with the potential of plastics for the composition of furniture, and new and unfamiliar design images resulted. Emphasis was on the transparent and collapsible—upon disposable, stackable, economical, mass-produced, multipurpose, and lightweight items.

Among the many designers in plastics was Vladimir Kagan of New York, a specialist in mobile, collapsible, and "suitcase" furniture, such as cabinets that could double as storage crates in moving. Designer-architect Paul Rudolph placed emphasis upon the modular and versatile by creating "architectural non-furniture"—plastic units two feet by two feet and eight inches high. Each milk-white unit of his could serve as either a storage unit, light source, table, case for electronic gear, or seat (with cushions on top). Units could be combined into platforms or wall hangings.

In minimal design the Frenchmen Jean Aubert, Jean-Paul Jungman, and Antonio Stinco simplified their furniture to two basic transparent inflatable units, a log and a square pillow; these were sufficient to create a roomful of furniture. Hung vertically, six to eight logs could form a room divider. Built in tabs with snaps on, the logs and pillows made possible the construction of a wide variety of armchairs and sofas.

The Vietnamese designer Quasar Khanh explored flexibility in the use of plastic units, and using only two versatile components, added more innovative features. A hard plastic frame shaped like a U standing upright with a plastic pillow served as a chair; on its side it became a see-through table. The pillows could be filled with colored water and on cold nights could be turned into cozy hot-water cushions. Other designers created waterbeds, which provided totally new sensations for people to experience.

20-5 *Niki de Saint Phalle.* Black Venus, *1967. Painted polyester. An example of plastic used for figure sculpture. Collection, Whitney Museum of American Art, New York.*

Plastics for Architectural Purposes

Plastics are unique as building material because they are light yet sturdy, both flexible and rigid, translucent and shatterproof, and easily maintained. Among their many uses are translucent walls, partitions, roofs, lighting fixture panels, dome lights, screening, louvered windows, wall coverings, and vinyl-coated aluminum siding.

To show the versatility and adequacy of plastics, in 1957 the Monsanto Chemical Company of St. Louis, Missouri, set a precedent for the architectural use of plastics in housing by constructing the "Plastics Home of the Future" at Disneyland, in Anaheim, California, in conjunction with the Massachusetts Institute of Technology. The experimental shell was built and furnished entirely with plastics, from the latex paint that covered the house to the polycarbonite tumblers used inside. The architect, Vincent Bonini, took advantage of the plastic medium and avoided the conventional cube shape of American architecture in favor of fluid curved lines. The furnishings, too, were custom-contoured in new forms to correspond with the design of the interior. Periodic testing and measurement have attested to the house's excellent structural performance.

Since then, plastics' potential for shelter has been increasingly realized. The American Iron and Steel Institute in its "Hospital of the Future" has created tent designs of translucent plastic supported by steel cylinder poles for structures that can be increased through the addition of more poles and plastic sheathing. In the future it is predicted we will have "add-a-room housing," where machines will blow up pads or rooms that can have door and window framing inserted. A process is currently being developed in the United States whereby one-thousand-square-foot buildings can be erected from molten plastic ejected from the arm of a truck in six hours by two men for less than half the cost of a similar steel or concrete structure. Thus plastics, hopefully, will make it possible for more of mankind to be housed adequately in the future.

In Europe, Gérard Grandval, a French architect, designed the La Plagne ski resort of prefabricated polyester and plywood shells. He has proposed using a huge transparent plastic form to house the French Air Ministry. His credo with respect to materials is expressed in these words: "I am interested in a consumer architecture, which we can eventually throw away like paper,

20-6 *Nicolas Vergette. A colored transparent window of laminated polyester resin, approximately 4' square. In its varying orbs and rays it is highly reminiscent of the sun. Courtesy Nicolas Vergette.*

20-7 *Douglas Deeds' pop-up shelter and/or display kiosk with frame of aluminum tubing over which is stretched nylon fabric, which may be made permanent by spraying with polyester resin. Within is Charles Gibilterra's chaise of steel and canvas; both shelter and chaise featured in* Design in *California XI. Photograph, American Home Magazine, June, 1971.*

20-8 *Kay Sekimachi, handweaving. A flowing three-dimensional woven form in clear nylon monofilament, 1965, length 15". American Crafts Museum, New York. Photograph by Don Pittman.*

allowing people to be free in their taste . . . an adventure on the level of the imagination."

In the fall of 1968, New York's Museum of Contemporary Crafts presented an exhibit, "Plastic as Plastic," in which new forms for today's shelter were displayed that used plastics as the primary structural material. Inflated and sprayed forms were used for the designs of temporary structures. Spraying with fiberglass and laminating metals between foam panels provided sufficient strength for permanent structures. Finnish Matti Suuronen's weekend house of polyester, reinforced with fiberglass and with acrylic windows and polyurethane insulation, looked like an efficient flying saucer of minimal design that had descended to earth.

Although many of the new forms made from plastic for furnishings and architecture have seemed cold, sterile, and unimaginative, to some the direction has been toward dispelling prejudices about materials and extending man's vision. Instead of creating designs to suit materials as he had been required to do in the past, man was now creating materials to fulfill his multiple and specific human requirements, thus increasing his autonomy over the environment. Concerning these experiments Louise Boger advised: "Out of new materials and new methods new and strange forms will come. Let us accept them; let us at any rate be adventurous. History has taught us that some extravagant designs originally ridiculed have in time become the basis for a popular fashion."[1]

[1] Louise Boger, *Furniture Past and Present* (New York: Doubleday, 1966), p. 462.

20-9 *Freda Koblick, American sculptress,* Column I. *Autoclave casting, 1954, first of an edition of five, height 47". Property of The Johnson Collection of Contemporary Crafts. The Museum of Contemporary Crafts, New York.*

Artistic Uses of Plastics

Plastics also served as a favored material for art in the 1960s. Acrylics displaced oils to a great extent, and plastics became the favorite medium of sculptors interested in light, space, time, and movement. Sculptor James Davis has stated that transparent plastics and artificial illumination are the two most significant tools for a movement consistent with our time.

Plastics have been particularly useful to the contemporary artist-craftsman interested in mobile constructions in which movement is integrated with image and time. Artists have accomplished this through identical repetition of details, changing forms, lineal patterns in three-dimensional space, and transparent materials, which create ambiguous space. Plastics are assembled and printed so that changing linear configurations are formed with the movement of the viewer. (See Figures 4-33 and 4-34.)

Plastics are also used in textile design for their color, transparency, and textural contributions. The potential of laminating objects such as rocks, shells, butterflies, and leaves between plastic sheets and of hardening plastic at different rates to create contrasting areas of form and light has been exploited aesthetically by several designers. California sculptress Freda Koblick's monolithic "Column I" is an exemplary illustration of plastics' unique potential for sculptural aestheticism. Sculptor Alexander Archipenko, who has carved lucite panels for transparent wall screens in domestic interiors, has recognized plastics' unique contribution to the aesthetics of architectural design:

There is no material that has such conductivity of light as plastic. There is a refraction effect from certain angles, but the refraction is not like crystal, which breaks the design. The design is not destroyed in plastic.[2]

[2] Eleanor Bittermann, *Art in Modern Architecture* (New York: Reinhold, 1952), p. 168.

Part Five
The Consumer of Design

Foreword

In this section, some of man's most immediate design concerns are presented: food, clothing, and shelter. Whether rich or poor, educated or uneducated, high or low in social status, there are some basic kinds of human activities in which all people engage daily with greater or lesser degrees of aesthetic concern. Among these are choosing food, clothing, shelter, and art. Selecting designed objects is done for a number of reasons: survival, convenience, and social influence. This part of the book ends with consumer issues and reminds us of the role of design in the lives of everyone. The interaction of visual expression and individual decision-making takes place in the consumer's market and the consumer's home. Still, artist-designers use visual expression for self-expression. They manipulate materials either as individuals or as team-members, and the result of this effort is considered art if it stands the test of time. Advertising and marketing campaigns, conspicuous consumption, and fashion are all part of the test of time. But so are the lasting qualities of materials, visual evaluation of the quality of design, and the object's existence. Saving objects and repeating traditions within one's daily life provide a laboratory for part of this test of time. Evaluation of design quality often is done by critics, curators of museums, and historians.

But as far as design influencing the consumer, we find that food, clothing, and shelter are essential items in one's near environment. While evaluating one's alternatives, design tradition and materials (the media for design) are essential for visual happiness. These areas will be explored briefly here.

Designing with Food 21

Medieval and Renaissance man did not employ our contemporary refinements of table service. Trestle tables often were covered with a cloth to hide the supports. Guests sat on a bench on one side in order to free the other for service. Those of wealth and hospitality would have food available throughout the day, as described by Chaucer in the Prologue of *The Canterbury Tales:* "His table dormant in his halle alway Stand redy covered al the longe day."

A large dish placed in the middle of the table served all. Until the sixteenth century, forks were unknown, and fingers were used for delivering food to the mouth. Knives would have been used beforehand to cut the food up, but these were personal equipment that the possessor carried in his belt. A slice of bread served as a plate and later silver was used.

An increase in culinary wares came along with imports of porcelain from the Orient by the East India companies during the seventeenth century, and with Western fascination for the novel drinks of tea, coffee, and cocoa, which required especially designed wares for their service. The increase in the number of liquids and kinds of drinking vessels required a correspondingly more formal art of service, both with respect to the design of wares and the manner of serving.

This formality persisted through succeeding centuries in those societies whose upper class utilized a full complement of servants to polish the silver, the pewter, and the brass, to prepare multicourse dinners, and to serve and clear away the food.

In modern times, which are marked by the absence of such a class, formality is on the wane. Formality is no longer a daily practice to many, but a special service reserved for uncommon occasions, such as ceremonial

21-1 *A formal table setting by Virginia Saale. The blue chinaware has a border design in intricate relief, and the pink cloth has bands of shimmering metallic threads. The delicate pink misty stemware repeats the color of the cloth. Photograph by Vincent Bernucci.*

Table Coverings

Although linen is a flaxen fiber, the term *linen* has become sufficiently generic to denote any table covering of fabric construction, whether of cotton, jute, or synthetic composition. Among these, however, linen made from flax remains the aristocrat of textiles for covering tables. Linen damasks in formal designs are traditional favorites. Appliquéd organdy, embroidered cut-work patterns, and lace cloths also convey formality.

One can compose intermediary studies between formal and informal by foregoing coverage of a wood surface by cloth or other materials. Instead of tablecloths, place mats with lace, embroidery, or appliqué, or those constructed with gold and silver metallic thread can suggest a semiformality and simultaneously produce a pleasing contrast between exposed wood surfaces and other materials. Informality is also suggested by tablecloths of plaid, striped, or colorful floral patterns and by fabrics of rough texture or irregular weave construction. Place mats of reed, hemp, bamboo, and pineapple fiber and those combining a variety of novel materials appear more casual.

or commemorative events. Vestiges of it do remain in the home, however. Entertaining friends often calls into play a greater formality than does the daily serving of family meals.

An arrangement may require some or all of the following: a table or other surface, a centerpiece, linens, dishes, flatware, and glasses.

The Surface

Among serving surfaces, the trestle, gate-leg table, and bar suggest informality. Among woods, pine and birch are not considered to be as formal as mahogany, rosewood, or walnut. Painted and plastic surfaces are less formal than satiny or reflecting wood finishes.

Dishes

Porcelain, or "china," is a semitransparent ceramic containing kaolin and feldspar. It is particularly suitable for formal occasions because of its fine ceramic quality. Being fired at high temperatures, it is completely vitrified, nonporous, glasslike, and resonant. Bone china, containing bone ash instead of feldspar, is very white and translucent in color. Placing one's hand behind it in a bright light should reveal the outline of the hand.

Of lesser formality are stoneware and earthenware.

Stoneware is made from coarser clays than porcelain, but when fired at high temperatures, it also becomes completely vitrified. Its textural quality and intermediate weight make it flexible and adaptable to many contemporary uses. Earthenware is made of coarser clays than either porcelain or stoneware. Being fired at low temperatures, it is porous and requires a glaze to prevent penetration by moisture. Unglazed terra cotta frequently is used for flower pots, because it allows movement of air and moisture. In warm countries it is used to keep water cool through evaporation. A disadvantage of earthenware is that a chip in the glaze will allow the moisture from food particles to penetrate.

In decorative application of design, motifs that are symmetrically structured and ordered to the form on which they are applied are more formal than those placed randomly on a vessel. Splashes of bold, bright colors seem casual. So do genre scenes. With respect to density, heavy wares seem less formal than those that are lighter in weight. So do those that are intense in color or roughly glazed. Borders of gold or silver and highly ordered patterns using classical motifs always suggest formality. Extensive decoration and refinement of detail also appear formal, because they are associated with periods when craftsmen could devote endless hours to production. Those dishes that have no applied decoration are flexible for use in either formal or informal settings.

Glassware

Crystal is the aristocrat of glassware. Because of the lead in its composition, it is highly refractive and scintillating in light. Lead also contributes to crystal's bell-like tone. Because of its appeal, designers have subjected its surface to embellishments of engraving, etching, enameling, casing, and carving. All these contribute to its decorativeness, and this tradition has created an association of crystal with the elite, elegant, and formal. Bottle glass and ordinary table glass contain lime and do not possess crystal's scintillation and resonance.

In structural design, associations also hold. Squat, cylindrical shapes, such as tumblers, seem informal. Height connotes formality—a tall tumbler seems more elegant and hence more formal than a low one. Stemware, which provides a base and stem for the elevation of a bowl, carries a formal message, particularly if it is delicate and tall. Glassware that is bold, low, and sturdy in construction tends to be intermediate in spirit. Hand-blown Mexican glass shows much variation and imperfection in handling, and so appears casual. Milk glass is less formal because it is opaque and comparatively heavy. Glass with handles seldom seems formal.

Metalware

Knives, forks, and spoons, collectively called flatware, have come a long design route from former times when man fashioned them from stones, twigs, and shells. Among the cool colors are silver, silver plate (silver electroplated to a baser metal), and stainless steel, which may be either satin-finished or glossy. For warmer tones, silver may be gold-plated and is known as vermeil. Dirilyte, a gold alloy, also provides warmth of color in flatware. Although the more traditionally aristocratic metals of gold and silver suggest heightened elegance and formality, today's design of stainless steel has become so refined that it can be used for both casual and formal occasions. Moreover, although silver, since Roman days, has traditionally been valued as most prestigious, today's golden tones of vermeil and dirilyte lend variety and often harmonize to a greater degree with colors of food and surrounding objects in interiors.

21-2 Georgian *stemware. The pleasing elegance of the design suggests a degree of formality. Fostoria Glass Company, Moundsville, West Virginia.*

Centerpieces

Centerpieces that are symmetrically structured are more formal in aspect than those that are structured asymmetrically. As with hollow ware, the materials of the container also carry a message. Gold and silver vessels suggest greater formality than those made of copper, tin, and reed. Containers of irregular form and those of rough or matte finish appear natural and unassuming.

The contents also communicate. Although one can make a formal arrangement through the symmetrical structuring of pansies, marigolds, or field daisies, our natural associative patterns do not grant these the same degree of formality as a formally structured arrangement of roses, chrysanthemums, or gladioli. Flowers of the field, which respond to the whims of the wind or seem jocose and undisciplined, are usually not selected when one wants to suggest dignity and elegance. Likewise, grasses and willowy forms seem to resist control. Dramatic and vertically erect plants are more responsive to being manipulated into formal arrangements. Although all materials can be structured formally (and even defiantly), a respect for the nature of materials may lead one to design more freely with some than others.

The whole world of the wild and random, and the cultivated and landscaped is within man's reach. From the garden come succulent foliages, fruits, vegetables, dried beans, and sunflower aureoles. In fields and alongside the roads and railroads are wild asters, daisies, Queen Anne's lace, wild strawberries, dried grasses, and milkweed pods. Swampy lands grow cattails. From trees hang all kinds of sculpturesque pods, winged seeds, and berries; branches drop apples and nuts; trunks yield bark. A branch itself can create an interesting line arrangement. The seashore provides stones, pebbles, washed fragments of glass, sand, shells, and driftwood. All that is needed is a seeing eye, an awareness for the potential of materials, an experimental mood, and indulgence of one's urge to create. Extending the range of materials, one can combine the natural with the man-made: glass bubbles, marbles, sculptured objects, books, bricks, and candles.

The arrangements that are most satisfying communicate a vitality of life and seem like a fresh presence, a new growth in a new surrounding. Flowers may lose their identity with the flora of the field, but, when empathically and skillfully arranged, they can find new life in relationship with other companions selected by man to grace his interiors.

21-3 *Roy Lichtenstein.* Still Life with Crystal Dish, *1972. This shows food, a long-time subject matter of art, commonly called still life. Collection, Whitney Museum of American Art, New York.*

21-4 *Food presented aesthetically is even more appealing, as seen here. Photograph by Steve Tregeagle for cover of* Jonathan's Dining Guide, Salt Lake Area (*Salt Lake City: James Klum, 1980*).

Practical Considerations

If one's supply of china is limited, selection of a light, undecorated service of simple design makes possible combinations in both formal and informal settings. It also allows greater variety in the color, texture, and decorativeness of place mats or table linen and it can be combined with both colored and textured glassware. Assuming one has sufficient storage space and income to have a wide range of table service, various combinations can be selected to coordinate the design of the food, centerpiece, linens, and tableware.

Inspiration for table design can come from anywhere. The choice of table linen or tableware may be influenced by the colors of foods to be prepared, by the season, or by personal mood. Taking a few minutes to study the characteristics of materials not only intensifies one's appreciation for the composition of objects, but increases sensitivity to the potential combinations. Interpreting the nature of materials and combining them on the basis of their expressive qualities is much more creative and rewarding than attempting to master a list of possible combinations. The evocative qualities of nature's materials then become the guide for the decision about whether and how they can be combined. Interpretation prepares one to meet the multiple new situations beyond those that are learned by rote with study, practice, and experience; one can develop the ability to make truly imaginative combinations for food and table.

Food

Food has long held the eye of artists. One common example of this is the *still life,* a painting that depicts small objects and food on table. The fact remains that food can also be arranged in an aesthetically pleasing manner. It is interesting that the different food groups for a balanced diet are often color keyed; for instance, leafy greens and orange foods and grains are food groups needed to maintain a healthy body. The art of arranging food is in using the combination of the visual and the olfactory and taste sensations of the human body. Food must look good as well as taste good. In fact, when foods are colored nontraditionally they are unpalatable for people.

Designing Clothing and Adornment 22

Dress is the most complex and difficult of all arts; for resting on the framework of the human body, an adjunct and accomplice in all man's expression, it requires the broadest knowledge of humanity and of individuality to understand its mysteries.[1]

Elizabeth Stuart Phelps

Functions of Dress

Of all the arts, designing his costume is one of man's most personal expressions, and the design of his cos-

[1]Quoted by Bernard Rudofsky in *Are Clothes Modern?* (Chicago: Paul Theobold, 1947) p. 183.

tume constitutes one of his most important social and historic documents. Throughout the ages clothing has fulfilled numerous functional, decorative, social, political, religious, and psychological needs of mankind. A few of these motivations for dress, some of which are closely interrelated, are listed:

comfort and protection from the elements of heat, sun, and other cosmic elements
providing the modesty prescribed by a society
ritual and ceremony
decoration and embellishment
conspicuous consumption to display wealth and status
identification and recognition: royal crowns, clerical vestments, uniforms
differentiation of the young from the older: mini- and maxi-skirts, see-throughs, hot pants, baggies

22-1 *Wool tapestry,* Courtiers with Roses, *Franco-Flemish, circa 1435–1440. Dress is for modesty. Our conventional bridal garments frequently have the lineaments and fragility of these maidens' hennins and a similar extension to the bodily structure through trains and billowing gowns. The high waistband is often repeated in dress of the Empire style. Collection, The Metropolitan Museum of Art, New York.*

22-2 The Original grizzly bear, *on a Tlingit ceremonial shirt. Alaska. Note the formal balance, expression of boldness, and the background areas, which also form pleasing units. The University Museum of the University of Pennsylvania, Philadelphia.*

22-3 *Tori Kiyonga. A standing woman, decoratively dressed and adorned, in the costume of a daimyo, Japanese, 18th century. Emphasis is on the vertical line movement in the stature of the woman and in the wall scroll. Curved forms relieve the uprights. Compare linear similarities to gowns in the* Age *of* Innocence, *Figure 22-4. Collection, The Metropolitan Museum of Art, New York.*

extension of one's self: billowing gowns, resplendent
   crowns
transformation or change of personality: a new hat, wig,
   or hair style
satisfaction of the urge to create
revealing one's body structure for enhancement
self-expression: "The apparel oft proclaims the man"—
   Shakespeare
   attraction of the opposite sex
   sufficient modesty to promote sex appeal: "The greatest provocations of lust are from our apparel"—Robert
Burton

22-4 *Age of Innocence, a three-panel mural. The tapestry panels, printed on linen, can be transferred from one wall, room, or home to another. The suede davenport is by Directional. Jack Denst Designs, Inc.*

22-5 *Walnut statuette: Saint Catherine, Flemish, first half of 16th century, height 15". Decorativeness and complexity of dress are coordinated into a rhythmic and provocative whole. The ability of wood to show fine fabriclike detail is apparent. The Metropolitan Museum of Art, New York.*

uncovering: Salome's dance, Gypsy Rose Lee and the
    art of the striptease.
social protest.
competition with one's own sex.
fun and recreation.
escape from boredom.
securing attention.
convention.
satisfying a desire for change.
bringing one's body into closer alignment with an ideal-
    ized image of a particular culture—shaping as well as
    covering.
displaying technological advance.

The Materials Used

For covering and adorning his body man has used a gamut of materials from conventionally woven fabrics to electrically wired and lighted ones. Today, we are finding pleasure not only from the use of new technological materials such as paper, plastic, and nonwoven textiles, but also from new uses of old materials with sensuous appeal. Furs and leather, once functional to ancient man for protection from the cold, are now luxury and novelty items. Among designers to whom these materials appeal is Maximilian, who not only has shown

22-6 Maenad Leaning on Her Thyrsos. *Roman copy of a Greek work of the late 5th century B.C., pentelic marble. The rhythmic line movement is fluid and enhances the maenad's body structure to make it more appealing than nudity. Much of our sleepware resembles the costume of this ancient Maenad. The Metropolitan Museum of Art, New York.*

mink pants but floor-length dresses made of fur. Bonnie Cashin found satisfaction through designing with leather. Imported embroidered pigskin costumes from Afghanistan have provided a new distinctiveness to dress. Feathers from the quetzal bird were used by

22-7 *Gold headdress of lady of the court, with some restoration, Egyptian, 18th Dynasty. The design is consistent with the materials and technology of that era. Collection, The Metropolitan Museum of Art, New York.*

the Aztec chieftains of Mexico for headdresses that indicated their rank. In contemporary American society, Adele Simpson has found their variety useful for vests, belts, neckties, and evening dresses. With respect to new materials, in the 1950s Mary Quant used poly-vinyl chloride (PVC) for clothing to provide a "wet look."

Metals, which in medieval times were used for armor and coats of mail, in the 1960s were used for jewelry, which so enveloped the costume as to become an integral and sometimes a dominant part of it. Entire costumes were made of lightweight aluminum or silver-colored plastic. Wood and metal shavings have been made into wigs. These reflect man's continual ingenuity and resourcefulness in converting materials to practical, novel, and exotic uses. James Russell Lowell, a New England conservative of the last century, sounds modern with his statement: "Fashion must be forever new, or she becomes insipid."

22-8 *Figures of Ny-kau-Hor and Eldest Son. Tomb of Ny-kau-Hor, detail, "false door," Egyptian, 5th dynasty, circa 2490 B.C. This detail shows two males, one clothed and one unclothed. The larger and more important male has a cloth garment, jewelry, and a distinctive hair style. Collection, The Metropolitan Museum of Art, New York.*

what stouter than women, the ideal for them too is to be tall and muscularly slim. George Bernard Shaw referred to this as the "cylindrical ideal." Artful manipulations of dress can create the illusion of having a more acceptable figure.

Evaluating Costume Design

Today's revolution in fashion design can be attributed in part to technological innovations and the introduction of new materials that influence what one expects to see in dress. This was well expressed by the English designer Mary Quant: "I want to invent new ways of

Creating Illusion to Secure the Desired Image

One of the main purposes of dress is to modify the apparent structure of the human body in order to bring it into closer correspondence with a desired norm. Each society has its own standard of beauty, which may change through the years. Today in American culture the slightness of figure associated with youth is a pronounced criterion for beauty. The Venus de Milo was long ranked as the world's most beautiful woman, but her proportions are not admired by men and women today. Nor do many appreciate the mature "bosom and bottom" silhouette of the Edwardian era. That some African tribes actually prefer the appearance of women who look well-fed may also seem strange to Americans. In our society, though men are permitted to be some-

22-9 *Andy Warhol,* Before and After, Free, *1962. Synthetic polymer on canvas. This shows how cosmetic surgery is part of people's desire to design with their bodies. People from other cultures have tattoos and some pierce holes in their ears. Body manipulation is just as important as choice of clothing itself. Collection, Whitney Museum of American Art, New York.*

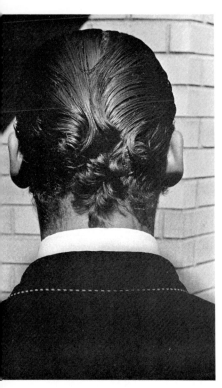

22-10 *Photograph by Ralph Gibson from* Quadrants, *1975. This photograph shows the importance of hair style as a form of body adornment. Courtesy of Ralph Gibson.*

making clothes in new materials, with new shapes and new fashion accessories that are up-to-date with the changing ways of life."[2]

French designer Paco Rabanne has declared: "I like being contemporary—not a yesterday man, not a designer for the year 2000. I combine traditional and contemporary materials. To new materials, one must apply new ideas. At the moment we are witnessing the end of an era—the needle is about to give way to the mold."[3]

In an age where science, innovation, and instant visual communication by mass media are constant factors, former considerations of what constitutes good taste can be contrasted with those that are satisfying for the moment and disrespectful of former values. As with any other art, one needs to have an appreciation of the intent of the designer and an appreciation of the function clothing is serving for the male or female wearer in order to evaluate or appreciate its design. A few broad, inclusive principles which hold can be stated. Clothing should be

comfortable.
complementary to the individual.
structured according to the principles of design.
appropriate to the occasion for which it is worn.
consistent with the role the individual is playing.
able to provide one with satisfaction and pleasure.

As man assumes many roles today and experiments with numerous others, his expressions take many forms and sometimes only the individual himself is aware of his trial roles. As men move farther from traditional, conservative, and limited roles, their clothing will reflect changes within their self-image. That designers of woman's clothing such as Bill Blass, Yves St. Laurent, and Oleg Cassini are also designing imaginative nontradi-

[2]Mary Quant, *Quant by Quant* (New York: Putnam, 1966), p. 152.
[3]Paco Rabanne, "Clothing: Theater of the Self." *Craft Horizons* **27**: 23 (May/June 1968).

tional clothing for men reflects man's changing attitude toward himself.

However, certain styles of fashion recur periodically. It would seem that in his clothing expression, man finds values perennially present in the design of some former periods. As Gabrielle Chanel said: "Mode passes but style remains. Mode consists of a few amusing ideas meant to be used up quickly so they may be replaced by others in the next collection. A style endures even as it is renewed and evolved.

A few frequently occurring or continuous styles are:

The sheath of ancient Egypt, the design in harmony with the contours of the human body, and one which suggests the beauty of vertical columns.
The simplicity of early Renaissance costume, with its soft shoulder line and becoming décolleté.
The empire style of early nineteenth century France rhythmically follows the lines of the human body and repeats the classical beauty of Greek form.
A short skirt allows freedom of movement.
A full skirt, as in the shirtwaist, allows for movement.
The pullover sweater.
Trousers for men and women generally provide for freedom of movement and protection against the elements.

In some costume designs of the past, clothing was constructed so that the structure lines of the garments were in close harmony with the structure of the body. The lines of clothing broke with the major skeletal junctures: the waist, knee, wrist, or ankle. Moreover, clothing was much more in harmony with the individual, so that he was not aware of it. In the words of Anthony Trollope, "Clothing should complement, not supplant the man." Clothing that was considered the most successful did not call attention to itself but subtly reinforced the personality of the individual wearing it. This position was also taken by Gabrielle Chanel, who insisted that woman should carry her clothes instead of being carried by them.

22-11 *Antonio Pollaiuolo (1433–1498), Italian, Florentine.* Portrait of a Young Lady, *tempera on wood, 18½ x 13". Emphasis results from visual involvement with the decorative pomegranate blossom on the shoulder of the costume and the hair jewelry. The expression is one of serenity. The harmony of the costume and adornment with the feminine form has a recurring appeal. Collection, The Metropolitan Museum of Art, New York.*

22-12 *Saul Steinberg,* Wedding Wallpaper, *1950. The ritual of dress for a wedding often supersedes all other rituals in a wedding ceremony. This wallpaper illustrates through repetition of line the uniformity of costume. Courtesy of the Cooper-Hewitt Museum of Decorative Art, Smithsonian Institution, New York.*

In contrast to the conventional view that clothing should complement the man and possess an understated beauty is today's treatment of body coverings as independent "objects" with new functions to be explored. Mary Quant, an English designer, expressed her philosophy:

Fashion is the product of 1,001 different things. The whole host of elusive ideas, influences, cross-currents, and economic factors, captured into a shape and dominated by two things . . . impact on others, fun for oneself. It is unpredictable, indefinable.[4]

Clothing in the Western world often reflects fashion. In many cultures whose technology is simpler, clothing is a matter of tradition and the availability of materials. Also, clothing reflects the climate and a particular culture's response to it: protecting one's body from extreme temperatures, for example. Clothing functions on many levels of human society, as do other forms of physical adornment.

[4]Op cit., p. 90.

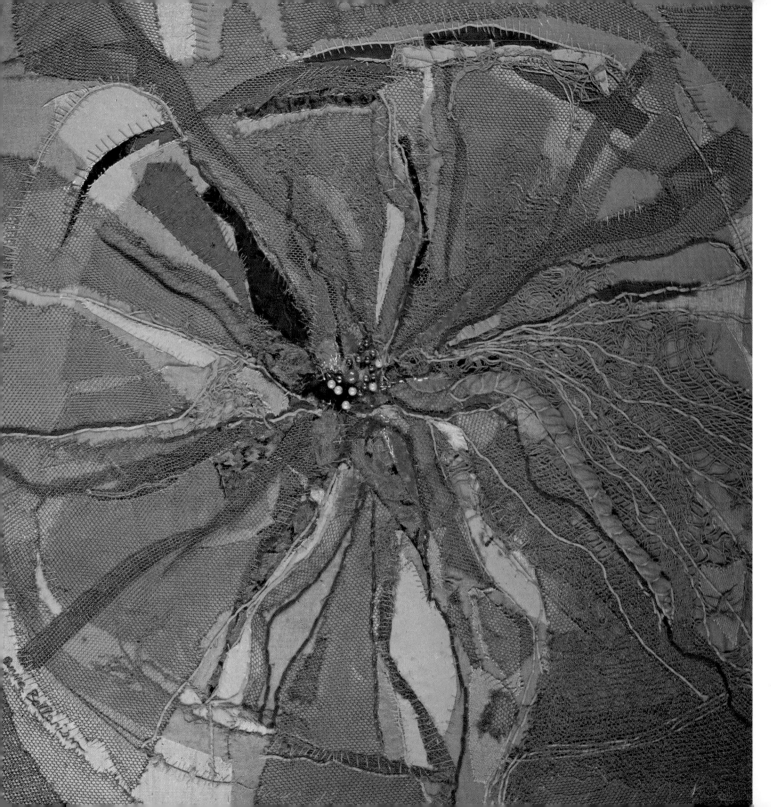

Anna Ballarian. *Burst of Joy*. A stitchery designed with warm colors evokes a happy mood. Courtesy, Anna Ballarian, Photograph by Vincent Bernucci.

(Overleaf) The famous Chinese Parlor at Winterthur, Delaware, which illustrates the interchange and harmony of East and West. Chinese elements include 18th century wallpaper. Coromandel black lacquered screens which were brought from China before 1800, and Chinese rugs that unify the room. Two sets of rococo chairs by Philadelphia craftsmen are designed in the spirit of Chippendale. Early 18th century green damask with blue fringe dresses the windows and furniture in winter—gold, in autumn. Courtesy, the Henry Francis du Pont Winterthur Museum.

Designing Shelter 23

There are many aspects to designing shelter. This book has concerned itself so far with visual communication, cultural concepts, materials, and consumer issues. All of these affect shelter as well. There are also social and behavioral issues to consider in shelter design. The finest of art reflects the visual best of a given time and place. The immediate test is the test by consumers. Does an item function? And shelter design includes two design professions: interior designers and architects.

Professional Designers

One's expectations of an interior designer vary and many stereotypes abound. Interior designers are among the leaders of the fields of interior design. Their educa-tional experience is in design and they are trained to make decisions about enclosed spaces. Presently, there are no governmental regulations in the United States to determine who can use the name *interior designer*. Many interior designers have worked hard to gain professional status. Professional organizations such as the American Society of Interior Designers, ASID, are estab-lishing high standards for their members so that the ini-tials ASID following someone's name are a professional distinction. Today designers are required to pass a na-tional exam to use such initials. Accordingly, a con-sumer, when seeking quality service, can look for these letters after a designer's name as an indication of profes-sionalism.

Architects are trained in universities and examined and then licensed by states; their professional organiza-tion is the American Institute of Architects. The letters

and an interior designer to be members of a shelter-designing team.

Elements and Principles of Design

All the elements and principles of design apply to shelter as to other aspects of the consumer's world. Both the interior and the exterior benefit from good principles of design. Consumers involved in custom designing a home will profit from using a professional architect or interior designer. Unfortunately, most people don't begin with choices of space or even choices of furnishings, but are inheritors of ill-conceived spaces and furnishings. Or, sometimes consumers make judicious selections of furniture but do not arrange it in an effective or satisfactory way. Therefore, taking a look at furniture arrangement in light of some of the principles of good design can be beneficial to the consumer.

Furniture is best selected in *scale* and *proportion* to the size of the room. In comparing closed to open space, a room is more satisfying if the amount of space occupied by furniture is not equal in proportion to the amount of uncommitted area. Many rooms can be improved by removing pieces whose utility does not justify the space they occupy.

In selecting other furnishings, consideration should be given to *rhythm,* as well. One means of establishing rhythm is through the continuous flow of line. Furniture pieces of similar height can be more easily arranged than pieces of extremely different heights. The repetition of similar patterns also promotes unity.

The movement of horizontal lines seems more rhythmic than that of vertical ones, because less visual energy is required to follow lines that are parallel with the horizon. Hence, modular furnishings, which have been designed to correspond with each other to provide single or related levels, are selected by those whose need for rhythm is pronounced. Many period pieces are structured vertically and vary more in height.

23-1 *Shaker dwelling room from the early 19th century community at Enfield, New Hampshire. Note the built-in storage as part of the architectural design to create serenity. The simplicity of the chair bears resemblance to the 1933 chair of Danish Kaare Klint and the simple folk chairs in French and Italian churches. Courtesy, the Henry Francis du Pont Winterthur Museum, Winterthur, Delaware.*

AIA after a person's name is what a consumer should look for when choosing an architect.

A consumer should choose a professional designer with care: the designer and consumer should be able to communicate well. Architects and interior designers charge a commission for their work or they work as consultants on a retainer or hourly fee. Some designers specialize in particular areas: residential design, kitchen design, or office design. Asking to see a designer's portfolio is sensible for good decision making. Architects differ from interior designers in their knowledge of and training in structural design. Some architects do interior design work as well. It is not unusual for an architect

Furnishings can be *balanced* either symmetrically or asymmetrically. Symmetrical balance involves placing identical objects on either side of a main object, such as a sofa. In equivalent or obvious balance the objects may not be the same, but they will be of equal visual weight in their power to attract. Hence, a chair on one side may be balanced by the table on the other. Symmetrical balance is formal in spirit and creates a heightened sense of order, restraint, dignity, and security.

Asymmetrical balance is achieved by spacing varia-tions of like or unlike objects. Space itself is used as a visual weight so that a small object placed at a great distance from a central object balances a larger one placed much closer. A small object can also balance a larger one by commanding more visual attention—for example, by being a brighter color. Asymmetrical balance is considered more lively, natural, and visually stimulating than symmetrical balance; through its infor-mality it is more consistent with much of contemporary living.

23-2 *Richard Neutra. Kaufmann Home, California. The ensemble of pavilion, house, pool, and mountains, with its interplay of light and shadow, has an unparalleled beauty and serenity. Notice how space is created. Forms are more sharply defined and values are in deeper con-trast in the foreground, as compared to the distant mountains whose lineaments are shrouded in mist. Photograph by Julius Shulman.*

23-3 *Eames House. Notice how the eucalyptus trees and greenery are reflected in the wall panels and seem to soften and hallow the man-made. Courtesy of Charles Eames.*

23-4 *In this Haverhill Room with American Hepplewhite furnishings, the furniture is rhythmically related to the architecture, being approximately the same height as the dado (lower part of the wall), except for the buffet. Even then the lower drawer section follows the basic architectural line. The mural contributes an illusion of depth. Collection, The Metropolitan Museum of Art, New York.*

A focal point is also important in interiors. The point of *emphasis* may be the fireplace, a picture collection, sofa, chair arrangement, or view of the outside. When the areas of design command equal attention so that one does not know where to look, psychological as well as visual fatigue may result. One feels a need not only for predominance of form—a kind of balance and an area of interest—but also for the elements of color, line direction, and textural qualities.

Designing with furnishings usually provides greater visual satisfaction when a dominant theme or an idea is realized. Although one may have a collection of objects from the past, present, or from varying cultures, a space needs a sense of dominance. Through furnishings one can emphasize any number of things, whether it be a dominant color, dominant texture, or a dominantly shaped object.

Illusion

The art of *manipulating space* to create illusion has many classical as well as aesthetic components. It is of particular interest to the professional designer and a value for a consumer to learn to create space illusion. The illusion of space may create dimension by manipulating line, form, space, light, color, texture, transpar-

23-5 *George Nakashima's home and furnishings are constructed in a simple forthright manner. There is a repeat of the rectilinear form with other subordinate forms for diversity. The textures of the room—wood, rush, and shoji paneling—are keyed to the concept of unity with variety. Courtesy George Nakashima and American Crafts Museum, New York.*

23-6 *Interior of Eames home. Walls need not divide if space is valued. Plants integrate indoors and outdoors. The grid patterns are an example of repetitive line; with the furnishings they suggest a musical composition. The armchair is a contemporary classic—Ero Saarinen's "womb" chair. Photograph by Julius Shulman.*

ency, and motion. Some of the devices that increase illusion of spaciousness are listed here:

Murals

More horizontal lines than vertical ones, using low furnishings, furniture, or wall panelling, for example

Diagonal line movement

Furniture that is built in or custom made to relate to the architectural design of the room

A minimum number of furnishings

Furniture small in scale and structured to provide a flow of space under the seat

Light colors

A restricted number of colors

Neutral colors

Colors with close values

Limited variety of textures and pattern

Small pattern repeats

Transparent materials

Smooth textures

Glass to extend indoors to outdoors (Figure 23-2)

Same material used indoors for walls or floors as on an adjacent terrace

Mirrors or metal foils on the walls to reflect the room's inside and outside

Room dividers that permit penetration of space; walls that do not continue all the way to the ceiling, for example

Built-in lighting to free space from the floor and also allow existing room space to be more visual

Architectural devices such as arches, cornices, and mouldings to join areas and make them seem integrated

Minimum contrast between window fabrics and walls

Furniture placed slightly away from the walls instead of tightly against it

Special Behavioral Issues

Some of the social and behavioral issues that relate to interior design are symbolism, social order, culture, group behavior, family interaction, privacy, crowding, territoriality, and personalization. Traditionally, aesthetic decisions involving art and design have been the basis of shelter-design decision making. But now, human factors are considered equally valid criteria in decision making—that is to say, aesthetic decisions include human factors. An interior or a structure is a nonverbal communication; people consciously or unconsciously say a variety of things with interiors. The most obvious social behavioral issue is symbolism. Symbolism has long been used in shelter. In interiors, the throne has long been a symbol of importance as well as a seat. In the year 1972, Claire Cooper Marcus wrote "The House as the Symbol of the Self" for *Design Environment*. Her theory is that the housing problem in America is an emotional problem because of the interrelationship of self and self-image and the home. Social order can also be indicated by shelter. That is, a person's socioeconomic status can be indicated by the style, the neighborhood, the exterior structure, and the size of the house. The value that a particular culture puts on differing materials and house size will vary. In cultures with simple technology, uniformity in housing and owner-built housing are more the norm than living in a home built by others. The behavior of non-family groups inside the family home will affect family interaction. In contemporary society the importance of privacy, alone-time, the effects of establishing territory, and the ability to personalize or put one's mark on an interior seem to affect satisfaction. When crowding takes place within a dwelling, the ensuing stress often has a negative effect on family interaction.

It is important that a shelter be aesthetic and functional, since it provides a space for many activities. Interior designers and architects provide services that can aid the consumer who desires a well-designed shelter.

24 Selecting Art

I would not paint a face, a rock, nor
 brooks, nor trees
Mere semblances of things, but
 something more than these.
That art is best which to the soul's
 range gives no bound,
Something besides the form,
 something beyond the sound.
—Eighth-century Chinese poet

Difficulty in Assimilating the New

Although it is not necessary to understand art in order to enjoy it, appreciation and acceptance can be en-hanced by trying to see as the artist sees. This chapter is a brief résumé of some of the considerations artists have had that may help to develop further insight into their motivation and art and increase our receptivity to new expressions.

The artist is a person who is sensitive to the social climate of his time. Ezra Pound designated the artist as "the antennae of the race." The artist seeks ways to make public his private responses. Because doing so necessarily involves new symbols and expressive de-vices, he is usually ahead of the general populace, who are attuned to the tried and familiar. In fact, in attempt-ing to give objective reality and visual description to the status quo, he may not be so much ahead of his time as congruently with it. The Fauves, the "wild beasts" of 1905 (the painters Matisse, Dufy, Dérain, Rouault, and Vlaminck)—so-called because of the intensity and brutality with which they painted—and other artists who displayed their work in the New York Armory Show in 1913, unleashed the fury and indignation of even the most knowledgeable critics whose vision was not prepared for acceptance of change. Such epithets as "Huns of the Art World," "anarchic hordes," "heart-rending and sickening," and "most hideous monstrosities ever perpetrated" indicate the wrath provoked by the exhibit. It was even asserted that the Armory's art would bring about the disintegration of society. Yet the same artists who contributed are now acknowledged as being integral with or ahead of their day and are credited with representing their culture well and intuitively. Matisse no longer seems to have been "mad, insane, and depraved," as he appeared to be to the traditionalists who were his contemporaries.

The passage of time has made the aesthetic deviates of the nineteenth century seem mild in their attempts to redefine the legitimate province of the artist. Notwithstanding, disputes over appropriate content continue to this day. Although the boundary between the acceptable and nonacceptable has been expended to make the furor of former days seem ludicrous, as recently as 1966 county officials threatened to ban from the Los Angeles County Museum the Edward Kienholz exhibit with its pop environments that included smells, sounds, and sordid sights in bars and male-female back-seat encounters. However, the museum's board of trustees decreed that it is not a museum's function to determine the appropriate content of art and the palatability of its format for public consumption. The society will pass judgment. Picasso spoke of an artist's internal tensions which compels one to communicate.

Former Purposes of Art

The emphasis upon individual feelings and perceptions and upon the artist's prerogative to give them personal expression is a modern concept of the artistic function. In past ages, the artist was engaged in activities reflecting the collective values of a society. In ancient Egypt, the Pharaohs had imperial workshops attached to the royal palaces, whose artisans worked in the established idiom. Their artists observed regulations that prescribed drawing the entire figure from an angle that most readily established its identity: the head in profile; feet and arms from the side; eyes, shoulders, and chest from the front. Other regulatory devices included seated statues having their hands on their knees and men being painted in a darker color than women.

The Greeks, seeking truth and beauty, studied the functioning of the human body in movement and added to its representations the ability to depict bone and muscle, the foreshortening of limbs, and an ideal-

24-1 *Edward Kienholz. The Beanery, 1964–65, 22' x 84" x 72". The Dwan Gallery, New York.*

24-2 *Inscriptions, Egyptian funerary papyrus of Gausen, Chantress of Amon, 21st Dynasty (1090–945 B.C.). Collection, The Metropolitan Museum of Art, New York.*

24-3 *Detail of a wounded Amazon in Pentelic marble, a Roman copy of a Greek statue attributed to Polykleitos, Height 6′. The Amazon illustrates the Greek idealized beauty in its common universality of features. Collection, The Metropolitan Museum of Art, New York.*

ized beauty. The practical-minded Romans added accuracy and detail in representing individuals. Byzantine art served a symbolic function, that of suggesting heaven's splendor. For this purpose, ivory, gold, jewels, and colored glass tesserae were used in mosaics. The flatness of design resulted from the employment of Syrian and Persian artisans who were accustomed to Eastern and Oriental two-dimensionalism, which is devoid of modeling techniques. In the Gothic period, cathedrals with glowing stained glass windows and pinnacles that pierced the sky in their upward thrust reflected man's celestial aspirations.

The Renaissance brought renewed fascination with Greco-Roman ideals and sculptural three-dimensionalism. The artist, commissioned by the pope or by royal and noble patrons to paint Madonnas and portraits or to sculpture religious and heroic images, was

24-4 *Roman bust of Empress Livia (57 B.C.–A.D. 29), bronze, height 9½″ (including base). Unlike the Greek Amazon, Empress Livia's features reflect the individual realism of a particular, identifiable woman. Collection, The Metropolitan Museum of Art, New York.*

24-5 *Rembrandt van Rijn.* Young Girl at an Open Half-Door, *1645, oil on canvas, 40⅛″ x 33⅛″, illustrating a magnificent and subtle use of light. The girl is portrayed in the classical tradition of highlighting one side of the face by using light reflected from an open door or window and then graduating the tones to the darkness of the background. Courtesy of The Art Institute of Chicago.*

not allowed the freedom of today's artists. His tensions were not only those that accompany any attempt to convert inner perception into outer reality, but they included concern with pleasing a patron whose eye was conditioned to conventional images and who had preconceived expectations. The classical tradition continued throughout Europe, receiving its greatest impetus from the French Royal Academy of Painting and Sculpture. The Academy clearly defined the acceptable in art and discouraged innovation and deviation by refusing to exhibit work that did not correspond to its standards. Content was decreed as well as method. Idealism took precedence over the ordinary and actual. In striving for the generalized ideal, individual emotions and sensations were not considered. Classical, religious, and mythological content were highly favored. Flemish and Dutch genre paintings and still lifes, which reflected man's attention to his temporal and mundane homely functionings and the fulfillment of creature comforts, were assigned a low status. The scenes that were encouraged tended toward the picturesque, with inclusion of Greco-Roman ruins or theatrical settings.

Composition also reflected the collective ideal. Drawing that involved mental activity was emphasized rather than color, a sensual element. Artists, visually bound to the sculptural models of the classical world, clearly outlined and carefully modeled forms from light to dark in three dimensions. As a result, painting was deliberate and studied, with emphasis upon technical skill, refinement, and sound craftsmanship. Nature was not painted as it appeared, but in the orderly and beautiful state man wished it to be. The Academy, in rejecting the ugly, the ordinary, and the real, was also rejecting man in his totality.

Events That Led to Change

Because of the European preoccupation with science and exploration during the nineteenth century, and because of French interest in northern Africa and the Near East, many catalytic changes took place with respect to man's view of himself and his universe. European commercialism spread to the far corners of the world and Europeans became familiar with the powerful and simplified design of primitive cultures. During this time many men were jarred from their long-established beliefs, and as old props disintegrated, new concepts were formed by both scientists and artists.

The chief event that led to this change was Darwin's evolutionary theory of man as a descendant of a long line of prehuman forms, as presented in his *The Origin of Species,* published in 1859. The theory shook men's minds, causing them to question traditional concepts about the origin of man and of life itself. Moreover, in an age of increasing scientific exploration, not only biology but anthropology and ethnology were developing as branches of science. Europeans could see the work of primitive peoples, for during the latter nineteenth and early twentieth centuries ethnological museums were being established in one city after another for the systematic investigation and evaluation of cultural artifacts.

The French acquisition of New Caledonia in 1853 and their colonization of Africa brought direct contact with the artifacts of primitive cultures. Since Napoleon's abortive invasion of Egypt in 1798, France had had an increasing commitment there. The French government developed the area bordering the Mediterranean into orchards, vineyards, and farmland as a valuable supplementary breadbasket for Europe. Here the colonists came into contact for the first time with African masks, sculptures, costumes, and other artifacts. These strange and sensational objects were collected to show to those at home, and eventually contributed to changing the direction of art on the European continent. The young

24-6 *Joseph Dufour.* Les Francais en Egypte. *A four-panel wallpaper screen of the French entering Egypt, designed from paintings by Dentil in 1814. Courtesy of the Cooper-Hewitt Museum of Decorative Arts and Design, Smithsonian Institution, New York.*

The tenacious hold that classical antiquity and the academic tradition have had upon the sculptor and painter is well explained by Irving Stone in his biography of Michelangelo, *The Agony and the Ecstasy,* and by David Weiss in *Naked Came I,* a biography of the French sculptor Auguste Rodin. The struggles of artists and sculptors to overcome long-established biases and the abuses they suffered from entrenched conservatism are common in the life histories of many artists of the latter nineteenth century.

24-7 *Large dance mask of the Bachams, a sub-group of the Bamileke in the Cameroun Grasslands of Africa. Note the exaggerated facial rhythms and the geometrically faceted features, which excited and inspired European artists to new visual formats. Museum Rietberg, Zurich.*

with the Arab countries. With the Canal's completion in 1869, the cord of commerce no longer needed to extend the long route of six thousand miles around the Cape of Good Hope. As the attention of the world became focused upon the Near East, the unfamiliar began to lose some of its strangeness. Persian costumes, rugs, and artifacts became popular. Many homes had Turkish corners with Turkish draperies and low tables and divans.

The opening of the Mohammedan Exhibit in Paris in 1903 additionally brought the European artist into contact with Near Eastern art forms. These included the colorful and flatly designed Persian manuscripts, minia-

24-8 *Pablo Picasso.* Les Demoiselles d'Avignon, *1907, oil on canvas, 8' x 7'8". Compare Picasso's violent rhythms and faceted cubistic forms to those of the Bacham dance mask. Collection, The Museum of Modern Art, New York.*

artists were particularly enamored with the Africans' way of depicting life. Both Picasso and Braque recognized their artistry and transposed elements of primitive design into the sophisticated Cubism of the early twentieth century.

The building of the Suez Canal under the direction of Ferdinand de Lesseps also provided new contacts

24-9 *James McNeill Whistler, American. Detail of* The Peacock Room, *1876–1877, taken from the Leyland Residence. Oil color and gold on leather and wood, 167⅞″ x 398″ x 239½″. Courtesy of the Smithsonian Institution, Freer Gallery of Art, Washington, D.C.*

tures, ceramics, and rugs. Matisse's use of burgundy color, his two-dimensional, stylized motifs, and his emphasis on textural patterns can be partially attributed to this Near Eastern influence; so can his penchant for depicting odalisques clothed in Turkish trousers and bolero jackets.

Of the many influences that led to change, none was more all-pervasive in art and interior design from the 1860s onward than that of the Orient. Japan had appeared as an exhibitor in the Western world for the first time at the World Exhibition in London in 1862, and at the close of the exhibition the firm of Farmer and Rogers was allowed to sell Japan's contributions. In the same year, Madame de Soye opened her shop "La Port Chinoise" in Paris's Rue de Rivoli. S. Bing, whose shop "L'Art Nouveau" opened in Paris in 1895 and gave its name to the whole Art Nouveau movement, began his career as an importer of Japanese arts and crafts.

The American artist James McNeill Whistler studied in Paris until 1859 and then brought his love for Japanese linear quality and color to London, where he influenced the interior design of his day. In his paintings he combined impressionism with echoes of Japanese woodcuts. His famed Peacock Room, built between 1876 and 1877 for the Leyland residence in London, influenced Art Nouveau designers such as Aubrey Beardsley in the later nineteenth century and popularized the peacock as a favorite motif. He is also associated with launching the craze for blue and white china, and in his interiors he used tatami rugs and gold wallpaper. He promoted the aesthetic of Oriental interior design with its simplicity, lightness, and delight in natural objects: "A few movable screens . . . a few vases for flowers and a few small objects of daily use . . . are the decoration that a Japanese man of taste deems sufficient for his room. . . . He does not know of the multitude of unnecessary things that crowd our houses . . . accumulation is alien to his feelings and he likes air, light, and unencumbered space."[1]

[1]Robert Schmutzler, *Art Nouveau* (New York: Abrams, 1962), p. 76.

Exhibitions, galleries, and prints also helped to familiarize the West with the refinement of Far Eastern interiors. By 1859 books had begun to appear in England that dealt with every aspect of Japanese life and art. In 1869, Charles Eastlake influenced interior decoration by his *Hints on Household Taste*, which called attention to Japanese models. Articles on Japanese flower arranging appeared in periodicals. Christopher Dresser, who had served as England's official representative in Japan, in 1876 published his observations of the country, entitled *Japan, Its Architecture, Art, and Art Manufactures.*

The open-door policy of the Orient during the later nineteenth century also facilitated communication and exchange between nations. Since 1615 Japan had been completely sealed off from foreign intervention by the closing of its ports and its oppression of Christianity under the rule of the Tokugawa Shoguns. After Commodore Perry's naval expedition in 1854, however, the country was reopened to the rest of the world. During this period of isolation the woodblock artistry of Japan, begun in 1658 with Hishikawa Moronobu's first illustrated book, led to the production of thousands of prints depicting the homely urbanity of daily middle-class life. Some Japanese did not think them worthy of collection and used them as wrapping paper, but the prints were avidly collected by Europeans during the latter nineteenth century and excited the imagination of many artists, among them Van Gogh, Matisse, Degas, and Toulouse-Lautrec.

During the late nineteenth century, photography came into its own, almost simultaneously with the possibility of production of multiple illustrations through the new arts of lithography and wood engraving. The camera challenged art's reportorial and descriptive functions. Formerly many artists had functioned as a mirror to nature, depicting it in minute detail. In seconds the camera could now duplicate the work the artist had painstakingly labored to produce over extended periods of time. In order to distinguish their efforts from mere illustration, many artists attempted to outdo the camera by painting in sepia tones. Others in the 1880s took their

24-10 *Honoré Daumier, French.* The Third-Class Carriage, *oil on canvas, 25¾ x 35½". In dispelling former academic biases, the ordinary as well as the beautiful became appropriate content for expression in art. Collection, The Metropolitan Museum of Art, New York.*

easels outdoors and experimented with color (which the camera could not do), thus leading to the development of impressionism and pointillism.

Nor could the camera take a picture of man's psychic interior. Psychology, which was first being recognized during the late nineteenth century, had declared itself a science by the early twentieth. The experiments with hysteria conducted by Josef Breuer and Sigmund Freud led to the latter's making known to man the wonderfully strange world of his own unconscious. Henceforth the artist too would include the unconscious as an appropriate realm for his artistry. Mind and emotions would be as valid for depiction as the outer, tangible manifestation of objects. Ideational and emotional imagery necessarily involves abstract symbolism, because such data are conceptual and nonobjective. The arts and sculpture of the mid-twentieth century have continued to mirror man's deep concern with his inner experiences—hence much of its abstract quality.

Past Revolutionaries

Among the nineteenth-century revolutionaries was Whistler, whose famous painting of his mother aroused so much public indignation as to have the respected art critic Ruskin accuse him of "flinging a pot of paint in the public's face." Whistler, aroused by this condemnation, was one of the first to define the function of painting as organization of a field, the canvas, to a higher level of significance than the individual objects themselves represent.

The vast majority of folk cannot and will not consider a picture as a picture, apart from any story which it may be

supposed to tell. . . . As music is the poetry of sound, so is painting the poetry of sight, and the subject matter has nothing to do with harmony of sound or of color.[2]

It is considered illogical to expect one of the arts, such as painting, to be representative and narrative whereas another (i.e., music) is accepted for its abstract harmonies and rhythms. The fact that music is not expected to tell a tale in order to have validity has led artists to label their paintings with numbers or giving them such titles as "Nocturne" and "Opus." Gauguin referred to his work as musical, "composed of rhythms and har-

[2]Alfred H. Barr, Jr., *What is Modern Painting* (New York: Museum of Modern Art, 1956), p. 10.

24-11 *Vincent van Gogh.* **The Starry Night,** *1889, oil on canvas, 29 x 36¼". The recurring spiral executed in vigorous strokes lends movement and life to the canvas. Collection, The Museum of Modern Art, New York.*

24-12 *Auguste Renoir.* Bal à Bougival, *oil on canvas, 70" x 34". Renoir was a postimpressionist who extolled the sensuous delight of women and through his paintings recorded the human vivacity of Parisian street life in the latter part of the 19th century. Courtesy, Museum of Fine Arts, Boston, Mass.*

monies." Kandinsky considered his paintings to be compositions and improvisations. Mondrian's last painting, made in 1965, is titled *Broadway Boogie Woogie.* (See Figure 5-4.)

Many late nineteenth-century artists were concerned with portraying the condition of man in lower-class situations. Jean-François Millet in 1853 chose as content for a picture that has become famous, not dignified personages in graceful poses, but lowly peasants of the field bending to their task. The growing scientific attitude in which truth and reality were respected more than traditional correctness and allegorical referents was objectively realized by Gustave Courbet, who in 1855 defiantly organized his own one-man show *"Le Réalisme"* in Paris. Honoré Daumier carried reality further with his social commentary on the life of the poor in many expressive lithographs and paintings. Detached from past glories, he was true to his day, concerned only with the inglorious, which he saw everywhere around him. He is ranked today among the greatest expressionists of all time, but an ironic commentary upon man's visual bias toward accepting only the familiar and accepted is the fact that Daumier was buried in a pauper's grave.

Other artists were involved with resolving problems concerning the artistic presentation of form. Their interest in veracity led them to study light, color, shadow, and reflection as these impinge upon man's senses. It is necessary to understand the traditional method of recording light and shadow before one can fully appreciate the deviation of those who came to be called impressionists. The impressionists were interested in truth—not convention. The Academy had decreed that models pose in studios, with light from the window showing one side in high relief and the other gradually receding toward darkness. Figures and objects so treated assumed a solid sculptural three-dimensionalism. The practice of *sfumato,* the gradual blending of tones from light shining on the forms to shadow and darkness in the background, effected a unity between foreground and background and prevented a strong contrast between positive and negative space. Traditionally, artists painted indoors.

Edouard Manet was among the first to record his actual visual experience while painting outdoors and to develop what he considered a scientific theory of color, *"en plein air."* He found that when looking at nature, one does not see individual objects, each with its own single hue, but instead a wide range of shimmering colors that tend to blend in the eye and mind. Lights from neighboring objects, reflected on the surface of forms, tend to fragment form. In sunlight and open air, there is no gradual transition of color from light to dark as in the modeling practiced in studios. Instead, harsh contrasts often exist. Strong sunlight can also wipe out differences in color and between foreground and background. Partial delineation of forms was found sufficient to suggest the whole, with the participation of the viewer being required for their completion.

Claude Monet also explored the effects of outdoor light, to find that objects change from moment to moment with the sun's position, with passing clouds, and with winds ruffling the waters. To capture a moment or mood, one cannot take time to mix colors but must work rapidly, juxtaposing yellow and blue to create the sensation of green; green, orange, and purple in close contiguity produce blackness. Combinations of this kind result in more intense luminous color. Rapidly dashed brush strokes also suggest the movement and energy inherent in life and nature. It was Monet's *Impression—Sunrise,* shown in the famous 1874 exhibition of paintings and rejected by the Academy, that earned the designation "impressionism" (an opprobrium at that time) for any work done in a similar manner.

Vincent van Gogh worked in much the same technique as the impressionists but instead of depicting the outer world of nature, his paintings became an expression of man's inner world. Man's deep emotions constituted part of life's most intense reality to him, placing him with those later artists known as expressionists because of their portrayal of strongly felt psychic states. Such portrayal may necessitate the distortion of objects,

24-13 *Georges Seurat.* Sunday Afternoon on the Island of La Grande Jatte, *1884–86, oil on canvas, 81 x 120⅜". Lively stipples of color (pointillism) help the viewer to fuse the varied sparkling hues into consistent, well-integrated forms. Well-ordered patterns of light to dark values are handled with masterful precision. Courtesy of The Art Institute of Chicago.*

background out of the most intense and richest blue the palette will yield. The blond luminous head stands out against this strong blue background mysteriously like a star in the azure.

Others who also absorbed, borrowed from, and then outgrew the bounds of impressionism with its concentration upon light and color were the post-impressionists—among them Renoir, Seurat, Gauguin, Toulouse-Lautrec, Matisse, and Cézanne. Their interest gravitated to the architecture of a picture—to organized form, to the massing of consistent colors, and to the structuring of planes. Organization of space into vertical and horizontal planes is particularly evident in the painting of Georges Seurat. The name *pointillism* was given to his work because he achieved form by a concentration of colored dots made with the point of his brush, which gave the canvas the quality of a shimmering, translucent screen.

Cézanne was particularly dissatisfied with the limitations of impressionism as he saw them. He wished to retain all the light and color of impressionism but simultaneously to realize what he considered a vital criterion for effective composition—solidity of form. To achieve this he developed a technique that has become so standard today as to make him the contemporary artist's forebear.

Traditionally, form had been roundly modeled by gradually changing the values of a single hue from light to dark. The impressionists, with little concern for structure, had trasmitted the optical quality of light as reflected by surfaces into multiple hues. To them an apple was not red nor was a banana yellow, but an aggregate of colors, if one painted the variations he sees instead of the generalization he has learned.

In his composition Cézanne reclaimed emphasis on form but not by contour and modeling. Exploring the geometry of nature he devised abstract geometric compositions. The varying planes gained depth and solidity, not by gradual change of values, but by employing planes of different hues for the same object. Spatially,

the extreme gesture, and elimination of all unnecessary details to make the desired impact. Van Gogh's work reflects his emotions: "The emotions are sometimes so strong that one works without being aware of working . . . and the strokes come with a sequence or coherence like words in a speech or a letter." They also reflect the distortion and selective process used by van Gogh to achieve certain effects:

I exaggerate the fair colors of the hair, I take orange, chrome, lemon colours, and behind the head I do not paint the trivial wall of the room but the Infinite. I make a simple

24-14 Paul Cézanne. The Basket of Apples, *1890–94, oil on canvas, 24¾ x 32". The tilted table top has space created by the placement of object behind object and by some placed higher than others on the picture plane. Banished is the vanishing point to project the illusion of distance. Courtesy of The Art Institute of Chicago.*

24-15 *Paul Gauguin.* La Orana Maria, *oil on canvas, 44¾ x 34½".*
Background areas are almost as significant in the design as are the
human figures, making a tightly knit composition. Collection, The
Metropolitan Museum of Art, New York.

too, he made visual innovations. He avoided the conventional hazy atmosphere and diminution of form to show recession into distance. Instead, he used the eye as a telescopic lens to bring the background into equivocal focus with the foreground and manipulated the elements of line, form, and color to produce a tightly knit defiant composition. With these techniques he presaged Cubism.

Paul Gauguin, the businessman who fled to the South Pacific to paint and escape the materialism of his day, also used the elements for their potential to evoke emotional responses. In his paintings natives with orange-brown skins wear garments in complementary hues of blues and purples. Where red appears in a composition, green is immediately adjacent or not far distant in order to create intensity through polarity of hue. With his "barbaric" harmonies, he antedated the abstract expressionists of the 1950s, who likewise used color arbitrarily, frequently juxtaposing complements for their emotional impact.

Edgar Dégas also made a contribution to vision. Dégas noted the technique employed in Japanese prints of showing not an entire view, but figures cut by interceding structures. So he devised his ballet studies with ballerinas only partially seen or so far in the foreground that the canvas could not contain them. In the same way, he achieved depth by the placement of smaller figures in total view and by strong diagonal movements directing the eye into the composition. In addition, a heightened sense of drama was achieved by depicting the figure from its most convincing angle.

Matisse also showed little respect for colors and forms as they exist in nature. Ordinary photographic realism repelled him. He preferred to use intensity of form, line, and color, and to design arbitrarily in a decorative manner, free from any troubling subject matter. Like the abstract expressionists of the 1950s, he saw the elements as sufficient in themselves to create harmonious compositions that depend entirely upon the manipulation of the artist. Like other artists, among them van Gogh and Cézanne, he distorted certain elements purposely to gain the effects he wanted. As an example, when a complaint came to Matisse that he had drawn a figure with only three fingers, he replied:

But I couldn't put the other two in without throwing the three out of the drawing. It would destroy the composition and unity of my ideal. Perhaps some day, I may be able to get what I want of sentiment, of emotional appeal, and at

24-16 *Pablo Picasso. "Ma Jolie" (Woman with a Zither or Guitar), 1911–12, oil on canvas, 39⅜ x 25¾". Facets of fragmented light facilitate seeing not only some of the external lineaments of objects but also some insights into their internal dynamics. "You paint not what you see, but what you know is there," Picasso has said. Collection, The Museum of Modern Art, New York.*

the same time draw all five fingers! But the subjective idea is what I am after now. The rest can wait.

This response is typical of artists who create such tightly knit compositions that no one part can be altered without changing the whole.

Picasso, like Cézanne, valued form, so much so that his work is sometimes referred to as "sculpture in painting." In reviewing the temper of the early nineteenth century, Naum Gabo, who pioneered in the use of welding, which later revolutionized modern sculpture, wrote:

The artist of today cannot possibly escape the impact science is making in the whole mentality of the human race . . . both the artist and the ancient scientist are prompted by the same creative urge to find a perceptible image of the hidden forces in nature of which they are both aware. . . . I do not know of any idea in the history of man's culture that developed in a separate and independent compartment of the human mind and I do not believe there is any aspect in nature or life which is communicable exclusively through the means of one particular discipline. . . . To my mind it is a fallacy to assume that the aspects of life and nature which contemporary science is unfolding are only communicable through science itself.[3]

Was Picasso responding to the radar of scientific investigation, which permeated the thoughts of men during the early twentieth century, when he took upon himself in some of his work to analyze the nature of solid forms, to seemingly dissect and X-ray an object

[3]Quoted in György Kepes, *The New Landscape in Art and Science* (Chicago: Theobald, 1957), pp. 61–62.

in order to divulge its multiple facets? He broke open the volume of objects, spread them out upon the surface of the canvas, and showed their plural faces simultaneously—fragments of their inside, outside, sides, front, and back.

Another technique he used in his search for reality was transparent overlays to show both the inner and outer aspects of things. He presented for men's scrutiny the component parts of ordinary objects. He did not rely, as many of his predecessors had done, upon the external frontal image of things, but took as his province the multilateral and internal. In powerful visual statements he proclaimed that man the artist has both the prerogative and the necessity to transpose and reconstruct objects according to his arbitrary will and vision. Concern is not with beauty, but with revealing life and its true reality. "You paint not what you see, but what you know is there."

Picasso's work presents both the enigma and fascination of a paradox. In his painting, although only a trace

24-17 *Marc Chagall.* I and the Village, *1911, oil on canvas, 75⅝ x 59⅝". The dreamlike recall of childhood images is labelled by some as surrealism, but others may regard it as a truer or more comprehensive level of reality because it recognizes one of our significant human experiences. Collection, The Museum of Modern Art, New York.*

of the original semblance of an object may remain, one can see the object more intensely and comprehensively than ever before. It is as though a psychoanalyst has laid bare the hidden structure and sentience of objects. In this sense an artist's free association of thought has been subjected to aesthetic organization.

The expressionists and the surrealists further explored the subconscious as well as the conscious. The expressionists—Ernst Kirchner, Oskar Kokoschka, Max Peckstein, Emil Nolde, and Edvard Munch—shocked the bourgeois from their complacency by depicting the reality of the human condition. They painted with savage intensity to express their disgust with the accepted values of art and civilization. The ugly as well as the beautiful, the brutal as well as the benign, anguish as well as joy, and violence as well as restraint became valid content for the artist. With the surrealists—Marc Chagall, Paul Klee, Max Ernst, and Salvador Dali—man's dream life as well as his waking hours became a worthy subject for artistic effort. For these artists, things in their symbolic relationship could be more important than the things themselves. For them, subjective art had its own valid rationale.

An interesting phenomenon in man's presentation of the nature of meaningful reality is what was labelled Futurism, a movement begun in 1909, in which the artists painted dynamic and simultaneous action. Marcel Duchamp, interested in showing movement, painted a nude descending a staircase in a photographic sequence of multiple exposures (see Figure 4-26). Exhibited at the 1913 Armory Show in New York, it excited violent reaction and extreme derogation; among the many negative descriptions was that of an "explosion in a shingle factory." Yet Duchamp fathered many techniques employed by contemporary artists. He produced accidental and chance art by dropping pieces of thread on a canvas and varnishing them where they fell. His selection of ordinary machine-made objects as suitable material for compositions was endorsed by the pop artists of the 1960s, who decided to approach the ready-made objects of an industrial society in a positive manner (just as

Ferdnand Léger had accepted the machine as a potential for artful composition). Furthermore, in 1913 he painted a mustached and goateed Mona Lisa, in much the same spirit as in 1968 the artist portrayed Russia's Svetlana on the cover of *Esquire* magazine. In the same decade, his use of the box as an art form was adopted by Louise Nevelson and other contemporary sculptors. His dazzling eye baffler (a rotating disc), which was spun at 33 revolutions per minute, was a forerunner of contemporary kinetic art and sculpture. Duchamp also created in the Dadaist manner, a movement following World War I in which the artist deliberately intended to outrage and scandalize, much as was common in funk art expressions of the 1960s.

Recent Developments

Many movements in art such as abstract expressionism, optical art, and kinetic art and sculpture have been included in previous chapters, so not all are presented here. In summary, one could say that the art of the 1950s, with abstract expressionism a dominant form of expression, was more inner-oriented than that of the 1960s. With the 1960s, the youth culture became an internationally recognized force, and buoyant, blatant, and extroverted forms of art abounded. Disrespect for the establishment and for commercial values, similar to the Dadaist anti-art anticulture movement following World War I, was reflected in a variety of art forms. Easel painting and static sculpture seemed timid and irrelevant to many artists living during this turbulent decade. Pop art, assemblage art and sculpture, process art of various forms, and psychedelic art expanded the boundaries of conventional art forms. No longer was art regarded as "precious," but as ever-changing, quickly constructed, temporary, and expendable. Man's total environment was taken as subject matter, including such elements as light, air, noise, smell, electric shock, and the earth

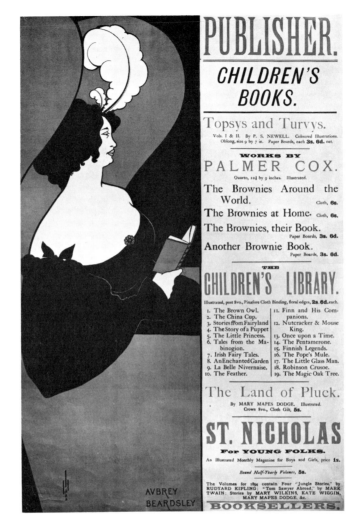

24-18 *Aubrey Beardsley. Poster for a book publisher. The undulating, bold curves and the power of contrasting values of the neutrals of black, gray, and white make an arresting statement. Victoria and Albert Museum, London. Crown Copyright.*

itself. And youths could identify and find pleasure both in dress and in art forms from the past that paralleled in expression their own inner tensions and experiences.

The Poster

Among the old forms that have gained renewed popularity is the poster. The poster is a message expressed in graphic form whose purpose is to advertise or publicize; in France of the late nineteenth century and in the United States during the 1960s, however, it received acknowledgment as an art form. Cro-Magnon man depicted his hunting expeditions and rituals on the walls of his caves; the governments of antiquity published their laws on large stone plaques for the public to read; armies waved banners and flags; merchants established their identity by signs of their trade hung outside their shops. Their aims were to be visibly accessible to all, to convey a message with as much expediency as possible, and if possible to produce a haunting reminiscence. For these needs poster art proved an ideal medium. Famous poster artists included Toulouse-Lautrec, who painted the characters to be seen at the famed Moulin Rouge, and Aubrey Beardsley, who worked in the black-and-white value scale. In the 1960s, there was a renaissance of interest in poster art as young people were attracted to the qualities of a poster: immediacy, impermanence, colorfulness, change, expressiveness, and decorativeness. Among the artists were Peter Max and Osborn/Woods. Through them and others, the poster became a most expressive and versatile medium suitable for expressing the many moods of the 1960s. Its content ranged from politics, astrology, personalities, announcements of rock band concerts, words, places, and superimpositions of multiple images to the visual equivalencies of rock sound.

24-19 *Osborn/Woods*. The Sign of the Rainbow (*from the Genesis Series*), *silk-screened, 1967. Courtesy of Osborn/Woods.*

The Assemblage

An assemblage is a collage in three dimensions made from objects instead of pasted papers and textures. In the 1960s, articles manufactured out of fragments were incorporated into wall or free-standing sculptures. Reflecting the visual vernacular of the day, they were described by art critic Harold Rosenberg as "materials talking back to the civilization that is producing them." There were also assemblages *en tableau,* in which a collection of people in a setting of daily living were presented as in the Argentinian Marisol Escobar's wooden forms (Figure 19-6) with photographs and paintings of people depicting *The Family;* George Segal's *The Diner,* composed of plaster figures in a lifelike scene; and pop artist Edward Kienholz's beanery assemblage.

Supergraphics

Graphic art is a general term that has encompassed every form of visual communication by means of which man has reproduced his knowledge and visual impressions on a multiple scale. As early as A.D. 880, the Chinese introduced relief wood-block printing as the first graphic hand process for artistic reproductions. Also commonly associated with graphic arts have been serigraphy, etching, lithography, and linoleum block printing. Through these means the works of masters such as Braque, Kandinsky, Munch, Miró, and Chagall have passed into greater circulation.

With the 1950s and 1960s the graphic arts, influenced by pop and psychedelia, moved away from their relatively conservative tradition and became a pulsating movement, climaxing in "supergraphics." Applied to interior design, supergraphics makes use of superscale forms in vivid colors that sweep in racing stripes up and down walls and ceilings and across doors and hallways to bind a room into a unified whole. Supergraphics has destroyed the concept of the room as a box, for ugly radiators or unattractive or poorly placed doors can be screened out by skillful use of the arresting colors and movement.

Ripples of color running from the walls were also carried through in rugs designed specifically with the room and wall graphics in mind. Some wallpaper companies, caught up in the movement, no longer created timid, repeated patterns but murals to cover an entire wall. Wall-mounted systems, supergraphic in dimension, were designed that could encompass the length of a room, be moved up and down the wall's surface, and house bins, bar, record changer, and other domestic objects. With supergraphics, interiors became vivid, exciting environments with pronounced rhythms.

Funk Art

Funk art is a form of assemblage with pronounced Dadaist characteristics. Like the Dadaists, the funk artists

24-20 *Nils Anderson.* #205 *Kinetics II, 48″-wide large-scale zigzag geometric wall design. Nils Anderson Studios, Inc., New York.*

24-21 *Robert Arneson. Rose, ceramic, funk art, 19½″ x 12″. The softness and delicacy of a rose are transposed into harsh, resistant clay. There is a paradoxical play in juxtaposing elements to extend our taken-for-granted expectations. Courtesy Robert Arneson.*

juxtaposed unexpected objects for their shock value. Though senseless and absurd, and often irreverent and disrespectful of traditional values and materials, their art reflects a sense of humor and an appreciation for subtleness. The artists have delighted in exploiting the vulgarity of common objects from our daily environment and changing elements from them into artistic imagery. They have shown us that even our anatomical organs— the viscera, kidneys, and lips—have design value. Basically enigmatic, funk's character was described by artist William Tunberg as "Art is not a science or a picture anymore. It is an object that exists for itself but it also conveys something more than just pure decoration— not exactly a message but a hunch."

Process Art and Happenings

The term *happening,* coined by Alan Kaprow in 1959, could also be considered a collage, a collage that might include time, space, people, music, and an activity. The elements of wonder, surprise, and excitement are often present when one expects that something unknown is going to happen. In this respect, happenings reflect the Zen Buddhist attitude of homage to the spontaneous and the now. Happenings have ranged in activity from the process of wrapping things up with plastics, such as galleries, monuments, women, and even entire cliffsides, to filling in a grave, and to more complex theatrical shows such as Robert Morris's thirty-nine minutes for thirty-nine autos in which people on Twin Peaks in San Francisco followed a program for sounding of horns and blinking of headlights with the action presented simultaneously televised. In all these, emphasis was upon collective activity and participation. Unlike theatrical productions, happenings require no consecutive plot, continuity, or related scenes. Events are often unconnected, unstructured, and unrehearsed and reflect a delight in paradoxes. Though a collective activity, through participation and involvement in the happening, the individual produces and becomes the work of art. The aim is a total sensory experience, as expressed by French artist Jean-Jacques Label:

I think art is supposed to provoke a crisis that will change a person's whole idea of himself.

Don't worship art—let it happen to you. The truth is that art is just the experience. The way you feel at a happening, the way you evade it or participate in it—these things make up your portrait, and your portrait *is* the work of art.[4]

Psychedelic Art

Of the art forms of the 1960s, psychedelic art was the most joyous expression and a celebration of the self. In it, youth found an expression to match its own restlessness and vibrancy. Whereas the surrealistic artist often painted images to reflect bizarre, dreamlike states and the hallucinations of a distorted mind, the psychedelic artist sought out images and sensations in the depths of the normal but expanded mind. The aim was to communicate spiritual and aesthetically beautiful experiences. In common with other art forms of the 1960s, the intent of the artist was often to shock the viewer into increased awareness and intensified perception.

The psychedelic artist is one whose artistic expression has been created during or after a psychedelic experience, which could be either chemically or self-educed. During a psychedelic experience one may experience synesthesia, a cross-sensory sensation in which one hears colors and sees sounds. (See Marcel Breuer's poem, p. 196.) There is often a richness and overload of sensations and a feeling that one is inside his own body. The artist tries to depict these simultaneous and heightened states in order to awaken the viewer's dormant feelings. As such, psychedelic art could be identified as any work that "turns one on."

[4]*Life* (Feb. 17, 1967), p. 92.

Impersonal Expressions

In the late 1960s, some artists showed not only a rejection of conventional artists' materials and techniques, but a marked impersonality as well. As an example, pop artist Andy Warhol clipped a picture of Marilyn Monroe from a magazine, had a silk screen cut, and then printed the same head over and over again without his hand ever touching the canvas. The sculptor, too, could order a steel beam to be painted a certain shade of red with instructions that it be delivered to the particular door of a particular museum. He would then supervise the leaning of the steel beam at the desired angle against an inside wall of the gallery—his "work of art" accomplished without his touching the beam. Carrying the expression still further, the artist might pile all his paintings in a heap and, after the arrival of his friends and the press, who had been invited to witness the act, he would set fire to his work. This was considered his true and final work of art, referred to in the vernacular of the day as "doing one's thing."

These are expressions of our time as all art is and always has been. Such gestures call for a new and strange appreciation, but like new music, poetry, dance, and like the rise and fall of hemlines, the more we see, the more we accept. Likewise, familiarity in art can breed respect as well as disrespect.

Where will the artist go from here? The only certainty is that his expression will be different and related to the world of tomorrow. Meanwhile in our space age, art is geared to light, space, movement, physics, electronics, computers, energy, the inner dynamics of man and materials, and above all—to experimentation.

Definition of Design Terms

Abstract expressionism: A term first applied to the work of a number of abstract painters in New York after World War II in which emphasis was placed upon the act of painting as being of prime importance, rather than the content of the painting, and which also emphasized art as an expression of the emotions.

Action painting, or *tachisme*: Producing a painting by means of unorthodox painters' tools. This can be accomplished by splashing, trickling, and throwing with sticks or trowels. Jackson Pollock devised the technique in 1947 to "feel near, more a part of the painting."

***Amor vacui*:** Refined sparseness, appreciated by Mackintosh, Voysey, and Whistler at the turn of the twentieth century. Antonym: *horror vacui.*

Amphora: An ancient vessel for wine or oil first created in Egypt, later developed and refined in Greece. It had a flat base, a slightly shouldered body connected by two handles, and a wide neck crowned by a distinct rim.

Annealing: A process of subjecting metal to heat in order to change it from a hard, nonmalleable state, which results from hammering, bending, or forging, to a soft state that can be worked.

Appliqué: An assemblage of materials made by stitching materials to each other in order to create a more exciting design.

Beauty: "The perceived harmonious relationship of all the parts." John C. Simonds, landscape architect.

Bessemer process: Converting iron to steel by blowing air that has been enriched with oxygen through molten iron to burn out the carbon content to exceed no more than 2 per cent. In the open hearth method the process of removing impurities and carbon is practiced on cold stock in steel-making furnaces.

Cantilever: A projection supported at only one end. In engineering, two beams that project from piers toward each other and that, when joined, form a span, are cantilevered.

Calico: A cotton, exported from Calcutta, India, that was usually textured with flowers, seed pods, vines, and trailing grasses. Sometimes called chintz.

Ariel glass: Patterns are created in glass by sandblasting into the core of the glass and laying a casing over the forms to enclose channels of air. The technique was invented by Edwin Öhrstrom for Sweden's Orrefors glassworks.

Arabesque: French for "in the Arab manner." A linear surface decoration with swirls of flowers, foliage, and scroll work fancifully intertwined.

Assemblage: The creation of three-dimensional objects by taking things or fragments of things from their accustomed structures or environments and combining them in a new context.

Baccarat: The name given to exotic glass produced in Baccarat, France, by the *Compagnie des Cristalleries de Baccarat*.

Baroque: A term applied to seventeenth- and eighteenth-century art in which stylistic features were often turbulent and bold, as can be noted in the twisted columns of Baldini's chapel in Saint Peter's, Rome, and in Michelangelo's frescoes in the Sistine Chapel.

Batik: A resist-dyeing process in which wax is painted on a fabric; when dipped in a dye solution, the waxed portions resist the color.

Biomorphic: Related to nature and its patterns of growth, therefore often irregular.

Block print: A relief design cut into wood or linoleum, whose surface is then inked and brushed with a roller that transfers the colored design to a material.

Bonsai: A Japanese miniature tree, from *bon,* "a pot," and *soi,* "a plant."

Calligraphy: Beautiful or elegant writing made with a pen, brush, or similar tool.

Cameo-carved cased glass: Glass in which the outer colored layers have been cut away to produce a surface relief pattern, as in the famous Portland vase.

Capital: The uppermost section of a column, which is placed above the shaft and supports the entablature.

Carat: A measure of the purity of gold. Pure gold is 24 carats; an alloy with 50 per cent gold is 12 carats.

Cartouche: A decorative frame enclosing an inscription, a coat of arms, or a similar motif.

Caryatid: A draped female figure, which serves as an architectural column, such as those used as supports in Greek temple architecture.

Cased or flashed glass: Glass in which a layer of contrasting colored glass has been superimposed onto the glass bubble before blowing, to increase its color potential.

Casting: Pouring molten metal into molds structured to the desired form, or with stamps that impress the design into a metal sheet. The impressive Shang bronzes of China were cast in a mold of hard clay in which the design was carved in reverse. In the archaic Greek period of 600 B.C., bowls of vessels were frequently hammered, whereas the feet and handles were cast and riveted or soldered to the bowl.

Celadon: A glaze associated with Chinese porcelain, which ranges in color from gray-green to olive-green.

Chasing: The use of hammer and punches to delineate line on the face of metals by a series of oblique indentations of the punch.

Chiaroscuro: Italian, meaning "light-dark." The science of dealing with light and shade in painting to produce strongly contrasting tones.

Champlevé enamel: A decorative process of cutting troughs into a metal into which a glassy material is poured and fused by heating.

Chinoiserie: A term from the French word *chinois,* which evolved in the mid-eighteenth century to describe works of art emanating from China, Japan, and the Dutch East Indies, and also European products inspired by them. In Europe, the motifs were used on many forms of decorative art. As a result, the original forms often became debased because they were combined with European fanciful motifs or created from word-of-mouth descriptions brought back by travelers and Jesuit missionaries.

Classicism: Art that favored the Greco-Roman ideals and placed emphasis on reason, objectivity, discipline, restraint, and order. A contrast to romanticism.

Cloisonné: An Oriental technique of enameling that was much used in the early Middle Ages. The glass materials (frit) were melted into areas defined by wires soldered to the surface being decorated.

Collage: A term derived from the French word *coller,* "to paste, or glue," hence the glueing of miscellaneous bits and pieces of newsprint, colored papers, photographs, string, fabric, etc., to a canvas, paper, or panel. Among early artists to use the technique were Max Ernst, Braque, and Picasso.

Contrapposto: An Italian term in which the posture of the body's hips and legs face in one direction and the torso in the opposite.

Constructivism: A twentieth-century movement with Naum Gabo and Antoine Pevsner (Russian brothers) and Lásló Moholy-Nagy as its chief proponents. Their three-dimensional abstract sculptures abandoned the monolith as the central core around which volumes were organized and were constructed instead in harmony with new concepts in physics and mathematics and the materials of modern technology.

Coptic: Name given to the Early Christian period in Egypt between the fourth and seventh centuries. Their artistic work tended to be flat rather than three-dimensional.

Crystal: A term derived from the Greek *krystallos*, "clear ice," originally applied to the transparent fifteenth-century Venetian glass. High-quality crystal today must contain at least 18 per cent lead oxide, which provides the necessary clarity and a bell-like resonance when the glass is tapped.

Cubism: An art form popular between 1909 and 1914. In analytical cubism, the first stage of cubism, forms were analyzed and reduced to their basic geometric constituents. In synthetic cubism the fragmental forms were reorganized into novel, many-faceted configurations. Gris, Léger, Picasso, and Braque were influenced by the movement.

Dada: The expression through art forms—painting or assemblages—to show disdain for current cultural standards or modes of design. The movement began during World War I and was revitalized as "funk art" in the 1960s.

de Stijl: A movement that took its name from a review published in 1917 by a group of Dutch painters, architects, and sculptors. Mainly inspired by the work of Mondrian, its design was orderly, intellectual, and impersonal.

Deutscher Werkbund: A society, formed in 1907, which is recognized as one of the most significant movements in the history of industrial design, antedating the Bauhaus, aimed at improving the standards of design and industry by collaboration of manufacturers, architects, and craftsmen.

Earthenware: Relatively unrefined clay that, when heated at low temperatures, produces porous vessels that must be glazed to become waterproof.

English East India Company: Company launched by Queen Elizabeth in 1600 that first brought the wealth of decorative design to European shores. The Netherlands United East India Company likewise helped disseminate the strange and fascinating visual imagery of the East.

Diatretra glass: A term given to a small group of highly valued glasses from the fourth century A.D. of Rheno-Roman origin. They consist of a solid vessel surrounded by a basketlike network of interlaced ornaments. This outer ornamental layer is joined to the solid inner core of the vessel by short glass struts.

Eclectic: An adjective that describes the selection and combination of forms and ideas from earlier and contemporary art forms.

Embossing, or repoussé: Hammering the reverse side of a sheet of bronze placed over an asphalt block, which yields to the hammer's blows, producing an alternation of concave and convex contours.

Electroplating: A process, introduced about 1842, whereby a layer of silver is deposited by electrolysis onto a baser metal.

Enameled decoration of glass: Metal oxides are applied to the surface of glass vessels by means of an oily medium. The glass is then fired at 700–800°C. and the areas to which lead content has been applied fuse into the glass to produce a reflecting surface.

Engraving, a. glass: A method of decorating glass by means of attrition. A glass is pressed against rapidly rotated copper wheels.

b. metal: Incising a line in a metal, which removes part of the substance to create a design.

Etching, a. glass: Decorating glass by coating negative areas with wax and exposing the design to a solution of hydrofluoric acid, which bites into the glass to create a frosted texture.

b. metal A printing process by which a design is cut into a metal plate, coated with wax, by a sharply pointed tool. The plate is then placed in an acid bath, which bites into the unwaxed areas to create a design that can be inked and rolled through a press.

Expressionism: A term applied to art when form, line, and color are governed by an artist's need to express emotion. Distortion, exaggeration of form, marked simplification of line, and strong color are frequently present. The works of van Gogh, Munch, and El Greco are representative.

Expressiveness: A quality of vitality imparted to forms created from inert materials such as stone and clay, which results in dynamic design relationships through the material's unique qualities and the designer's incorporation of some of his own particular life force.

Famille verte* and *famille rose: In the green family and in the red family, respectively.

Forging: Working metals by massive hammer blows.

Forth bridge: An iron bridge over Scotland's Firth of Forth, with a span of 1,710 feet, designed by Fowler and Baker, 1881–1887, which has been considered the most splendid of all cantilevered bridges.

Found object (French *objet trouvé*): Any natural object found by chance, such as a pebble or a shell, that is cherished because it contains aesthetic elements paralleling those in a work of art.

Futurism: An Italian movement (1905–1915) that embraced the machine aesthetic and interpreted its dynamism, speed, power, and motion through a continual transformation of forms.

Genre painting: A type of small-scale painting showing scenes from everyday life rather than idealized or exalted forms. Representative examples: Vermeer, Chardin, Gainsborough.

Glaze, a. ceramics: A vitreous coating of minerals and silicates that produce an impervious coating to earthenware or can increase its decorative quality.

      b. painting: A thin layer or layers of paint applied to a canvas to increase its transparency or luminosity. It can also be scraped back to achieve more complex textural and color nuance.

Golden means (golden section): A system of proportion formulated by Vitruvius, the Roman architect, that was thought to possess an intrinsic aesthetic virtue. Through it a line could be divided in such a way that the smaller would be to the larger as the larger to the whole.

Gothic: A period from the twelfth to as late as the sixteenth century in some parts of Western Europe in which painting, sculpture and architecture were nonclassical. It was characterized by intense religious feeling, which produced a soaring elongation of forms, pointed arches, ribbed vaulting, and the use of window tracery filled with stained glass.

Graal glass: Glass that has been made by cutting patterns into layers of casings of glass and then firing the glass to regain some of its quality of fluidity.

Grand manner: Representation during the High Renaissance period of human figures in noble and exalted themes as prescribed by the academies. Subject matter for painting was codified in order of ideal preference with historic painting ranked first and genre painting low. Numerous rules were devised that included how to depict sentiment and passion.

Grotesque: Decoration, often three-dimensional, with human and animal forms fantastically interwoven with foliage and scrolls. These were derived from Roman murals, where bizarre, exaggerated, or distorted forms were common.

Haniwa: Clay cylinders at the margins of Japanese burial mounds that presumably served to check soil erosion. Later sculptural figures were used to decorate the tops of these tubular forms.

Hollow ware: China or metal wares in the form of hollow vessels such as bowls and pitchers, as distinguished from flatware.

Horror vacui: A human psychological reaction that implies fear of a vacuum or unfilled area.

Hyperbolic-paraboloid: A doubly curved surface that has the important property that it can be generated by straight lines.

Impasto: Paint applied thickly to a panel or canvas, often with a palette knife, which creates a low relief.

Impressionism: A term used to describe the process of artists who painted dabs and dots of color, leaving unpainted areas of white canvas between colors to compound the sunlight reflected by the pigment and to create an outdoor ambience.

Inlaying or damascening metal: The art of encrusting metals, which originated in the Orient with the goldsmiths of Damascus. Fine cuts are made in the surface of metals to admit gold, silver, or copper threads that are hammered into the fine groovings to produce variations in color and light reflection.

Integrity of materials: Each material, having its own chemical composition and physical properties, will react differently under forces of compression, tension, or torsion. Each has its own color and textural potential, depending upon its molecular composition. The designer who respects the integrity of materials is responsive to these.

Jigger: A machine carrying a revolving mold in which clay is shaped.

Kaolin: Chinese for "high hill," named for the fine white clay of China where it was originally found and used to form the paste of porcelain.

Kinesthetic: The sensation of movement, which can be realized either physically or visually through structuring the elements of art.

Lalique: An Art Nouveau glass artist who concentrated on bringing out the qualities of materials in creating jewelry, whereas previously the value of jewelry had been based solely upon its preciousness.

Lithography: The art of reproducing printed impressions on stone, zinc, or aluminum by use of an oily or water-repellent substance.

Lost-wax process (*cire perdue*): A process employed by Egyptians, ca. 2500 B.C., by the Sumerians in the dawn of civilization, and by the Chinese during the late Chou period. A wax model is bathed with successive washes of diluted clay to form a firm mold. Runners are made in the clay to allow the wax to escape when subjected to heat. The vacuum is then filled with molten bronze and when sufficiently cool, the clay mold is removed to reveal the image. Hollow forms are made by providing a central core of clay over which wax is modeled and washed over with a clay mixture. Removal of the inner and outer layer of clay leaves a hollow shell.

Majolica: Term for pottery glazed with tin to produce a white background, to which is then applied richly decorative design with metallic oxide. First developed in Majorca, during the sixteenth century, it parallels Holland's Delft, a generic term for all pottery produced in the Low Countries, and the faïence earthenware produced in France.

Malleable: Able to be molded or shaped.

Metal: A glassmakers' term for the material after it has been fused in the furnace.

Millefiori glass: "Thousand-flowered glass": bundles of small glass rods, with a pattern in cross section, are fused together and cut to a desired thickness. These pieces may then be fused side by side to make larger designs.

Mosaic: A method of decoration used for floors, walls, and vaulted ceilings since ancient times, which involves the use of tesserae, small cubes of colored glass, stone, marble, or enamel set into cement.

Motif: The recurrent theme or dominant form of a design.

Negative space: The area surrounding motifs (positive space) that functions as background or field.

Niello: An ancient form of applied decoration used to heighten the contrast in color and reflectance of metals. A powdered compound of metals is inlaid in a receiving metal and then fused and burnished when cool. Niello was also applied to French furniture during the periods of Louis XIII through Louis XVI, but then became a lost art, which only recently has been revived.

Odalisque: A voluptuous inmate of an Oriental harem, who appealed as a design subject particularly to Ingres, Renoir, and Matisse.

Optical art: A surface topography in which the manipulation of the elements of design into multiple and equivocal configurations may cause one's vision to become overstimulated and fatigued.

Optical illusion: A visual experience in which a discrepancy exists between one's perceptual judgment and the actual physical character of the original stimulus.

Ormolu: A colored alloy of copper, zinc, and tin used to create gilded bronze for decorating furniture, particularly during the eighteenth century.

Parthenon: The Temple of Athena on the Acropolis at Athens, designed by Ictinus and other Greek architects between 447 and 438 B.C. It is considered to be one of the world's most significant structures and to incorporate the chief principles of design.

Patina: An oxide produced naturally or artificially on the surface of a metal.

Photogram: Image taken on light sensitive paper without use of film.

Pierre Brassau: A chimpanzee (with a penchant for paint) whose daubings were entered by his owners in a competition of abstract paintings. His work was reviewed by one art critic as "Pierre Brassau paints with powerful strokes, but also with clear determinism. His brush strokes twist with furious fastidiousness. Pierre is an artist who performs with the delicacy of a ballet dancer." (*Time*, February 21, 1964).

Pilotis: Free-standing columns at ground level, often employed by architect Le Corbusier to free the lower level of his buildings for aesthetic enjoyment or landscaping.

Planishing: Smoothing the surface of a sheet of metal by beating it on an anvil with a special hammer.

Pontil, or punty: The iron rod to which glass vessels are transferred before their removal from the blowing iron for further working.

Pneumatic: Inflated with air, such as a plastic shelter.

Popular or pop art: An art form of the 1960s that exploited the ordinary and commercial aspects of the environment by the use of large-scale and mechanical repetition of forms.

Pointillism: A technique of painting favored by neoimpressionists, which consisted of small dots or strokes of pure color whose placement in relationship to each other was so calculated that they fused to create forms and colors in the eye of the beholder.

Porcelain: A ceramic containing feldspar and kaolin that can be fired at high temperatures to produce a semitranslucent ware that is impervious to moisture. Adding bone increases the translucency of the china. Stoneware is of the same nature but is made from coarser clays.

Pre-Columbian Art: Art of the America's before Spanish and other conquests; it includes such cultures as the Aztec, Mayan, and Peruvian.

Prestressed concrete: A reinforced concrete strengthened by stretching high-tensile steel strands within concrete forms before the concrete sets. When the tension is released, the strands encased in the concrete attempt to return to their former length, simultaneously squeezing the concrete particles to greater density and strength.

Pressed glass: Molten glass, poured and pressed into a mold.

Raising, metal: A hand-hammering process by which a sheet of flat metal is formed into a seamless hollow vessel.

Repoussé: Ornamental metalwork produced by hammering a metal into relief from the reverse side. The design may be further accentuated from the right side by *chasing*, in which hammer and punches are used to strengthen the line of the decorative detail and deepen the relief.

Rococo: A style that reached its peak during the reign of Louis XV. Derived from the French word *rocaille*, meaning "pebble or rock," it indicated a line that was free flowing, profuse, and often asymmetrical.

Romanesque: A Western European style of architecture, sculpture, and painting based upon Roman prototypes, which was dominant from the ninth to the twelfth century and characterized by bold, rounded curves.

Romanticism: In opposition to classicism, a dominant style or attitude of mind developed during the late eighteenth and nineteenth centuries that placed emphasis upon natural phenomena, imagination, emotions, individuality, and asymmetry.

Rya: A Swedish word meaning rug in English. Formerly a bed cover in Sweden, with knotted pile, soft sheen, and warmth, used to replace the fur-skin bed covers.

Sfumato: A term derived from the Italian *sfumare*, "to tone down, disappear, or blend." Technique of painting used in the Renaissance to dissolve the outlines of objects by subtle series of color gradations.

Sgraffito: Italian for "scratching," a method of decorating ceramics by coating an object with a glaze and scratching through it to produce a design by revealing the color beneath.

Shōsō-in: The Japanese repository of Imperial household objects created in 756 for the preservation of Chinese and Japanese artifacts.

Silk-screen printing: A process by which a stencil is placed on a piece of silk stretched over a wooden frame. The background of the design can be masked out by several means. Ink is then pulled over the silk by a spatulate tool and the ink passes through the part of the stencil not treated by a substance to form a design.

Soldering: Joining pieces of metal by another metal or alloy that flows in the presence of heat.

Space: A variously defined element of design. Practically any line, color, splotch, or hole made on a planed surface can generate the sensation of space.

Spinning: A method of metalcraft used for the softer metals, such as gold and silver, in which a sheet of metal is placed over a model of the desired form, which is secured to a lathe. With rapid revolution of the lathe, the metal is formed into shape.

Sterling silver: The word *sterling* stamped on the back of a piece of silver indicates that it meets the U.S. government standard for solid silver. The National Stamping Act passed in 1907 standardized sterling content at 925 parts silver to 75 parts of an alloy.

Streamline: A contour to decrease air resistance in the design of airplanes, automobiles, and steamships for greater speed and fluidity of movement. Through study of the structure of porpoises, fish, and falling raindrops designers learned that gliding forms can more easily overcome resistance when passing through air or water than can those with projections. The designers of everyday objects in the United States were particularly influenced by its stringency.

Style: A design expression in a particular historic era that reflects the philosophical and material forces of the time.

Surrealism: A movement launched in 1924 to indicate a super-reality, that of the unconscious, dreams, and fantasies. The surrealist manifesto assigned the artist the task of liberating the soul of man from the chains of reason and inhibition. Max Ernst, Salvador Dali, Marc Chagall were active surrealists.

Symbol: A shorthand form of belief expressed in terms of line, form, and color. A symbol suggests something by reason of relationship, association, or convention—such as a flag representing a country.

Tempera: A painting medium made by mixing ground-up pigment with a binding agent, such as egg or casein, and diluting it with water.

Terra cotta: "Baked earth" pottery of a brownish red color that is hard and unglazed.

Tie-and-dye: A process by which fabric is variously tied with string and then dyed. The tied sections act as a resist to the dye.

Trailing: A method of decorating glass known since Roman times in which a lump of softened glass is drawn into thread and attached to the surface of a heated vessel. Italian *latticino* glass is created by this method.

Tree of Life: The tree of life, exotic and asymmetrical, was a synthesis of many trees of the ancient Eastern fertility cults, dating back possibly to the tree in the Garden of Eden from which man was expelled. The motif was popular in both Persian and Oriental arts.

Triptych: Three panels or panels hinged together, as in the ivory triptychs of the Middle Ages.

Trompe l'oeil: A French term meaning "deceives the eye." Painting in which still-life objects are rendered so realistically that they seem three-dimensional and tangible.

Ukiyo-e: Japanese for "mirror of the transient world." The wood blacks of seventeenth-century Japan depicted everyday scences of people at work or at their leisure. The works of Utamaro, Hokusai, and Kiroshige are representative.

Unity with variety: Areas of concentrated interest are countered by areas of rest.

Vermeil: Gold-plated sterling silver.

Waldglass: Glass of a heavy primitive quality produced in glassworks fired by wood (*wald*) in Central Europe between the fifteenth and eighteenth centuries, which contrasts with Venetian crystal.

Sources of Reference

The following is a list of sources to which the author referred or which relate to the designated topics. Newspapers, periodicals, and the *Encyclopaedia Britannica* also provided a wealth of information.

Design Inspiration

Ballinger, Louise, and Thomas Vroman. *Design: Sources and Resources.* New York: Reinhold Publishing Corporation, 1965.

Barford, George. "Form and Structures: A Pictorial Essay." *Everyday Art,* **45** (Winter 1967).

Barr, Beryl. *Wonders, Warriors, and Beasts Abounding: How the Artist Sees His World.* Garden City, N.Y.: Doubleday Company, Inc., 1968.

Eisenstaedt, Alfred, *Witness to Nature.* New York: The Viking Press, 1971.

Fabun, Don. *You and Creativity.* Beverly Hills, Calif.: Glencoe Press, 1971.

Horst, H. P. *Patterns from Nature.* New York: J. J. Augustin, 1946.

Howard, Constance. *Inspiration for Embroidery.* London: Batsford, 1966.

Linderman, Earl W. *Invitation to Vision: Ideas and Imaginations for Art.* Dubuque, Ia.: William C. Brown Company, Publishers, 1967.

Ritchie, James. *Design in Nature.* New York: Scribner, 1937.

Elements, Principles, and Evaluation of Design

Anderson, Donald M. *Elements of Design.* New York: Holt, Rinehart and Winston, Inc., 1961.

Beitler, Ethel, and Bill Lockhart. *Design for You.* New York: John Wiley & Sons, Inc., 1961.

Bevlin, Marjorie. *Design Through Discovery.* New York: Holt, Rinehart and Winston, Inc., 1970.

Birren, Faber. *Creative Color*. New York: Reinhold Publishing Corporation, 1961.

Cornford, Christopher. "Cold Rice Pudding and Revisionism." *Design* 231 (March 1968), pp. 46ff.

Downer, Marion. *The Story of Design*. New York: Lothrop, Lee and Shepard Co., Inc., 1963.

Drexler, Arthur, and Greta Daniel. *Introduction to Twentieth-Century Design*. Collection of the New York Museum of Modern Art, 1959. Distributed by Doubleday.

"The Dynamics of Shape," *Design Quarterly* **64.**

Goldstein, Harriet, and Vetta Goldstein. *Art in Everyday Life*. New York: The Macmillan Company, 1954.

Grillo, Paul Jacques. *What Is Design?* Chicago: Paul Theobald and Company, 1967.

"A Guide to Well Designed Products," *Every Day Art Quarterly, Nos.* **15, 16, 20.** Walker Art Center, Minneapolis.

Gump, Richard. *Good Taste Costs No More*. Garden City, N.Y.: Doubleday, & Company, Inc., 1951.

Kepes, Gyorgy, "Light and Design," *Design Quarterly* **68.**

Kepes, Gyorgy. *The New Landscape*. Chicago: Paul Theobald and Company, 1967.

"Knife/Fork/Spoon," *Design Quarterly* **18-19.**

Kojiro, Yuichiro. *Forms in Japan*. Honolulu: East-West Center Press, 1965.

Kranz, Stewart, and Robert Fisher. *The Design Continuum: An Approach to Understanding Visual Forms*. New York: Reinhold Publication Corporation, 1966.

Krause, Joseph H. *The Nature of Art*. Englewood Cliffs, N. J.: Prentice-Hall, Inc., 1969.

Moholy-Nagy, László. *The New Vision and Abstract of an Artist*. New York: George Wittenborn, 1949.

Moholy-Nagy. László, *Vision in Motion*. Chicago: Paul Theobald and Company, 1947.

Piene, Nan R. "Light Art," *Art in America* (May–June 1967), pp. 24–47.

Pye, David. "How Will Furniture Develop?" *Country Life* 23 (March 1967), pp. 47ff.

Read, Herbert. *Art and Industry: The Principles of Industrial Design*. New York: Horizon Press, 1954.

Rosenberg, Jacob. *On Quality of Art*. Criteria of Excellence, Past and Present. Mellon Lectures in the Fine Arts. Princeton, N.J.: Princeton University Press, 1964.

Simonds, John C. "A Search for Quality," *Interiors* (October 1967), pp. 22, 180.

Smith, Laura J. *The Development of a Symbol*. Designed and submitted in partial fulfillment of the requirement for the MFA degree in Graphic Design from the Yale University School of Art and Architecture. New Haven, Conn.: John H. Graaf, printer, 1966.

"Tradition in Good Design," *Design Art Quarterly* **16.**

Warner, Esther. *Art: An Everyday Experience*. New York: Harper and Row, Publishers, Inc., 1963.

Decorative Objects

California Design, Eight, Ten, and Eleven. Pasadena Art Museum publications, Pasadena, California., 1962, 1968, 1971.

Moody, Ella, (editor). *Decorative Art in Modern Interiors*. New York: The Viking Press. Published in yearly editions.

Slivka, Rose. *The Crafts of the Modern World*. New York: Horizon Press, 1968. (Published in collaboration with the World Crafts Council, New York City.)

Architects and the Modern Movement

Bittermann, Eleanor. *Art in Modern Architecture*. New York: Reinhold Publishing Corporation, 1952.

Breuer, Marcel, *Design Quarterly* **53.**

Bush-Brown, Albert. *Louis Sullivan*. New York: George Braziller, Inc., 1960.

Choay, Françoise. *Le Corbusier*. New York: George Braziller, Inc., 1960.

Drexler, Arthur. *Ludwig Mies van der Rohe*. New York: George Braziller, Inc., 1960.

Fitch, James Marston. *Walter Gropius*. New York: George Braziller, Inc., 1960.

Huxtable, Ada Louise. *Pier Luigi Nervi*. New York: George Braziller, Inc., 1960.

Madsen, S. Tschudi. *Art Nouveau*. New York: McGraw-Hill Book Company, Inc., 1967.

McMullen, Roy. "Gaudi." *Horizon* **10:**4 (Autumn 1968), 28ff.

Naylor, Gillian. *The Bauhaus*. New York: E. P. Dutton & Co., Inc., 1968.

Papadaki, Stamo. *Oscar Niemeyer*. New York: George Braziller, Inc., 1960.

Pevsner, Nikolaus. *The Sources of Modern Architecture and Design*. New York: Frederick A. Praeger, 1968.

Rheims, Maurice. *The Flowering of Art Nouveau*. New York: Harry N. Abrams, Inc., (N.D.).

Rosenthal, Rudolph, and Helena Ratzka. *The Story of Modern Applied Art.* New York: Harper and Row, Publishers, Inc., 1948.

Saarinen, Aline, (editor). *Eero Saarinen on His Work.* New Haven: Yale University Press, 1968.

Schmutzler, Robert. *Art Nouveau.* New York: Harry N. Abrams, Inc., 1962.

Scully, Vincent, Jr. *Frank Lloyd Wright.* New York: George Braziller, Inc., 1960.

Shinkokai, Kokusai Bunka. *Architectural Beauty in Japan.* New York: Studio Publications, 1956.

Wright, Iovanna Lloyd. *Architecture: Man in Possession of His Earth.* New York: Doubleday and Company, Inc., 1962.

The Near and Far East

Arakawa, Hirokazu, et al. *Traditions in Japanese Design.* Tokyo: Japan, and Palo Alto, Calif.: Kodansha International, 1967.

Carver, Norman F., Jr. *Form and Space of Japanese Architecture.* Tokyo: Shokokrusha Publishing Company, 1955.

Forman, Werner. *Japanese Netsuke.* London: Spring Books, 1960.

Grube, Ernst J. *The World of Islam.* New York: McGraw-Hill Book Company, Inc., 1967.

Iwamiya, Takeji. *Design and Craftsmanship of Japan: Stone, Metal, Fibers and Fabrics, Bamboo.* New York: Harry N. Abrams, Inc., 1965.

Iwamiya, Takeji. *Katachi: Japanese Pattern and Design in Wood, Paper, and Clay.* New York: Harry N. Abrams, Inc., 1963.

Lee, Sherman E. *A History of Far Eastern Art.* New York: Harry N. Abrams, Inc., 1964.

Mehta, Rustam J. *The Handicrafts and Industrial Arts of India.* Bombay: D. B. Taraporevala Sons and Company, 1960.

Noma, Seiruku, compilator. *Japanese Sense of Beauty.* Tokyo: Asahi Shimbun Publishing Company, 1963.

Oka, Hideyuki. *How To Wrap Five Eggs.* Japanese Design in Traditional Packaging. Foreword by George Nelson. New York: Harper and Row, Publishers, Inc., 1967.

Okakura, Kakuzo. *The Book of Tea.* New York: Dover Publications, Inc., 1964.

Roy, Claude. *Zao Wou-Ki.* New York: Grove Press, Inc., 1959.

Textiles and Lacquers: Pageant of Japanese Art. Edited by staff members of the Tokyo National Museum. Rutland, Vt: Charles E. Tuttle Company, 1958.

Tseng, Yu-ho. *Some Contemporary Elements in Classical Chinese Art.* Honolulu: University of Hawaii Press, 1963.

Wright, Frank Lloyd. *The Japanese Print: An Interpretation.* New York: Horizon Press, 1967.

Scandinavian Design

Design From Scandinavia. Copenhagen, Denmark: World Pictures. Yearly editions distributed in the United States by Trade Publishing Associates, New York.

Hård af Segerstad, Ulf. *Modern Scandinavian Furniture.* Totowa, N.Y.: The Bedminster Press, 1963.

Hård af Segerstad, Ulf. *Scandinavian Design.* New York: Lyle Stuart, 1961.

Karlsen, Arne, and Anker Tiedemann. *Made in Denmark.* New York: Reinhold Publication Corporation, 1960.

Kontur. Swedish Design Annual.

Ratia, Armi, (editor-in-chief). *The Ornamo Book of Finnish Design.* Helsinki: 1962.

Zahle, Erik, (editor). *A Treasury of Scandinavian Design.* New York: Golden Press, 1961.

The United States and Canada

"American Design," *Design Quarterly* **29.**

America's Arts and Skills. (Editors of *Life*). New York: E. P. Dutton & Co., Inc., 1967.

Cheney, Sheldon. *Art and the Machine: An Account of Industrial Design in 20th Century America.* New York: McGraw-Hill Book Company, Inc., 1936.

Douglas, Frederic H., and René D'Harnoncourt. *Indian Art of the United States.* New York: The Museum of Modern Art, 1941.

"Fifty-seven American Weavers and Their Work," *Design Quarterly* **48-49.**

Friedman, William, editor. *Twentieth Century Design: USA, 1959–1960.* Holling Press.

Gunther, Erna. *Northwest Coast Indian Art.* Washington State Museum, University of Washington. (N.D.)

Kauffman, Henry J. *Pennsylvania Dutch America.* New York: Dover Publications, Inc., 1964.

Lichten, Frances. *Folk Art of Rural Pennsylvania.* New York: Charles Scribner's Sons, 1946.

Robadrer, Earl F. *Touch of the Dutchland*. New York: A. S. Barnes and Co., 1965.

Teague, Walter Dorwin. *Design This Day*. New York: Harcourt, Brace, Jovanovich, Inc., 1940.

Wallance, Don. *Shaping America's Products*. New York: Reinhold Publishing Corporation, 1956.

Italian Design

"The Expression of Gio Ponti," *Design Quarterly* **69–70**.

Forme Nuova in Italia. Roma: Bestetti, 1962.

Michener, James A. "Those Fabulous Italian Designers," *Reader's Digest*. (Sept. 1969), pp. 157–166.

English Design

Henderson, Philip. *William Morris: His Life, Work and Friends*. New York: McGraw-Hill Book Company, Inc., 1967.

Thomas, Gertrude. *Richer Than Spices*. How a Royal Bride's Dowry Introduced Cane, Lacquer, Cottons, Tea and Porcelain to England and So Revolutionized Taste, Manners, Craftsmanship, and History in Both England and America. New York: Alfred A. Knopf, Inc., 1965.

Watkinson, Ray. *William Morris As Designer*. New York: Reinhold Publishing Corporation, 1967.

Design from Many Nations

Fernández, Justin. *Mexican Art*. London: Spring Books, 1966.

Forman, W., and B. Forman. *Art of Far Lands*. London: Spring Books, 1958.

Forman, W., and B. Forman. *Exotic Art*. London: Spring Books, 1956.

Keleman, Pál. *Medieval American Art*. New York. The Macmillan Company, 1956.

Shipway, Verna, and Warren Shipway. *Decorative Design in Mexican Homes*. New York: Architectural Book Publishing Co., Inc., 1966.

Swarup, Shanti. *5,000 Years of Arts and Crafts in India and Pakistan*. Bombay: D. B. Taraporevala Sons and Company, 1968.

Primitive, Folk, and Indigenous Design

Christensen, Erwin. *Primitive Art*. New York: Bonanza Books, 1955.

Duerden, Dennis. *African Art*. London: Hamlyn Publishing Group, Ltd., 1968.

Lommel, Andreas. *Prehistoric and Primitive Man*. New York: McGraw-Hill Book Company, Inc., 1966.

Murdock, Peter. "Designers Without Portfolios." *Industrial Design* (March 1968), 34–37.

Trowell, Margaret. *African Design*. New York: Praeger Publishers, 1966.

Stone and Clay

Desautels, Paul E. *The Mineral Kingdom*. New York: Ridge Press, Inc., 1968.

Gary, Dorothy Hales. *Sun, Stones and Silence*. New York: Simon and Schuster, 1963.

Feininger, Andreas. *Man and Stone*. New York: Crown Publishers, Inc., 1961.

Haniwa. Introduction by Seiroku Noma. Circulated with co-operation of an International Program of the Museum of Modern Art, New York. New York: The Asia Society, Inc., 1960.

Mitsuoka, Tadanari. *Ceramic Art of Japan*. Tokyo: Japan Travel Bureau, 1956.

Jade

Nott, Stanley Charles. *Chinese Jade Throughout the Ages*. Rutland, Vt.: Charles E. Tuttle Company, 1962.

Savage, George. *Chinese Jade*. New York: October House, Inc., 1965.

Metals

Kauffman, Henry J. *Early American Ironware*. Rutland, Vt.: Charles E. Tuttle Company, 1966.

Koczogh, Akos. *Modern Hungarian Metalwork*. Budapest, Hungary: Athenaeum Printing House, 1964.

Kühn, Fritz. *Decorative Work in Wrought Iron and Other Metals*. London: George Harrap & Sons Ltd., 1968.

Lynch, John. *Metal Sculpture; New Forms, New Techniques*. New York: Studio-Crowell, 1957.

Strong, D. E. *Greek and Roman Gold and Silver Plate*. Ithaca, N.Y.: Cornell University Press, 1966.

Sutherland, C. H. V. *Gold, Its Beauty, Power and Allure*. New York: McGraw-Hill Book Company, Inc., 1968.

Taylor, Gerald. *Art in Silver and Gold*. London: Studio Vista Limited. New York: E. P. Dutton & Co., Inc., 1964.

Thomas, Richard. *Metalsmithing For the Artist Craftsman.* New York: Chilton Company, Inc., 1959.

Williamsburg Reproductions: *Interior Designs for Today's Living.* (Pewter). Virginia: Williamsburg Restoration, Incorporated, 1966.

Glass and Related Decorative Arts

Ashton, Dore, et al. *The Mosaics of Jeanne Reynal.* New York: George Wittenborn, Inc., 1964.

Bufano Sculpture, Mosaics, Drawings, published for the Bufano Society of the Arts, San Francisco, by John Weatherhill, Inc., Tokyo.

Kämfer, Fritz, and Klaus G. Beyer. *Glass: A World History.* New York: New York Graphic Society, 1966.

Koch, Robert. *Louis C. Tiffany, Rebel in Glass.* New York: Crown Publishers, Inc., 1965.

Plaut, James S. *Steuben Glass.* New York: H. Bittner and Company, Publishers, 1948.

Poetry in Crystal. Steuben Glass, a division of Corning Glass Works. New York: The Spiral Press, 1963.

Polak, Ada. *Modern Glass.* London: Faber and Faber, 1962.

Purtell, Joseph. *The Tiffany Touch.* New York: Random House, Inc., 1971.

Savage, George. *Glass.* New York: G. P. Putnam's Sons, 1965.

Smith, Ray Winfield. "History Revealed in Ancient Glass," *National Geographic* **126: 3** (Sept. 1964), 346–369.

Stennett-Willson, Ronald. *The Beauty of Modern Glass.* New York: Studio Publications, Inc., 1957.

"The Story of Orrefors Glass," *Design Quarterly* **34.**

Unger, Hans. *Practical Mosaics.* New York: The Viking Press, Inc., 1965.

Grasses: Cane and Bamboo

Ball, Katherine M. *Bamboo.* Berkeley, California: The Gillick Press, 1964.

"Bamboo" *Ciba Riview,* Basle, Switzerland: Ciba Ltd. 1969-3, pp. 2–39. (Represented in U.S.A. by Ciba Chemical and Dye Company, Fair Lawn, New Jersey).

Ivory

Beebe, Maurice. *Ivory Towers and Sacred Founts.* New York: University Press, 1964.

Beigbeder, O. *Ivory.* New York: G. P. Putnam's Sons, 1965.

Maskell, Alfred. *Ivories.* Rutland, Vt.: Charles E. Tuttle Company, 1966.

Sanderson, Ivan T. "A Passion for Ivory." *Horizon* (May 1960) pp. 88ff.

Wood

Andrews, Edward Deming, *Religion in Wood; a Book of Shaker Furniture.* Bloomington, Indiana: Indiana University Press, 1966.

Monies, Finn. *Wood in Architecture.* New York: F. W. Dodge Corporation, 1961.

Röttger, Ernst. *Creative Wood Design.* New York: Reinhold Publishing Corporation, 1961.

Paper and Papier-mâché

Entwisle, E. A. *The Book of Wallpaper.* London: Arthur Barker, Ltd., 1954.

Greysmith, Brenda. *Wallpaper.* New York: Macmillan Publishing Co., Inc., 1976.

"The World of Wallpapers." *Architectural Digest* (Summer 1967) pp. 24–41.

Röttger, Ernst. *Creative Paper Design.* New York: Reinhold Publishing Corporation, 1968.

Toller, Jane. *Papier-mâché in Great Britain and America.* Newton, Mass.: Charles T. Branford Company, 1962.

Textiles

Birrell, Verla. *The Textile Arts.* New York: Harper and Row, Publishers, Inc., 1959.

Brushan, Jamila Brij. *The Costumes and Textiles of India.* New Delhi: D. B. Taraporevala Sons and Company, 1958.

Dilley, Arthur Urbane. *Oriental Rugs and Carpets.* New York: J. B. Lippincott Company, 1959.

Dongerkery, Kamala S. *The Indian Sari.* New Delhi: The All India Handicrafts Board. (N.D.)

Freeman, Margaret B. *The St. Martin Embroideries.* A Fifteenth Century Series Illustrating the Life and Legend of St. Martin of Tours. Distributed by the Metropolitan Museum of Art. Greenwich, Conn.: New York Graphic Society Limited, 1968.

Harvey, Virginia I. *Macramé: The Art of Creative Knotting.* New York: Reinhold Publishing Corporation, 1967.

Hobson, June. *Batik Fabrics.* Leicester, England: Dryad Press, 1965.

Johnston, Meda, and Glen Kaufman. *Design on Fabrics.* New York: Reinhold Publishing Corporation, 1967.

Kaufmann, Ruth. *The New American Tapestry.* New York: Reinhold Publishing Corporation, 1968.

Krevitsky, Nik. *Batik: Art and Craft.* New York: Reinhold Publishing Corporation, 1964.

Kybalová, Ludmila. *Coptic Textiles.* London: Paul Hamlyn, 1967.

Scholôsser, Ignace. *The Book of Rugs Oriental and European.* New York: Crown Publishers, Inc., 1963.

Van Dommelen, David B. *Decorative Wall Hangings: Art with Fabrics.* New York: Funk and Wagnalls Company, Inc., 1962.

Wilson, Erica. *Embroidery Book.* New York: Charles Scribner's Sons, 1973.

Plastics

Watkins, Wilbur L. *A Study of Plastic As a Design Medium and Its Place In the Art Curriculum.* Master's thesis, California State University, San José, 1961.

Dietz, G. H. *Plastics for Architects and Builders.* Cambridge, Mass.: MIT Press, 1969.

Designing His Costume

Craft Horizons (May/June, 1968). Issue on Dress.

Garland, Madge. *The Changing Face of Beauty.* New York: M. Barrows and Company, Inc., 1957.

Quant, Mary. *Quant by Quant.* New York: G. P. Putnam's Sons, 1966.

Rudofsky, B. *Are Clothes Modern?* Chicago: Paul Theobald, 1947.

Furniture Design

Andrews, Edward Deming, and Faith Andrews. *Shaker Furniture.* New York: Dover Publications, Inc., 1950.

Aronson, Joseph. *The New Encyclopedia of Furniture.* New York: Crown Publishers, Inc., 1967.

Downs, Joseph. *American Furniture.* Queen Anne and Chippendale Periods. New York: The Macmillan Company, 1952.

Ecke, Gustav. *Chinese Domestic Furniture.* Rutland, Vt.: Charles E. Tuttle Company, 1962.

Faulkner, Ray, and Sarah Faulkner. *Inside Today's Home.* New York: Holt, Rinehart and Winston, Inc., 1968.

Gloag, John. *A Social History of Furniture Design.* New York: Crown Publishers Inc., 1966.

Hatje, Gerd, and Ursula Hatje. *Design for Modern Living.* New York: Harry N. Abrams, Inc., 1962.

Hayward, Helena, (editor). *World Furniture.* New York: McGraw-Hill Book Company, Inc., 1965.

Hicks, David. *David Hicks on Decoration.* New York: The Macmillan Company, 1967.

Joy, Edward T. *English Furniture.* New York: Arco Publishing, 1962.

Please Be Seated. The American Federation of Arts, 1968.

Revi, Albert Christian (ed). *The Spinning Wheel's Complete Book of Antiques.* New York: Grosset & Dunlap, 1972.

Robsjohn-Gibbings, T. H., and Carlton W. Pullin. *Furniture of Classical Greece.* New York: Alfred A. Knopf, Inc., 1963.

Savage, George. *A Concise History of Interior Design.* New York: Grosset and Dunlap, Inc., 1966.

Stepat-DeVan, Dorothy. *Introduction to Home Furnishings.* New York: The Macmillan Company, 1971.

Van Dommelen, David B. *Designing and Decorating Interiors.* New York: John Wiley & Sons, Inc., 1965.

Viaux, Jacqueline. *French Furniture.* New York: G. P. Putnam's Sons, 1964.

Whiton, Sherrill. *Elements of Interior Design and Decoration.* New York: J. B. Lippincott Company, 1963.

Flower Arranging

Ohi, Minobu, *History of Ikebana.* Tokyo: Shufunotomo Co., Ltd., 1962.

Riester, Dorothy W. *Design for Flower Arrangers.* Princeton, N.J.: Van Nostrand, 1959.

Sparnon, Norman, *Japanese Flower Arrangement.* Rutland, Vt.: Charles E. Tuttle Company, 1960.

Appreciation of Art

Brown, Milton W. *The Story of the Armory Show.* New York: The Joseph H. Hirshhorn Foundation, 1963.

Burnham, Jack. *Beyond Modern Sculpture: The Effects of Science and Technology on the Sculpture of this Century.* New York: George Braziller, Inc., 1967.

California University. Art Museum. *Funk.* Berkeley, Calif. 1967.

Carraher, Ronald G. and Jacqueline B. Thurston. *Optical Illusion and The Visual Arts.* New York: Reinhold Publishing Corporation, 1968.

Clark, Kenneth. *Civilization*. Crawfordsville, Indiana: R. R. Donnelley and Sons Co., 1970.

Elsen, Albert E. *Purposes of Art*. New York: Holt, Rinehart, and Winston, Inc., 1962

The Epic of Man, Editors of *Life*. New York: Time Incorporated, 1961.

Faulkner, Ray, and Edwin Zeigfeld. *Art Today*. New York: Holt, Rinehart, and Winston, Inc., 1969.

Feldman, Edmund B. *Art as Image and Idea*. Englewood Cliffs, N.J.: Prentice-Hall, Inc., 1967.

Giedion-Welcker, Carola. *Contemporary Sculpture*. New York: George Wittenborn, Inc., 1960.

Janis, Harriet, and Rudi Blesh. *Collage: Personalities, Concepts, Techniques*. Philadelphia: Chilton Company Book Division, 1962.

Janis, Harriet, and Sidney Janis. *Picasso*. Garden City, N.Y.: Doubleday and Company, Inc., 1946.

Kennedy, John F., et al. *Creative America,* published by the National Cultural Center. New York: The Ridge Press, Inc., 1962.

Kirby, Michael. *Happenings*. New York: E. P. Dutton & Co., Inc., 1966.

Linton, Ralph. *The Tree of Culture*. New York: Alfred A. Knopf, Inc., 1964.

Lips, Julius E. *The Savage Hits Back*. New Haven, Conn.: University Books, 1966.

"Los Angeles County Museum," *Time* (April 8, 1966), 78.

Lynton, Norbert. *The Modern World*. New York: McGraw-Hill Book Company, 1965.

Masters, Robert E. L., and Jean Houston. *Psychedelic Art*. New York: Grove Press, Inc., 1968.

Myers, Bernard S. *Art and Civilization*. New York: McGraw-Hill Book Company, Inc., 1967.

Noguchi, Isamu. *A Sculptor's World*. New York: Harper and Row, Publishers, Inc., 1968.

Rader, Melvin Miller. *A Modern Book of Aesthetics: An Anthology*. New York: Holt, Rinehart, and Winston, Inc., 1960.

Robb, David M., and J. J. Garrison. *Art in the Western World*. New York: Harper and Row, Publishers, Inc., 1942.

Sypher, Wylie. *Rococo to Cubism in Art and Literature*. New York: Random House, Inc., 1960.

The Exterior Environment

Abrams, Charles. *Man's Struggle for Shelter in an Urbanizing World*. Cambridge, Massachusetts: MIT Press, 1964.

Coats, Peter. *Great Gardens of the Western World*. New York: Putnam, 1963.

Engel, David H. *Japanese Gardens for Today*. Rutland, Vt.: Charles E. Tuttle Company, 1959.

Fabun, Don. *Dimensions of Change*. "Shelter, The Cave Reexamined." Beverly Hills, Calif.: Glencoe Press, 1971.

Fuller, R. Buckminster, and John McHale. *Inventory of World Resources Human Trends and Needs*. Under auspices of Southern Illinois University, Carbondale, Illinois, 1963.

Halprin, Lawrence. *Cities*. New York: Reinhold Publishing Corporation, 1963.

Kassler, Elizabeth B. *Modern Gardens and The Landscape*. New York: Museum of Modern Art, 1964. Distributed by Doubleday.

Moholy-Nagy, Sibyl. *Matrix of Man: An Illustrated History of Urban Environment*. New York: Praeger Publishers, 1968.

Mumford, Louis. *City Development*. New York: Harcourt, Brace, Jovanovich Inc., 1961.

Schuler, Stanley. *America's Great Private Gardens*. New York: The Macmillan Company, 1967.

Simons, John Ormsbee. *Landscape Architecture*. New York: F. W. Dodge Corporation, 1961.

Soleri, Paolo. *Arcology: The City in the Image of Man*. Cambridge, Mass: MIT Press, 1969.

Spreiregen, Paul D. *Urban Design: The Architecture of Towns and Cities*. New York: McGraw-Hill Book Company, Inc., 1965.

Consumer Issues

Gordon, Leland J., and Stewart M. Lee. *Economics for Consumers*. New York: Van Nostrand Reinhold Co., 1972.

Index

P

Pabst, Walter, *Fig. 10-40*
Paleolithic art, 162
Paper, 120, 271–273
  contemporary uses of, 272–273
  historical uses of, 272
  Made with Paper exhibit, 272
Paper folding, 275–276
Papier-mâché, 273–275
Parthenon, 77, 162, 335
Paul, Bruno, 125
Paulin, Pierre, 74
Peckstein, Max, 324, 347
Pepys, Samuel, 292, 266
Persian design, 96, 248–250, 312, 315–316, *Figs. 4-40, 13-10, 18-20*
Peruvian design, 109, 231, 232, *Fig. 18-26*
Pevsner, Antoine, 86, 333, *Fig. 4-15*
Pewter, 160, 186–188, *Figs. 13-13, 13-14*
  historic uses of, 186–188
  properties of, 186
  types of, 186
Philippine design, *Fig. 4-44*
Photogram, 335, *Figs. 2-2, 5-1*
Picasso, 25, 64, 106, 156, 192, 278, 315, 323–324, 333, *Figs. 4-1, 4-13, 24-8, 24-16*
Pilotis, 336
Piranesi, Giambattista, 27, *Fig. 4-25*
Plastic as Plastic exhibit, 286
Plastics, 30, 162, 280–286
  architectural purpose of, 284–286
  artistic uses of, 386
  carpeting of, 283–284
  composition and kinds of, 281–282
  fabrics of, 283
  furnishings of, 284–284
  historical background of, 281
  household wares of, 282
  molded components and surface laminates of, 296–297
Pliny the Elder, 164, 194, 234
Plunkett, William, 148
Pointillism, 44, 320, 336, *Fig. 24-13*
Pollock, Jackson, 48, 104, 118, 331, *Fig. 4-44*

Pop art, 120, 325, 327, 329, 336
Porcelain, 168, 336
Poster, 325–326
Pre-Columbian art, 156, 336, *Figs. 6-8, 15-8*
Prestini, James
  theory of design, 14–15, *Fig. 3-1*
  woodwork of, 266
Primitive art, 156, *Figs. 5-13, 13-8, 13-12, 7-1, 19-3, 24-7*
Principles of design, 5, 50–64
  in other cultures, 63–64
Process art, 325, 328
Proportion, 51–53
Psychedelic art, 83, 325, 327, 328
Pucci, Emilio, 147, 259
Pueblo Indians, 73
Pyramids
  Egyptians, 24
  Peruvian, 162

Q

Quant, Mary, 299–300, 302

R

Rabanne, Paco, 300
Radio-carbon tests, 162
Ratio, Armi, 259
Rattan, 147, 224–225
Ravencraft, George, 210
Read, Herbert, on importance of education in aesthetics, 66
Rembrandt, use of light, 34, *Fig. 24-5*
Renaissance design, 25, 218, 244, 312, *Figs. 18-14, 18-15*
Renoir, 320, 335, *Fig. 24-12*
Reveillon, *Fig. 4-9*
Reynal, Jeanne, *Fig. 16-16*
Reynolds, Sir Joshua, 15
Rhythm, 56–59
  by continuous line movement, 57, *Figs. 5-11, 5-12, 5-13, 5-14*
  by graduation, 59, *Figs. 5-15, 13-9*
  by radiation, 57, *Figs. 5-15, 5-16, 5-17*
  by repetition, 57, *Figs. 5-12, 5-13*